GUIDE TO
Vacation Rentals
IN EUROPE

GUIDE TO

Vacation Rentals

IN EUROPE

by
Michael
and
Laura Murphy

A Voyager Book

The Globe Pequot Press

Old Saybrook, Connecticut

Library of Congress Cataloging-in-Publication Data

Murphy, Michael, 1927-
    Guide to vacation rentals in Europe / by Michael and Laura Murphy.
       p.   cm.
    "A Voyager book."
    Includes index.
    ISBN 1-56440-493-5
    1. Vacation homes--Europe--Guidebooks. 2. Rental housing--Europe-
-Guidebooks.   I. Murphy, Laura.   II. Title.
TX907.5.E85M86   1994
647.944--dc20   94-23035
                                              CIP

Manufactured in the United States of America
First Edition/First Printing

Contents

The prices and rates listed in the guidebook were confirmed at press time.
We recommend, however, that you call establishments before traveling to
obtain current information.

Acknowledgments

Our thanks go to the owners and representatives of the many rental companies that responded helpfully to our inquiries and took the time to meet with us on a personal basis. We are especially grateful to those who offered their friendship and hospitality during our travels through Europe, both recently and in the past.

Preface

Spending a week or more in a short-term vacation rental in Europe opens new avenues of enjoyment for North American travelers. Compared to a series of stays in hotels, the obvious benefits of renting include a lower accommodation cost, more space, kitchen and dining facilities (which reduce the cost of meals), play space for children, and a home base to return to after day trips exploring the area. Vacationers renting in Europe may also become part of a community for a short time by shopping at local markets and interacting with local people. Whether you choose to rent a place in an English village or on a working vineyard in the Tuscany hills, you will become a foreign visitor, rather than a tourist.

More and more North American travelers are choosing the rental option, which has been enjoyed by European vacationers for decades. Of course, they are there and we are here, on the other side of the Atlantic. We have always had the difficulty of locating the right rental property in the right place at the right price—from a distance.

Our decision to write this guidebook arises from the obvious: North American travelers should have the same opportunity to pay the same price for vacation rental properties in Europe as Europeans do. With the advent of fax machines, both here and in Europe, there is no reason why anyone willing to put in a little extra time and effort cannot save a considerable amount of money by communicating directly with the European rental companies. Even international telephoning has become swift, simple, and modestly priced, making it easier to locate and book a rental over the telephone. The amount of money spent on overseas communication is small in terms of what can be saved by booking directly.

Not everyone will want to make this extra effort, but for those who do, this guide will prove to be very helpful. And even for those who don't, a number of U.S. agencies are included because they represent a broad array of dependable rentals and because they charge little or no commission. As for the difficulty of making arrangements in foreign lands, a word about the authors and their research for this book will help put things into perspective.

We have always enjoyed travel, and have made pleasure trips to Europe, Mexico, around the United States and Canada, traveling on a modest budget, avoiding the heavily traveled tourist paths. In 1984 we moved to Europe for almost a year on a book assignment. It was all very new, learning to live independently in foreign countries. We not only learned how to conduct business there, we also gained experience in renting places for ourselves for extended periods.

In 1988 we began work on our first book on vacation rentals, which emerged from the good experiences we had with this style of travel, and was reinforced by the escalating costs of travel in Europe and the declining dollar. Working several months in advance, we set about making appointments with European rental company owners and other authorities to see their operations and visit a sampling of their properties.

We set out on our three-month itinerary by car, having arranged for a Renault on that company's Purchase/Buyback Plan (see chapter four). We never had a car problem in over nine thousand miles and rarely became even temporarily lost.

We found stores in which to buy groceries and the other few things we needed for our many cottages, apartments, villas, and chalets, and enjoyed the fun of choosing easily prepared foods for our own kitchens. Language was never a barrier to our buying what we needed, even though some basic Spanish is our only other language.

We often wished that each stay could be longer, but usually the few days we needed to work in each region were all we could schedule. Our stays in rental properties not only gave us a needed break from hotels, but enabled us to make a fair comparison between the two styles of travel. Vacation rentals have our unqualified vote, for ourselves and anyone else who is not compelled, for one reason or another, to travel great distances in a very limited time.

We found almost all of the rental companies to be well run, proud of their properties, and staffed by helpful, knowledgeable persons. Any that do not meet these basic standards are not included in this guidebook. We regret that not all good European companies appear in the pages—they number in the hundreds and simply could not all be investigated and included.

As for the effort needed to select the place you dream of and then book it, travel to it, and get your groceries for it, we recommend it for the challenge, the fun, and the rewards. We hope this guidebook will make your planning easier.

Chapter One

ABOUT RENTALS AND RENTING

Overview

There is no mystery to booking and staying in a property in Europe—the process is much the same in North America, the Caribbean, Hawaii, and elsewhere in the northern half of the western hemisphere. In Europe there are many more rentals, though, and they are much more diverse in age, condition, and character. Rarely seen in the New World, thatched-roof stone cottages, stuccoed villas, renovated farm houses, mountain chalets, and even castles for rent are common throughout Continental Europe, the United Kingdom, and the Republic of Ireland. There are, of course, city apartments, which range from elegant rooms to simple flats in modern apartment blocks. Then there are the ubiquitous beach-front condos of the type popular in Hawaii, America's southeast coast, and the resorts of Mexico and the Caribbean.

Referred to by most English-speaking Europeans as "self-catering" or "holiday" rentals, vacation properties can be rented by the week or by the month, and come furnished with fully equipped kitchens, table service, usually linens and bedding, and maid service.

Thousands of these vacation rentals are available, and it is not difficult for Europeans to locate and book a villa, or flat, or cottage in some favorite foreign or domestic spot away from home. They know the ropes and they know how and where to look, while most of us on this side of the Atlantic do not.

Direct Contact

Until a few years ago, finding and renting an apartment in a village on the Rhine, a small villa in Tuscany, or a flat in central London by directly booking with a European company was not an easy task. The prevailing requirement of having to pay rent in advance by bank draft in foreign currency made financial transactions awkward. This inconvenience, coupled with the expense of trans-Atlantic telephone calls and the slow speed of communicating by mail, plus an absence of information on rentals, explain why North Americans visiting Europe in the past have usually stayed in hotels and taken meals out. But as the dollar slumped relative to European currencies, and travelers began to seek alternatives to expensive hotels and restaurants, renting became increasingly popular.

People who looked for economy found a new approach to visiting Europe, one that offered a sense of independence, greatly reduced the pressures of packing and unpacking every few days, and enabled families with children to have more enjoyable and relaxed vacations. Rental agencies began to proliferate in the United States and Canada and now number over sixty. Although they are few compared to the number of travel agencies, rental agencies are specialized. It is to these agencies that travelers (and many travel agencies) turn to find rental accommodations in Europe. But of course there is a price to pay—usually a commission to a North American agent.

Concurrent with the growth of agencies in the United States and Canada, the European companies (many of which are represented by agencies here) awoke to the North American market and set about making things easier for individuals to make contact, specifically by installing fax machines, accepting credit cards, and having English speakers on their staffs.

Although U.S. and Canadian agencies receive a discount from the European companies they represent, many add a commission of between 10 and 20 percent (a few as high as 40 percent) for their services. If you book through a domestic travel agency, there may be an additional percentage tacked on to the rental agency's commission, meaning that three layers of commissions are built in to the rental price. There are, however, some agencies that do not add on commissions—usually U.S. or Canadian branches of European companies, or larger companies for which vacation rentals are part of a broad spectrum of travel-related services. A selected few are included in this guidebook. Since the price of a rental must cover the commission paid by the property owner to the European rental company, the price will be lower when the rental company itself is the property owner. Usually this arrangement is more common in major cities, where the rental companies market their apartments directly to the public rather than through a broker. Some apartment-block owners do both.

Depending on the price of the rental and the length of time it is rented for, the difference between what a North American pays and a European pays can amount to hundreds, even thousands, of dollars. One objective of this guide is to present the best combination of fair pricing and convenience. If a North American agency knows the properties of the European companies it represents, charges no commission (or a very modest fee), and simplifies the process of booking and paying, then we consider it for inclusion in this guide.

If money is of little consequence, or if you would prefer to have it all done for you, then we suggest you contact one of the North American agencies or a travel agency and pay the extra commission. This guidebook will be invaluable, however, if you are willing to put a modest amount of energy into booking a rental yourself.

Selections for this Guidebook

It would be virtually impossible to include all of the European rental companies in one manageable volume, so we made selections according to a number of criteria. These criteria were designed basically to indicate the interest and ability of the companies to work with English-speaking foreign travelers. We sent out a questionnaire to all companies we were interested in including in the book. The speed with which the companies responded gave us a good indication of their interest. From those that replied in a reasonable time, we chose those that responded well to the questions. Positive responses made clear some key points: (1) bookings are accepted directly from overseas, (2) English-speaking staff, (3) property descriptions and location directions are in English, (4) fax machine on-line, (5) reasonable deposit and final-payment terms, (6) fair and clearly stated cancellation and refund policy, (7) credit cards and/or dollar checks or travelers cheques accepted. Any company that did not respond favorably was not considered.

We also looked at other factors such as length of time in business, availability of someone at or near all rental sites in case of problems, availability of linens and towels, and, when possible, reputation. Size of the company was of no concern, because we had earlier learned that there was no consistent relationship between size and quality of properties or service. With these criteria in mind we made personal contact with the companies that interested us to determine whether their operations and rental properties met reasonable American standards and seemed to be fairly priced. By "fairly priced" we do not mean modest or inexpensive—we mean good value, priced appropriately for the property, whether it is a $400-per-week studio or a $14,000-per-week castle or luxury villa.

One subjective criterion we used for inclusion was the distinctiveness of a company's rental properties. We asked ourselves whether the rustic cabin on a resort in the Bavarian woods was much different from one we might find in the Adirondacks or the Rockies. Would a chalet in the Austrian Alps just to the south be preferable? If we had just arrived for a vacation, would we be disappointed to find that our rental on the Mediterranean coast was one in a row of motel-like stucco cottages?

We feel that it is a long way to travel to stay in places much like those available here at home, so we wanted to include the alternatives to such places. And there are thousands of them: a thatched-roof cottage in Ireland, a stone house in the hills of Tuscany or above the Côte d'Azur, or a villa in Portugal's Algarve. As for the high-rise condominiums that line stretches of the southern coasts of

France and Spain—they are like high-rise condos everywhere. Although they make good home bases from which to spend time on the beaches or savoring the fare of a foreign country, we looked for other rental options.

The Cost Advantage

Price and Locale

Rental prices are primarily affected by type, size, services provided, quality of construction, furniture, decor, and amenities. They are also governed by the economy of the country in which the rental units are located, and by specific locale. For example, those in the prime European vacation spots such as France's Côte d'Azur, the hills of Tuscany, and major cities are among the most expensive. Luxury villas in Portugal's Algarve can be costly, despite the fact that overall prices in Portugal are among the lowest in Europe.

When reading a description of a vacation rental, watch for catchphrases like "sea view" (you may be on a hill ten blocks from the sea), and "accommodates six" (which may describe a double bed, a sofa bed, and a rollaway for children, all in one or two rooms). Generally, we found that bargain prices (except for off-season) rarely exist—they are usually low for a reason. In this guide we have attempted to weed out those companies that provide inaccurate property descriptions.

Rates: Hotels vs. Rentals

It is difficult to be precise when comparing hotel prices with those of vacation rentals. A modest room in a fashionable area of London or Zurich will cost more than a deluxe room in a less convenient or less fashionable part of town, so a simple cottage on the beach front will cost more than a larger villa inland. Most of the European rental companies, however, carefully counsel property owners about their rental prices, and make sure they are kept well below hotel rates, all other factors being equal. Several European agents told us they like to keep rents at about 65 percent of the rate for an equivalent hotel room.

Although there are thousands of properties that rent for low to moderate prices and keep below equivalent hotel rates, many others have no equivalent in hotels. These are the luxury rentals, which range from spacious jewels in the centers of cities to expansive villas on cliffs overlooking the sea, and even include English manor houses. They offer a totally different way of visiting abroad. Most properties in this category include in the price daily maid service and often a private swimming pool, tennis court, choice location, and perhaps a gardener, cook, and driver, if desired. The lower end of the deluxe category includes spacious villas or townhouses in resort settlements. Rents for deluxe properties range from $1,500 to $20,000 per week, but the properties are usually large enough to be shared by four to six persons, and even up to a dozen or more. We visited some manor houses and estates that were often rented for large family gatherings or by a large group of friends.

General Notes on Paying

Credit Cards. A few of the companies that accept credit cards allow clients to pay the deposit by card when they book and then make the final payment upon arrival. This is especially true of some of the larger apartment hotels in major cities. When noted in the company descriptions, the general rule is that the final on-site payment can be made by credit card. If otherwise, this information is always made clear in the confirmation documents.

Travelers Cheques. When payment by travelers cheque is accepted, the cheques may be in either U.S. or other major currency equivalents or in the currency of the destination country. We suggest using whichever you have decided to use for your other expenses overseas; that is, there is no reason to purchase both U.S. (or Canadian) cheques and foreign-fund cheques.

Value Added Tax (VAT). This add-on tax varies widely from country to country but is almost always included in the quoted rent price or the price figures in published price lists. Exceptions are always made clear, but on the rare occasion where no reference to VAT is made, be sure to ask about it. If a change in the VAT rate takes place after price lists for the year have been published, the companies always adjust the final price accordingly.

Value by Country

Value in rentals can be simply described as the best for the money. That is, the largest, or the most comfortable, or the best furnished, or the best located, or usually a combination of these measures, for a given price. The following recommendations take into account all of these factors. They summarize our estimation of where the best values lie among the countries covered in this guide, irrespective of price.

The best values overall are to be found in rural Great Britain and Portugal.

For neat, scrupulously maintained rentals in scenic grandeur, the values in alpine Austria can't be outdone, even by neighboring Switzerland and Germany's Bavaria.

For space and elegance in historic settings, the large homes in the rural areas of England and the Republic of Ireland are an excellent value in the luxury category. Because Italy's hill-country rental properties have become relatively expensive, the cost must be balanced against the delightful experience of a stay in an ancient Tuscan or Umbrian villa.

For well-serviced, spacious villas, it's back again to Portugal's Algarve. For elegance and location at any price, a villa in the hills of France's Côte d'Azur above Nice, Cannes, or St. Tropez is hard to beat in the off-season or shoulder season.

(These coastal towns become very crowded and expensive in July and August.)

For tranquil simplicity in a culturally unique area with interesting historical sites and small market towns, France's southwestern river valleys of the Dordogne, Tarn, and Lot are excellent. Prices are higher than in Britain, but less than on France's southern coast.

For skiing vacations, the villages of Austria's Vorarlberg Province, especially those of the Montafon Valley, offer good value. Rent and food are far less than in the "international" resort towns of Austria (Lech, Zürs, St. Anton-am-Arlberg, Innsbruck, Kitzbühel) and Switzerland (Zermatt, Davos, St. Moritz).

As for city apartments, London offers the best value and the greatest selection. There is also a good selection in Paris. Although the rentals are expensive, the savings over hotels and meals out is considerable. Vienna offers a small selection with only a few in the city center, but prices are lower than in other major cities. There are few apartments in Rome, and they are expensive. In Italy, Florence is a better bet, although still expensive.

Apartments in Cannes, Cap d'Antibes, Golfe Juan, St. Tropez, and Nice offer the best selection of rentals along the coast of southern France, but they are not good values in summer. For bargains in this area, travel in spring or late fall if you can.

Madrid and Barcelona offer surprisingly few apartments; the prices are modest, but so is the quality. The best bet for the Barcelona area is to go during shoulder or off-season and drive through the nearby coastal towns looking for FOR RENT (*alquiler*) signs. Among the smaller cities of England, Bath is an outstanding and well-located place in which to stay, with a fair selection of modestly priced apartments. Edinburgh, Scotland also has a reasonably good selection, especially off-season.

One advantage city apartments have over their rural counterparts is that they can often be rented for a three-day minimum rather than a week. Consider a three-day stay in the city, followed by a move to the country.

Factors Other Than Price

In addition to cost considerations, there are many good reasons to stay in a vacation rental. European hotels, of course, offer daily maid service, fresh towels and soap, a bar and lobby, and often a continental breakfast. On the other hand, rentals offer more space, the convenience of a kitchen, and, we discovered, a sense of independence, privacy, and homelike comfort not found in hotels. Maybe it's the appeal of making your own morning coffee, or raiding the refrigerator in the evening. Maybe it's being able to shop at the local market for a sampling of local foods and wines and the opportunity to try them out in your own dwelling. It depends not only on what you can afford, but on what is important to you. And there are still other considerations.

From quaint country cottages to this fourteen-bedroom Irish castle, there is a European rental property to suit every traveler's needs, tastes, and budget. (Courtesy Elegant Ireland)

In-Depth Exploration

Vacation rentals are for travelers who enjoy setting their own pace, exploring a city or two, and spending time in villages or regions of interest, as opposed to making a rapid, demanding tour where only the highlights of a half-dozen cities can be touched.

Anyone who has traveled on an extensive itinerary fitted into a limited stretch of time knows about the energy and time expended in constantly packing and unpacking, finding hotels and railway stations in unfamiliar cities, looking for a place to eat after a late arrival, and deciding what to see and visit in what always seems like far too short a period of time. By renting, however, you will always have a home base to return to, whether you have been gone on a day trip or one of several days' duration. You will have a place to unpack, unwind, and make plans for the next adventure into the surrounding country.

In order to derive the most pleasure from short-term rental, the selection of the right location is vital. In the United Kingdom, for example, if two weeks exploring the London area is your aim, then it would be better to look for an apartment in the city or its environs. If a few days in London will be enough, then maybe a cottage base from which to explore Wales or Scotland would be best. It could still be within easy travel distance of London, but your time would be apportioned differently.

The descriptions of regions and cities in each country chapters will help you choose a location within the best striking distance of the things you want to include.

European Variety and Standards

There is no "typical" rental property. Unlike the sameness among short-term tourist and resort rentals in Hawaii, much of Florida, Mexico, and the Caribbean, the variety found in Europe is amazingly wide. Large or small, modern or rustic, urban or rural, modest or luxurious, all the rental units included in this guide are designed and equipped to meet the needs of travelers. All have completely equipped kitchens and table service for as many guests as the unit accommodates, but expect oddities. For example, to most Italians a coffee maker is an espresso pot. The British lean toward tea and instant coffee, so the device of choice is often an electric kettle. You may have to improvise with a cone and filters.

Some rentals are furnished exquisitely, and some simply. Many are conversions from a former existence—a winery, an oast house for drying hops, a gate house to a manor, or the manor itself. Some are in new resort developments, and others in older, elegant developments such as the Riviera towns of Cannes, Antibes, and Villefranche-sur-Mer.

Bedding and towels are always available—although sometimes for an extra fee. It seems that many Europeans are accustomed to packing their linens and towels in their suitcases when they leave on holiday in their own or neighboring countries, and, of course, most travel by car. Fortunately, many rental companies seem to be learning that it's too much to ask North Americans to fly their clean towels to Europe and their damp ones back. We have noted where special arrangements should be made for North Americans by the rental companies. To play it safe, if you are unsure whether linens are provided, especially if you are renting in rural Britain or in France, tell the rental company that you will need them.

Some rental arrangements include weekly or semiweekly laundry service. Other rentals have washers, a few have dryers, and some agencies leave instructions on how to get to the nearest launderette. In most rentals from northern Scotland to southern Portugal you will find a booklet or a collection of information and instructions about the accommodation and its vicinity.

In the meantime, check the chapters for the countries you plan to visit to see if there is anything unusual to watch for, but most important, carefully study the material and descriptions you receive from the agencies. What Europeans take for granted may well catch you by surprise.

Rental Periods

There are minor differences from country to country in the policies and customs of the rental agencies, but throughout Europe their operations are surprisingly similar. Idiosyncrasies that may affect you are noted in the appropriate country chapters.

One practice that will affect your plans is that virtually all weekly rental periods run from Saturday to Saturday. Typically, as with most hotels, you will be asked to observe check-in and check-out times.

Saturday is called the "changeover day," the day when maids and maintenance persons go to work cleaning and setting things up for the next renters. One reason that it is usually Saturday is because many of the cleaners and service people are students, free to work on Saturdays, but not on weekdays, during the school year. Suggestions on how to deal with this rather rigid rule are made in chapter three under Planning Your Trip.

Making Choices

From the wide variety of vacation rental properties available, how do you decide which one to choose? It's usually a process of elimination, beginning with the two most basic determining factors: location and budget. Only you know where you want to visit and how much you're prepared to spend.

The first step is to decide what country, or perhaps two, you plan to visit; then turn to the appropriate country chapter of this guide. Scanning it will give you an idea of where rentals are available, enabling you to zero in on specific locales that appeal to you. The companies that own or offer short-term rentals in each of these locales are described at the beginning of each country chapter.

It is helpful to work with two good maps. Unless you plan to spend all of your time in one country, you'll need a map of the whole of Europe, plus one of the country you're considering for your home base. Often, the government tourist authority will send you a map for the asking. The best maps are Michelin and Halwag and, for Britain, those of the British Automobile Association and Royal Automobile Club. The American Automobile Association also has a selection of good maps of Europe, but some are less detailed and often fail to show small towns. Because Britain is crossed by an intricate network of highways and roads, we suggest that on arrival you purchase a large-scale ordinance map of the area where your rental is located.

Once you find one or more locales you'd like to investigate further, refer to the rental company list in the appropriate country chapter to determine which offer properties in those locales. The next step is to make contact, ideally by telephone or fax, to get things rolling. This procedure is the main topic of chapter three.

For the Wanderer or Off-Season Traveler

Unlike vacationers, who usually have some specific time frame into which a journey or visit must fit, wanderers are usually fortunate enough to have no such time restraints. These independent travelers, as well as the few vacationers who do have that luxury, should consider off-season visits to Europe. During these months, normally between mid-September and the end of May (except in the ski resorts), most rentals either stand empty awaiting an occasional booking, or are not offered for rent. If you are in an area of interest and would like to stay for a few days, look around for a short-term rental. These are often less difficult to find in the smaller towns and resort areas than in major cities. Some villages, most towns, and all cities have a tourist assistance office with listings of places to rent. If you are in an area that is heavily touristed in the high season, there should be many rentals and you can simply wander through the streets looking for an appealing place to rent.

We took this independent approach when we went to Europe several years ago to do research for our first travel guide. We leased a car in Paris and headed toward the vicinity of Barcelona, where we wanted to set up a home base. We drove into Spain down the north Mediterranean coast, spotting numerous *alquiler* (for rent) signs along the way. We found a place we liked in the pleasant little coastal town of Sitges, some twenty miles south of Barcelona. It was a small, modestly equipped apartment with a view, just across the street from a beach. The off-season rent was about $290 per month, including utilities. We found it by scouting the beach-side street, and lived there for four months, taking extended drives and journeys by port-to-port ships. We went as far as Yugoslavia, Greece, and Tunis, always returning "home" to our apartment in Sitges.

We repeated this procedure when we moved to England later that year, in June, but found that we were very close to the high season, when everything is fully booked. We worked things out, but barely in time. In retrospect, had we arrived in Spain between mid-May and mid-September, or during the three weeks surrounding Easter, we would have had difficulties renting there as well, and the cost would have been double or triple the off-season rate.

The lesson we learned is that if you want to rent as you go, plan your visit during the low or shoulder season. Except for ski areas, low season is generally the winter months, and shoulder season is the months of April and May (except for Easter weeks) and from mid-September to November. In Britain, early June is also shoulder season in the countryside, but not London. The period from two weeks before Easter through the week after is a time of peak travel in Europe, especially in the Mediterranean countries.

In most ski areas, especially at the fashionable international ski resorts, be prepared for peak prices and dense crowds from December through the first two weeks of January. February is a better time to go. If you're planning an autumn ski trip, book at one of the high-altitude spots to be assured of good snow. Our suggestion is to go in November to one of the less prominent (and less expensive) lower altitude areas, such as in Austria's Vorarlberg Province, where there is a permanent population.

Chapter Two

USING THIS GUIDE

How to Begin

In addition to providing you with detailed information on rentals and rental companies, this guide will help you plan your trip. In order to familiarize yourself with the nature of European rental companies and the necessary procedures for making contact, getting information, and finally booking, begin by reading chapter three.

If you have not yet decided where you want to go, perusing the country chapters may help you focus your plans. Once you know where you want to go, turn to the country chapter or chapters of your choice to learn if vacation rentals are available in the locales of interest to you. Bear in mind that the vast number and variety of rentals opens up a new world of possible locations, so think beyond the conventional places where the hotels or B&Bs are. Consider a chalet perched high above the valley floor in the Alps, or a converted stone house on the grounds of an estate in England or Scotland, or perhaps an apartment in one of the large and ancient farmhouses overlooking the valley of the Arno River in Tuscany. If you have always wanted to stay in some elegant neighborhood of London or Paris, but find that hotels run beyond your budget, check the appropriate chapters for apartments in those neighborhoods, and make contact. You may be pleasantly surprised by the prices.

Once you've settled on the region or city in which you would like to stay, find the appropriate rental companies by referring to the regional descriptions of each country chapter, which note the companies in that region and describe where their rental properties are.

Next, select a company or two, and find their addresses and fax and phone numbers in the listing at the end of each chapter. Telephone the company or send a letter or fax telling them specifically what you are looking for. (See chapter three for details on what information you must provide and what questions you must ask.)

When you have found at least three rental possibilities in the locale of your choice, contact the appropriate company and begin the booking procedure.

The Organization of Information

Chapter three, *Finding and Booking Your Vacation Home Abroad,* describes in detail the nature of European rental companies and how they operate. This description is followed by step-by-step instructions on how to work with them, from initial contact through the process of selecting, booking, and finally occupying your cottage, castle, or chalet.

The Country Chapters

Each of the ten country chapters is divided into two sections: an overview of the country and a descriptive list of the European companies with short-term rentals in that country. These chapters are set up this way to enable you to find the companies with rentals where you want to be.

The information we provide is detailed enough to give you a good idea of the kind of organization you are dealing with and, in general, what their properties are like. Our comments might reveal a certain bias, born of spending enough time in rental properties throughout each country to make fair comparisons. Be forewarned that our bias is toward comfortable rather than the glitzy, moderately priced rather than costly, off-the-beaten-tourist-trails instead of better known but crowded. We are also committed to companies whose properties are as they are advertised and who demonstrate an interest in working with American and Canadian travelers.

If the company is headquartered in the country the chapter is dealing with, there will be descriptive information in addition to the contact address and phone and fax numbers. For companies with headquarters in some other country, only the contact information is provided, and the reader is referred to the home country for more detailed information. For example, both PEGO and Interhome offer properties in Austria. PEGO is based in Austria and Interhome, in Switzerland. PEGO, therefore, is described in the chapter on *Austria,* Interhome is only listed, along with a referral to the *Switzerland* chapter, where a more complete description of Interhome can be found.

The Country

To help you find a desirable location in which to rent for a week or more, each chapter begins with a general description of the country, its regions, and its cities. These overviews are not substitutes for a good guidebook; they provide general observations on rentals and describe any unusual factors that could affect your choice of locale or time of year to visit. Suggestions on when to go to a particular country may be included in the overview if the country is small or has a fairly consistent climate and tourist pattern. Otherwise, this advice is covered in the regional descriptions.

La Bolomière, situated on an acre of rolling land along the banks of the Lot River in southwest France, offers a taste of rural French living. (Courtesy French Home Rentals)

Environs and Accommodations. These paragraphs describe the regions in the vicinity of rental units. If the rentals are in a city, their neighborhoods are described. The terrain, scenery, and nature of the villages are given for rural areas. The typical styles of rentals, if any, are noted, for example, mountain chalets, flats, estates, condos, converted farmhouses, beach apartments, or villas. Suggestions on the best time to visit may also be included here.

Location and Transportation. This section of each regional description describes important cities or sites in the region that can be visited on day or overnight trips from the rental properties. It also may note more distant destinations that can be reached on round-trips of two days or so. For example, from a rental in the vicinity of Cannes, on the south coast of France, a trip into Italy as far as Milan, Pisa, Genoa, and even Florence is reasonable. Visits to Geneva and certainly Marseille and Aix-en-Provence would also be feasible.

As you work on deciding where to locate it is helpful, even essential, that you use a good map of the area. The line maps contained in this guide help as a quick locator and reference, but are not a substitute for a good highway map.

Also noted in this section is the accessibility of the towns or areas where rentals are located to railway lines, primary and secondary highways, ferry terminals, and other forms of transportation. If a car is essential to isolated properties or locales, this will be noted. If you are not planning on having a car, be sure to get specific transportation information for your particular rental before you book. Appropriate suggestions are made regarding the best means of traveling throughout the area.

Prices. All rental companies list their prices for the *entire unit,* so the cost per person can be easily figured. Be careful when making price comparisons with hotels; many European hotels show prices per person rather than per room. General prices for each region are provided.

Some larger properties may seem expensive, but upon examination you may learn that they accommodate six, eight, ten, or more persons. These are ideal for families, or for sharing among travel companions. A three-bedroom villa, for example, is always less expensive than three rooms in a hotel of equal standard.

Advance Booking Time. Here you will learn how many weeks or months in advance of your planned arrival you must book in order to be assured of having a place to stay. The differences in booking times depend on locale and time of year. This section will alert you to holidays that can affect the required booking time; for example, Britain's Bank and midterm school holidays.

The Companies

Because choosing the right rental agency is so important to the success of your vacation, a substantial part of each country chapter is devoted to an overview of the agencies in that country. In addition to contact information for each company (address and telephone and fax numbers), it briefly describes the rental company's policies and how it operates. You'll learn how to get the latest informational materials, and in what other countries and regions of Europe each company offers properties. If an agency specializes in deluxe or modest properties, this information is provided. Also indicated are price ranges, the general nature, variety and quality of a company's properties; services available (such as cooking, a cook, housekeeper, or other staff) and amenities generally provided or specifically excluded (towels and linens, for example). Method of payment is described and any idiosyncrasies in the booking procedures are noted.

The Appendices

In Appendix A you will find a few North American rental agencies that represent or are branches of European rental companies. Although there are more than sixty such agencies, those included are moderate in their commission charges or represent especially desirable properties.

Appendix B is a list of government tourist offices (known as GTOs in the trade) in the United States and Canada. Upon request many of these offices can provide a list of rental properties in their respective countries. The tourist offices cannot make rental arrangements for you but will provide other relevant information. They will often send country, regional, and city maps upon request.

Chapter Three

FINDING AND BOOKING
YOUR VACATION HOME
ABROAD

The Rental Companies

As in any business transaction, it is important to know something about the person or organization with whom you are dealing. One of the European agents we met asked, "Can you think of any other holiday enterprise in which customers are required to put up all the money in advance to rent a place they have never seen from someone they've never met?" The answer to this very good question is no, which is why it is worth making an effort to choose a sound and reliable company. The information provided below on how rental companies work will help you make a good informed choice when you select a rental company and, eventually, a rental property.

What They Are

The business of seeking out and listing rental properties throughout a region or country began in Europe long before it was started in the United States, and it is practiced more aggressively abroad. European companies advertise and compete with each other in their continuing quest for owners who will rent short-term to vacationers. Their staffs comb the countryside looking for new properties and the companies attempt to make sure that the owners they represent are keeping up their part of the bargain by maintaining standards set by the companies. Many of these companies also promote the restoration and conversion of ancient buildings and crumbling stone cottages into apartments, comfortable villas, and cozy bungalows. Some even help owners with the process of securing loans and grants to convert their properties for vacation use. The rental companies produce illustrated catalogs describing hundreds of properties and distribute them to potential customers and sometimes to agents in the United States and Canada.

Some companies are two- or three-person operations, and some have dozens on their staffs, including those who work with sophisticated computer systems, multilingual professionals who deal with an international clientele, and overseers of the quality and maintenance of the properties they represent. Some of the companies are highly personalized, working closely with their owners and clientele and limiting their operating area to properties that can be reached within a fairly short drive. Others are large, offering properties throughout an entire country and, in a few cases, throughout Europe and even North America. These larger companies rely on their networks of regionally based staff to deal with owners, properties, and clients. Some do this well and some not so well.

How They Operate

There are basically two types of short-term property rental companies in Europe. One type functions as a brokerage; it represents many private individuals who own cottages, chalets, apartments, or villas that they do not regularly occupy. The brokerage solicits their listings, then sets standards of cleanliness, furnishings, service, and the like, and, as we mentioned earlier, lists these properties in a catalog. In the cities, the broker companies offer accommodations in apartment blocks in various areas. These may be the same apartments that can be booked directly with the individual apartment managements (described below), but the brokers have the advantage of offering a wide selection and will scan the city for an apartment that meets your specifications. Because their commission is paid by the apartment owners, the price to the renter is usually the same as if the booking had been made directly with the owners.

The second type of vacation rental company owns its rental properties and markets them directly to the public as well as to brokers. These are usually urban apartment blocks and what many Europeans refer to as "aparthotels." An aparthotel usually offers rooms as well as residence apartments and *some* may provide services typically found in hotels, including twenty-four-hour porterage and reception and sometimes a restaurant. Many of the elegant apartments of London, Paris and Rome are in aparthotels, so don't expect low prices, but do expect good value.

Company Locations

Rental company offices are literally scattered throughout the length and breadth of Europe. With a few exceptions, which we note in the country chapters, we favor companies whose properties are within their own country; their lines of communication with their staff and with property owners are shorter, and in all likelihood they know the territory better than a company headquartered in another country. The exceptions are those international companies that our experience shows are well managed, and which have staff in the vicinity of the foreign properties they offer. To obtain a complete list of rental companies for a given country, write the national tourist office (see Appendix B for contact information). Not all countries have such lists, though. These lists vary in length and level of detail. Some only list the agents, while others, such as Germany and Ireland, give brief descriptions of individual properties. The United Kingdom has the most comprehensive publication.

Company and Property Ratings

The British are well along in developing a property rating system similar to that for hotels, while the French have long rated the country rentals of members belonging to the national organization, Federation de Gîtes Ruraux.

The rental business is very competitive in Europe, and most of the companies we dealt with are doing a remarkable job, offering well-described, well-maintained properties at fair prices. Companies that offer shoddy, misrepresented or grossly overpriced properties will generally fall by the wayside. The trick is to avoid dealing with them during their predictably short lives. One purpose of this guidebook is to attempt to sort these companies out. We cannot, of course, guarantee satisfaction with particular properties, but we have been careful not to include companies we know little or nothing of and we make recommendations when we feel they are especially merited.

European Company/North American Agency Relationships

Despite the tendency of European companies to establish relationships with overseas agencies in order to better reach the North American market, there are many that prefer to work directly with American and Canadian customers without an agent. They can offer their rental properties without the added fees and commissions of an agent, while providing good service and ease of booking.

A few European companies put caps on the prices charged by their foreign agents, but most have no such control. They give the agents a discount, but seldom know how much more is being added. These European companies are concerned that the layers of administration between the property owners and the renters could increase rental prices unreasonably, bringing them into the price ranges of comparable hotels. There is also the worry (both in Europe and here) that a North American client will discover two prices for the same property: the one paid to agents on this continent and the one Europeans are paying.

Finding and Booking: The Process

Trip Planning

The thought of being at a particular property in some remote, unfamiliar locale between 3:00 p.m. and 7:00 p.m. on a Saturday six months from the present could be worrisome. On the other hand, one tends to be focused on planning and working out details in advance. But once the arrangements are made you don't have to worry about time schedules again as you would on an extended travel itinerary with trains or busses to catch, stations to find, and reserved hotels or B&Bs to arrive at.

Often the most awkward part of the planning process is meshing flight-arrival times with the traditional Saturday start days for the rental. In terms of cost, transatlantic fares are normally less from Monday through Thursday, which means arriving at your destination airport between Tuesday and Friday, at the latest one day before you can occupy any Saturday-start-day rental. This arrangement actually works out well. If you have rented in some rural area away from your destination city, you will need to figure time to clear customs, pick up your car or travel to the railroad station, and travel to the rental itself. This is an exhausting effort when suffering from sleep deprivation or jet lag. Your best bet is to reserve a room in a hotel or B&B within easy reach of your destination, relax, get a good night's sleep, and depart the following day. Arrival even two or three days in advance makes the journey more pleasant as well as enabling you to take advantage of lower air fares. If working six months or so in advance on rental reservations, you may wish to delay making airline reservations to assure the best prices.

If you are planning your trip for the off-seasons, there are two things working for you in addition to lower prices and thinner crowds. First, many rental companies offer midweek bookings and even rental periods for less than a full week. If this is not noted in the catalog or materials received, just ask the rental reservationist. Second, you probably will not have to book a hotel or B&B in advance for your brief pre-rental stay.

First Contact

Be sure to have a specific travel time frame in mind before contacting the rentals. If you are planning your trip for any peak or high season (see the appropriate country chapter and region for the seasons), contact these rentals at least six to seven months in advance. For the shoulder seasons, three months advance is usually adequate. In low season, four to six weeks is sufficient.

Once you have decided on the region you want to visit and have selected two or so companies with rental properties there (see chapter two), you are ready to contact the companies. If you are working well in advance, your first communication should be a request for a catalog sent to you airmail. If time is short, make the contact as if no catalog is available. For companies that do not offer descriptive catalogs or will not mail them overseas, prepare a list of your requirements and the important specifics about the dates, your party size, budget, and the like. Do this in letter form for the mail or fax or to use as an outline to follow when you telephone. (An example can be found at the end of this chapter.)

The more concisely and completely you convey your needs, the better the company can canvass its properties and respond with a choice of places that meet your requirements for the time period you want. Your communication, in whatever form, should include the following subjects:

Location: Where do you want to be—on or near the beach, in the center of a village, in a remote rural area? Perhaps you would like a historic urban area, like Bloomsbury, or you want to be on the Rhine. Which *arrondissements* (districts) in Paris do you prefer, or will any do? Do you want to stay in Florence proper or in the nearby Tuscan hills? Keep your budget in mind and prioritize your list. You might even draw a line between those locale features that are essential (you won't settle for less) and those that are desirable but not essential; perhaps they will be unaffordable or unavailable. If you are inflexible, the odds are that even if you find a place that seems almost right, you'll be disappointed if it doesn't meet your precise requirements and budget.

Size: How large must your rental be? Do you know how many meters (square feet divided by 10.5) you would like? Is a studio adequate, or do you need one or more bedrooms? How many bathrooms are required? Is a sofa bed in the living room okay, or definitely not okay? Note that most Europeans do not include the kitchen in the room count (a two-room apartment may be a three-room by most counts, with a bedroom, sitting/dining area, and kitchen). Ask if it is not clear.

Number in Your Party: The total should include children as well as adults. If children are to be included, indicate their ages. (A few properties have age restrictions or do not allow children at all.)

Dates: Allow some flexibility if possible, and aim for shoulder or off-season travel. If you have seasonal flexibility, ask the company for the price during your preferred time, and for an off-season price.

Budget: Indicate the amount per week you are comfortable with, and the maximum amount per week you are willing to pay. As you reconcile your budget and your rental preferences, you may discover later in the process that you will have to lower your sights, or you may be pleasantly surprised that you can spend less. If you are traveling with friends, be sure you are all involved in working out these details, especially those having to do with the budget.

Style: Are you looking for something contemporary, ancient, or historic? Do you want a stone cottage, castle, farmhouse, or mountain chalet? Or perhaps style just isn't important to you.

Type: You may prefer a freestanding (detached) house, or you may be happy with an apartment. If you envision an apartment for your vacation, is one level (flat) okay, or would you like two or more levels?

Quality Standards: Define the quality of furnishings, construction, and appliances you want. Many vacation rentals are not the principal homes of the owners, so they may not be furnished or equipped like your own home. The exceptions are usually in the luxury category. The common descriptive terms in the rental business are "economy," "standard," "deluxe," and "luxury." In addition, the stars system used to evaluate hotels is increasingly being applied to rentals. Bear in mind that even five-star accommodations may have been built well before the age of inside toilets, in the cities as well as the country, so don't be surprised by exposed pipes and bathrooms in odd places. Garbage disposals are rare, and dishwashers are uncommon but are becoming less so. You'll sometimes find washing machines but, less often, clothes dryers.

Transportation: Will you have a vehicle, or must you be within walking distance of public transportation and grocery stores? If you have decided to have a car in a city, you would be wise to insist on allocated parking.

Amenities and Service: Is a swimming pool essential? Is weekly maid service and linen change sufficient? If you want more frequent service, how much are you willing to pay? Is a full- or part-time cook required? Do you want a car and driver? Bear in mind that except in the luxury standard, the more stringent your requirements, the fewer properties will be available.

Special Needs: Are there any features required by a handicapped person in your party? Do you need a baby-sitter? Is there anything else you can think of?

There are important reasons for working out and writing down this information. Many companies *do not* send catalogs to prospective customers overseas but instead ask for a complete description of what you are looking for. After receiving this information by fax, mail, or telephone, they match your description with properties they have available in your time period and mail or fax to you a collection of property profiles that seem appropriate for you. The property descriptions should include the prices for the period you want; if they do not, ask for these prices and read them carefully. If you are planning for a stay of more than one week, the prices are sometimes quoted per week and sometimes for the full period you have requested. They are always for the entire unit, not per person.

Selecting the Right Company and Property

Choose a company that presents itself well, is quick to respond, and provides good detail on its properties and terms. Choose a rental that is well described to meet your needs at the price you want to pay. Both are there waiting for your contact.

Step 1. Much can be determined about the companies from the appearance of their catalog: the layout, the completeness of the descriptions, the photography or drawings, the nature and directness of the terms and conditions, the booking forms, and the like. Companies that have no catalog but operate by matching your requirements with their property inventory, should not be considered inferior in any way—they just operate differently. If you are working without a catalog, it is important to receive the company's terms and conditions as well as photos and written descriptions of several properties they are proposing. In all cases, the timeliness of a company's response provides a good clue to the nature of the company, whether it is sending a catalog at your request or sending selections in reply to the requirements you have sent.

Specific responses to your requests should be contained in the catalog description or profile sheet. The rental company should convey the atmosphere of the property as well as accurately describe its style and type. The standard of the rental should be very specific. Although most countries require accuracy in such terms as "luxury" or "four-star," look beyond these words to the descriptions and photos themselves. You can then choose one or two companies that are best suited to your taste. Refer to the company descriptions in this book to see if there are any caveats or other idiosyncrasies about your choice.

Step 2. Narrow your choice to the company that offers the best rental prospects and make your contact. If it is a catalog company, rank at least three properties, complete the rental form in the catalog, and mail or fax it, depending on your sense of urgency (fax for high-season and shoulder-season trips). The company will confirm the booking of the top-ranked property available for your dates. If you have included your credit-card number, consider it booked (but play it safe with a final confirming fax, phone call, or letter). If you are sending a bank draft, they will advise you how long they will hold your booking.

If you are selecting one of the properties proposed by a company with no catalog, simply phone or fax them your selection, re-stating your dates. Give them your credit-card number, or, if they accept only bank drafts, advise them that a draft for the deposit (or in full) is being airmailed. If nothing is of interest try other companies or catalogs or ask for more proposals from the company you are working with. Select only one company, however, and work with it until the booking is made or you run out of acceptable options. In all cases ask the company to confirm your booking by fax or telephone.

If you are especially concerned about specific location or atmosphere, appro-

A look through a window of a rural stone house in the central highlands of Scotland. (Photo by Michael and Laura Murphy)

priateness of the property for children, special requirements for disabled persons, or precisely how far to the railway or bus station, a telephone call should be made. In larger companies the person with whom you are dealing may have no personal knowledge of such details, but they will usually try to find out.

Key Instructions and Three Basic Rules

You should never have to leave for Europe without all the information you need to find and settle into your self-catering unit. To help ensure this, be sure to follow these three rules:

1. Be thoughtful and careful in deciding where you want to stay.
2. Don't sign a rental agreement or make a deposit unless the information you receive on any rental unit coincides with what you are looking for.
3. Don't send your final rental check or credit card authorization until you are comfortable with all the arrangements.

Note: Few if any rental companies will give you final directions on how to reach the property or instructions on how to get the key until your full rent has been received.

If the answers to the following questions are not contained in the brochures, rental terms, and other materials you receive, ask them of the company in your subsequent telephone conversation or fax.

In case of problems with the property, is there anyone on or near the property who can be contacted? If not, whom do we contact?

What are your policies regarding refund of the deposit or rent paid in the event of cancellation before departure? What if you or the owner cancel the agreement before we depart or take occupancy? Is cancellation insurance mandatory?

Cancellation Insurance

Although it is not mandatory with most rental companies, cancellation insurance should be considered if you think there is any chance that you will need to cancel your booking for reasons of illness or another unavoidable event. Insurance covers the loss of a deposit or the full rent payment if you must cancel because of any of a number of legitimate reasons: the illness of one of the traveling party or of a member's immediate family (confirmed by a physician), a death in the family, a fire, or the destruction of someone's home, jury duty, or imprisonment. Cancellation insurance does not cover a change of mind or other frivolous reason. Obtaining this insurance (which can include other coverage, such as payment for forfeiture of nonreimbursable airline tickets) is easily done. Just contact one or more of the following for information and application: Tele-Trip Company (Mutual of Omaha) at (800) 228–9792, Travel Assistance International at (800) 821–2828, The Travelers Insurance at (800) 243–3174, or International Travelers Assistance Association at (800) 732–5309.

Problems and Complaints

For on-site problems, such as a faulty appliance, leaking pipe, or a missing utensil you cannot do without, you are expected to contact the caretaker, manager, or the owner who is on or near the property. If there is none, contact the company representative whose name and phone number have been provided before your departure. If you have not received this information soon after you have booked, be sure to request it. Complaints of a more serious nature, such as finding that the property is not as it was advertised, or its location is not as it was described, must be dealt with immediately by contacting the rental company. Do not wait until your return home: Despite the best intentions of the Europeans, it can be difficult and costly to resolve problems across the Atlantic.

When the company must cancel, which is rare, it will find another comparable property, or perhaps offer one that is even more expensive at the price of the cancelled rental. If a cancellation should occur, remember that you're legally in the driver's seat. You should never pay more for a replacement, regardless of its listed rental price, unless *you* initiate the substitution.

When we know of any company that departs from this standard procedure, the differences are noted in the company profiles in the country chapters or, more often, the company is not included in the guidebook.

Booking Two Locations

You may enjoy renting in two or more locations on your visit to Europe. In the peak tourist seasons, especially July and August, you will need to rent for a minimum of two weeks, one week in each rental. On the popular French Riviera and in the Lugano/Locarno area of Switzerland, the minimum is often two weeks from late July through August, or four weeks altogether. There are, however, some companies that offer combination options, such as two weeks in a London flat and one week in a cottage in Scotland, or vice versa. Combination options are noted in this guide, but even if they are not specifically mentioned, don't hesitate to inquire when you contact the company with your first call or fax. A variety of arrangements is often available, especially during the shoulder seasons.

One awkward aspect of the Saturday to Saturday booking arrangement is that it doesn't allow for the travel time between rental properties. Unfortunately, this cannot be avoided except in the low season, when companies and owners become quite flexible.

Damage Deposits

In many cases the refundable damage deposit may seem rather large. Apparently travelers who rent have been known to neglect or even steal from the homes they occupy. We have heard stories of stolen paintings, lamps, art objects, and even china and tableware. The owners, therefore, have had little choice but to require substantial deposits. As a rule, the more luxurious the property, the higher the deposit.

Sample Message

The message on the following page is an illustration of a typical letter to be mailed or sent by fax to a European rental company. The family and the rental company are imaginary, but the information is the minimum required for the first inquiry. *Please note: In Europe, the date is written in a different numeric sequence of day, month, and year than in North America.* Europeans put the day first and the month second, while Americans do the reverse. Thus, we write the fourth of July as 7/4/94. To a European, this is the seventh of April. An error in sequence can obviously have serious results. To keep it straight, think in European (and U.S. military) terms and spell out the date: 4 July 1994.

2 December

To: Villas Ligure   (Fax: 011—33—93—22—22—22)
    Boulevard Jules Grec, Menton, France

From: Matilda X. Billingslea
      1234 S.E. Hollingsbeck Rd.
      Portland, OR 97222 U.S.A.
      Fax: (503) 305—5432

Number of persons: 4 (2 adults, girl age 11, boy
  age 9).
Dates: 2 weeks. First choice: 10 June—24 June 1995.
Second choice: 17 June—1 July 1995.
Location: First choice in hills or in hill village
  within 20 km (kilometers) of Menton, Nice, or
  Cannes.
Second choice: in small coast town.
Size: Living room, 2 bedrooms (1 double bed, 1 twin
  beds preferred, but 2 twin ok). 1 or 2 bathrooms.
  Prefer dining room, but dining area ok. At least
  60 sq. meters (*use sq. ft. for Britain*).
Type: House or apartment in small house in hills or
  apartment in town.
Style: Prefer older, traditional property. DO NOT
  want modern high-rise.
Standard: Prefer moderate standard, comparable to
  ** or **½ hotel.
Price: Up to U.S. $1,000 per week, utilities, tow-
  els, and linens included.
Transportation: We will have a car.
Amenities required: Linens and towels, clothes
  washing machine, TV.
Amenities desired: Dishwasher, clothes dryer, nearby
  swimming pool.
Special: My husband uses a cane and prefers one-
  level house or flat. If a flat, ground floor or
  first floor, or elevator.

We want a property with the feeling of the south
of France, simple but comfortable; good place for
children; not crowded. Thank you.

22 August

To: Clube Ponta de Sagres   (Fax: 011—351—82—44—44)
    Figueira, Portugal

From: William and Joan Eveningshade
      222 Panorama Drive
      Roanoke, VA 24015, U.S.A.
      Fax: (703) 345—6789

Number of persons: 4 adults (2 couples)
Dates: 1 week. First choice: 29 October—5 Nov.
Second choice: 5—12 November
We are sorry to be so late, but since this is for
  your low season we hope that you will have something available.
We are two senior couples who wish to share a two-
  bedroom deluxe villa with a view of the ocean. We
  want this to be well located and quiet, with a
  private swimming pool. We believe that your rent
  price includes daily maid service; please confirm
  this. If possible, we would like to arrange for a
  cook to prepare dinner two or three times for us.
We want a spacious villa with living room and dining room, two bathrooms, and a deck or grounds.
  Bedrooms: one double bed, one with twin beds preferred, but either is ok.
Price: As this will be low season, up to around
  U.S. $1,000 per week.
Transportation: We will have a car and will drive
  from Lisbon.
Amenities required: We assume these villas are completely furnished and equipped with all modern
  amenities. Please fax brochure if possible, along
  with description of the villa you are proposing
  to us. We also need a map, or explicit directions
  to the villa or your reception office. Because it
  is so late, perhaps you should fax this also. Oh,
  can we rent golf clubs? Thanks.

Chapter 4

GROUND TRANSPORTATION IN EUROPE

Rail and Bus

Because the public transportation systems differ between countries, most of the country chapters include a short section on transportation. These are not detailed, but offer overviews and tips, as well as comments on whether a car is essential or merely convenient.

Travel by rail sounds romantic and is indeed exciting and enjoyable, but in addition to racing through the countryside on some great international express, there is the reality of arriving in a town or village and finding yourself some distance from your rented cottage or apartment. This may mean only a few blocks, but it might be much farther: not bad on a pleasant, sunny day, but miserable if you are returning late on a rainy night from a day trip to a nearby city or a longer excursion through some other region of the country.

Because most of the regions described in this guide are rural, anyone considering travel exclusively by train or bus should think of it as though it were the United States or Canada, where homes are rarely located next to the railroad or bus station. Although many European villages are on train lines and *remarkable* trains go to mountain villages located high in the mountains, railroads are very thin threads through a wide countryside.

If you do not plan to rent or lease a car, make this clear to any rental company you are working with so that they can advise you if the properties proposed to you are actually within walking distance of the local railroad station or on a bus route accessible to the station. With the exception of bus schedules that are associated with rail transportation, local bus schedules and taxi situations can only be investigated upon arrival.

Intercity schedules and routes for railroads are contained in the *Thomas Cook European Timetable*. We strongly recommend it to anyone planning to use trains exclusively. If you fall in this category, purchase this timetable early, when planning your trip. It will help you plan excursions away from your home base and confirm that the town or village you choose to stay in is served by rail (or a bus extension of the rail service). The timetables are available at offices of Thomas Cook travel agencies, many large bookstores, or by contacting: Forsyth Travel Library, P.O. Box 2975, Dept. TCT, Shawnee Mission, KS 66201; Tel: (800) 367–7984 or (913) 384–0496. The price by mail is $24.95 plus $4.00 for postage.

Rail Europe or Britrail

The best approach to rail travel for anyone who plans to cover great distances, take in large areas, or move through two or more continental countries is to purchase a pass issued by Rail Europe. For travel limited to Great Britain (which is not included under Rail Europe) there are BritRail passes. These full passes, however, are usually not appropriate for travelers locating in a rented home base, from which shorter journeys are usually the rule. Both systems do sell flexipasses for more limited travel.

Rail passes must be purchased in North America before departing, but before doing so obtain the most current information and prices. You may decide that renting a car makes better financial sense, especially if there are two or more in your family or party. Two regular fifteen-day EurailPasses, for example, will cost nearly $1,000; this is more than the rent of a moderately priced car for the same period. And, as we have noted before, there is also the matter of convenience for renters of rural properties.

The opening of the 31.4-mile-long Channel Tunnel, popularly called the Chunnel, has reduced train travel time between London and Paris to a remarkable three hours. The passenger train is called *Eurostar,* the latest generation of France's sleek TGV train. In addition, rail shuttles between Folkestone and Calais, designed to transport vehicles, offer drivers a choice between boarding a car ferry or hovercraft or taking the tunnel beneath the sea. Because drivers and passengers remain in their cars aboard the shuttle, the trip is said to be a strange adventure, traveling at high speed for half an hour in a featureless gray atmosphere. The decision on which mode is best, below the sea or upon it, lies partly on the cost difference at the time, partly on one's need for haste, and partly on one's personal preferences. On the one hand a two- to five-hour sea voyage (depending on the route) can be a relaxing pleasure or, if the weather is foul, it can be quite unpleasant.

Travel on the passenger train and vehicle shuttle is currently not included under BritRail and Eurail pass plans. Information and booking for all tunnel transportation as well as BritRail programs is available by contacting any travel agency or by telephone direct: BritRail International, (800) 677–8585 or (212) 575–2667; for BritRail and Eurail passes, telephone Rail Pass Express (800)

722–7151; for Eurail passes and programs, telephone Rail Europe (800) 848–7245.

The prices are set and are the same regardless of the source.

Automobile Rental: Money-saving Options

The mysteries of renting a car abroad are enough to confound anyone; there are deals and deals within deals. There are arrangements through hotel chains, and combined rail and highway plans, fly and drive plans, and the like. There are corporate discounts, and AAA and AARP discounts. One can spend a frustrating period just shopping around, but it usually pays off in savings.

The basic rule is to *always make your transportation arrangements before leaving for Europe.* To simply walk up to a rental counter at the destination airport will virtually assure that you will pay the highest price possible, unless you find a combination fly and drive, stay and drive, or rail and drive, which usually involve one of the major car rental companies such as Hertz, Avis, National, Europcar, or Eurodollar. Renting directly from one of these companies, however, is more costly than some of the alternatives described below.

Car Rental Brokers

There are three types of organizations through which vehicles can be rented. One is the major companies such as those noted above. Another type is an agency in the United States that represents European and international car rental companies (including those based in the United States and Canada). The third group directly or indirectly represents one or more of the three automakers of France: Renault, Citroën, and Peugeot. These rental companies offer the unusual purchase/buyback (lease) plan described in the next section. Some of the brokers offer discount rentals and lease plans.

Although there is very little advertising by the U.S. agencies, they are all legitimate, booking is easy, and the car you rent may well be identical to the one you would have received by booking with one of the majors. The brokers, in fact, have contracts with the majors, both American and European. If, for example, you book a car with AutoEurope for the south of France, you might be instructed to go to the Europecar/National counter at your destination airport. The brokers can be trusted, and can save you up to 30 percent.

Arranging a booking through a broker is the same as booking through any car rental agency: Telephone them toll free, get price quotes on the type of car you want, and location of the pickup and drop-off points (ask about drop-off charges in another location if this will be required). Call one or two of the other companies to compare prices for your particular circumstances. Some have lower prices in some cities, some in others, so shop around. The cars are categorized by type, such as a two-door subcompact or a four-door midsize and are each assigned a letter by the rental companies. The important thing is to compare prices within the same category. Only rough standards have been accepted within the industry regarding what type car fits into what category. Generally, they are:

A	B	C	D	E	F
Subcompact	Compact or midsize	Intermediate	Large sedan	Luxury	Wagons, minivans

Once you have ordered a car, you will be given a reservation or confirmation number and will soon receive the confirming paperwork in the mail. Be sure to study it because the pickup instructions will be included, informing you of the appropriate rental counter to go to on arrival.

Remember, in most European rental cars, automatic transmissions are the exception rather than the rule, so they add considerably to the rental price. The same is true with air-conditioning.

If you are working with a travel agency, ask them to book your car through one of the brokers and pass the saving on to you. We suggest, however, that you contact a broker directly. These are a few we recommend:

Auto Europe
Maine
(800) 223–5555
(207) 828–2525

Europa-Let, Inc.
Oregon
(800) 462–4486
(503) 484–5806

Europe By Car
New York
(800) 223–1516
(212) 581–3040

Eurorent
Florida
(800) 521–2235
(305) 351–9006

Foremost Eurocar
California
(800) 272–3299
(818) 786–1960

ITS
Florida
(800) 521–0643

Town and Country
Florida
(Rentals in U.K.)
(800) 248–4350

Kenning
Florida
(U.K., Ireland, and Portugal)
(800) 227–8990

Kemwell
New York
(800) 678–0678
(914) 835–5555

Our experience has been with Kenning, ITS, and Auto Europe, all of which gave excellent service both in the booking process and in the quality of the cars we drove in Europe.

Le Case Gialli, one of the houses of the Italian vineyard estate of Villa Saulina, looks southward across the vineyards of the farm I Mori.
(Courtesy Villa Saulina)

Insurance (And How to Avoid the Collision Premium)

Liability and comprehensive insurance are included in the price of the vehicle rental, but collision is not. In fact, along with Value Added Tax, collision coverage is one of the two items that add appreciably to the cost of a car rental. There is, however, a way you can be covered at no extra cost.

Most major credit card issuers offer as a service to their clients damage (collision) insurance coverage on rental cars at no cost to the cardholder if the vehicle is paid for with their card. American Express, for example, at present covers the cost of collision insurance for the first thirty-one days for overseas rentals. Most VISA and MasterCard issuers cover the insurance, as does Diner's Club, but if it is not spelled out in the conditions page (or if you have misplaced it), call the customer-service number of the issuing bank or other institution and ask. And ask if there is a special number in the United States to telephone in the event of an accident overseas.

If satisfied that you are covered, tell the car rental agency that you want to waive the added collision coverage (it is called CDW, Collision Damage Waiver). At the overseas car pickup point you will be asked to sign or initial the waiver. This is where your credit card insurance coverage will come in. You may also be asked for your credit card to imprint so that in the event of a collision, the damage costs will be charged to your account *up to the deductible amount,* typically from $500 to $2,000, depending on the car and the country. In case of an accident where there is serious collision damage, notify your credit-card issuer by telephone. They should give you instructions, but in any case be sure to bring all bills, charges, and the police report back with you. Your collision coverage will pay the charges made against your account by the car rental agency.

Losses from your car by theft are normally covered by your home-owner's insurance. In case of such loss, it is important to report it to the local police and obtain a copy of the police report.

VAT: Value Added Tax

With one exception, the purchase/buyback program described below, the VAT is unavoidable if the car is picked up in any country that charges the tax. This includes all western European countries except Switzerland. VAT runs from 12 to 28 percent, depending on the country. The range of VAT in the western European countries covered in the guide currently runs from 0 percent in Switzerland to 21.2 percent in Austria.

If you are shopping for quotations from car rental agencies, be sure to listen carefully when insurance charges and VAT amounts are given. Although the agencies should volunteer these figures, few emphasize them.

"Lease" or Purchase/Buyback Programs: Legally Avoiding the VAT

There is actually no such thing as a short-term lease for vacation vehicles— there are simply longer term rentals by the week, often with full insurance and VAT included in the price.

Another program, to which the term "lease" is commonly applied, is actually a purchase/buyback plan. The word "lease" is used because few North Americans know what a purchase/buyback plan means or how it works. It is thought by some to be the purchase of a vehicle for shipment back to the States or Canada, and by others to be a complex and costly rental scheme. It is neither. It is, in fact, an ideal way to obtain a car for anyone planning to stay in Europe for more than three weeks. Although there are some inconveniences, it is certainly the most economical approach, as well as having numerous benefits. Under this lease plan you pay no Value Added Tax, and complete insurance (no deductibles, no damage waiver fees or deposits, full collision) is included in the single price. These features alone can save several hundred dollars, in addition to the lower basic price. Also, we especially like the twenty-four-hour emergency road service that is included, and the fact that the car you get is brand new. You become the registered owner and are handed title.

The car can be driven anywhere in Europe, and the insurance is in force in all but a few countries, where additional premiums must be paid.

The lease programs are available only through the French automakers Renault, Citroën, and Peugeot, and although free pickup and drop-off is offered only in France, pickup and drop-off is available in other countries (in major cities) for a modest surcharge. Even with the surcharge, the overall cost is lower than renting, especially for longer terms.

There is no extra cost for picking up the vehicle in one city and dropping off in another if both are in France. If it is picked up in one of the out-of-France surcharge cities, it can be dropped off in any of the French cities for no additional charge, and vice versa.

All arrangements are made in the United States before departure. In the case of Renault, it is the company itself that handles the arrangements from its New York office. It is called Renault Eurodrive and is the most prominent of the three programs. Renault vehicles can also be obtained through several independent agents, or brokers. Neither the Citroën nor Peugeot companies have lease/purchase offices in the United States, but agents handle the business very effectively.

The Purchase/Buyback Procedure

Because Renault is the only one of the three French automakers with a company office in the United States, we suggest that you call them for a Eurodrive brochure. Also contact at least two agents (telephone numbers below) to ask for the brochure and price list for the purchase/buyback plan for the vehicle make you are interested in (including Renault for comparison).

The price lists will show the various models of the manufacturer and the price for each model for a number of set periods, starting with three weeks (twenty-two or twenty-three days, actually), then in weekly increments thereafter. These will be prorated if you need the vehicle for less than the full final week.

Compare prices, pickup and delivery cities, and services. As with booking a regular car rental, decide the make, size, and model of vehicle you want, then with your dates and pickup/drop-off information at hand, call the agent, confirm the price for the period you wish, and ask them to send the documents.

These will include a contract and an application for registration. In essence, you agree to purchase a specific car at a specific price, to be picked up at the specific location of your choice on the date you designate. The company (Renault, Citroën, or Peugeot) agrees to purchase that car back from you for a specific price, on the date of your choice, at the location you specify. Count on it—it's a legal contract with one of the three largest companies in France.

In actuality, you will not pay the price of the vehicle, nor will the company pay you the agreed price; this is done on paper. The cost to you is the difference between the purchase and sale prices and will be the amount shown in the price schedule. The document you will receive will make all this clear. Suppose, for example, that from the brochure you have selected a Renault CLIO RL 1.2 five-door sedan for about six weeks (forty days). You want to pick up your new car in Amsterdam and want to return it in Paris. The financial end of the contract document for this transaction will look something like this:

Total price of car (including touring documents and full insurance) $14,000.00
Guaranteed repurchase price   – 13,040.00
Subtotal (purchase price minus repurchase)   960.00
Delivery (pickup) charge: Amsterdam   + 55.00
Return charge if other than free city   -0-
Value Added Tax   -0-
Total Payment $ 1,015.00

This example turns out to be about U.S. $170 per week; not bad for a brand new car, fully insured with no deductible, and twenty-four-hour road service. Had both pickup and drop-off been in France, the price would have averaged $160 per week. In either case the subsequent weeks would be $105 each for this particular car.

The selling and buyback prices are immaterial; it is only the *difference* that you pay, and the difference depends on the size of the car and duration of the "lease," just as for regular rentals. It is a completely legitimate program approved by the French government. The brochures issued by the automakers tell exactly what the price will be by means of the table that you will receive. But there are some important details and terms.

The minimum duration for a contract is from twenty-one to twenty-three days, although you don't have to keep it that long. The reason for this minimum is so that the programs will not compete with the short-term rental business. It is this first three-week period that is the most expensive part; the price for subsequent weeks is considerably lower.

Bookings must be completed at least six weeks before the pickup date, except for a pickup to be made in Paris, where four weeks is usually adequate. For a surcharge, the delivery can sometimes be expedited. The reason for this time requirement is that a new car of your choice is going to be delivered to you at whatever point you choose, which, of course, entails shipping the car to London, or Amsterdam, or Frankfort, if that is where you want it.

Pay attention to the size of the trunk as well as to the overall car size, type, and style. Among the compacts, the Renault CLIO five-door and Citroën AX10 have the greatest luggage capacity. Among the midsize cars, the Citroën BX models and the Renault 19 RN (with trunk) have the best space; in the full-size models, the Renault 21 and Citroën XM both offer 17 cubic feet.

A tip: Renault Eurodrive, as a subsidiary of the parent company, cannot discount their published prices, but the consolidators that handle Renault can, and usually do. It makes no difference to Renault—they handle the arrangements regardless of whether the booking is made directly with them or with one of the agents. So, unless you prefer to work directly with the car company, you can save money and lose nothing by calling one of the agencies listed below.

Renault Eurodrive
    Eastern and Midwestern United States: (800) 221–1052 Renault
    Western United States: (800) 477–7116
    New York City and Canada: (212) 532–1221

Auto France, Inc. (800) 572–9655 Peugeot
Kemwell (800) 678–0678 Peugeot
Europe by Car (800) 223–1516 Renault and Citroën
Foremost Eurocar (800) 272–3299 Renault, Citroën, Peugeot
Europa-Let, Inc. (800) 462–4486 Renault
Bon Voyage by Car (800) 253–3876 Peugeot

Our first experience with Renault's Eurodrive program was a decade ago when we picked up a new Renault 11 in Paris, traveled some 28,000 miles in Continental Europe, Scandinavia, the United Kingdom, and Ireland over a period of ten months, then returned the car in Brussels. (Six months is now the maximum limit for these programs.) We were so satisfied with the Renault operation that we repeated it several years later for a ten-week period.

As a final point, we emphasize that full insurance coverage is included in the price—it is a French law.

In summary, if your planned trip is for three weeks or more, call Renault and two agents that handle Peugeot and Citroën and obtain prices and car descriptions. Also obtain quotes from one or two of the car rental brokers described earlier in the chapter (these might be the same agencies that handle the purchase/buyback programs) and compare prices.

If you are planning a stay of less than the minimum twenty-one to twenty-three day lease period you must pay for, you can return the car early; just figure where the breakeven point is relative to a regular rental or rail travel.

Chapter 5

AUSTRIA

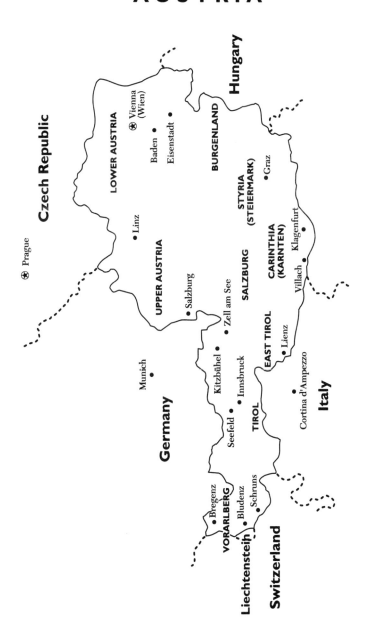

Austrian National Tourist Offices:

500 Fifth Avenue	500 North Michigan Avenue, Suite 544
New York, NY 10110	Chicago, IL 60611
Tel: (212) 944–6880	Tel: (312) 644–5556
4800 San Felipe	11601 Wilshire Boulevard, Suite 2480
Houston, TX 77056	Los Angeles, CA 90025
Tel: (713) 850–9999	Tel: (213) 477–3332

International Telephone Country Code: 43
City Codes: Bludenz 55 52; Innsbruck 52 22; Vienna 222
Example: To telephone agency PEGO in Bludenz from the United States or Canada, dial 011–43–55–52–65–666; fax 011–43–55–52–63–801.
Passport: Yes, but no visa.
Language: German; English is the leading secondary language.
Currency: Austrian schilling, abbreviated AUS or AS, sometimes S in Austria. Divides into 100 Groschen (g).
Value Added Tax (VAT): 21.2%
Electricity: 220v AC, 50 cycles.
Credit Cards: AMEX, VISA, MasterCard widely accepted; some Diners Club. Oil company cards are not accepted in service stations.
Main Destination Cities From North America: Vienna (for eastern and southeastern Austria), Munich (central and western Austria), Zurich (western and central Austria).

The Country

This chapter covers vacation rentals throughout the most interesting and rewarding regions of Austria and in the major cities of Bregenz, Innsbruck, Salzburg, and Vienna (Wien). Austria is slightly smaller than Indiana, and can be easily traversed in less than a day in a north–south direction, despite having to cross the Alps. Along its east–west axis, however, it is a long day's drive (650 km/400 mi.), even on the autobahns, between Bregenz at the west end and Vienna near the east. A look at a map of Europe will show that Bregenz is only about half way between Paris and Vienna.

Austria is an amazingly beautiful country, and not one to hurry through. Its mountains, lakes, and vast river valleys offer some of the finest scenery in Europe, and its villages and ancient cities are rich in architectural wonder and steeped in historical interest. The musical tradition of the country is well known. It is manifested in its famous opera and the renowned festivals at Salzburg, Vienna, and Bregenz, as well as the joyous smaller ones held in such places as the Montafon Valley of Vorarlberg Province. Of course, Austria's reputation for skiing and other winter sports is known worldwide. To skiers, names such as the Tirol, St. Anton am Arlberg, Lech, Zürs, Kitzbühel and St. Johann have long been associated with the origins of Alpine skiing. But from May through September the same slopes that beckoned skiers in winter become grassy, flowered alpine meadows, which draw walkers, hikers, climbers, bikers, and trekkers from all over the world. Many of the snow fields become some of the best golf courses in Europe.

Less athletic visitors come to be immersed in a world of mountains, music, the arts, and history. There seems to be something for everyone to see and do throughout most of the year.

Best Times of Year to Visit

Because of the almost year-round attractions, in many areas of Austria there are two high tourist seasons, characterized by crowds and elevated prices: July through August and in winter. The winter ski season usually peaks two weeks before Christmas through early January and again in February (some regions into March). As the periods of peak, high, shoulder, and low seasons vary throughout the country, it is important to check the property catalogs carefully, or determine from the rental company the exact dates of the seasons. There can be a marked difference in rental prices. Low-season prices are often less than half of those in high season and often include incentives such as a free week if you rent for three and better rates for groups. Austrian rental companies can provide you with more detailed information about rental seasons and low-season bargains than their Canadian and U.S. counterparts.

If skiing isn't a priority, the best times to visit are mid-April through early June and October, when the weather is mild, there are fewer tourists, and low prices. For virtual isolation, the month of November and the period from mid-March to mid-April are the real off-seasons. The first lies between the end of the warm days of autumn and the beginning of the ski season, and the latter after low and mid-altitude skiing has ended and spring has begun. There are no crowds, low rates apply, and the changing seasons lend even more beauty to the mountain scenery. Hikers tramp the high country, bikers ride the mountain roads and trails, and fishermen flail the alpine lakes. If you plan to visit rural areas during this period, tell the agent you want a place above the valley fog.

In addition to the general seasons there are local holiday periods that often influence rental prices. We have suggested to the companies that a leveling out of seasonal and holiday prices, perhaps down to three or four calendar periods, would be helpful to potential clients. As it stands, the main Austrian rental company, PEGO, has six different rates to cover *thirteen* different time periods. Although their price list is not hard to deal with, it is awkward. Its heading looks like this:

Ref. num.	num. pers. price per week	21.12-04.01		26.10-21.12 04.01-08.02 14.03-11.04 18.04-25.04		08.02-14.03 11.04-18.04		25.04-30.05 03.10-31.10		30.05-04.07 22.08-03.10		04.07-22.08	
		AS	DM	AS	DM	AS	DM	AS	DM	AS	DM	AS	DM
V100-1	1 - 8	5670	810	4515	645	5110	730	4515	645	5040	720	5740	820
V100-2 a	1 - 4	10150	1450	8120	1160	8120	1160	8400	1200	8400	1200	10150	1450
V100-2 b	1 - 4	10920	1560	9310	1330	9310	1330	9660	1380	9660	1380	10990	1570
V100-5	1 - 4	4060	580	3815	545	3815	545	3815	545	3815	545	5425	776

The confusing numbers are the date periods, but because they are typical of European date writing, a little practice will make travel and travel planning easier. (See chapter three, Sample Message.)

The letters AS and DM heading the six columns show the prices below them in Austrian schillings and Deutschemarks (Germany). The letter V in the reference number column indicates the property is in Vorarlberg. Other listings would be marked T for Tirol, S for Salzburger, ST for Styria, K for Karnten (Carinthia), and W for Vienna (Wien).

General Information About Rentals

The terms "holiday house," "chalet," or "bungalow" are the names applied to separate dwellings, to be occupied only by the booking party. "Holiday flat" or "apartment" indicate that there are other units in the building. The style of most rural or village apartment buildings is what Americans think of as chalet style—with peaked but gently sloped roofs, balconies, and shuttered windows. Most accommodations include sheets, towels, and linens, and this information is usually provided in the rental catalog or the property descriptions. If it is not, make a point of requesting it.

For many rural rentals, especially those owned by families or private individuals, there are four possible charges in addition to the rent: heat, electricity, final cleaning, and local tax. Normally they are not expensive, and are usually paid directly to the owner or key holder upon your arrival. The rental company price quote or catalog will show these additional charges: a set amount for cleaning, and tax, and a variable rate for utilities, depending on use. Unlike most North American vacation rentals, where all these charges are included, the thinking in Europe seems to be that each renter should pay only for what is used. Despite being a small nuisance, perhaps it is a more democratic approach than spreading the cost across all renters. If these additional charges are not shown in the property description, ask the company about them.

Regular rental periods are Saturday to Saturday, but other times can be arranged during low seasons. Rents are often reduced for stays longer than three weeks, and there are some reductions for older persons and larger parties. These and other bargains are spelled out in the catalogs and property descriptions of the two principal rental companies, especially PEGO's, less so Interhome's.

In addition to the rental companies, most of the provincial tourist offices in Austria maintain lists of available short-term rentals and will help travelers find one. We advise against this in the high seasons, and certainly during festival periods, but if you plan an off-season visit and feel comfortable going to Europe with no reservation in hand, try the tourist office. Booking directly with the owners or apartment block saves considerable money in commissions. You should, however, check the accommodation before committing to it. The provincial offices are located at the following addresses:

Vorarlberg: Römerstrasse 7/I, Bregenz

Tirol: Bozner Platz 6, Innsbruck

Salzburger Land: Alpenstrasse 96, Salzburg

Styria: St. Peter Hauptstrasse 243, Graz

Carinthia: Halleggerstrasse 1, Krumpendorf

Upper Austria: Schillerstrasse 50, Linz

Burgenland: Schloss Esterhazy, Eisenstadt

Vienna: Obere Augartenstrasse 40, Vienna

Where to Stay: The Regions

Vacation rentals are available throughout the country, but bear in mind that Austria is too large and too varied to explore easily from a single location. For a stay of one week it makes sense to locate reasonably near the places that are of special interest to you. If you want to explore the entire country, plan to spend at least a week in each of two locations. For a visit during the months from mid-march to mid-October, the Vorarlberg and Tirol provinces offer numerous good rentals for exploring the western area. A village location anywhere in Salzburg Province is ideal for day trips to the central and western parts of the country, even as far as Innsbruck. All of the eastern area, including overnighters to Vienna, can be explored from a rental base in Carinthia (Kärnten), or Styria (Steiermark).

If you must visit in the high summer season or during a festival event, we recommend that you avoid making your home base in the cities of Bregenz, Salzburg, Innsbruck, or Vienna; rather, book a rural property in a nearby town and commute. For Bregenz, this means anywhere in Vorarlberg Province. From anywhere in Tirol or eastern Vorarlberg, the wonderful city of Innsbruck can be easily reached. Near Salzburg, the villages of the lake country just to the north and east offer beauty and easy access to the city; try St. Gilgen, Faistenau, Mattsee, St. Wolfgang, or Mondsee. Near Vienna are the towns of Baden and Willendorf, good locations if visits to Vienna in high season are unavoidable. As for the provinces of Styria or Carinthia, they are more rural, dotted with lakes, ideal for getting away from the crowds in high season, and lovely at any time.

If it is to be a skiing vacation, the choices are almost as numerous, but additional factors should be considered. Many of the ski resorts are communities created to cater to skiers, and are basically a cluster of hotels, apartments, ski shops, gift shops, discos, and restaurants. They are communities that, as an Austrian friend noted, have little life of their own. Outside of the ski season, or when summer tourists are not riding the gondolas, the towns are dead. They lack a sizable permanent population, and usually have little history. These are the higher-altitude resort towns, crammed and festive in the ski season, generally dull the rest of the year.

During ski season, the prices of accommodations, meals, lift tickets, and entertainment seem to reflect the altitude: the higher the town, the higher the prices. The high-altitude resort towns are peopled by the international wealthy and pretenders. They are places to be "seen," as well as to enjoy great skiing in mountains high enough to offer the best snow conditions and longest seasons. Among these towns are Lech am Arlberg and Zürs in Vorarlberg Province; and St. Anton and Seefeld (near Innsbruck, famed for Nordic skiing), Igls, St. Johann, and Kitzbühel of Tirol Province.

Among the many lively villages in which skiing and tourism are important but not the sole source of revenue, our favorites lie in the Montafon Valley, in Vorarlberg. Most of these are at lower altitudes than the international ski resorts, so their winter seasons begin later and end earlier. Nevertheless, they are beautiful villages to stay in at any time of year. In fact, if the international ski set is not your dish, or if between $250 and $600 per night for a hotel room seems extravagant, rent a chalet or apartment in one of the valley towns and commute. For example, it is less than an hour's drive between the Montafon Valley towns and the high-altitude resort of Zürs. As average skiers of modest means, we prefer staying in the valley towns, and capitalizing on the great slopes that surround them; they are usually far less crowded than those of the more fashionable resorts.

As for staying in the cities of Salzburg, Vienna, or Innsbruck, an apartment is ideal. Although most are not as centrally located as the premium hotels, they cost far less, saving you several hundred dollars if a stay of a week or more is planned. During the high winter ski season, you can stay in one of these cities and commute to a resort. If you stay in Salzburg, for example, you can drive to St. Johann or Kitzbühel.

We chose to explore five regions that are the principal destinations of visitors to Austria. Although we visited them before the ski season, we tried to view these areas from the perspectives of both skiers and summer travelers. Following are the provinces from west to east.

Vorarlberg Province
Environs and Accommodations

This westernmost province has it all. There is Lake Constance (Bodensee), Liechtenstein, and Switzerland on the western border; the high valleys, peaks, and villages of the Bregenz Woods, which rise eastward from the lake toward the great mountains and ski resorts of the Arlberg; and the Montafon valley, with its beautiful little villages, alpine meadows, great peaks, streams, and lakes.

We stayed in the Montafon Valley in a pleasant apartment in the village of Schruns (pop. 4,000), one of over three hundred vacation rental properties in Vorarlberg Province, most of which are handled by PEGO, the oldest and most accommodating rental company in Austria. Peter Godula and his staff at PEGO know the area and the properties very well. We spent hours with Godula driving and walking the alpine slopes above Schruns, getting a feeling for the area before there was any discussion of his company and the properties it handled.

There are twelve villages scattered along the Montafon valley, with an aggregate permanent population of 17,000. Dozens of gondolas, cog railways, and chair lifts rise from the valley floor into spectacular mountains, making the region not only one of Austria's best ski areas, but affording access to the peaks and high country meadows and lakes by summer hikers and climbers.

There are good ski schools, climbing schools, and even tennis schools for interested summer visitors, but as we mentioned earlier, this is not one of the high-fashion resort areas; it is more relaxed and less expensive. Ernest Hemingway, who enjoyed skiing in the Montafon, favored the Taube hotel.

The Montafon valley rises toward the south into the Silvretta Alps, so if downhill skiing is your aim, the southern villages, at the highest altitude, are the best choices. These include Gaschurn (1,000 m/3,250 ft.) and St. Gallenkirch (900 m/2,925 ft.). Just above the main town of Schruns (700 m/2,275 ft.) is Bartholomäberg (1,100 m/3,575 ft.). The villages of the Montafon Valley are close to each other, so select the most appealing chalet or chalet apartment rather than allowing altitude to determine your choice.

Elsewhere in Vorarlberg are holiday chalets and apartments in small villages in the alpine meadows of the Bregenzerwald (Bregenz Woods). They are well located for lovers of nature, scenery, and tranquility and, in winter, Nordic skiing. From the eastern area it is a short commute to the big alpine ski resorts at Lech, Zürs, and St. Anton-am-Arlberg.

Bregenzerwald comprises several hundred square miles of forest and meadowland with high peaks in the east. Rentals are available in and near the villages of Hittisau, Sibratsgfäll, Mellau, Au, and Mettelberg. A stay in any of these towns is rewarding, especially for persons interested in getting away from it all, summer or winter.

Although there are properties in the area of Lake Constance and along the

Rhine we suggest the Montafon valley or Bregenz Woods for best year-around enjoyment.

Location and Transportation

Vorarlberg occupies extreme western Austria. The main cities are Bregenz and Bludenz, but a visit to the ancient and interesting Rhine valley town of Feldkirch is essential. Within a few hours by car or train are Innsbruck to the east, Zurich and Switzerland to the west, and Munich, Germany, to the north.

Mainline rail service is excellent, and there is even commuter service between Bludenz and Schruns, about halfway up the Montafon Valley. A vehicle is essential for a stay in the Bregenz Woods area but not for a stay in the Montafon Valley, although a car opens up vistas otherwise not accessible, and makes for better access between Montafon villages and the high Arlberg ski resorts.

If you want to be near a railroad station, be sure to make clear your requirements at the time of your first contact with the rental company. In Vorarlberg, the rural towns with rentals available and railroad service include St. Anton im Montafon, Vandans, and Schruns (all in the Montafon Valley), and Lech in the high Arlberg mountains, with rail connections to St. Anton-am-Arlberg, just across the border in Tirol (not to be confused with St. Anton-im-Montafon).

Prices

Rents run the gamut in Vorarlberg, dictated not so much by the quality and size of the accommodation as by its location. For example, a three-room apartment we stayed in (called a two room in the catalogs because the kitchen is not counted) is three blocks from the center of the village of Schruns. It is the equivalent of a three-star hotel, and rents for about $600 per week for two persons in peak ski season (two Christmas weeks), $510 in high summer season (July and August) and $300 in low season (January, April, May, and October). It accommodates four persons (two on a studio bed in the living room or in bunks in the bedroom), at a slightly higher rent.

By comparison, in the peak ski season a similar apartment in the ski resort town of Lech will run about 30 percent higher, and in fashionable St. Anton-am-Arlberg, some thirty miles from Schruns, peak rent for a similar apartment is almost double. A hotel room in Lech of equal standard will cost about $300 per night in peak (demi-pension required).

A deluxe four-bedroom holiday home in Schruns rents from $900 per week in low season to about $1,150 in high, and $1,300 during the two weeks of Christmas. There is a garage, dishwasher, telephone, washing machine, TV, stereo, outdoor grill, and a great view. It will accommodate eight persons comfortably. The comparison with hotel prices is obvious.

These illustrations represent a good average for the province, but are lower than in the winter resorts of the Arlberg area; there are also simpler places, and more deluxe.

Advance Booking Time

For December, July, August: six months
For January, February, September: four months
Rest of year: zero to two months

Tirol Province

Environs and Accommodations

This province, the best known outside of Austria, adjoins Vorarlberg on its west. With Vorarlberg it shares the mountains and ski areas of the Arlberg; to the east is the Province of Salzburg. It is described as the heart of the Austrian Alps, and it is the most spectacularly beautiful.

Chalets, holiday houses, and apartments can be found in virtually every village and town in Tirol, with others dotting the high meadowlands and alpine slopes.

Because it is better known internationally than neighboring Vorarlberg, and because Innsbruck has been the site of two Winter Olympics and is an interesting historical town, Tirol Province attracts more foreign visitors than do other parts of the country (except the cities of Vienna and Salzburg). With this long-running popularity have come more crowds and elevated prices during high seasons (see Prices, below).

At the suggestion of an Austrian friend, we stayed in one of the apartments in a large building styled like a chalet in the center of the resort/spa village of Seefeld. At an altitude of 4,000 feet, the town lies in a wide, mountain-ringed saddle on a plateau high above the broad Inn River Valley, and only twenty minutes from Innsbruck, seemingly straight down the palisade of the valley. It is the area where the Nordic races of the Winter Olympics were run, evidence of its importance as a winter sports center. Its terrain makes Seefeld a fine area for cross-country skiing in winter and a perfect place for hiking, golf, horseback riding, bicycling, tennis, swimming, or just loafing in summer. Alpine chair lifts and gondolas can take the visitor to higher country and even more spectacular scenery. Seefeld is just one of many such villages in Tirol; it's hard to go wrong wherever you decide to stay. Apartments are also available in Innsbruck, a centrally located, beautiful, international sort of small city.

About halfway between Innsbruck and Salzburg, rental chalets dot the lake country in pretty villages such as Zell am Ziller, Wörgl, Itter, and the medieval village of Kufstein. Rentals in famous Kitzbühel are a bit more costly than in lesser known villages, especially in winter, but a chalet or apartment anywhere in this area would be delightful. Being near both Innsbruck and Salzburg is a real advantage.

Location and Transportation

The major town of Tirol is Innsbruck. Within a three- to four-hour drive or train trip are Zurich and Bludenz to the west, Salzburg and Linz to the east, Munich to the north, and Bolzano, Italy, to the south. The main east–west freeway (*autobahn*) and the mainline railroad between Zurich and Vienna run through the center of the province.

As elsewhere in Austria, a car expands a visitor's options for exploring the beauty of Tirol Province and makes more rental properties accessible. Mainline and spur rail lines serve many villages, however, so if you are not planning to rent or lease a car, tell the rental company that you must locate in a community served by rail. Among the Tirolean towns with both rentals and rail service are St. Anton-am-Arlberg, Imst, Otzal, Seefeld, Kufstein, Wörgl, Westendorf, Kitzbühel, St. Johann, and Zell-am-See.

Prices

All other factors being equal, prices in Tirol run a little higher than in the Montafon and Bregenzerwald areas of neighboring Vorarlberg Province. There is also a difference here in prices of accommodations between resort villages and those that are not. Villages in the Arlberg ski areas and close to Innsbruck command higher prices. For example, Seefeld, where we stayed, fits both criteria for higher prices: It's a summer and a winter resort, and it's close to Innsbruck. Our small, stylish, nicely appointed one-bedroom flat in a chalet-styled building rents for about $520 per week in winter high season (November through mid-April with a dip in February), $425 in summer high season (July and August), and $280 most of the rest of the year.

If you have a car and are looking for more remote tranquility, ask for a rental in a smaller nonresort village. A simple two-bedroom holiday house, perhaps on a high country farm, can be rented for between $220 and $300 per week throughout the year. You can count on it being neat and clean, although the less expensive ones might be simple in their furnishings and managed by owners who do not speak English.

Advance Booking Time

Summer and winter high seasons: six months
For midseasons: four months
Low (January, March, May, October): zero–two months

Salzburg Province

The Environs and Accommodations

East of Tirol lies the province of Salzburg, sometimes referred to as Salzburger Land. Near its northern border, the high mountains that dominate most of this province give way to rolling hills, which spread into Germany's southeastern state of Bavaria (Bayern). Despite the beauty of the lake country and the rugged alpine core, it is the city of Salzburg that attracts the majority of the province's visitors. The birthplace of Mozart, Salzburg is a center for music, art, and learning, as well as a city of festivals (Mozart Week in late January, Easter, Whitsuntide in late May, and the Salzburg Festival in late July and August). It is an outstanding city in which to stay, not only because of its own attractions, but as a base for day trips into the surrounding area.

If you are planning a stay in Salzburg, timing and advance booking are essential. During any of its many events and festivals, accommodations of any kind are difficult to find and should be arranged for at least six months in advance. Many Europeans book a year in advance, so expect to be in a city crowded with foreign visitors. An alternative during these peak periods is to book a vacation rental within reasonable commuting distance of the city and make day excursions.

To the east of Salzburg, about an hour by car, bus, or rail, lies an area of low mountain lakes and lakeside villages well worth making excursions to, or staying in, for a week or so. Rentals are available in Mattsee, Seekinchen, Fuschl-am-See, St. Gligen on Wolfgangsee, and Fastenau on Hintersee. Whether you stay in Salzburg and travel to the countryside or vice versa is entirely a matter of personal choice. During high festival times, car drivers will save parking headaches in Salzburg by leaving the car and taking the train between any of these towns and the city. You can also stay south of Salzburg and take the train from and to Bischofshofen. Consult the *Thomas Cook European Timetable* for train schedules or let the rental company know that you want to travel by rail. In the off-seasons finding parking in Salzburg is no more difficult than in any city.

Toward the southwest from Salzburg, Zell-am-See is an ideal town to stay in. Also delightful, and closer to Salzburg, are the towns of Marie Alm, Leogang, and Unken. In fact, it is hard to go wrong in selecting any of the lake region villages, still remarkably unspoiled. The best resource for finding rentals in this area is PEGO, followed by Interhome; together they offer rentals in eight villages in this outstanding area.

South from Salzburg toward Werfen, the Salzach River Valley narrows as one moves deeper into the Alps, changing from the open pastoral area in the north until, squeezed by the mountains, it becomes more narrow. There are four villages in which PEGO has apartments, Werfenweig, Werfen, Kuchl, and St. Golling, each typical of the area and of Austria: neat, charming, and old. Kuchl and Golling are in the lower, wider part of the valley, while Werfenweig and Werfen are more alpine, but the area immediately surrounding each is scenic. The towns are small enough that a car is not needed to explore one or another, but rail service south along the Salzach River is limited to a single line between Bischofshofen and Salzburg.

Location and Transportation

The main city of Salzburg Province is Salzburg (pop. 150,000), which can be reached within two hours by car or train from almost anywhere in the province. Major cities within five hours' drive include Vienna, Munich, and Linz. Toward the south, a visit to Austria's southern provinces Styria and Carinthia are worthwhile, and a round-trip journey of three days or so to Trieste, Italy, for a total change of scene is feasible.

The main east–west autobahn between Zurich and Vienna runs through part of Salzburg Province. Since the other main highways are all excellent, however, there is no need to stay on the autobahn.

If you are depending on rail and are staying in the lake country north and east of Salzburg, trains run between Salzburg and the town of Bad Ischl, with stops at Strobl and St. Gilgen.

Many villages to the southwest and west of Salzburg are served by rail. A car is essential, though, to truly explore the beauty of the mountains and the villages that dot them.

Price Ranges

Rents vary widely, and are generally higher in Salzburg city. We stayed in a modest, well located one-bedroom apartment ten minutes by car or bus from the heart of Salzburg, for which the rent is about $635 per week year-round. A typical apartment in the lake region north and east of Salzburg for between two and four persons runs about $420 per week in July, August, and the Christmas season, and $340 per week the rest of the year.

Larger holiday chalets (single-dwelling, three-bedroom homes housing up to ten people) are about $1,250 per week in high season and $775 in low. It is obvious that Austria rentals are among the most reasonably priced in Europe.

If you stay in the city of Salzburg, bear in mind that many apartment buildings are old and unusual. But don't let outside appearances concern you—once inside the apartments are comfortable enough.

Advance Booking Time

Summer and winter high seasons: six months
For midseasons: four months
Low (January, March, May, October): zero–two months
Salzburg: Easter and festivals: six–eight months

Carinthia and Styria

Environs and Accommodations

The southeastern provinces of Carinthia and Styria encompass the southern slopes of the Alps; Carinthia is also influenced by the marine climate of the

Adriatic. They have the reputation of being the warmest and sunniest regions of Austria, while still offering rugged mountain beauty, excellent skiing, and some of the most fascinating cities, villages, castles, and churches in Austria. In addition, they enjoy an early spring, long, warm and sunny summers, and extended autumns, especially Carinthia. In spite of their many virtues, these two provinces are the least known by North Americans.

Although Graz, the capital of Styria, is the second largest city in the country, the entire area seems unhurried, uncrowded, and undiscovered. Prices of virtually everything from hotels to restaurant meals and holiday chalets to groceries are less expensive than in the provinces to the north.

In Carinthia, the most appealing area to have a home base is in the lake country in the vicinity of the capital city, twelfth-century Klagenfurt (pop. 95,000). Many of the rentals in the area are on or near one or another of the many lakes. Fish from the Worthersee, Faaker See, and the Osslacher See are specialties at lakeshore restaurants and are amply available in the markets.

Styria is a less popular destination, a bit less spectacular than Carinthia, with lower mountains, more pasturelands, and wooded forests. Graz, the capital, is the second largest city of Austria (pop. 245,000), well worth a visit of several days to take in its old, architecturally distinguished buildings and the more ancient remains of fortifications. Although Styria is a good area for laid-back vacations, and there are many interesting itineraries to take, a week here is ample.

Location and Transportation

Especially pleasant among the lake district communities are Villach/Magdalenensee, Seeboden, Weissensee (an alpine lake with good summer swimming), Badesee, Spital, Velden, Maria Worth (warmest weather, best sunshine), Falkertsee (for skiing as well as summer recreation), and Portschach. Within a four-hour radius by highway or rail from the approximate center of the two provinces are the cities of Vienna to the northeast, Salzburg to the northwest, Innsbruck to the west, and Trieste, Italy, to the south. If you are planning to drive deeper into Italy, enjoy spectacular mountain scenery, and don't mind tightly winding roads, we suggest that in good weather you drive via Lienz (East Tirol), south to Cortina d'Ampezzo, Italy, and across the passes through the Dolomites to the autostrada south of Bolzano. A detailed map will also show a remote road through the mountains south to Venice.

Mainline railways intersect at Villach to the cities noted above and beyond, and there is extra service between Villach (where rentals are available) and Klagenfurt, but not all the smaller communities are served. There is also public bus transportation.

Price Range

This part of Austria is more popular in summer than winter (although there are lesser-known but excellent ski resorts), with crowds peaking in July and August. Some properties are in fact unavailable between November and March. The best time to go is in May and between late September and late October, when rates are more modest and the region is less crowded. A pleasant typical three-room lakeside apartment or small, independent chalet for four in the Carinthian lake district runs about $350 per week in those months, and $650 per week in July and August. In the mountain villages, in ski areas, winter is the high season. Prices in Carinthia and Styria are among the lowest rental prices in Europe, except for Greece and parts of Portugal.

Advance Booking Time

For summer and winter high seasons: six months
For April–May and October: 2 months
For January–March and November–December: zero–two months

Vienna, Lower Austria, and Burgenland
Environs and Accommodations

There is little about Vienna that has not been written in everything from spy novels and travel guides to scholarly books on history, art, architecture, music, and politics. The only subject left to discuss is how to find a city apartment or a home-base chalet or flat in the vicinity. By vicinity we mean close enough to make short day trips to the city from one of the easternmost of Austria's nine states, either Lower Austria, which surrounds the city and province of Wien (Vienna), or Burgenland. The advantage of staying somewhere outside of Vienna is purely economic; there is no particular excitement in the landscape, which is mostly an area of low hills, flatlands, vineyards, farms, and market towns.

Both PEGO and Interhome have rentals in Vienna as well as a few scattered throughout the surrounding area, within an hour by car or rail from Vienna center.

A stay in Vienna is a splendid idea except during one of the festival times or the high-season month of August. Of course it is exciting at those times—a city filled with people and activity—but hard to deal with unless you have been there before or you revel in crowds. If you plan a stay during the festivals or in August, book early and try for an apartment in the first, eighth, or eleventh districts. (PEGO and Interhome have a few; the former will offer advice on the best location.) You will not need a car in the city.

In the vicinity, if day trips into Vienna are your aim, consider Baden. It is an ideal out-of-Vienna location; 25 km south of the city, and served by bus. A dozen flats at modest prices are found in a pleasant building beside the notable Sacher Hotel. Baden is an historical town, a spa (with sulphur springs), and resort. Beethoven wrote his Ninth Symphony in Baden, which has long been an attraction to European notables.

Location and Transportation

Vienna, at the eastern end of Austria, is an ideal point from which to explore eastern Europe. That is, of course, if you tire of the city and its environs. A journey to Prague in the Czech Republic or Budapest, Hungary, is a four-hour trip by car or train. Salzburg is four hours to the west, and a day-long round-trip south will take you into the province of Styria and the city of Graz. Vienna is on mainline rail routes to all major cities and the towns in between. Within this area, it's easy to travel to and from most of the towns of Burgenland and Lower Austria. Among the regions of Austria, a car is dispensed with most easily here, especially if your stay is limited to Vienna proper or nearby Baden.

Price Range

Among the major cities of Western Europe, prices overall in Vienna are among the lowest. This does not mean that rates for accommodations and food are low, just that they are considerably less than in Paris, London, Zurich, and Rome, all else being equal. A room in a typical three-star hotel goes for around $200 per night, varying somewhat with location. A modest, well-located studio apartment in the first district will cost $700 per week; a one bedroom about $820. The most elegant one-bedroom apartments offered by PEGO, which accommodate between two and four people, are about 45 square meters (475 sq. ft.) and rent for $1,350 per week year-round. Apartments in the city are usually in apartment buildings not unlike those in any American or Canadian city, except from a different period in time. Unlike some rural or village rentals, the city apartments come complete with everything and include all utilities. A final cleaning may be extra, about $45.

As in most cities, there is very little seasonal price change in Vienna, but oddly, some rates are lower in the high-season months of July and August, when Europeans leave their own cities for a holiday in the countryside.

Rents in the outlying towns are not particularly lower than in Vienna, but you get much more for the shilling. For example, a two-bedroom, 1,250-square-foot house for four to six people on a farm near Schwarzenbach rents for $700 per week in July and August and $450 the rest of the year. The flats in the spa town of Baden rent for about $600 per week for two persons (add $200 per week per additional person).

The Rental Companies of Austria

With only two major rental companies with properties throughout the country, finding and booking is comparatively easy. Both are reputable companies but are quite different from one another. PEGO is comparatively small, Austrian owned and operated, and very interested in the North American market. Although PEGO catalogs can be ordered from the Austrian Government Tourist Office in New York, booking is a bit harder than with Interhome because international fax and calls to Austria are necessary. Interhome is immense, Swiss, and has an American-owned office in New Jersey, which makes booking easier. As for prices, we feel that PEGO has the edge—there is no commission added. Another PEGO advantage is that the office in Austria is easy to contact should any problems or questions arise after you arrive. We suggest studying both of these company's catalogs and price lists.

PEGO   Throughout Austria

Sägeweg 1
A-6700 Bludenz
Vorarlberg, Austria
Tel: 55–52–65–666 Fax: 55–52–63–801

With over nine hundred fifty properties throughout Austria, PEGO is the major source of rentals in the country. Based in the capital city of Vorarlberg Province, it has a high concentration of rentals, most chalet-style, in Vorarlberg itself and adjacent Tirol. It is owned and managed by the amiable Peter Godula and has a capable staff and thoroughly modern operations. The properties are carefully selected, and owners must meet the standards set by the company. Mr. Godula and others on his staff speak English.

A colorful catalog is available from Austrian Government Tourist Offices in the U.S. and Canada as well as directly from the company. The price list is a little hard to deal with because of the many seasonal rates, but it is well organized and relates to reference numbers in the catalog. Prices are shown in German deutschmarks (DM) and Austrian schillings (AS).

All the booking and payment details and terms and conditions are contained in the price list; the deposit at time of booking is 30 percent of the rent, payable within fourteen days of booking, along with a flat booking fee of about U.S. $25. If using a credit card, you can pay your deposit when you book. A confirmation will be mailed or sent by fax; all directions to the property and information about the keyholder will be sent upon receipt of full payment. Price reductions are possible for stays of three weeks or more, so be sure to inquire. There are often discounts for seniors (known there as pensioners), so let them know if you are

Many luxury vacation apartments can be found in picturesque Tirol, Austria's most popular vacation paradise. (Courtesy Interhome Vacation Rental Network)

over sixty. A damage deposit, specified in the confirmation sheet, **must be paid in schillings** to the owner or keyholder on site.

If you prefer not to work with a catalog and if you know where you want to be, your dates, the size accommodation you need, and your approximate budget, telephone or fax this information to PEGO, and they will respond with several options. For rural properties be sure to state whether you want an independent chalet/bungalow or an apartment.

Rent prices are surprisingly modest; in our view they are among the best values in western Europe. Each year PEGO seems to persuade more owners to provide towels and linens, but be alert to those that do not. PEGO is eminently fair and we recommend this company with no qualifications.

Interhome (USA), Inc.   **Interhome**   Throughout Austria
124 Little Falls Road   Alpenstrasse 54
Fairfield, NJ 07004   5020 Salzburg, Austria
Tel: (201) 882–6864   Tel: 662–845–586
Fax: (201) 808–1742

The New-Jersey–based office is the independent U.S. agent for Interhome of Switzerland, the largest rental company in Europe, representing some 21,000 rentals. It operates by sending a country catalog upon request then quickly responds to the client about availability of the selected property choices. The catalog property descriptions are not very complete, but there are small photos of the exteriors and a more complete description is sent when a choice of two or three possibilities are zeroed in on by a client. In effect, what you give up in display and descriptive information is compensated for by range of choices and moderate prices.

This is a very efficient operation: Interhome USA communicates with the mainframe computer in Zurich, which keeps track of their thousands of properties, making possible the quick reply time to inquiring clients. Simply choose two or three as possibilities, let them know what you are looking for, and be prepared for a fax or call about availability, usually within twenty-four hours. Or you can call or fax with your requirements as to size, type, location, budget, and dates, and several possibilities that meet your criteria will be proposed.

We are sometimes concerned about the long strings between an office in New Jersey and the rental owners in Europe, but there is an Interhome operation in each country, such as the one in Salzburg, which finds properties and looks after client interests. It's not very personalized but it works. The procedure is easier than making the overseas contact, but there is a commission charged. In shoulder and off seasons, always ask about discounted prices.

The first step is to phone or fax for their catalog; specify the country because there are several catalogs. The cost ranges from $3.00 to $5.00 and is well worth it. If using the catalog, select and rank three choices and call or fax again with the reference numbers. Once the choice is made and deposit paid, all directions and instructions will be sent. Payment can be made by personal check (US$) or credit card. The damage deposit, electricity, and other charges, such as tax, are paid on site. Cancellation insurance is automatic with this company at a cost of 3 percent of the total rent. This is a fair rate, but if you do not want insurance or prefer to go to another source, be sure to say so at the time of booking. More information on Interhome can be found in chapter 12.

Domino Apartments	**ALDA Travel Agency**
Sonnenfelstrasse 3/2D	Sonnenfelstrasse 3/2D
1010 Vienna	1010 Vienna
Tel: 1–513–4597	Tel: 1–42–1626

Neither company markets internationally, but if you are in Vienna and need an apartment, these are good contacts. No commission.

Chapter 6

FRANCE

French Government Tourist Offices:

628 Fifth Avenue
New York, NY 10020
Tel: (212) 757–1125

645 No. Michigan Avenue
Chicago, IL 60611
Tel: (312) 337–6301

2305 Cedar Springs Rd.
Dallas, TX 75201
Tel: (214) 720–4010

9454 Wilshire Blvd.
Beverly Hills, CA 90212
Tel: (310) 271–6665

Box 8, 1 Dundas St. West
Toronto, Canada
Tel: (416) 593–4717

International Telephone Country Code: 33
City Codes: Paris 1; Marseilles 91; Cannes, Nice, Antibes 93; Villefranche-sur-Mer 93; Villeneuve-sur-Lot 53
Example: To contact the Regional Tourist Office in Nice, dial 011–33–93–37–78–78
Passport: Yes, but no visa.
Language: French; English secondary language in tourist cities and areas.
Currency: French franc, abbreviated ff or Frf.
Value Added Tax (VAT): 18.6%
Electricity: 220v AC, 50 cycles.
Credit Cards: AMEX, VISA, MasterCard widely accepted; some Diners Club; No oil company cards accepted. (Use charge card.)
Special Events: Contact French Government Tourist Office for annual calendar of events, especially in cities or regions you plan to visit.
Main Destination Cities From North America: Paris, Nice

The Country

Equalling, or perhaps surpassing, the United Kingdom in numbers and variety of vacation rentals, France offers something for everyone: from simple, inexpensive rural houses (*gîtes*) to elegant châteaux, from apartments of every description in Paris to villas along the French Riviera and chalets in the ski resorts of the Alps. It is not a country that can reasonably be explored from a single home base. It is important, therefore, to plan rental periods in two areas or decide what part of the country you most wish to visit and settle in. In any event, it is safe to say that wherever you decide to stay, if you book appropriately in advance, there will be a rental property available.

Because France is so large and variable, the regional descriptions in this chapter cannot do it justice. Rather, they are summaries, written from the perspective of renting a vacation property. We suggest that you contact the nearest French government tourist office to ask for general information plus regional information for any area in which you are especially interested. Our personal preferences for nonwinter visits include the hill country above the Riviera (southern Provence), the southwest regions of Dordogne and Tarn et Lot, the coastal area of Brittany, the town and vicinity of Megève for alpine beauty, and the lower Loire Valley. Then, of course, there is Paris. These areas are described later in the chapter.

Best Times of Year to Visit

Where you plan to go and what you want to do will determine the best time of year to visit. The French habit of taking vacations in August and, to a lesser degree, July suggests some patterns if you must visit in those summer months. It is the coastal and mountain areas that become most crowded as vacationers flee from the cities. These are also the months in which prices in those areas peak. As a consequence of this migration, the cities are vacated by many of their residents but refill with foreign tourists. If you must visit from mid-July through August, avoid the coasts and mountains and stay in cities. As the head of Paris Sejour Reservation, the largest rental agency in Paris, told us, these months are good times to visit the city because hotels and apartments have lost many of their business clients to the beaches. Another Parisian wondered, however, who would want to come to Paris if the French were gone and only the tourists were left.

If you are fortunate enough to be able to go any time, discover why people love Paris in the springtime (especially mid-April through May). It is equally lovely anywhere in France. Move with the seasons: In early spring, head south for the Mediterranean coast. To visit cooler, wetter southwestern France (Dordogne, Tarn et Lot), go later in spring (May and June) and earlier in fall (September to mid-October). These same periods are good times to visit the lower Loire Valley, Brittany, Normandy, and the Burgundy regions. Avoid the two weeks before Easter and the week after if possible. More information on best times can be found in the regional sections of this chapter.

Ski Vacations

If you're planning to ski, there are dozens of winter resorts to choose from. The best time to go is dependent on such variables as the snowfall in any particular year and the altitude of the area. Most reliable include the areas of La Plagne, Val d'Isère, Megève, Chamonix, and Les Trois Vallées. The principal towns are, respectively, Courchevel, Méribel, Les Menuires, and Val Thorens. Avoid the two weeks before Christmas through the first week of January unless you don't mind crowds and elevated prices. In general, November, January 7 to

February 1, and late April are good months to go. (For more information on ski areas, see the Haut Savoie region later in this chapter.)

The Seasons and Prices

In France, as in many large countries with a variety of climates and terrains, seasonal tourist prices are not necessarily dictated by the calendar. High season for prices in the alpine ski resorts is midwinter, a time when the Riviera is virtually empty and rents are at bottom. In September, mountain chalets can be had for very little, while villas in the Dordogne and Provence hills still command near high-season prices. Rental companies (and hotels) often deal with this by showing their seasons according to the calendar but not tying their prices to the conventional calendar months. For example, high is considered to be roughly during the months of July and August, but prices in ski resorts shown in the "high" column are well below those shown in "Low," which range from November through March. Also, prices might be lower in the summer high season if the area becomes unbearably hot. If you have flexibility in your travel time and are looking for the best prices, don't assume that they rigidly adhere to the conventional rate schedules. It's important to look closely at the rates, surveying the prices for all the seasons, and paying special attention to seasonal idiosyncrasies. Christmas and Easter seasons, for example, tend to show upward price spikes in the southern climes.

General Information about Rentals

In the French rental business the term "villa" means a detached house that may be above average in quality, size, and amenities, but not necessarily. We often think of a villa as being located in pleasant suburbs, or a resort, or holiday area. In common usage in France (and elsewhere in Europe), the term can mean almost any kind of freestanding house, from large to small, and it can be either a private, single-family place, or a large one divided into several apartments. In alpine villages and ski resorts, the term "chalet" indicates a villa distinguished by a sloping roof, balconies, and shutters. "Bungalow" often refers to a single-family type of dwelling, and is the term to use if you are requesting a modern, freestanding, private house. The terms "apartment" and "flat" are used interchangeably, so if for any reason you want a one-floor apartment, avoid confusion by making clear exactly what you mean. Apartments are available in villas, chalets, and châteaux as well as in the larger buildings we often think of. A "château," originally a feudal castle, has also come to mean an exceptionally large and usually elegant country home. A "gîte" (pronounced "zheet") is a privately owned farm or rural village house, or part of a house, furnished and equipped for short-term renting.

The Gîtes Ruraux de France

Among rental properties available in France there are 35,000 or so *gîtes* whose owners are members of an unusual organization. These properties offer the possibility of truly experiencing what French rural life is like, not only by taking up a brief residence, but by doing the marketing, buying farm and dairy products from the owners or the neighbors, and myriad other ways of experiencing the local culture.

The *gîtes* tend to be modest in their character and in their prices, virtues that, along with offering a chance at enjoying rural tranquility, make them desirable and popular rentals. The history of their availability for rent is interesting (and bears upon renting one).

With decreasing rural populations and the concurrent abandonment of farm and village homes, it became evident that France needed to take steps to avoid the ultimate dissolution of traditional rural life and the cultural richness of centuries past. At the same time, there was the fear that tourism, seen as a means of bringing new life to rural areas, would bring uncontrolled modern development, as was evident in the high-rises and fashionable hotels and resorts along the Mediterranean coast. Controlling the development of tourism was the key, and the answer was the establishment of an organization that brought together the government of France, local and regional governments and authorities, and representatives of rural property owners and agricultural interests.

Named the *Federation Nationale des Gîtes Ruraux de France*, a quasi-governmental, nonprofit organization was formed to ensure that the cultural richness and variety of rural France remains. From the cliffs of Brittany to the vineyards of the Bordeaux and the valleys and forests of Champagne-Ardenne, much of rural France remains unspoiled and can be seen (and inhabited) by vacationers and travelers. For information on renting a *gîte,* see the listings for the Federation and for the French Experience at the end of this chapter.

Supplies and Equipment

In almost all Paris apartments, bed linens and towels are supplied, and utilities are included, as they are in most deluxe properties. In moderately priced apartments and villas, including linens and towels is not a universal policy. In most farm and rural properties, including *gîtes,* linens and towels are rarely included, but can be arranged for in advance (through the booking company). There may be an additional charge.

Although pots and pans, cutlery, and dinnerware are always furnished, some items may be different from what North Americans are used to. For example, in France a coffee pot may be either an espresso maker or cone filter, but it is not predictable which. If you are coffee drinkers, either carry instant coffee for emergencies or buy a small filter cone, filters, and coffee. Except in luxury rentals, few microwaves or dishwashers will be found; washing machines are provided in moderate and luxury rentals, but they are seldom accompanied by clothes dryers. The owner of a $3,000-per-week villa on the Riviera seemed outraged that a dryer was expected. After all, there is plenty of sunshine, and it is better for the clothes.

Where to Stay: The Regions

For purposes of identifying areas of interest to vacationers, France is variously divided into anything from ten to twenty-five regions. This guide carves it into the nine most prominent vacation destination areas in the country.

One of the great advantages to renting a home base is that the immediate surrounding area can be explored. But it is also important to feel free to roam beyond these surroundings and take longer day or overnight journeys. This means, of course, that it is not necessary to choose one style of vacation to the exclusion of others. A trip to Paris from Brittany or Burgundy isn't that difficult, nor is a visit to Pisa or Florence from the *Côte d'Azur* (Riviera), or a trip into Spain from the Languedoc or southwest France. It is a relatively large country, however, between 600 and 700 highway miles north to south and almost that far between east and west, so plan your vacation carefully.

Paris and Environs *(Île de France)*

In Paris, as in any major city, prices are high and, in general, you get what you pay for. If you rent an apartment for a modest cost, you'll be in a modest accommodation and, more often than not, Parisian standards for "modest" are something less than those in North America. Yet simply being in Paris is worth a great deal, and older buildings, higher ceilings, narrower hallways, small kitchens, unusual elevators, and odd adaptations of twentieth-century bathrooms installed in eighteenth-century buildings are all part of the package. On the other hand, the elegance and ambiance of some of the Parisian apartments available for short-term rent would be difficult to find in the United States or Canada.

Environs and Accommodations

The Île-de-France includes and surrounds Paris, encompassing a region rich in outstanding attractions within easy day trips from the city center. Most are accessible by bus, train, and car. (A car is usually more trouble than it's worth if you are staying in the city.) Plan trips to Fountainebleau, Versailles, Danpierre, Melun, and Chartres. High-speed trains make Brussels, the Loire Valley, the coast of Normandy, and even Bordeaux accessible on excursions of two days or so. We suggest, however, that if you have only a week, stay within the immediate region and save the more distant areas for another visit.

One problem for first-time visitors is where in the city to stay. Although there is an attraction to staying near Paris, staying in the city proper, is one of the important experiences of a visit to France.

There are apartments available in almost every district (*arrondissement*, pronounced ah-RON-deez-mont) of the city, and their locations bear as much upon the rental as do size and quality. One approach to finding where you want to stay is to study a good map and a reputable guidebook with clear descriptions of the various neighborhoods of the city. You will see that the famous points of reference: the Eiffel Tower, Arc de Triomphe, Louvre, Montmartre, the Church of the Sâcré-Coeur, Pompidou Center, Nôtre Dame Cathedral are spread widely throughout Paris. But as the metro (subway) and bus systems are very good, you need not make a decision based solely on being near one of these landmarks. Try to select an area where you'd like to be on a daily basis.

If it is to be your first visit, or if you are not committed to some special place as a result of a former visit, the best approach is to let someone who knows the city decide for you, within the parameters you set.

In either case, outline your interests in a converging order: Do you prefer to stay in old Paris or new? Are you generally more interested in shopping in the flea markets and antique stores or the designer shops and fashionable stores? Do you prefer to be close to some of the finer restaurants or will the more modest ones do? Do you prefer to be in an area popular with North Americans and other tourists, or do you want to be in a more "Parisian" part of Paris? Do you plan to concentrate your time along any special lines, such as historic art, modern art, music and opera, architecture, monuments and other historical places? A definite leaning helps the rental company find the best location for you or helps you choose an area from a Paris guidebook. The final factor is your ideal budget (and an absolute maximum rent you are willing to pay).

Location and Transportation

Be careful about selecting a location simply because you have heard of it—the chances are that everyone else has, too, making it touristy and high priced. For example, if you stay just off the Champs-Elysées near the Arc de Triomphe in the eighth *arrondissement*, you will find a premium locale rich with shops, stores, and restaurants, one of the Prisunic department stores (which also sell groceries), theaters, and an easy walk to the Seine and the Eiffel Tower. But because of these assets and because tourists know the names Champs-Elysées and Arc de Triomphe, rents in the eighth *arrondissement* are relatively high, as are prices for very ordinary food in the ordinary tourist restaurants that line the boulevard. Apartments farther out, in the sixteenth, for example, or in less well known areas will run 20 to 40 percent below those in the eighth, all else being equal. Again, unless you know Paris, see what locales and prices some reputable agencies will propose to you.

It helps to know that the *arrondissements* of Paris are numbered like a spiral, beginning in the city center. The Louvre and Palais Royale are in the first *arrondissement*. The second is just to the north of the first, the third is to the east of the second, the fourth is to the south of the third, and so on. Do not assume that a high number means a distant district; the eleventh and twelfth, for example, are adjacent to the third and fourth *arrondissements*.

The postal codes for Paris indicate the *arrondissement*. For example, the code 75008 indicates that an address is in the eighth *arrondissement;* 75017 is for the seventeenth, and so forth. Thus, when an apartment postal code is shown in any literature, it's easy to find roughly where it is.

Paris is the hub of France; all mainline railroads and most major highways run there, the latter making Paris a difficult city to drive in. A car is unnecessary and, as noted, the public transportation system is usually quite adequate, even for a trip to areas outside of Paris proper. If you are planning a short stay in Paris followed by a longer stay elsewhere and need a car for the latter, delay the pickup date until you are ready to depart the city. If you feel that you must have a car in Paris, be sure to advise the apartment management or rental company of the fact, and insist on a garage or parking spot. If none is available, try another apartment elsewhere or give up having a car—don't plan to park on the street unless you are staying well in the suburbs.

Prices

Apartment rentals begin at $700 per week for a modest studio in an outer *arrondissement,* and around $900 for a well-located studio. One-bedroom apartments rent for $1,000 to $2,000. Although the prices seem high, they remain a bargain at about 60 percent of the rate at comparable hotels and offer much more room.

Prices remain fairly steady year-round, slightly lower in the dead of winter. There are often short-term price increases during especially popular events (art shows, the International Dance Festival, the Le Bourget Air Show, the annual Jazz Festival). Check the list of events and celebrations in the *France— Discovery Guide* available from the French Government Tourist Offices.

Because of the high prices of restaurant meals, much can be saved by eating at least some meals in the apartment. We found grocery stores easy to find and food prices like those in most United States cities. In addition to regular (but small) grocery stores and the open-market stalls, the urban Prisunic department stores (called *magasins*) have fairly well-stocked grocery sections. Prices are a bit higher there, but the convenience is usually worth the difference.

Advance Booking Times

Although the turnover rate among apartments is faster than among rural properties, there is an ever-increasing demand, and many foreign corporations are booking apartments for their personnel rather than putting them up in expensive hotels. In addition, Paris is a city for conventions and events, some of which fill virtually all accommodations. Our recommendation, therefore, is that you book at least two months in advance for any time of year.

Brittany and Normandy
Environs and Accommodations

These are the provinces of northwestern France, meeting the sea at the English Channel to the north, and, in the case of Brittany, jutting into the Atlantic. The coast is punctuated by craggy cliffs and white sand beaches, while the interior is filled with wooded hills and farmland. From a base anywhere in this region all of Brittany and Normandy can be explored. It is an area, however, in which we recommend travel by car; there are too many fascinating places that are out of the way of easy access by rail or bus.

A round-trip visit of two or three days to Paris is feasible, but the chances are that there is so much to see and do here that you may not want to take the time. Even a day or two in England, and especially on the Channel Islands of Jersey and Guernsey, can easily be managed from Brittany. Ferries run out of Roscoff, St. Malo, and Cherbourg.

Vacation rentals are scattered throughout the region, and tend to be individual cottages, private homes, and *gîtes*.

As the months of July and August are pleasantly warm (while the south tends to be hot), the coasts and their beaches are a magnet for vacationers, especially French and British. May and June and September through October are ideal months to visit, when the coastal crowds are not too large. The relative scarcity of properties that can easily be booked from this side of the Atlantic adds to the problem, so plan ahead, book early, and don't discount going in the months of November, February, or March. It's a mild climate year-round, although winter storms sometimes rage.

Especially desirable are the north coastal towns of Brittany's *Côte d'Emeraud* in the vicinity of St. Malo, followed by some of the inland market towns and *gîtes* in the farm areas.

As for Normandy, there are scattered rentals available, mostly along the beautiful peninsular coast; the western area will provide interesting days of exploration, from Mont St. Michel to the city of Rouen. Normandy's proximity to England makes a vacation divided between France and England worth considering. The east of Normandy is not as physically beautiful as the west, and given the other possibilities in France, one may need to have special, perhaps personal, reasons to select this as a destination.

Location and Transportation

As noted above, having a car in these regions is a considerable asset. Many rentals are rural or on the outskirts of towns, making reliance on public transportation difficult. If you plan to depend on bus and rail, tell the rental company that you need reasonable access to a terminal. Unfortunately, this will limit your selection considerably.

There is direct mainline rail service between Paris and the north coast terminal cities of Brest, Granville, Cherbourg, Le Havre, Dieppe, Boulogne, and Calais. On the south Brittany coast the Paris rail service connects Le Croisic via St. Nazaire and Rennes. For details on rail service, consult a Eurail guidebook or, if you are considering a trip on an island or cross-channel ferry, the *Thomas Cook European Timetable.*

Prices

Rental prices are moderate, peaking in the high season of July and August. A one- or two-bedroom *gîte* can be rented for about $350 per week, a two-bedroom cottage or small villa will run about $650 per week, and a typical two-bedroom house for four to six persons is about $1,000. These prices drop considerably, from 25 to 40 percent less, in the low seasons—May and June and September to early October. During winter, the rates drop even more: a one-bedroom *gîte* is $275, a cottage can be rented for about $325 per week, and a comfortably spacious house for four to six persons is about $400. Grocery prices are modest.

Advance Booking Time

July and August: six months
May, June and September and October: two months
Rest of Year: five weeks from abroad, zero locally

The Loire Valley

Environs and Accommodations

The broad valley of the Loire River wanders almost the breadth of France; its long east-west axis is often called the garden of France. Although many rentals, especially *gîtes,* are available in the upper valley, south of Paris, most are concentrated in the region between the city of Orléans and the Atlantic. Since the climate is mild, this is a good area to visit in spring and fall, as early as April and as late as October. It is a valley of châteaux and of engaging small towns and remarkable cities such as Tours and Angers, and of castles and fortresses like Chambord and Chaumont.

In addition to the *gîtes,* scattered villas, and apartments, there are almost two dozen elegant châteaux in the Loire Valley between Vichy and Nantes that are members of an organization called *Châteaux Accueil* (welcome), an association of château and manor house owners who offer a glimpse of château life by renting guest rooms and apartments on their estates. These are available elsewhere in France, but the Loire Valley offers the most. (See booking information in the last section of this chapter.)

This is one of the most delightful areas of France to spend a few weeks in, ideally in the shoulder seasons of fewer tourists and crowds. And to savor the Loire in its entirety, consider renting somewhere in the lower valley, west of Orléans, for a week or so, and somewhere to the south of Orléans for a second week.

Location and Transportation

From a rental anywhere in this region of the Loire, it is easy to explore the entire area and also make easy visits of a few days to Paris and the Île-de-France and to the Atlantic coast area. (We suggest the train if you go into Paris.) As with most of France, although local public transportation is available, the Loire is best explored by car, especially as most of the rental properties are rural.

Mainline railroads connect Paris with the principal Loire Valley cities of Chartres, Le Mans, Angers, Tours, Nantes, and Orléans, stopping at many smaller towns in between.

Prices

Except for *gîtes*, rental prices are fairly high, partly because there are few rental properties in this region and partly because they are typically larger than in, say, Brittany. They peak in the high season (July and August); a one-bedroom *gîte* can be rented for about $350 per week, and a typical two-bedroom house for four to six persons for about $1,100. These drop 20 percent in the low seasons (May and June and September to early October) and during winter they drop even more: a one-bedroom *gîte* can be rented for about $250 per week, and a modest house for four to six (hard to find) for about $400.

Advance Booking Time

July and August: six months
May, June and September and October: two months
Rest of Year: five weeks from abroad, or go without reservations

Southwest France:
The Dordogne, Lot et Garonne, and Tarn et Garonne
Environs and Accommodations

Foreign lovers of the Dordogne River Valley might decry the inclusion of the valleys of the rivers Lot, Garonne, and Tarn as part of a single region, but indeed they are all part of the system of rivers and tributaries of a single watershed draining into the Atlantic by way of the vast estuary of the Gironde, on whose shores lie the vineyards of Bordeaux. This is an area of rolling countryside rising toward the east, of lakes for summer swimming, forests of pine and oak, vineyards and wineries, farms with produce to sell, market villages, Romanesque churches, and ancient fortified towns. At one time the Dordogne River was the border between England and France, necessitating much in the way of battlements and fortifications. Many of them still stand, whole or in part, today.

This is a region popular with those who love tranquility. Toward the south, into Tarn et Garonne, the villages are frequented by fewer tourists and remain even less touched by modern civilization than elsewhere in the area.

Rental properties, many of them individual stone or stuccoed houses, range from simple to modest, with a few in the near-deluxe category. There have also been some excellent conversions of rural estate properties, turning former wineries, stables, fruit storage buildings, and the like into comfortable accommodations. In addition, many of the rural houses (*gîtes*) are fairly large, often divided into apartments or split into duplex arrangements.

French Home Rentals, the company owned by the amiable Michel Tessel, is the only rental organization based in the region (at Villeneuve-sur-Lot) that markets its properties in the United States. M. Tessel has spent time in the United States and seems to understand what North Americans are looking for: comfort combined with French provincial style.

The rentals are liberally scattered throughout this region, and where you locate is probably less important than the character of the property itself, unless you have no car and must find a place near one of the three railway lines crossing the area.

Location and Transportation

The principal cities of the Dordogne region are Bergerac, Périgueux, and in the flatland near where the Dordogne River blends with the Garonne, the port of Bordeaux. In the valleys of the Garonne, Lot, and Tarn rivers to the south are the towns of Agen, Villeneueve-sur-Lot, and the beautiful walled city of Monflanquin. To the east is the city of Cahors, and within an easy day round-trip toward the southeast are Toulouse, and a bit farther, the walled city of Carcasonne, well worth an overnight trip.

Toward the southwest, again only a few hours away by car, is the Bay of Biscay and the coast cities of Bayonne and Biarritz. The latter is a living monument to the resort pleasures of the nineteenth and early twentieth centuries. A round-trip of several days can include the eastern Pyrenees and the principality of Andorra.

Delightful and interesting weeks can be spent living in and exploring this entire region. The countryside is beautiful (except for the flatlands southwest of the Garonne), the manifestations of medieval history are many, and the local foods are excellent. The scores of ancient *bastides,* free towns, founded mostly in the twelfth and thirteenth centuries, are varied and enjoyable to visit. A stay within 40 miles or so of Villeneuve-sur-Lot (itself a large *bastide*) is ideally central to the region.

There are mainline railroads that connect with Paris, Bordeaux, and Toulouse; stops in the region include Périgueux, Bergerac, Libourne, and Le Buisson. It is easy an striking distance from these stations to Carcassonne and Montauban. Toward the southwest lie Biarritz and San Sebastián, Spain. There is a big hole in the middle of the region that is devoid of rail lines, so if you must travel by rail or bus, advise the rental company before booking so that a rental near a transportation center can be found.

Prices

Prices are moderate in this region, far less than rentals in Paris, the Riviera, and winter ski resorts. They peak in the high season (July and August), when a one-bedroom apartment or farm conversion will cost about $600 per week. In the shoulder seasons (May and June and September to early October), prices only drop 15 to 20 percent. Off-season rates drop more; a small *gîte* or a one-bedroom apartment in a house can be rented for about $300 per week, and a typical two-bedroom house for four for about $400 (through a rental company). In the off-season months (November to March), however, it is possible to travel into this region without reservations and check with the local tourist office (*syndicat d'initiative*). There will always be something available. Not many travelers, it seems, spend their vacations here in the winter.

Advance Times for Reservations

July and August: six months
May and June and September and October: two months
Rest of the Year: four weeks from abroad; zero locally

The West and the Atlantic Coast
Environs and Accommodations

From the southwest corner of France, where it meets Spain and the sea, north to Finistère, the peninsula of Brittany, the Atlantic coast and its beaches seems to be the place for family summer holidays, when swimming, boating, surfing, and lying in the sun are the principal activities. But all of western France is steeped in some of the most significant events of European history. The signs are still very much in evidence, from the scenes of battles between the French and the British at Poitiers and the defeat of the French king during the time of the Black Prince, to the outstanding Norman architecture of the cathedrals of Angoulême, Luçon, Poitiers, and Saintes.

Boating on the inland waterways of the Poitou marshes near Niort, and eating at restaurants famous for mussels, oysters, and fresh fish are all part of the appeal of the region. And for visitors with a vacation rental, utilizing the fine array of seafoods and locally grown products in your own kitchen, accompanied by the wines of Anjou and Saumur, can be another happy pastime if you tire of sightseeing.

There are many rentals along the 375 or so miles of coastline, including a good selection near the shoreline that capitalize on the miles of white sand beaches. Some are in rural areas, some in scattered villages. It is a long way to go from North America to a beach, and there may be better ones closer to home, but in this region, consider the sea and beaches a bonus.

Location and Transportation

A week could easily be devoted to the Atlantic coast, especially north of the estuary of the Gironde, beginnng with Royan. Although there are properties available south of the Gironde River, excursions throughout the region of Poitou-Charentes are most rewarding. Along with clean beaches and offshore islets, the area offers visitors fields and forests, vineyards, farms, and the ruins from pre-Christian and Roman times, the coastal city of La Rochelle, and excursions to the important inland cities of Niort and Poitiers. Some pleasant coastal towns include Carnac, La Baule, Erquy, and Sables d'Olonne.

The mainline railroad follows the coast, serving Biarritz, Bayonne, Bordeaux, Saintes, Roquefort, La Rochelle, Nantes, and on to the end of the peninsula of Brittany at Brest. Four spur lines connect the mainline with Royan, Les Sables d'Olonne, La Baule, and Quiberon. If you do not plan to have a car, tell the agent you must locate in or near a town with rail service; the area is well served by rail, so this should not be hard to do. If you prefer a more rural area or want to explore away from the busier towns, having a car is essential.

There are two ways of planning a stay in this area. One is to time your visit with the spring or, better, fall shoulder season and drive around looking for a well-located rental. But if you must travel in summer, book well ahead, as you would for any popular beach area.

For first-time visitors to France, we suggest that there are many other interesting areas in which to locate: just to the south in the Dordogne, for example, or just to the north, in Brittany. When deciding where in this large region to stay, consider the centrally located town of La Rochelle.

Prices

Between mid-September and early June the rental rates are comparatively low, but many of the accommodations are large, private villas. Typical is $700 to $1,000 per week for a villa for six to ten persons in this off-season; the rent is double that in July and August. Smaller places are available, but the choice is limited. Nevertheless, to rent a good size private villa for under $200 per night is indeed a bargain. *Gîtes* are also available; modest ones are around $300, moderately good ones cost $400 to $450, and *super-gîtes* are priced like small villas.

Advance Times for Reservations

July and August: six months
May and June and September and October: two months
Rest of the Year: four weeks from abroad; zero locally.

Languedoc-Roussillon

Environs and Accommodations

This long region stretches from the Spanish border and the eastern Pyrenees eastward along the Mediterranean coast, almost to Marseille. Despite the obvious appeal of much of the area, in our many journeys there we have run across relatively few Americans. It seems only recently to have been discovered as a region for coastal resorts, and it is changing rapidly. Outside of the quiet old canal town of Sète, the port for the long-route ferries to Tangier and the Ballearic Islands, new resort communities, featuring clusters of white stuccoed apartments and villas, shimmer in the Mediterranean sunshine. Yet even now agents list only a very few properties in the region, and most of them are inland, in the valleys of the upper Tarn and lower Rhône rivers. This is just as well, because the beaches are always accessible by day trips, and the greater beauty of the area and its cities is not on the sea. For a seaside stay, look to the resort area of Cap d'Agde (midway between Sète and the city of Narbonne), a miles-long stretch of white sand beach on one side and a lagoon on the other. Although Cap d'Agde is a resort, nearby Montpellier, Sète, and Narbonne are not: They are interesting each in its own way.

Location and Transportation

The major cities of Languedoc-Rousillon are all worthy of extended visits, as are many of its ancient, smaller towns. Among the former are the walled city of Carcassonne to the west, Narbonne, Bezier, and Montpellier in a line along the curve of the coast, Nîmes up the Rhône Valley, Ales in the western mountains. One could easily and happily spend a week or more in this region, ideally renting a place in a village fairly close to one of the main cities noted above. Outside of the region, but within range of an overnight stay, are the major cities of Marseille, Avignon, and Aix-en-Provence.

For a special, longer journey, consider a voyage to Spain's Ballearic Islands on one of the large ocean ferryliners out of Sète. Trasmediterranea (Spanish) and COMANAV (Morrocan) both operate ships from spring to fall; the fare is modest, so book a cabin and take a first-class ticket. Contact S.N.C.M., 4 Quai d'Alger, Sète, France; Tel: 67–74–70–55. Toward the west and south, a visit to Barcelona by rail or car is reasonable from this region of France.

Three north-south rail lines intersect with the east-west coastal mainline (Geneva-Barcelona) at Bezier, Nîmes, and Tarascon, providing service to even some of the smaller towns, including Sète and Agde.

Prices

There is considerable variation, depending on location, season, and type of rental. The properties all tend to be large and attractive, commanding generally higher prices than, say, the West Coast. A simple one-bedroom house is about $400 per week in off-season and $700 in peak; top properties in terms of location, style, size, and quality begin at $800 per week in low season and $1,200 to $1,700 in high. Most houses in this category will accommodate six or more persons. *Gîtes,* as always, are simpler and more modestly priced, and are widely scattered throughout the region.

Advance Times for Reservations

July and August: six months
May and June and September and October: three months
Rest of the Year: four weeks from abroad; zero locally

Provence and the Riviera (Côte d'Azur)
Environs and Accommodations

Between the Languedoc region and the border of Italy to the east lies what is probably the most famous and varied region of France, so much so that it can rightfully be divided into three areas of different topography and climate. To the northeast of Provence are the Alpes Maritimes, a land of mountains, lakes, and villages. Toward the west the mountains soften, then give way to the broad valley of the Rhône. Between the two is the coast of Provence, the Riviera, of which the section from the town of St. Raphael east to the Italian border is known as the Côte d'Azur.

Despite the crowds that pack the area in summer and late into fall, and despite the high-rises that compete with each other for a glimpse of the Mediterranean, despite the yachts that pack the harbors at St. Tropez, Cannes, Nice, and Villefranche-sur-Mer, despite stony beaches and the high prices of virtually everything, the Riviera continues to draw people, newcomers and old-timers alike. The climate, pleasant almost year-round, the physical beauty of the area, and the Mediterranean style of its cities and towns all contribute to the

Riviera's popularity. Together they produce a distinctive ambiance, difficult to explain but apparent to all. Even if you don't go to one of the casinos, don't go to horse races, can't afford night after night of the tariff at the elegant restaurants, they contribute to the atmosphere. Sunshine, the sea, strolling through the seaside and hill towns, shopping for nothing in particular, picnicking, and watching people are available to all.

The wonderful week or two that can be filled in this area can be accomplished with ease from any of dozens of home-base locations. Accommodations in this tourist-impacted area are on the expensive side, and a basic understanding of this complex area helps. Three factors dramatically affect rental prices on the Riviera: location, season, and style.

The First Tier: The Seaside Towns. Refer to a good map of this area, and begin to think of the Riviera as three physical environments. First are the cities and towns that border the sea: the first tier. From east to west the main towns are Menton, Monte Carlo (in Monaco, not part of France), St. Jean-Cap-Ferrat, Beaulieu, Villefranche, Nice, Cagnes-sur-Mer, Villeneuve Loubet, Cannes, Antibes, Juan-les-Pins, and Golfe Juan. Farther southwest are Ste. Maxime and St. Tropez. In the center of this string of cities and towns, between Nice and Antibes, there is a sweep of hotels, apartments, and restaurants along thirty-five or so miles of the Bord de Mer, a broad seaside boulevard that sometimes changes name as it runs through one city or another. As desirable as it may sound to have an apartment directly on the Mediterranean, virtually all of the buildings from Nice to Antibes face the sea across this crowded boulevard. Many of the grand hotels and apartments were built when carriages, or at most a few automobiles, traveled the boulevard. Now the noise level is high, and you have the choice of keeping the windows closed or suffering the sound. East of Nice, however, from Villefranche to Menton, the cliffs rise more abruptly from the sea and the high-speed boulevard does not intervene; the same is true from La Napoule west to St. Tropez. The key, if you prefer an apartment in any of the seaside cities or towns, is to choose one that does not front on the Bord de Mer where it is wide and heavy with traffic. You should make this clear to any agent. In Nice, stay in the *centre* or *hors centre* in the areas of La Conque and La Mantega or, for less expensive apartments, toward St. Roch. In Cannes, the expensive hotels and apartments are along the Boulevard de la Croisette, and prices drop significantly a few blocks away in Le Cannet and Super Cannes. Of the adjacent coastal communities of Juan-les-Pins and Golfe Juan, rental prices are less in Golfe Juan. St. Tropez prices are high and can be avoided by staying away from the seashore, or across the bay in Ste. Maxime.

Also in this first tier are small communities, often like suburbs, in which rental properties tend toward the elegant, offering visitors quiet luxury and four-star standards at much less than a comparable hotel. (See Prices, below.) In these towns the rentals are often privately owned vacation homes of well-to-do Europeans that, for ten or eleven months of the year, are managed by rental agencies. Most prominent of this type of coastal community are St. Jean-Cap-Ferrat, Cap d'Antibes, and Juan-les-Pins. A little less expensive are Villefranche-sur-Mer, Golfe Juan, La Napoule, St. Raphael, and Ste. Maxime, all of which are delightful. Unusual among the coastal towns is Villeneuve Loubet, a newer planned resort community of privately owned villas set in several hundred acres on the highlands immediately above Antibes. (For rental information, see Interhome at the back of this chapter.) A town we stayed in, Cagnes-sur-Mer, is about halfway between Nice and Antibes; it is unusual in its unpretentiousness and modest prices, but look for an apartment at least a block back from the Bord de Mer, or better, north of the throughway in Haute de Cagnes.

The Second Tier: The Hill Towns Near the Coast. The hills that rise just back from the sea and parallel to the coast contribute to the pleasant climate of the Riviera and provide a setting for villages that perch on hilltops and even larger towns that spill down the slopes. The rentals are mostly in rural settings, often with broad views of the Mediterranean and the cities below. Many are apartments in individual villas, but most are villas of moderate or large size, many with pools. A few are less elaborate cottages, and a few are available in the towns themselves. Prices are less than in the coastal towns, but as the properties are larger, expect to pay high rent (or share with friends). These hilltop locations are very desirable, away from the dense population and tourist throngs that crowd the coastal band, yet accessible to the beaches and the cities below. Rentals in the areas of Vence, Mougin, and Grasse should be of special interest; just ask the rental company to provide specific information on the hill properties of the Côte d'Azur. A car is essential for staying in this hill country. The fields around Grasse, incidentally, provide the bulk of the flowers for France's perfume industry.

The Third Tier: The Interior. This is the country well back from the sea, characterized by small villages and winding roads. Here is the essence of old Provence, slower paced, traditional. British expatriots and other Europeans live scattered about in the villages, having taken up the tranquil life. Unfortunately, there are not many rental accommodations, but they can be found. Study the catalogs of Riviera Retreats, French Home Rentals, and Interhome. (See the back of this chapter for private listings.) You might also check the vacation rentals in classified sections of *Atlantic Monthly* and *Harper's* magazines, and the *New York Times* and other major newspapers. Most villages in this tier are within an hour's drive of the coast. A car is essential.

The Seasons. As in most resort areas, prices on the Riviera vary greatly with the seasons. Minimum stays also vary. During the peak season a month may be the minimum for a private villa, but two-week minimums are more common, dropping to one week at other times. The peak season is July and August; shoulder seasons are June and September, and low season is October through May. There are some variances, but these times generally apply. The price difference, coupled with the crowds in the peak season make April through June and September through October the best times of year to stay in this area. The weather in spring and fall is usually delightful. For swimming, sailing, and surfing, September can be ideal. The International Film Festival at Cannes (late May) seems to fill the entire Côte d'Azur with people, and prices spike upward, so unless you have a large budget and can book well in advance, avoid the area.

Style. Some places along the coast are considered to be more stylish, or fashionable, than others. All else being equal as far as accommodations are concerned, prices are higher in these more fashionable areas; they are where people go to be seen and to see others. They are hard to sort out, but an agency should be able to help. If you prefer to be in a fashionable community or area, make it clear what you are looking for, but you can live equally well in a less chic community. For example, an apartment or private villa of equal standards in less expensive Golfe Juan is just as nice as one in Juan-les-Pins, a mile up the coast. St. Tropez is thought of as more fashionable than Ste. Maxime; the part of Cannes near the luxury hotels is more fashionable than the Le Cannet district. If you do not know the Riviera, the key is to carefully compare the property descriptions and prices, and be specific with the companies about what you are seeking. Of course some of the most quietly fashionable areas are also the most desirable: Cap d'Antibes, Villefranche-sur-Mer, St. Jean-Cap-Ferrat, Eze-sur-Mer, and Juan-les-Pins.

Location and Transportation

From the Riviera all of Provence can be explored, from Avignon, Aix-en-Provence and the port city of Marseille in the west to the interesting towns of Digne and Sisteron in the north. Day trips can easily be made into Italy to visit nearby San Remo and even the city of Torino. From the commercial harbour at Nice there are inexpensive, port-to-port sailings daily from June through September to the island of Corsica and its ancient towns of Bastia and Ajaccio and to the resort town of l'Île Rousse. It is a five- to seven-hour voyage, depending on origin and destination, and you can arrange a car rental there before departing. If you want to take the round-trip and stay for a few hours, make Bastia the destination. Contact any travel agent on the mainland or the offices of the shipline S.N.C.M. at the ports of Nice or Toulon for schedules and tickets.

The mainline railway between Paris and Genoa runs along the coast, stopping at almost every town along the Riviera. Northbound out of Nice the line runs to Digne, Grenoble, and on to Lyon or Geneva. There are also buses that serve the hill towns in addition to running along the coast.

Prices

A brief note on price ranges is usually enough, but the large seasonal differences and the sometimes elevated prices of properties on the Riviera call for a more comprehensive sampling to give you a better idea of what to expect.

The following are examples of average prices listed by various real estate agents (*agences immobilières*) along the Riviera, and by local tourist offices and the *Comité Regional du Tourisme*. They are approximate, intended to show the order of prices, not exact figures, and are shown in francs due to the fluctuations of currency rates. Just check the newspaper or phone a bank for the current rate and apply to the francs. If you compare the prices shown here with any quoted by U.S. agencies, bear in mind that these do not include the commissions normally charged a U.S. agent. A few sample hotel room prices are included to give an idea of what they run.

The locations of the studio and one-bedroom apartments are in and around Menton, Nice, Cannes, and the hill cities of Grasse and Mougin. The luxury villas sampled are in residential areas of Cap d'Antibes and Cap Ferrat. Many include swimming pools and most are on or within an easy walk of the sea.

The rental figures are approximate. The ratings for the apartments and villas are comparable to three hotel ratings:

°°° = Superior °° = Comfortable ° = Standard

The first figure shown is French francs (ff); the second is U.S. dollars at 5 francs to the dollar, an approximate exchange rate that makes calculating easy. The longer the period rented, the less the weekly rate. Utilities and final cleaning are usually extra.

	July & August	*Studio Apartments* June & September	Rest of Year
°°°	4,500 $900	2,800 $560	1,800 $360
°°	3,000 $600	2,500 $500	1,800 $360
°	2,500 $500	1,900 $380	1,500 $300

		One Bedroom	
°°°	5,500 $1,100	4,000 $800	2,800 $560
°°	4,000 $800	3,000 $600	2,000 $400
°	3,000 $600	2,000 $400	1,600 $320

Private Villas, prime locations
Standard 2 br, 1 ba, yard, sea view, standard furnishings:
> July & August - $5,500/month (1 month minimum)
> June & September - $1,100/week (2 week minimum)
> October through May - $900/week (1 week minimum)
Luxury 4 br, 3 ba, terrace, pool, yard, beautifully furnished:
> July & August - $18,000/month (1 month minimum)
> June & September - $2,500/week (2 week minimum)
> October through May - $1,500/week (1 week minimum)
Luxury 7 br, 5 ba, terrace, large pool, gardens, art, elegant furnishings
> July & August - $35,000/month (1 month minimum)
> June & September - $5,000/week (2 week minimum)
> October through May - $3,500/week (1 week minimum)

After visiting these properties we were told by the agent that we could not see their prime property, an eleven-bedroom estate on the sea. It was occupied, and booked for several months. The peak-season rent is $77,000 per month.

In general, the cost of apartments runs from 10 to 40 percent less than hotel rooms of equal standards. From October to May you can rent a private four-bedroom luxury villa with garden and pool at about the rate of a one-bedroom suite at the Cap Eden Roc Hotel in Cap d'Antibes.

Advance Times for Reservations
July and August: six months
May, June, September: three months
Rest of Year: five weeks from abroad; 0 locally

If you are planning an off-season visit (excluding the Easter holidays), simply check into a hotel for a day or two (they are also available at lower rates) and contact a local Tourist Office or go to one of the many agencies *(agences immobilières)* you'll spot along the Bord de Mer.

Savoie and Haute Savoie
Environs and Accommodations
This is the principal mountain country of France, an area lying north of *Haute Provence* between the valley of the Rhône to the west and Switzerland and Italy to the east. Not only is this the ski and winter sports area of the country, it is one of the most popular for summer visitors who love hiking or driving through mountains and spending a holiday in alpine towns. Summer is the time to visit Aix-les-Bains and nearby Annecy, partly for their beautiful settings and partly because they are towns that are fun to be in. For the gourmet, the place to visit is Bourg-en-Bresse, a town of fine restaurants.

Despite the summer pleasures provided by the area, it is nevertheless winter in the Alps and the ski resorts that draw the dedicated skiers, the rich and famous, or their onlookers.

Most of the vacation rentals in the region are either in rural areas or in mountain towns, and although they tend to be a little less expensive than on the Riviera, they are priced on the high side given overall prices in France. The fashionable winter resorts are quite expensive. In general, the chalets and apartments in large chalets are of deluxe standard. Chamonix is the town for skiing on Mt. Blanc, with cable cars running to within 2,000 feet of the 13,000-foot summit. Megève is another favorite, especially for those who prefer an older village for the home base, and Courchevel offers ninety lifts and a great variety of slopes. Most rentals in these towns can be best described as modern, rustic apartments, usually for two to six persons in a chalet. They are attractively furnished, comfortable, and warm; and they blend in well with the alpine surroundings. The exception is the area of Les Trois Vallées, including the towns of Courchevel, Mèribel, Les Menuires, and Val Thorens, which offer the *least* of what many Americans are looking for in European skiing. They are mostly large, modern apartment blocks, rather than attractive chalets replete with cozy comfort.

The best approach to renting, except for the low months of November and May, is to select one or two rental companies (listed in the last section of this chapter) and book ahead. Another approach is to telephone the local tourist office of the resort area of interest and ask for a listing to be sent air mail. Specify whether you want an apartment or a cottage. They will send instructions and a descriptive listing from which to choose. The organizations and managements are accustomed to dealing with an international clientele. Apartments are especially popular and numerous in La Plagne, Megève and Les Trois Vallées, Val d'Isère, Tignes, and Chamonix. The tourist offices are as follows:

Chamonix	Tel: 50–53–00–24;	fax: 50–53–58–90
La Plagne	Tel: 79–09–79–79;	fax: 79–09–70–10
Megève	Tel: 50–21–25–92	
Méribel	Tel: 79–08–60–01	
Courchevel	Tel: 79–08–00–29	
Tignes	Tel: 79–06–35–60;	fax: 79–06–45–44
Val d'Isère	Tel: 79–06–10–83;	fax: 79–06–26–11

(If you are a fan of the great skier Jean-Claude Killy, you might be interested in asking about chalet rentals from his sister Patricia's company: Mountain Lodges, 65 Les Andes, BP 37, 73150 Val d'Isère; tel: 79–06–20–77.)

It is also possible in low seasons to find a rental simply by going to the ski resort and checking with the local tourist office. Book a hotel in advance for a night or two to provide a base, then look around.

Location and Transportation

The major cities within a round-trip of a day or two from anywhere in Savoie or Haute Savoie are Lyon to the west, Grenoble to the south, Geneva and Lausanne, Switzerland, to the north, and Torino, Italy, to the east. Railways connect all the major towns in the area, with mainlines running between Lyon and Geneva, Aix-les-Bains, and Torino. Other lines connect Aix with Annecy, St. Gervais, and Chamonix. There are between five and eight daily runs of the high-speed TGV trains between Paris and Grenoble (three hours and ten minutes), with connections beyond. Many of the smaller alpine towns, however, including Val d'Isère and Courchevel, are well off the main railways and highways, but bus service extends from the stations to the smaller resort towns. If you are not planning to have a car, be sure to get specific instructions from the agent on how to get to the rental property.

Prices

In the summer peak season (July and August), a modest *gîte* in most areas of Savoie will run between $250 and $300. A comfortable studio apartment is about $550 per week, and a one-bedroom apartment between $600 and $750. Between mid-September and mid-June, prices are about 40 to 50 percent less. In the winter resorts during the months of December and January, expect to pay between $800 and $1,100 per week for a deluxe studio and $1,000 to $1,500 for a one-bedroom, depending on the location and altitude, which bears on duration of snow. Larger deluxe private chalets or three- to four-bedroom apartments can run up to $3,000 per week, but obviously can accommodate large groups. There are few simple and inexpensive rentals in the ski resort towns.

Advance Booking Time

July and August (summer peak): six months
December and March (winter peak): six months
June and September (summer shoulder): three months
Mid-January–April (winter shoulder): two months
Rest of year: one month from abroad to zero locally.

If you want the security of booking ahead, this should be done four to six weeks in advance for the "low" periods (generally November, January 5–February 1, and after mid-April) and three to four months in advance for other times. For the Christmas season, make it six months.

Northeast France

To the north of Haute Savoie lies northeast France and the winelands: Burgundy, Champagne Ardenne, Franche-Compté, Alsace and Lorraine. Despite the richness of the lands, villages, and cities of these regions, there are remarkably few vacation rental properties in the collections of either French, North American, or British rental companies. Perhaps one reason is that there is no principal destination, no special city or attraction considered of sufficient interest to tempt foreigners there for a week or two. This suggests that this large region is devoid of attractions, but, of course, it is not. Although there are far fewer North Americans visiting the great cathedrals at Metz and Reims than there are on the beaches of the Riviera, this is a wonderful part of France to visit. Like the Dordogne of southwest France, the northeast lends itself to a stay, not a pass-through.

In northwest Burgundy are some of the finest examples of eleventh- to sixteenth-century architecture in Europe, and the region is dotted with fascinating medieval villages and market towns. Except for the rise of the Jura mountains to the southeast, the slope of the land is gentle, much of it forested, and, of course, much of it devoted to the revered grape.

Accommodations and Transportation

Because of the relative paucity of rentals in the region, the best bet, oddly enough, is to contact two rental agencies in the United States, The French Experience and Interhome. The former offers *gîtes* in the area, which are otherwise very difficult to find and book directly with the federation of *gîte* owners. Interhome's selection is not large, but provides a good variety of modest houses at fair prices.

Worth considering is a stay in the western part of the region, from which trips to Paris can be accomplished with ease. By the west we mean in the vicinity of the cities of Auxerre, Troyes, Epernay, or Chalons-sur-Marne, which are on mainline railways. Fall and spring are the best times to go, but June and even July are not too crowded. We strongly recommend a car; there are too many interesting and unusual places in the region that are not served by rail.

South-central France

This region is south of the Loire Valley and southwest of Burgundy. Like the northeast, there is a relatively low number of rentals in the area, despite the beauty and tortured quality of the great mountainous area known as the Massif Central. Indeed, it is the complex topography of the Massif that makes the area hard to travel through, with few of the towns served by rail. There are of course towns and cities to visit, including Limoges, the city renowned throughout the world for its fine porcelain and enamel works, and Aurillac, with its seventeenth-century houses, a central spot from which to explore the wilds of the Massif.

Accommodations and Transportation

If you wish to explore this area, one good approach is to drive into it from a home base in the Dordogne region, which adjoins it to the west. Because so few of the towns are served by rail the best approach is by car. The best times are in spring and fall. In fact, late spring is best if you want to travel through the mountainous Massif Central itself.

During these times of year there is very little competition for accommodations, and any city or regional *office de tourisme* will provide a list of apartments and cottage rentals. However, if you want to stay in the region and book ahead, contact The French Experience for a *gîte,* or Interhome for other selections. Rents are modest, as are groceries and restaurant fare outside the main cities.

The Rental Companies and Organizations of France

The French term *à la carte* aptly applies to a style of renting apartments that has become common in France. It describes a system of offering guests a variety of prices and amenities. The system prevails in many of the high-quality apartments, which are equipped to offer a range of services typical of hotels. The apartments belong to chains or apartment hotels. The price schedules include a price per week for the basic rent of the apartment of your choice, stipulating the frequency of maid service and linen changes per week. Then there is an optional price list of à la carte services that may be added to the basic rent: maid service midweek (or every other day), change of towels daily (or twice a week), and the same for linens. Breakfast served in a communal breakfast room or room service are also options. If one were to request all the à la carte services, the total would be equal to a full-service hotel. The advantage is that you can stay in high-quality surroundings at far less cost than in a hotel of equal standard. You can pay for all, some, or none of the services and still enjoy a lobby, desk, lounges, and concierge. You do not have to commit to the style you want at the time of booking; just call the desk and ask for a cleaning, or linen change, or whatever. In some cases, if you see a price list that includes a "hotel" rate schedule, the prices shown include all services, and are usually shown by the day rather than by the week, sometimes with a three-day minimum.

Unique to France are chains of apartments intended for short-term renters. In addition to their city apartments, most of the chain companies have apartment accommodations in the most desirable locations of France: the Riviera; the Alps; the beach resorts of the western Mediterranean, Atlantic coast, and Brittany. Some are elegant and expensive, but most are in the modest to moderate price range. The apartments are comfortably furnished and adequately equipped, but are not distinctive. The prominent chains are Pierre et Vacances, Citadines, NPH Residentiale, and Les Residences Orion and Maeva, all profiled below. Together they offer apartments in more than fifty prime ski and sea locations, in addition to Paris, Aix-en-Provence, Biarritz, Montpellier, Lyon, and other cities. Dealing with them is like dealing with a hotel chain: There is much to choose from, competitive prices, good service, and dependable standards. For more personalized attention, out-of-the-way places, distinctive accommodations, and the privacy of simple farmhouse rentals or elegant villas, however, the smaller private companies excel.

When perusing French rental materials or driving about in France looking for a rental, watch for certain terms. *Residence,* or *hotel residence* typically means an apartment hotel. The word *location* means a rental, normally for the short term. The word *cabine* in property descriptions means a small room or alcove that is part of what is considered a studio; it is often two bunks in a small anteroom that has no dedicated closet and may or may not have windows. They are fine for preteen children or for two plus two adults for short periods, and enable families to share accommodations at a modest price. The *cabine* usually offers some, but not complete, privacy.

Barclay International Group   Paris and throughout France
150 East 52nd Street
New York, NY 10022
Tel: (800) 845–6636 or 212–832–3777   Fax: (212) 753–1139

This U.S. company is included because it charges no additional commission, has been operating for thirty years, and knows its territory. It is the agent for the French chain of apartments and resorts Les Citadines, which has apartments and resorts in many prime locations in France as well as in Paris. They also represent Riviera Retreats, a company with an especially desirable selection of deluxe and luxury villas on the coast and in the hills of the south of France. (These companies are profiled in this chapter and can be contacted directly for information, prices, and booking.) A fourth group represented is Residentiale Chambiges, modestly priced apartments in Paris and other areas of France. The company also has many London apartments, and is profiled more thoroughly in the chapter on England.

Obtaining information, booking, and paying are made easy. Telephone or fax for their brochure and price list; although the various apartments are not described in any detail, the official standards ratings are made clear and the prices suggest the quality and location variables. If you have no idea where you want to be, explain your interests and requirements to an agent at Barclay; they will give good and knowledgeable advice. The owners and staff make numerous trips to Europe checking on the properties in order to assure high standards. Personal checks or major credit cards are accepted.

B & V Associates   Throughout France / London
140 East 56th Street, Suite 4C
New York, NY 10022
Tel: (800) 755–8266; (212) 688–9464   Fax: (212) 688–9567

Headed by the affable Peter Bruneau, B & V Associates is the capable U.S. representative of the large chain of modestly priced apartments called Residences Orion (see listing, below). Orion has also opened up an apartment complex in central London. B & V is also an agent for "La Vie de Château," rentals of rooms and suites in some of the most elegant châteaux of France. They can also be contacted for information and booking of journeys on the canals of France. Payment by credit card or personal check. No commission is added.

Blakes International Group   Throughout France
Wroxham, Norfolk
Norwich NR12 8DH, England
Tel: 011–44–603–782–141   Fax: 011–44–603–782–871

A large and reputable British company, Blakes has a very good selection of rentals throughout France. All arrangements are made through their headquarters in England. A catalog will be sent and after a decision is reached the booking is made by phone or fax. Credit cards accepted. See chapter thirteen, United Kingdom, for more information on this company.

British Airways   Paris
Tel: (800) 876–2200

As a convenience (and savings) to people flying trans-Atlantic with British Airways, apartments in Paris can be booked directly through the airline. They are located in the fifteenth *arrondissement* in Montparnasse, near the Eiffel Tower and toward the north end of the district at 14 rue du Théâtre. The apartments are operated by Flatotel International and are pleasant and attractive. The fifteenth *arrondissement* itself retains the atmosphere of the twenties. Good restaurants include the immense and famous brasserie La Coupole as well as La Maison Blanche and Le Clos Morillons. It is a short metro trip to the city center (stops: Duplix and Charles-Michels).

Rents are for three-days minimum. Studios cost about $380 for the three days, one-bedrooms about $600, and two-bedrooms about $950, with slight seasonal variations. These are very good values for Paris. Book by telephone; pay by credit card.

Cannes Beach Residence   Cannes (Riviera)
11 Avenue Pierre-Semard
06150 Cannes la Boca
Tel: 92–19–3000   Fax: 92–10–3009

This independent apartment hotel is an immense, modern, low-rise Mediterranean building with balconies. It surrounds a large inner courtyard of palm trees, a garden, and swimming pool, a building style typical of Riviera resort apartments. Although only a block from the beach and on a busy street near the railroad tracks, the inner courtyard, which the apartments face, ensures relative quiet. Unfortunately, the view is of the courtyard, not the sea or the surrounding hills. The kitchens are small but well equipped and adequate, apartment sizes run from about 265 square feet in a studio for two to 320 square feet in a one-bedroom, up to a fairly good size 525 square feet in a deluxe apartment, which is rated for six persons.

The building has a restaurant, bar, ice cream parlor, fitness center, saunas, a game room, and for a fee, parking in the building. Prices are appropriate for the atmosphere and good quality of the apartments, ranging from the small studio in winter season for the very low price of about $220 per week to $950 for the same studio in August. This is called a studio *cabine,* which means that there are twin convertible beds in the living area and two in a small anteroom (best for children). The best bet for two is the larger studio at around $475 per week in June and September. The largest, most elegant apartment is about $300 per week in April, May, October, and November, and $920 in August, with many seasonal differences in between. There is a 30 percent reduction for stays of over a week. There is an extra charge for linens, up to about $10 per week per person.

A brochure, including drawings of the apartment layouts, will be mailed for the asking. Like any hotel, payment can be made by credit card: a deposit upon booking and final payment after arrival. English is spoken. The staff will help arrange water skiing, fishing, golf, windsurfing, and biking. The location and design of this large complex makes it attractive for families with preteen children, but don't look for Côte d'Azur glamour here. The town center of Cannes la Boca is quite simple and includes a good open-air market once a week. We suggest these apartments for families who plan to spend their time out and about, on the sea and exploring the hills and towns of coastal Provence from a modest, well priced home base.

Citadines   Paris and throughout France
163-167 avenue Georges Clemenceau
Batiment E
Parc des Fontaines
92022 Nanterre Cedex
(Central reservations, Paris) Tel: 1–47–25–5454   Fax: 1–47–25–4918
U.S. agents: Keith Prowse & Co. (USA), Ltd., and the Barclay International
Group, listed in this chapter.

Citadines is a large chain of apartments best characterized as moderate in
their standard and prices. They are generally attractive, comfortable, and well
maintained, and they are well priced. There are four locations in Paris:
Austerlitz (thirteenth *arrondissement*), Lyon-Bastille (twelfth *arrondissement*),
Montparnasse (fourteenth), and Trocadéro (sixteenth). Two more were about to
open in Paris near the Opéra and the Place de la Republique at the time of this
writing. The closest to the center of Paris (and, we think, the nicest) is in the
Trocadéro on rue Saint Didier, just south of Place Victor Hugo. These are good
apartments for travelers on a midrange budget: A studio in Austerlitz costs
between $700 and $800 per week; in Montparnasse between $800 and $900; a
one-bedroom in Montparnasse from $1,300 to $1,500. Neither Prowse nor
Barclay charge additional commission, but their rates may vary a little.

In addition to having relatively modestly priced studios and apartments in
resortlike destination areas such as Nice and Cannes, they are also available in a
large number of key cities and areas throughout France: Aix-en-Provence,
Montpellier, Lyon, Bordeaux, Marseille, and Lille. Their one ski area accommodation is opening at Grenoble, and there are others in towns farther off the
regular tourist track. Foreign travelers can book ahead with confidence in Port
Camargue, Strasbourg, Ferney-Voltaire (near Geneva), Gaillard (a French out-
skirt of Geneva), and Toulouse. The company has more properties in cities of
interest than it has in beach and ski resorts. For many travelling North
Americans this is a great advantage.

The Citadines apartments in Gaillard, a suburb of Geneva, are a good example. There is no reason to stay in Gaillard other than access to Geneva and the
fact that prices on the French side are considerably less. Here the apartments
are generally attractive, comfortable, and well maintained. It is not difficult to
get to Geneva central from Gaillard: It is a step across the border, then ten minutes by car or bus. We also stayed in a Citadines apartment in Nice. The apartments are somewhat formulaic in nature, but are neat and clean, comfortable
for a few days stay, and much more spacious than a hotel room of equal standard
and higher cost. A studio in Nice is $355 per week in the shoulder season, and
$665 in July and August. For the Riviera, this is quite inexpensive. (In Nice, we

prefer the Promenade building; ask for an apartment facing the garden.)

Citadines offers the best apartments possible in a modest price range by offering locations just beyond the high-rent urban areas.

The best approach is to ask for a Citadines brochure by calling or faxing Citadines, Keith Prowse & Co., or Barclay International Group. If you know where you want to be, and if you want to make contact directly, just phone the main reservations number in Paris. Ask about prices. Credit cards or personal checks are accepted. Neither U.S. company charges an additional commission.

Claridge   Paris
74 Champs Elysées
75008 Paris
Tel: 1–42–13–3333   Fax: 1–42–25–0488

This is a lovely, well-located apartment building on the Champs Elysées, a few blocks from the Arc de Triomphe. Although the boulevard is a busy, noisy thoroughfare, the apartments face an inner courtyard and are therefore quiet for their location. This is a lovely accommodation with attractive reception and lounge areas as well as exquisite apartments. English is spoken; service is excellent (including maid service three times a week).

Prices are constant year-round and vary, depending on size and location in the building. The least expensive is studio "Alsace" at about $1,225 per week; other studios range upward to about $1,540. One-bedroom apartments run about $2,100, and two bedrooms cost $3,060.

Major credit cards are accepted. The best approach is to pay the deposit (between $500 and $1,500) by credit card, then pay the balance on arrival. They will probably ask that you fax a signed note, authorizing the credit card charge.

Claridge is the kind of place you can feel comfortable booking with when you have minimal information, but a brochure will be airmailed for the asking. It is the sort of apartment seen in visitors' dreams of a stay in Paris.

Suzanne B. Cohen, Agent   Provence, Riviera
94 Winthrop Street
Augusta, ME 04330
Tel: (207) 622–0743   Fax: (207) 622–1902

Suzanne B. Cohen is a very small agency representing a fairly large British company called CV Travel, which seems to do an excellent job of locating, displaying, and renting properties—mostly villas and other independent houses in Spain, France, Portugal, and the Island of Corfu in Greece. It has marketed its rentals principally to British travelers and is now available to North Americans.

Although it appears that this company has one of the nicest selections available, we have not visited their properties and must rely on the taste and judgment of agent Suzanne Cohen, whom we regard well. She also represents an English company with some of the nicest rentals in Britain, and small Italian companies that offer good properties in Tuscany, so we know her standards and service. There is no added commission, and she makes finding and booking easy for the client.

Phone or fax for a catalog. The cost is $3.00 postpaid, but well worth it: It's colorful and descriptive. Payment can be made by credit card or personal check.

Federation Nationale des   Throughout France
Gîtes Ruraux de France
35 rue Godot-de-Mauroy
75009 Paris
Tel: 1–47–422–020   Fax: 1–47–42–7311
(U.S. contact: The French Experience—see profile below.)

This organization, mentioned earlier in the chapter, is the very large quasi-governmental organization composed of regional organizations that represent owners of modestly priced rural and small-town rentals. The controls of the Federation and its ratings-of-standards system virtually guarantee that the rental property you get will be as it is described. If you choose an inexpensive rental then there will be limited space, supplies, and amenities; if you rent a *"super-gîte"* you can count on it being adequate in size and fully furnished, supplied, and equipped.

The difficulty in renting property through the Federation is that it is a complex bureaucracy. If you are fluent in French, have considerable persistence, know the location you want, and deal well with foreign currencies, contact this organization and ask for their catalog of *gîtes* in the area in which you are interested. After receiving the catalog, all future contact (usually in French) is with the regional "Relais," (department) in which your choice of *gîtes* is located. Because the procedure is somewhat difficult, consider contacting The French Experience in New York (see following phone and fax numbers). Tell them you want a *gîte,* give them the area of France in which you want to be, size accommodation needed, dates, and other pertinent information. The rent range is $300 to $600 per week, the same as if booking direct. There are thousands of these rural properties for rent, and they are very popular, partly because of the modest rent prices and partly because the rentals represent true rural France. They are heavily marketed in Britain by British companies. **Book well in advance** (6 to 8 months for summer). Direct payment usually by franc bank draft.

If you are traveling through rural areas and smaller towns during the shoulder or low seasons, watch for signs that read "Gîte de France," signifying affiliation with this trustworthy organization. The standard of the rental will be displayed on signs as ears of corn, which, to us, are ears of wheat. Standards run from no wheats (very basic) to four wheats (top grade). The top grade is usually excellent, but don't look for luxury.

The French Experience   Gîtes Throughout France, Paris Apartments
370 Lexington Ave, Suite 812
New York, NY 10017
Tel: (212) 986–1115   Fax: (212) 986–3808

The French Experience books *gîtes,* which were described earlier in the chapter. The rents charged by this U.S. company range from $300 to $600 per week, the same as if booking direct through the Federation Nationale des Gîtes. Although there are thousands of these rural properties for rent, they are very popular. **Book well in advance** (6 to 8 months for summer). Call or fax with information on the area of France in which you want to be, size accommodation needed, your price range, dates, and so forth. They will go through the elaborate procedure of finding and booking for you. As agent for Paris Bienvenue (see profile later in the chapter), this company also has a good selection of apartments in Paris. It also offers self-directed tours with itineraries from three to ten days, with accommodations set up along the way. Payment by check or credit card. The company also offers car rentals and airline tickets.

French Home Rentals   Southwest France, Paris, and the Riviera
18 rue de Velours
Villeneueve-sur-Lot
Tel: 53–40–1407   Fax: 53–40–2426

U.S. Office:
P.O. Box 82386
Portland, OR 97282
Tel: (503) 774–8977   Fax: same (listen to message)

This relatively small company has a unique and excellent selection of rentals in this beautiful area of southwest France (including the valleys of the Lot and Garonne rivers, the Dordogne, and parts of Armagnac and Bordeaux). It also has a good sampling on the Riviera at Villefranche-sur-Mer, Cannes, and Ste. Maxime, and apartments in Paris ranging from modest to luxurious.

This is one of the rare French companies that actually has an office in the United States, which makes booking easy and assures good prices. The Portland office is small and busy and it often takes some patience to get information. In exchange, the manager is very helpful and will work hard to find the right spot for you. The approach is to call or fax the details of what you are looking for, where you would like to be, your price range and dates. You will shortly receive

Toits de Leauze, an ancient stone building in the Dordogne River valley between Sarlat and Montignac, has been artfully converted into two self-contained units that each accommodate up to four people. (Courtesy French Home Rentals)

a packet of property descriptions, with photos, of those rentals that fit your criteria. Once decided, call or fax again with two or three selections; availability will be verified by the office in France and the Portland office will call. Because that office is in the valley of the Lot River (some 100 miles east of Bordeaux), most of the rural properties are in this area, as far north as the Dordogne. This entire region is one of the most peaceful, beautiful, and historically interesting areas of France. We spent five days there in the large country villa called La Tuque, a modern home just outside of Villeneuve-sur-Lot on a hill near the ancient walled village of Pujols.

On the Riviera the company offers a choice of several apartments in the little seacoast town of Villefranche-sur-Mer, wonderfully located just east of Nice. There are two or three exquisite luxury villas, but most are modestly or moderately priced. Our suggestion is to book the better of the moderate apartments unless you are on a very tight budget. Others are in Cannes, and one group in the pleasant town of Ste. Maxime, across the bay from over-touristed St. Tropez. For Ste. Maxime, consider especially the apartments called Felix 1, 2, 3, and 4.

In Paris the apartments are scattered about, but all are in the central *arrondissements;* ask about the apartments called Perche, Ste. Croix, and Dauphine, or give agent Joanne Carlson in Oregon your requirements. Apartments are all moderately priced.

Beyond the rental business, M. Tessel directs the "Institut Français de Langues et de Services" which offers a variety of programs of cultural and linguistic nature. One, "Objectif France," is a 3-week program for adults of 50+ years presented in Paris and southwest France; another is for families, in which children are enrolled in bilingual English/French schools while parents run the gamut from language classes to cooking. There are even intensive English language programs for French speakers, conducted in North America. This is a truly intercultural institute, certainly worth looking into by anyone interested in France and the French language and culture. Although the rental business and the Institut are separate, the former can provide accommodations for the latter. The Portland office has material on the institute, but after reviewing it you might want to talk to M. Tessel directly (he is fluent in English and knowledgeable about the U.S.).

It is best to contact the Portland office, but if you want to discuss particular villas or apartments in more detail, feel free to call the main office at Villenueve-sur-Lot. Payment by personal or travelers cheque. (Canadian funds are accepted.)

Hoeseasons Holidays, Ltd.   Throughout France
Sunway House
Lowestoft, Suffolk NR32 3LT
England
Tel: 011–44–502–500–555 or 011–44–502–501–501 (for catalog only)
Fax: 011–44–502–500–532

This British company has developed a substantial selection of cottages, *gîtes,* and villas in France. Unlike its British rentals, which are often vacation parks and clusters of cottages, the French properties are an excellent assortment of independent houses, ranging from simple rural houses to quite substantial ones. They are especially strong in Brittany and Normandy, but there are good choices in virtually all of the most interesting parts of the country, from the Riviera and Dordogne to Picardy and Moselle.

Prices are very reasonable, and the company is easy for North Americans to book with. Credit cards are accepted. A catalog is available for the asking. For more information on this company, see chapter thirteen, United Kingdom.

Home Plazza Bastille   **Home Plazza Saint Antoine**   Paris
74, rue Amelot   289 bis, rue de Faubourg St. Antoine
75011 Paris   75011 Paris
(Central reservations) Tel: 1–40–21–2223   Fax: 1–47–00–8240

These are two very popular all-suite apartment hotels, which operate on the à la carte plan, providing complete flexibility for the guest. Apartments can be taken under the hotel plan (one night minimum, just like a hotel) or the residence plan (three nights minimum). The rate is about $20 per day less for the residence plan, regardless of the size of the apartment. For stays of seven days or more there is an additional 12 percent reduction, and 20 percent if rented by the month.

These handsome old apartment buildings have been refurbished to include a lobby, reception, lounges, bar, conference rooms, atrium dining room (in Bastille only), terrace gardens, and children's play area. They are the result of carefully supervised and government-controlled renovations and restorations of historical blocks of the city. Very well accomplished, the results are attractive, light, and pleasant. The apartments in buildings Ravel and Dufy in Home Plazza Bastille are almost all with twin beds. Eiffel apartments have mostly queen beds and the building is, indeed, where Eiffel once lived. Secure parking is available, but expensive, 95 FrF per day. The apartments are not large but afford considerably more space than regular hotels of similar standards. Most are studios (called junior suites) that encompass a living/dining room and a *cabine* of bunk beds; they accommodate up to three persons, four in a pinch if two are children. The executive suites accommodate up to five, and can be expanded by an adjoining studio to handle six persons fairly comfortably, although the kitchens may be on the small side for this many. In addition, the smaller studios can be joined, ideal where some privacy is required. All have kitchenettes and dining areas. The quality of the apartments is standard first class. To encourage stays of three days or more during the quieter months in Paris, there is a 50 percent rate reduction from November to March and in July and August; a 30 percent reduction in September and October and again in April and June. There are also price spikes during busy periods, such as special holidays. Be sure to settle on price. At roughly $950 per week for a studio for two in the summer season, discounted by 50 percent or 30 percent depending on the season in addition to the reduction for length of stay, these are very good values. Ask for a location as far back from the lobby as possible (Building Gauguin A or B); there are no street noises in the complex, but these are the most private.

Both apartments are well located in the eleventh arrondissement; the Bastille is closest to the city center, between the Place de la Bastille and the Place de la Republique. The splendid Boulevard Beaumarchais parallels rue Amelot, so there are a number of good restaurants and shops. The St. Antoine is near the Place de la Nation. These apartments are not designed to spend your days in—but in Paris, who wants to stay at "home"?

Phone or fax for a brochure; payment is by major credit card. A 30 percent deposit will guarantee the reservation. You can pay the balance upon arrival. Keith Prowse (USA) Ltd. (see listing, below) is an agent for Home Plazza. We suggest direct contact, however, to get best price quote.

Interhome USA, Inc.   Paris and throughout France
124 Little Falls Road
Fairfield, NJ 07004
Tel: (201) 882–6864   Fax: (201) 808–1742

This is the independently owned branch of the largest vacation rental company in Europe (perhaps the world): Zurich-based Interhome. It offers a large selection of mostly modest and moderately priced rentals in most regions of France. The approach is to phone or fax for their substantial catalog. The price is $3.00, but it is worth the small cost and is fun to peruse. Select several, note the reference numbers, and contact Interhome regarding availability. A direct hookup with the Zurich computer enables a very quick response. For details on Interhome, see the profile in the chapter on Switzerland.

International Cap d'Antibes   Cap d'Antibes and the Riviera
Le Royal
Boulevard du Cap 125
06600 Cap d'Antibes
Tel: 93–61–2217   Fax: 93–61–0982

For a moderate or elegant villa in the exclusive point of land on the Riviera called Cap d'Antibes, this is a good company to contact. Most of the properties they offer are within this small seaside residential area adjacent to Antibes and Juan-les-Pins, fifteen minutes from Cannes. The majority are private homes whose furnishings and amenities reflect the owners' tastes. Some are fairly plain, some luxurious, with pools and gardens. None are far from the sea. The cape that the town occupies is away from the main tourist area, ensuring quiet. This is an ideal location from which to explore the Riviera and southern Provence.

Contact the company with the details of what you are seeking and the dates. They will respond with two or three descriptive brochures. Advise them of your choices (ranked), and they will confirm shortly. Pay by bank transfer, or purchase and airmail a bank draft in francs for one quarter of the total rent. It is wise to fax a copy of the draft you are sending, in case there is a hold-up in the mails. On arrival, pay the balance due plus a damage deposit of one third the rent. The rents are moderate to high, depending on size, standard, and proximity to the sea. The company is helpful and prices are fair.

JRH Prestige   Paris
4, rue de Castiglione
75001 Paris
Tel: 1–42–60–1550   Fax: 1–42–60–2135

U.S. agents: Keith Prowse & Co., listed in this chapter, and
Grant Reid Communications
Box 810216
Dallas, TX 75381
Tel: (800) 327–1849 or (214) 243–6748   Fax: (214) 484–5778.

These moderately priced, serviced apartments are in eight good locations around Paris and range from studios to four bedrooms. The apartments closest to the city center are in the Quartier Latin (fifth *arrondissement*) and Gobelins in the thirteenth. Other excellent locations are just off the Champs Elysées on rue de Berri (eighth), and Trocadéro and Victor Hugo in the prestigious sixteenth *arrondissement*. One is in Montparnasse (fifteenth), one in Auteuil (sixteenth), and one outside the ring road in Neuilly, somewhat remote but priced accordingly.

This is a rapidly enlarging organization; four of its properties opened in 1993. Except for those in the Latin Quarter and Montparnasse, these are not new buildings, but historical ones, totally renovated for apartment use. None of them are large; they have between six and thirty-five apartments. Our impression overall is that any of them would make a comfortable home base for a stay in Paris; the location is a matter of personal preference (and price).

JRH Prestige is eager to be better known in the North American market and makes booking easy. They will accept direct requests for brochures and bookings, but the easiest approach is to contact Keith Prowse & Co. toll free in New York. Get the brochure, in which the apartments are pictured, briefly described and located, make the choice and book. The Keith Prowse company is profiled below.

Maeva Loisirs   Throughout France and International
30 rue d'Orleans
Neuilly-sur Seine 92200
Tel: 46–41–5050   Fax: 47–22–8314

Loisir is French for leisure, spare time, or time off, and pretty well characterizes the aim of the large Maeva chain of apartment accommodations. Their locations and style emphasize having active fun: skiing, boating, angling, windsurfing, parasailing, enjoying nightlife, and family recreation. It is an immense chain whose apartment properties are themselves large and normally include restaurants, bars, lounges, a laundry, and other facilities. They are located in twenty-five mountain ski towns from Alp d'Huez to Vars, with several buildings in many of these towns. In ocean resorts and coastal towns from Antibes to Saint Tropez there are at least thirty-five more, plus complexes in Canada, Cuba, the Canary Islands, Martinique, Guadaloupe, and even Tahiti.

They seem not to market actively in North America. Their 150-page catalog is descriptive and well illustrated, but it is in French. Their prices are remarkably modest; typical peak-season (December to March) rates in popular ski resorts like Val Thorens and Courchevel run from $700 to $800 per week for a studio for four persons, $450 to $600 in less glitzy resorts like Les Arcs, Tignes, and even Chamonix. Off-season prices are half that. In the ocean resorts, the prices are about the same, with the seasons reversed.

Phone or fax Maeva for their catalog (which includes prices); although written in French, it will give you an idea where the apartments are and what they are like. In the price schedule for the ski resorts, the term *"formula location simple"* means the price for an apartment; *"formula location + remontes mecaniques (6 jours)"* means price per person including lift tickets for six days. Like most of the other French chains, the studios and apartments are designed with the assumption that the renters will be spending most of their time on the slopes, on the beach, by the pool, in cafes, or exploring the countryside.

Mansley Travel Apartments International   Paris and other cities
No. 1 The Mansions
219 Earls Court Road
London SW5 9BN
Tel: 44–71–373–4689   Fax: 44–71–373–2062

U.S. agent: Grant Reid Communications
Box 810216
Dallas, TX 75381
Tel: (800) 327–1849 or (214) 243–6748   Fax: (214) 484–5778

This British company represents a very nice selection of apartments in Paris, Nice, Cannes, and other principal destination cities of France (and major cities of Europe). Its apartments and the French companies it represents are profiled in this section: NPH Residentiale and JRH Prestige, both of which can be contacted directly. The involvement of the British agency and its U.S. representative show the many layers possible in the vacation rental business. Although the prices seem very close, price lists printed annually in sterling or dollars have the disadvantage of not reflecting the true exchange rate. Since Mansley offers prices in both dollars and French francs, however, we suggest calculating the most advantageous price at the time of booking. If you prefer, contact the French companies directly for current prices and compare; paying by credit card at the exchange rate of the day is an advantage in times of a stable or strengthening dollar. This applies to paying the U.S. agent as well as paying directly.

Mansley is a fast-growing company that specializes in city apartments for short-term rent. We found the properties they represent—we have visited six and stayed in three—to be dependably good, mostly three- and four-star properties at fair prices. Contact the U.S. agent for a brochure and prices. (See also chapter thirteen, United Kingdom, for a profile on Mansley and their U.S. agent, and their excellent apartments in London.)

NPH Residentiale (Chain)   Paris, Riviera, southern cities
16, Avenue Hoche
75008 Paris
Tel: 1–42–25–01–49 Fax: 1–42–25–75–99

U.S. agent: Grant Reid Communications
P.O. Box 810216
Dallas, TX 75381
Tel: (800) 327–1849 or (214) 243–6748 Fax: (214) 484–5778

This is a company with seven apartment buildings located in Paris, Antibes, Cannes, Juan-les-Pins, Montpellier, Aix-en-Provence, and Biarritz, all excellent destinations for foreign visitors. Standards range from three- to four-star, but vary in their quality.

The location of their Paris apartment building is in the eighth *arrondissement,* considered the most elegant district, with many grand sights, from the Arc de Triomphe to the main stores of Dior, Givenchy, Nina Ricci, and other designers. Despite the decline of the Champs Elysées because of the growth of fast-food chains and the competing touristy restaurants, it remains a wonderful area of Paris. One can always take a bus or the metro to less expensive parts of the city after lunch at Cafe Fouquet's on Avenue George V. The NPH Paris apartment is in the center of all this at 8, rue Chambiges, just around the corner from the Hotel Plaza Athenée. The apartments are four-star and are well valued, located in a handsome, restored building with a stylish reception and adjacent bar and breakfast room. The studios are small but comfortable and convenient; the apartments are spacious and well designed. All are nicely furnished and appointed. Service includes twenty-four-hour reception and daily maid service. Rates are about $230 per night for a studio and $375 for the large apartment. This is the jewel of the NPH group, but the quality varies among them.

Although we did not visit all the NPH locations, we visited the ones in Juan-les-Pins and Antibes and stayed in apartments in Cannes and Biarritz. The Residentiale Cannes has a four-star apartment rating, but we were disappointed. It is in a beautiful setting of gardens, just a block from the seaside boulevard La Croisette and the beach, though the apartments themselves are rather drab and unimaginative. However, the peak rate of about $615 per week and low season rate of $270 make these a good value for the center of Cannes. There is twenty-four-hour reception, a bar, lounge, pool, garage, and laundromat. The

Residentiale Biarritz is one of the newest of the apartments, and although not on the sea, it is an easy walk and close to the city center. The lounge, bar, and breakfast area is particularly appealing; the apartments are a bit spartan but entirely satisfactory and a good value.

Prices vary with town location, apartment size, and season, so you might prefer to call or fax and ask that a brochure and price list be airmailed. They are very accommodating. Prices range from a low of about $300 per week in low season for a studio in Biarritz to $800 during peak. Year-round rates are about $500 in Aix-en-Provence. In the beautiful coastal town of Juan-les-Pins (near Cannes), a studio in the Residentiale runs from about $250 per week in winter to $700 in summer. A larger studio is $300 winter and $900 in range. The apartments are typically not very large (255 sq. ft. in a double studio) but have neat kitchenettes and more space than a hotel room for twice the price. Given the accommodations and amenities, these are good values. There may be modest extra charges for electricity and local tax. Prepare for a $200 refundable damage deposit. Among them, the Paris apartments are the most expensive. The apartments are available with full hotel services (daily maid service and linen changes) at the much higher hotel rate.

The procedure is like booking a hotel: If you want a brochure and price list, phone or fax and ask that they be airmailed. Or just let central reservations know your destination, the number in your party, and your arrival and departure dates and ask about availability. A deposit by major credit card is acceptable, with the balance due on arrival.

Residence Hoteliers OPEN   Golfe Juan (Riviera)
Avenue Georges-Pompidou
06220 Golfe Juan
Tel: 93–63–3300   Fax: 93–63–4484

The management of this three-star, low-rise apartment complex in the heart of the village of Golfe Juan has thought of everything, including a very complete and attractive brochure. Besides the private pool, a private beach is staked out a short walk from the apartments. If you are not inclined to spend all your time at the water's edge or lounging in the gardens, there is a gymnastics program (water and floor), a climbing wall for the rock enthusiast, golf practice, a weekly tennis tournament, table tennis, a Jacuzzi, and sauna. Besides the excellent main restaurant and beachside cafe, there is a poolside grill. This is a very good spot for families with children of any age.

There are two ways to stay: Rent an apartment only (which includes a weekly change of linens and maid service) or an apartment with full hotel services (including daily maid service, a mid-week linen and towel change, and free access to all sport and entertainment facilities). The apartments are ample size, with balconies or terraces; kitchens are well equipped. Rent for a studio with a *cabine* for two to four persons in winter runs about $270 per week, and $440 with full hotel service; the same studio is about $950 per week from mid-July to the end of August, and $1,100 with full service. An apartment for four without hotel service runs from $375 in winter to about $1,250 in high season. The best time for bargains is late October through March; the optimum times combining best prices and fair weather are May, June, and September.

Be sure to ask for a location facing the garden area, as high up as possible (with a balcony instead of terrace). The best apartments are in the main hotel building, overlooking the chess board (it is a large one); these are used as full-service hotel rooms in the high season, but they are sometimes available as apartments in the winter and shoulder seasons through mid-June and after mid-September.

Phone or fax the company and ask for their brochure and tariffs. Reserve and book by credit card. Conference facilities are available. This is a good value accommodation, well managed, well located, and very pleasant overall.

Residences Orion   Paris and throughout France (also London)
30 Place d'Italie
75013 Paris
Tel: 1–40–78–52–52   Fax: 1–40–78–54–55
U.S. agent: B & V Associates; 140 East 56th Street, Suite 4C
New York, NY 10022
Tel: (800) 755–8266 or (212) 688–9538   Fax: (212) 688–9467

Orion is a large chain of modestly priced rental properties throughout France, easy to book through its principal U.S. agent B & V Associates. These are apartments we would rate with two-plus stars; they are well priced, comfortable enough, all with adequate kitchens, well located, but not in high-rent locations. We consider these to be good value and recommend them to travelers more interested in being out and about than at the home base. They are especially good for families wanting reasonable prices and accommodations a cut above economy level. Because there are thirty-one locations (and more to come), they are also for travelers wanting to stay in unusual places as well as principal tourist destinations. These include Chamonix, Méribel, Les Dieux Alpes and Villard-de-Lans, Marseille, Lyon, Toulouse, Saint Malo, Les Sables d'Olonne on the Atlantic coast, Porte de Genève, Cap d'Agde on the new "Riviera" near Montpellier, and the Riviera towns of Antibes, Cannes, Menton, and Ste. Maxime.

There are three locations in Paris: at La Défense (outside the ring road at Pont de Neuilly), Place d'Italie in the thirteenth *arrondissement,* and near the city center, Les Halles in the first *arrondissement.*

Our experience with the company, including visits to a number of their properties and our stays at Chamonix and Cap d'Agde, were quite satisfactory. The Orions vary in style from chalet designs in the Alps to modern, rectangular, Mediterranean-looking buildings. The interiors are all very much alike: neat, efficient, and sparely but comfortably furnished. The studios all have *cabines* and can accommodate up to four persons; the main bed is actually a surprisingly comfortable convertible sofa. The design and furnishings are consistent and extend right down to the dinnerware and kitchen utensils (such as an oyster shucking knife we found in the ski town of Chamonix).

Prices vary considerably with size, location, and season. A studio for one to four persons at Chamonix, for example, ranges from about $210 to $645 in the winter ski season. At Cap d'Agde a studio runs from about $200 in winter to $575 in summer. Three-night "weekends" are available as well as nightly rates in Paris.

In Paris the main price difference between the three apartment blocks is location. A studio at the Les Halles is about $1,100 per week, at Place d'Italie it is $950, and at La Défense, about $800.

The rental procedure is to contact the U.S. office and request a brochure, or if you know the general area of France or the city you want to be in, call or fax the company in New York. They will take the next steps, including making suggestions and proposing some properties, if you wish. There are small general brochures available for the asking, and at the time of writing more comprehensive ones, written in English, are being planned. There is no additional commission, but you might want to compare rental prices. Payment can be made by personal check or major credit card.

Paris Bienvenue
10 Avenue de Villars
75007 Paris
Tel: 1–47–53–8081   Fax:1–47–53–7299
U.S. agent: The French Experience, listed in this section.

A well-established organization, Paris Bienvenue has an inventory of good, privately owned apartments throughout the city in the modest to moderate price range. They can be rented for short (five days) or long terms and include everything from simple studios in Montmartre to luxury three-bedroom apartments in prestigious districts. They seem to us fair in their prices, which include all utilities (except phone charges), three cleanings, and a linen/towel change per week. Prices of course depend on location, space, and quality, but typically a studio costs $610 per week at 5.7 francs = $1; a one bedroom is about $675, and a two bedroom costs about $1,100.

Approach: Like most other Paris apartment brokers, Paris Bienvenue matches your requirements with their apartments. Decide where you want to be, the size accommodation you need, style preferred, dates, budget range, and any special needs, then fax or telephone this information to Paris Bienvenue. They will respond with descriptions of apartments available for your dates. Or you can trust them to secure what you have described; they are a responsible company. Once confirmed, pay the deposit by credit card. There are no hidden charges. Although the cost may be slightly higher, an alternative is to book through the agent, The French Experience, a good French company with fair prices.

Paris Sejour Reservation   Paris and throughout France
90 Champs Elysées
75008 Paris
Tel: 1–42–25–4297   Fax: 1–42–89–4297

U.S. office: Paris Sejour Reservation (PSR)
645 No. Michigan Ave.
Chicago, IL 61611
Tel: (312) 587–7707   Fax: 1 (800) 582–7274

Canadian office: PSR Canada Inc.
1168 West St. Catherine, Rm 207
Montreal, Quebec H3B 1K1 Tel: (514) 875–4412   Fax: (514) 875–5635

This is one of two French rental companies with branch offices in North America, which we see as advantageous to clients as well as to the companies. Directed by the indefatigable Marie France Menage, PSR offers the widest selection of individual, privately owned apartments in Paris, ranging from tiny studios to large luxury apartments. With over 600 apartments in their inventory, there is everything in between. As these are privately owned, they differ according to owners' styles, but the company sets the standards.

Because of the vast number of apartments available, their locations are in virtually all arrondissements. There is no catalog available, just a general brochure. The key to booking the most satisfactory place is to know what you are looking for, including if possible the locations you favor. If you don't know where you want to be, talk it over with a company representative (especially Virginia Menage, who manages the Chicago office, or Michele Begot in Montreal).

There is no price list, except a general one; studios run from $75 per night to $200; one-bedroom apartments are between $110 and $250, and two bedrooms, $150 to $300. Price depends on location as well as standards, and we think these are fairly priced. Prices will be given in francs, so currency rates are of no concern.

Telephone or fax the Chicago or Montreal office with information about what you are seeking and when it is needed. The response will be a proposal describing several apartments that meet your criteria, including locations. The deposit can be made by credit card or personal check, with a final payment before departure or after arrival. The keys are picked up at the Paris office, so pay attention to the office hours. If your arrival time is outside of those hours, special arrangements will be made. An easy way to handle this is to take the chauffeur option; the company will send a driver with the keys to meet your flight or train, and you'll be driven to the apartment (for a fee).

We particularly enjoyed our stay on rue Bayard and in the little studio on rue d'Artois. In sum, if you want a privately owned apartment in Paris and are willing to let one of the company staff or management help with your selection, this is the right company for you. Prices are the same booked directly or through the branch office. Agent for Pierre et Vacances (see below). Highly recommended.

Pierre et Vacances   Paris and throughout France
54, Avenue Marceau
7508 Paris
Tel: 1–49–52–00–00 Fax: 1–47–23–03–49
U.S. and Canadian agents: Paris Sejour Reservation (PSR), listed in this section, above.

Vacances means vacations, which makes the name of this company a little unusual to those who do not speak French. It is one of the large French chains of principally resort apartment hotels with accommodations in some forty locations in France. Of these, there are a dozen in the mountains, in high Alps and Pyrenees towns, and the others rim the coast of France from Normandy, along the Atlantic, to the Languedoc and the Riviera. The resorts are deluxe in standard and are architecturally varied to fit the locale. The public areas are also varied, but the apartment interiors are surprisingly similar. The choice is large, and because they are located in important destination areas and towns they are listed below.

In the mountains
You will find apartments in Alpe d'Huez, Avoriaz, Belle Plagne, Chamonix, Les Coches, Les Menuires, Méribel, Villard-de-Lans, Val Thorens, and in the new ski resort called Pyrénées 2000, about 60 miles west of Perpignan.
On the Riviera
Pierre et Vacances has properties in Villefranche-sur-Mer, Cannes la Bocca (Villa Francia), Theoule, Cap Esterel, Ste. Maxime, Cogolin, and Pramousquier. Also at Marina Baie des Anges (a huge resort), Antibes, another called Cannes Verrerie, two in Grimaud, La Croix Valmer, and Cavalaire.
West of the Riviera

Here there are apartments in Sanary-Bandol, which is far less developed than the Riviera.

Corsica

On the quiet and rather remote southwest coast near Ajaccio is an ideal getaway called Terra Bella.

Western Mediterranean coast of Languedoc-Roussillon

In this "Riviera of the future" wide beaches of blonde sand (sables d'olonne) stretch from Sète (pronounced Set) west along the curve to the border with Spain. Access to the interesting cities of Beziers and Montpellier. There are apartments in four locations: Cap d'Agde, Port Gruissan, Port Lecaute, and Cap Courdalère. Because the construction in the area is new, these resort complexes and apartments are also new. Good for beach-loving and sailing families.

Atlantic Coast

Apartments can be found in the old resort city of Biarritz, on the golf course at Moliets just north of Biarritz, cottage-type rentals at Lacanau, small apartment clusters at Maubuisson, at La Rochelle, and near the sea at Port-Bourgenay.

Brittany

Here there are rentals on the south coast at Port de Crouesty and on the north coast at Perros–Guirec.

English Channel Coast

There is an apartment at one location, Le Touquet, just south of Boulogne.

These are all resort communities planned with families in mind, complete with pools and a reception desk. Most have bars and lounges, many have dining rooms and some include tennis and golf in the vicinity. À la carte services are available. Neat, comfortable, and well managed, the apartment interiors are rather formulaic, with similar layouts and virtually the same furnishings, appointments, and dinnerware. Although they are not distinctive, there is a good standard that can be counted on, and the sites seem especially selected to be interesting and inviting. Villa Francia in Cannes la Bocca, scattered and hidden in the steep hills just a short distance above the sea, is delightful. In addition the setting offers a striking contrast to the apartments and hotels that line the highway along the water's edge below.

The Paris apartment is located near the metro station Porte de Versailles and the Parc d'Expositions of south Montparnasse, a little out of the way from the city center, but in a pleasant area. The apartments are ample size, nicely furnished, and comfortable, accommodating two to four persons in one bedroom with additional sleeping accommodations in the living room and a fully equipped kitchen. There is twenty-four-hour reception, a bar lounge, à la carte breakfast, and the advantage of parking.

For all rentals except in Paris, contact the agent, PSR, in Chicago or Montreal; there is no add-on commission. For the Pierre et Vacances Paris apartments contact the company directly. It is also possible to contact the company in Paris directly for any booking, but the agent is easier to work with. There is a catalog of all Pierre et Vacances properties available, but if you know where you want to be, ask for individual brochures (they are in English). Payment to PSR in North America is by credit card or personal check; in France, by credit card or a bank draft in francs.

Keith Prowse & Co. (USA) Ltd.   Paris and throughout France
234 West 44th St., Suite 1000
New York, NY 10036
Tel: (800) 669–8687   Fax: (212) 302–4251

This agency represents Citadines, a chain of modest but comfortable and fairly priced apartments in Paris (in the twelfth, thirteenth, fourteenth, and sixteenth districts) and in numerous well-known and lesser-known cities and towns throughout France. They also represent Home Plazza Bastille and Home Plazza Sainte Antoine in Paris, and JRH Prestige, all profiled in this section. Apartments are also offered in many major cities in Italy, Spain, the Netherlands, Belgium, and in Scandinavian countries.

The company is a privately owned affiliate of a European company that has been in the business for many decades. Its principal strength is in London apartments (as well as theater tickets and tours). The company makes booking easy and stands behind the properties it represents. It adds no fee or extra commission, provides a price list, and accepts major credit cards. Payment by check or credit card is accepted. Call for a brochure and prices (and good advice if you need it).

Riviera Retreats   Southern Provence / Riviera
Attn: Richard Wolf
11 rue de Petits Ponts
Mougin le Haut
06250 Mougin
Tel: 93–64–86–40   Fax: 93–64–00–80
U.S. agents: Barclay International Group, New York and Suzanne T. Pidduck, listed in this section

This is a very responsible broker representing the prestigious Argosy Pollet, Ltd., with an excellent selection of some 150 rentals in the south of France. Most are along the eastern Riviera (the Côte d'Azur). This includes the hills, the second and third tiers described earlier in this chapter. The office at Mougin (just outside of Cannes) is managed by a Richard Wolf, who is knowledgable and helpful. The company is quite used to dealing with British, American, and Canadian clients.

Most of the villas represented by this company are what we would call estates. They are all large, elegant, with grounds, gardens, and pools. Some have tennis courts and some are rented complete with staff. They typically accommodate from eight to twelve persons. Rents average around $3,500 per week, with a few over $20,000 per week, topped by $57,000 per week for a luxurious place at Villefranche. The prices listed for the peak months of July and August are reduced by 30 percent in June and September, and even more the rest of the year (call or fax for quotes).

In addition to these outstanding villas, there are also a few more modest rentals of good quality. There are some lovely three- and four-bedroom apartments in the range of $1,500 to $2,000 per week during the shoulder months. There is also a small assortment of apartments available in the $700- to $1,000-per-week range, all carefully chosen. Two-week minimums are usually required in July and August.

Call or fax for a brochure, which will be sent for the asking; or you can describe precisely what your needs are, and several suitable properties will be proposed. The catalog of color photos describes the properties only briefly, but the company will mail detailed descriptions and color renderings of individual properties you are interested in. Payment is required in the form of a bank draft in francs or a bank transfer. (Instructions are provided during the booking process.) Alternatively, contact either the Barclay International Group or Suzanne Pidduck in California. Both accept personal checks or credit cards and charge no additional commission.

Victoria Gardens   Bordeaux city
127, Cours de la Somme
33800 Bordeaux
Tel: 56–33–48–48   Fax:56–33–48–49

A modern apartment/hotel near the center of Bordeaux, but in a quiet area. There are 100 fully furnished and well equipped apartments: studios for one or two persons rent for about $335 per week, larger studios for four with sleeping alcoves at $500, and fair-sized two-room apartments for families at $550 per week. Modern furnishings, the multilingual staff, bar/salon, sauna, desk service, and availability of parking, laundry, and breakfast make the Victoria Gardens an excellent value compared to hotels of the same rating. An apartment can be booked on a per-night basis for about 10 percent extra. À la carte services include breakfast and cleaning and a change of linens on demand. Victoria Gardens is quick to mail a brochure and price list if requested. Or simply call or fax and book your stay in Bordeaux city. A credit card will hold your reservation, and final payment is made on arrival.

Chapter 7

GERMANY

Denmark

Baltic Sea

North Sea

Fehmarn

Warnemünde
Rostock
Lübeck • Travemünde
Hamburg
Bremen
Oldenburg

Elbe River

Berlin ⊛

The
Netherlands

• Hannover
NORTHERN GERMANY

Poland

Leipzig
Dresden

Cologne (Köln)

HESSE

Belgium

Bonn

RHINELAND

Prague ⊛

Czech
Republic

Koblenz

• Frankfurt

Bayreuth •

BAVARIAN FOREST

• Trier

Worm

Nuremberg

Luxembourg

• Heidelberg

Neckar River

Baden-Baden

Stuttgart

BAVARIA
(BAYERN)

France

Strasbourg

BLACK FOREST

BADEN-
WURTTEMBERG

UPPER BAVARIA

• Munich (München)

• Salzburg

Lindau

• Garmisch-
Partenkirchen

Berchtesgaden

Switzerland

Austria

German National Tourist Offices

122 East 42nd St. - 52nd floor
New York, NY 10168
Tel: (212) 661–7200
Fax: (212) 661–7174

11766 Wilshire Blvd. - #750
Los Angeles, CA 90025
Tel: (310) 575–9799
Fax: (310) 575–1565

175 Bloor St. East
North Tower - Suite 604
Toronto, Ontario M4W 3R8
Tel: (416) 968–1570   Fax: (416) 968–1986

International Telephone Country Code: 49
City Codes: Berlin 30; Bonn 228; Frankfurt 69; Munich 89
Example: To contact ADZ (Tourist Board Accommodation Reservations), in
    Frankfurt, dial 011–49–69–7572–0 or fax 011–49–69–7519–03.
Passport: Yes, but no visa
Language: German; English spoken widely in the west.
Currency: Deutsche mark (DM) or mark; divided into 100 pfennigs.
Value Added Tax (VAT): 15%
Electricity: 220v AC, 50 cycles.
Credit cards: AMEX, VISA, and MasterCard widely accepted in the western
    portion (formerly the Federal Republic of Germany), less so in the eastern
    portion. No oil company cards are accepted.
Main Destination Cities from North America: Frankfurt, Berlin, Munich
    (nearby Luxembourg for the western areas).

The Country

Unified Germany is approximately 625 miles long and 420 miles wide, with an
area slightly smaller than the state of California—far too large to explore from a
single location. It is not only the size, however, that makes two home bases necessary for a rich exploration, but the diversity it affords the visitor.

Much of the countryside is very appealing, from the high alps of the south
to the rolling forests of the east and north. It is the multitude of unique cities
and towns, however, as well as the famed castles, that bring history to life in
Germany. Fortunately, there are so many worthwhile towns and cities to visit
that it is possible to rent an apartment or cottage in almost any rural or resort
area and find enough rewarding destinations nearby or within a short journey to
fill weeks of exploration.

The unification of East Germany and West Germany had very little impact,
thus far, on available rentals, so few descriptions of the "new" merged states are

included in this guide. East Germany was not much given to the development of vacation resorts, nor did it have much in the way of surplus housing to rent to vacationers. There are, however, a few rentals available in Thuringia and Mecklenburg–West Pomerania, described below in General Information About Rentals.

First, in trying to decide where in Germany to set up a home base from which to travel and explore, think of Germany in four general contexts: the Alps with their picturesque chalets, the cities and their old architectural wonders, the rolling forest lands and, fourth, the great rivers flowing through wine country, dotted with villages and brooding castles. With the exception of the interesting cities of Hamburg and Lübeck, this pretty well excludes the northern, flatter region, which is a third of the country. Then there is the state of Hesse, which rises eastward from the central Rhine and Frankfurt-am-Main to the forested rolling hills. Beautiful enough, but the rental accommodations are more often rustic cabins and small resorts to which city dwellers escape, places reminiscent of resorts found in North American mountain country. This leads us to look toward the Rhineland, to Baden-Württemberg, and to Bavaria (*Bayern*), and explains why we give limited attention to the other areas of Germany. Making comparisons is, after all, part of the planning for any journey for pleasure.

Best Times of Year to Visit

As with most of northern Continental Europe, the best times to visit Germany are in the spring and fall, before or after the majority of Europeans have taken their "holidays." The optimum periods are May through mid-June and the month of October. If your trip is to be a skiing visit in the Alps of Bayern, remember that December is the peak month for crowds and prices. They generally drop off in January through mid-February, then rise again until the end of the season.

General Information About Rentals

The countryside in the principal holiday areas of western Germany are dotted with vacation rentals, but relatively few are offered through agencies in Germany, and fewer still in the catalogs and listings of United States and Canadian agencies. This is not to say that there are not thousands of vacation rentals available—only that they are more difficult to find and book through private brokers. Finding a rental is made easier, however, through the consolidation of descriptions of privately owned properties in a publication of the National Tourist Board, Deutsche Zentrale für Tourismus (DZT). Booking is also handled by the DZT, but the procedure is different from private rental companies.

Begin by contacting the nearest office of the German National Tourist Board and ask for the booklet *Self-Catering in Germany*. You will find several hundred vacation rentals listed, nicely divided into regions and accompanied by photographs and descriptions. They range from cabins in the woods to large resorts, with a few privately owned houses. Most are apartments in buildings that reflect the contemporary architecture of their respective regions. Built principally for German vacationers, they are nonetheless popular with other Europeans, and the developments usually feature a clubhouse, swimming pool, tennis courts, and other amenities.

The listings and bookings are coordinated by the Tourist Board (DZT) in Frankfurt. This centralized system is a pretty good guarantee that the accommodations are clean and well maintained, and that the properties are as they are described in the catalog. You will also note that most of the properties are officially registered resorts of one kind or another: health resort, climatic health resort or spa, winter resort, and bathing resort and spa, etc. These labels serve as good thumbnail descriptions, but don't worry if the particular spot you are interested in is not "officially registered." Because of the seriousness with which many Germans view matters of health, it is essential to them that they know the nature of the various spots in which they stay. Some resorts are classified as health resorts by virtue of their clean air, prevailing winds, humidity, and the like; some because they offer warm medicinal springs, and mud treatments; and others because they offer health regimens from spa staff.

Because the property descriptions in the DZT catalog are limited, you should work with a good general or regional guidebook in order to link the catalog descriptions with the actual character of the areas you are interested in unless you are very familiar with the country. Details on the booking process are provided at the end of this chapter in the section on rental and organizations.

As for rentals in the eastern portion of the country (formerly East Germany), most available through the ADZ are cottages in a lakeland resort area of the state of Thuringia (*Thüringen*), near the town of Saalfeld. This is within an easy drive of Leipzig and Dresden. Another group of bungalows is in a small complex not far from Rostock, 135 miles north of Berlin.

For rentals such as private homes and apartments in private buildings, the best selections are available through the New Jersey branch of Interhome, a rental company based in Zurich. A commission will be charged, and prices are higher than direct rentals from the ADZ in Frankfurt, but their catalog is comprehensive. Incidentally, the New Jersey branch of Interhome markets to travel agencies and other rental agencies in North America as well as to the public; they sometimes have flexibility in their prices.

If you are traveling in Germany in the off-seasons, there are many vacancies to be found in all regions; just drive around looking, or check with the local tourist office or travelers' assistance in a railway station.

Where to Stay: The Regions

Germany comprises five regions for our purposes: Northern Germany, Rheinland, Hesse, Baden-Württemberg, and Bayern. This division will facilitate finding a home-base vacation rental from which visiting and touring may best be carried out. The majority of rentals are available in the Rhineland (including the Mosel River area) and in Baden-Württemberg, followed by Bavaria. These are the regions in which most foreign visitors are interested, with good reason. If the length of a planned visit between May and late October is limited to, say, two weeks, and you want to find a single location that is central to the area of greatest interest and diversity, Baden-Württemberg and southern Rheinland are good choices. If more time is available, two thirds of it should be allotted to these two southern regions, and one third either to the north or to eastern Bavaria and its Bavarian Woods. For a winter vacation, the area of southern Baden-Württemberg, especially southern Bavaria along the Swiss and Austrian borders, is where to go. The reasons for these choices are based on such subjective criteria as physical beauty, historical interest, wines and foods, access to great cities and quaint villages, and even ski slopes.

Northern Germany
Environs and Accommodations

This region is less frequented by North Americans than the better known areas to the south, such as the valleys of the Rhine (*Rhein*), Mosel, and Neckar rivers, the Black Forest, Swabian Alps, and Lake Constance (Bodensee). This is the coastal area of western Germany, whose Continental beaches and ocean resorts, along with those of the offshore *Ostfriesische* and *Nordfriesische* (East and North Frisian) Islands, are popular with vacationing Germans. The sea resorts and towns of the Baltic are popular as well.

In the north, the countryside is flat or gently rolling, much of it forested and dotted with lakes. Toward the south, the region rises into the Weser hills and, southeast of Hannover, to the Harz mountains; these are areas of forests, lakes, and holiday resorts.

Both the coastal vacation areas and mountains are similar in many ways to parts of North America. The rentals range from apartments in large seaside developments to cottages in smaller developments in the woods. Although these developments are not particularly magnetic destinations, the rentals can be used as spacious and relatively inexpensive home bases from which to visit the important cities and towns of the region. Where you locate is dependent upon whether you prefer mountains or sea, since all of the region can be explored readily from any part by means of day trips and a few overnighters.

Often windswept, the North Sea coast is flat, with long stretches of beach. It is very much affected by weather, especially from fall through midspring. Our personal preference is the coastal region to the east of the peninsula, the Baltic Sea coast along the Bay of Lübeck, from Fehmarn south to Travemünde. For rentals in this area, study the catalog of the DZT; the photographs, although small, depict pretty well what the resort areas are like.

Another approach to finding a rental, if you plan to have a car, is to visit between mid-May and mid-June, or between mid-September and late October, and contact the tourist office in any of the towns you want to visit. Check into a hotel for a day or so while you work with the tourist office listing.

Apartments in Berlin can be booked directly through the German Tourist Board in Frankfurt. A good bet is the Hotel Berlin, a full-service apartment hotel. The rates vary seasonally; a one-bedroom apartment costs about $1,500 per week from April 1 to mid-November and $1,200 the rest of the year. For a studio, the rates are about $1,000 per week in the high season and $800 during the rest of the year. The DZT also will send the catalog *Holidays in Germany* listing hotels, inns, and B&Bs.

Location and Transportation

The North Sea resort areas are central to several important cities, each of them easily worth more than a day of exploration. The most interesting of these is the garden city of Bremen, Germany's oldest port, which was one of the major cities of the Hanseatic League. The towns along the estuary of the Elbe River from Cuxhavn to Hamburg, and Hamburg itself, are well worth a visit.

Although much of it has been reconstructed since World War II, Hamburg retains a large city charm, with many of its Renaissance-style buildings still intact. The St. Pauli quarter is noted for its lusty nightlife.

From Hamburg there are three or four sailings weekly of large ocean ferry-liners bound for Harwich, England. It is a twenty-hour voyage featuring excellent food, pleasant cabins, and a delightful journey along the Elbe River estuary at a very modest cost. (Contact any travel agency in Hamburg, or the DFDS Seaways offices at the dock. For information in the United States, call 800–533–3755.) To the southeast of Hamburg, the medieval town of Lüneberg is worth the twenty-five-mile trip, and if you are driving, Lüneberg is a starting point for exploring the Lüneberg Heath, a vast reserve of wildlife. Kiel is more of an industrial port city, worth a visit if you are in the vicinity.

The Baltic Sea resorts center on the city of Lübeck, a picturesque and historically interesting place of twelfth- and thirteenth-century buildings along and back from the River Trave. Ten miles downriver from Lübeck is Travemünde (literally, mouth of the Trave), a beautiful old resort town, where pine forests meet the river and the sandy beaches along the sea. It is a place to come to relax and enjoy the food and the ocean, yet close to its companion city of Lübeck.

Travemünde is one of the Baltic's major ferry ports, with many departures daily by ocean ferryliners to Gedser, Denmark, Trelleborg, Sweden, and even as far as Helsinki, Finland.

The public bus system is good in this region. Although there aren't many long-route buses, there are a lot of local buses, which connect town to town. Virtually every town of any consequence has rail service. Bremen and Hamburg are the hubs, with mainline service between them as well as north into Denmark, east to Berlin, and south into the Rheinland. Since the principal sights of interest in this region are in the cities, and the resort areas are well served by bus or rail, having a car is a convenience but not a necessity.

Prices
There are many variables, but the principal one affecting price is the season. For example, a typical one-bedroom apartment for two to four persons in a modern seaside resort complex runs about $275 per week from March to mid-May, $450 from mid-May to mid-June and again in September, and $700 from mid-June through August. There is no real need to book ahead between September 5 and mid-May; there are plenty of vacancies, so just drive around until one strikes your fancy. Information is available at the local tourist offices, or use the DZT's self-catering catalog as a guide.

Advance Booking Time:
For July and August: six months
Mid-May to July and September: two months
Rest of the Year: four weeks from abroad, zero locally

The Rhine Valley
Environs and Accommodations
The valley of the Rhine (*Rhein*) River runs almost two thirds of the north-south length of western Germany, from Lake Constance (*Bodensee*) and the Swiss and Austrian borders at the south, through the region of Baden-Württemberg northward, dividing the Rheinland to the west from Hesse to the east, and finally departing into the Netherlands in the northwest. The valley narrows from north to south, and to this great river are added the waters of the Neckar, Mosel, Nahe, Saar, Main, and other smaller rivers. Together they have served as the major transportation network from pre-Roman times. Along the route are everything from the famed vineyards of the Rheinland to castles, forests, quaint towns, and great cities.

Northern Rheinland has the most concentrated population, and it is hard to tell when you leave the industrial city of Düsseldorf and enter the city of Essen or proceed on to Dortmund. But despite the industry and population, the new cities still hold the old within them and deserve a visit. Cologne (*Köln*) is the major city, and the northern beginning of the *Rheinland* as foreigners think of it: hills, gorges, perched villages, ramparts and fortresses, ancient towns, barges, and sight-seeing boats on the river. It is indeed a region in which many weeks can be enjoyed.

Vacation rentals are plentiful in almost all parts of the Rheinland, available through the ADZ in Frankfurt, but not very well represented in North America by the commercial rental agencies. As is the case with the other regions of Germany, the least expensive rents are obtained by booking directly with the ADZ, which lists rentals in the Sauerland, Eifel, Westerwald, and the Mosell and Pfalz/Saarland areas of the Rhine Valley.

Location and Transportation

In an area so rich in castles, walled towns, ancient cities, cathedrals, and vineyards it is difficult to name all the important places to visit. A good guide and good maps are essential. Of special focus should be Cologne, if only for a visit to the Cathedral; Trier, the oldest city in Germany, is a must, as are Worms and Koblenz and a trip to Aachen. A day or two spent in the Principality of Luxembourg is rewarding and easily accomplished from any of the rentals in the Rheinland. More distant, yet still possible, is a trip south to Lake Constance, the alpine Vorarlberg province of Austria, Zurich, and northern Switzerland.

Local bus service is good in this region, which is also crisscrossed with railroads, with mainlines following much of the Rhein along both its banks. One also connects Koblenz along the Mosel valley with Trier and Luxembourg; and another runs between Cologne, Düsseldorf, Bremen, and Hamburg. Yet with all the public transportation available, the region lends itself well to exploration by car, which is not essential but very convenient.

Prices

As in the rest of Western Germany, the main variable affecting price is the season, but prices tend to be higher in this region than in northern Germany and Hesse, all else being equal. The most expensive apartments we found through the ADZ were in the large, ancient, timbered building called Residenz Moselschlösschen in the twin towns of Traben-Trarbach, some 60 miles south of Koblenz. The largest and nicest (accommodating four to six persons) runs about $975 per week July through October, $710 in the spring and fall shoulder seasons, and $570 the rest of the year. We picked as another good example a typical modern studio in a small apartment house directly on the Mosel River near the town of Cochem, an ideal location. The rent is about $375 per week from November 1 through March 25, $440 through June 28, and $540 from then to November 1. Even at peak season this is only about $77 per day, plus electricity and a small final cleaning charge. An equivalent hotel room (without a kitchen or as much space) in Cochem is about $95.

Advance Booking Time:
For July to mid-September: six months
Late March to July: two months
Rest of the Year: four weeks from abroad, zero locally

Hesse
Environs and Accommodations
To the east of the Rheinland, including part of the Rhine Valley and on to the border with Bavaria and the state of Thuringia, lies the region of Hesse, the least familiar to North Americans except for its main city, Frankfurt-am-Main, where many of us land after the transatlantic flight to Germany.

One reason this area is not so well known to foreigners is the perceived greater richness of other regions that surround it. Unlike Rheinland and Baden-Württemberg, the castles and ancient towns are not numerous, but there are many, including the castle of Sababurg, near Gottsburen—the castle of Sleeping Beauty made famous by the Brothers Grimm. It is part of the Mittelgebirge (middle mountains)—hilly, heavily forested, and cut with rivers and small streams.

The government tourist board lists about half a dozen complexes, mostly tucked away in quiet woodlands, under the heading "Hessiches Bergland/Rhein/Odenwald/Vogelsberg." This is the countryside, an area to visit to escape the cities and commune with nature. For first-time visitors to Germany, we suggest that there are regions of the country that can better fill your precious days. This is not to diminish the beauty of most of Hesse, or the interest of Wiesbaden, baroque Fulda, ancient Limburg, or the bright and beautiful Rhenish town of Rudesheim. But if you cannot find a rental to your liking (due to the relatively small selection available), this is a region that can be reasonably explored from a home base in the central Rheinland. Or, if you visit during any months between late September and mid-June, it is not difficult to find rentals listed at local town tourist offices and simply find one you like.

There are two north-south mainline railroads and one cutting diagonally across Hessen between Frankfurt and Berlin, and most of the towns in the region are served. There are also town-to-town buses.

Baden-Württemberg
Environs and Accommodations
The western edge of this region, which occupies the southwestern corner of Germany, is the upper Rhine Valley, from which the land rises toward the east into the hill country of the Black Forest (*Schwarzwald*). It encompasses the

Schwabian Alps, making it the country's most diverse and picturesque region. Despite its popularity as a tourist destination, both for Germans on holiday and for foreigners visiting Germany, there are many areas that are not heavily impacted. In the spring and fall, especially, Baden-Württemberg is a delightful region in which to spend a few weeks.

This is a land of castles and woods, of alpine meadows, quaint towns, vineyards of the Neckar River Valley, abbeys, health spas around which towns have grown over the centuries, the shores and waters of Lake Constance, and villages famous for their craftsmanship in everything from gold to clocks.

Because this is such a popular area of Germany to visit, there are numerous rental accommodations available. During April, May, and early June, and from late September through October, it is not difficult to drive through the region and find a cottage or apartment to rent for a few weeks. The best approach is to take a hotel and then check with the local tourist offices; they have lists of chalets and apartments. In addition, even though you are not booking through them, contact the ADZ in Frankfurt and ask for the self-catering catalog—it will help you locate rental properties. For advance booking, essential from early June to mid-September and during holiday seasons such as Easter and Christmas, use the catalog to select rentals under the heading "Black Forest/Swabian Jura/Lake Constance." A relatively small percentage of everything that is available is listed by the ADZ in Frankfurt, but it is a fair assortment. As seems to be the case throughout Germany, many of the vacation rentals are apartments or bungalows in planned holiday parks, although in Baden-Württemberg there is also a fair selection of apartments in private homes and buildings available through the U.S. office of Interhome. The advantage of the ADZ rentals is that they are usually less expensive and often offer communal amenities such as a laundromat, swimming pool, and clubhouse. Rentals in private homes and smaller buildings usually offer more privacy and a better sense of the locale. Because of all that there is to see and do in the region, however, it is likely that you will be spending most of your time away from "home." Regardless of which type of rental setting you stay in, you can depend on comfort and cleanliness.

Location and Transportation

It is difficult to find an unattractive town in this region, including the industrial city of Stuttgart, capital of Baden-Württemberg, an ancient city surrounded by wooded hills. And although Heidelberg and Baden-Baden are the best known towns, both worthy of their fame and of extended visits, the entire region seems dotted with inviting places. Beyond the borders of the region, yet within reach for a stay of a day or two, are Basel, Lucerne, and Zurich, Switzerland, and to the southwest, a touch of Austria where it meets with western Germany on the shore of the Bodensee near the walled island town of Lindau. To the west, a sample of France of the Middle Ages (and some fine French restaurants) can be enjoyed at Strasbourg, one of the great cities of Europe.

The railway system in the region, as in most of the country, is very good, with mainline service connecting all the major cities and serving many of the smaller ones, and extending into France, Switzerland, and Austria as well as to Berlin and the north. The intercity bus system is good, but there are so many interesting and picturesque out-of-the-way places in the region that having a car is more than just a matter of convenience—it will heighten your enjoyment of Baden-Württemberg and its environs (especially if you stay off the *autobahn*).

Prices

Along with the Rheinland to the north, prices tend to be higher in this region than elsewhere in Germany. They are lower in smaller towns and in the countryside, however. An example are the apartments in Todtnau, a small town on Highway 317, southeast of the city of Freiburg. In a balconied apartment house with the improbable name of Wanderresidenz Roseneck, a one-bedroom flat that sleeps two to four people runs about $625 per week in the high season, between late June and mid-September; in the spring and fall shoulder seasons the rent is about $460. Typically, final cleaning is $35 and electricity $5 per day.

These prices are approximate, intended to give an idea of what rents should be in the smaller towns of this area; they also help in comparing prices offered by private rental companies.

Advance Booking Time

For July to mid-September: six months
Late March to July: two months
Rest of the Year: four weeks from abroad, zero locally

Bavaria *(Bayern)*

Environs and Accommodations

Between Baden-Württemberg and the borders of Czechoslovakia and central Austria lies Bavaria, the largest of Germany's regions. It is the region of the high Alps; summer hiking and winter sports are enjoyed in the south, the Bavarian forest is in the northeast, and a rich history is everywhere, manifested in the towns and cities from Augsburg to Würzburg.

Upper Bavaria (*Oberbayern*) is the most scenic area of the region, encompassing the Alps, which it shares geographically with Austria. It is just a little over 40 miles between West Germany's famous ski resort of Garmisch to Austria's pride, Innsbruck. The beauty of Oberbayern and the Allgäu argue strongly for locating in the southern alpine area. This does not mean that the rest of Bayern is hard to explore; it is only 180 miles from Garmisch in the Alps across the region to Bayreuth, near the northeast corner of the region. Along with the attraction of Upper Bavaria come higher prices than are generally found in central and eastern Bayern. But after the investment of air fare to cross the Atlantic, the few dollars more are comparatively little to pay for a place in this spectacular area.

Like neighboring Baden-Württemberg, much of Bayern is a very popular vacation destination, both for Germans and foreign travelers, so accommodations are plentiful. There are fewer large holiday park developments in Bavaria than in the Rheinland and northern Germany. The rentals tend more toward holiday homes, often chalet styled buildings with four to ten apartments, or small private apartment buildings, usually rustic in appearance but modern in all respects.

As in other regions of western Germany, the German Tourist Board has a good selection of rentals that can be booked directly with their central reservations service (ADZ) office in Frankfurt. This is the best bet if you are interested in eastern Bavaria and the Bavarian forest. These registered properties are all attractive, and like those represented by private agencies, are mostly in chalets and town apartments, although there are a few in large holiday parks. The Tourist Board rentals catalog breaks Bavaria into two sections, Eastern Bavaria and the Bavarian forest, and the German Alps. Our suggestion, unless you are seeking rural tranquility, is to stay in the south, see "German Alps" section of the ADZ catalog.

Location and Transportation

The major city of Bavaria is Munich (*München*), located in the central south. It is a city of 1.5 million people, rich in culture and history, good food, and night life. Many days can be spent wandering through its museums, churches, shopping streets, and parks; and in the evenings, enjoying its restaurants and theaters. For Wagner fans, Bayreuth becomes packed during the annual Wagner festival in late July to August, but a visit there along with Nürnberg, Bamberg, and Würzburg, the important cities of northern Bavaria, make for an interesting and rewarding journey from wherever you have selected a home base.

Two places in the south that still attract visitors by the thousands mid-June through August are Fussen and Berchtesgaden. The former because it is near Neuschwanstein, Mad Ludwig's castle, and the latter because people are drawn to its beautiful setting or wish to see the remains of Hitler's former retreat. The great attraction in the vicinity, however, is the city 20 miles down the highway, Salzburg, Austria.

If you cannot find the rental you want in the inventories of ADZ or Interhome, an alternative approach to visiting Oberbayern is to seek a rental in northern Austria. A look at a map will show five main highways (one an *autobahn*) across the border between Innsbruck on the west and Salzburg on the east. There is a good selection of rentals in the northern Vorarlberg, Tirol, and Salzburg provinces of Austria offered by the very good rental company PEGO.

See chapter five, Austria, for information on agencies.

Mainline railroads run between the major cities of Würzburg, Nürnburg, München, and Augsberg, extending to major cities of Austria, Switzerland, and other parts of Germany. There are spurs serving Füssen, Garmisch, Partenkirchen, Berchtesgaden, and Oberammergau, among others. There are fewer lines in the east and through the Bavarian forest, so a car is more important in this area. For example, Passau can be reached by train, but it is 10 kilometers to the nearest chalet rental; you can take a taxi, but once there, it's a long walk back to buy groceries.

In the south, the town-to-town bus system is very good, but if you truly want to explore the farther mountain recesses of Oberbayern, it must be done by car.

Prices

They are of course seasonally variable, but most rentals are less expensive in eastern Bayern and the Bavarian forest areas than in the south, especially in or near the German Alps. Typical rent for a one-bedroom flat in a high-quality small apartment building in the south (the Allgäu region southwest of Munich) is $750 per week in summer high season and in December in ski areas, and $550 per week in the off-season.

A typical Bavarian forest rental is a 700-square-foot two-bedroom apartment or half chalet, which rents through the German Tourist Board for around $650 per week in the high months and $400 the rest of the year. One reason for these very modest prices for modern, attractive accommodations in a beautiful part of Germany is that the Bavarian forest area is the hinterlands, not heavily visited by foreign tourists.

If you are willing to pay slightly more, book through a regular travel agent, but as we suggested earlier, make sure they are dealing with the DZT.

Advance Booking Time

For July to mid-September: six months
Late March to July: two months
Rest of the Year: four weeks from abroad, zero locally
Ski Areas: December and mid-February–April: four months
November and January to mid-February: one to two months

The Rental Companies and Organizations of Germany

Unlike in other countries featured in this guidebook, the majority of rentals accessible from overseas are listed and handled by a government agency. Although this means complexity, especially in terms of method of payment, it also means very reasonable prices. Thus the choice for anyone looking for a rental is between complicated booking procedures with low prices and simple booking procedures and higher prices.

DST - Serviceabteilung   Throughout Germany
ADZ Central Reservations
Corneliusstrasse, 34
D-6000 Frankfurt-am-Main,
Germany
Tel: 69–74–07–67   Fax: 69–75–10–56

This is the large government central booking agency that handles bookings for vacation rentals as well as hotel and B&B reservations. The ADZ-listed rentals *cannot* be booked through the German Tourist Offices in North America. The details on how to book are shown in their catalog, but basically it is a process of either contacting ADZ directly in Frankfurt or through a travel agency. Because the commission is controlled, the price difference is small, and many travel agencies prefer not to trouble themselves with German rentals. If you choose to work with a North American travel agency, however, we suggest that you make sure that they are dealing with the ADZ and not with some domestic rental agency that will likely add on a considerable commission.

The best approach is to call or fax one of the three German Tourist offices in North America and ask for their catalog *Self-Catering in Germany*. The catalog lists and briefly describes the hundreds of rentals that have listed with the ADZ. Each shows the prices for the various types, sizes, standards, and seasons. Select at least three properties of interest and jot down the names of your choices (they do not use reference numbers) and their respective catalog page numbers. Communicate this information by letter, telephone, or fax to the ADZ along with your dates, number of persons, name, address, and fax or phone number. If you telephone, ask for someone who speaks English (most of the reservationists do). They will be able to advise you of the availability of your choices. If you are ready to book and are satisfied with one of the properties, notify the ADZ of your choice, and they will mail to you a confirmation of the booking along with instructions. A bank form will be enclosed, and you are asked to make a deposit in the form of a wire transfer of funds in marks, payable to the account of either the ADZ (or DZT) or to the property owner or management. The amount is normally 50 percent of the full rent and is due four to six weeks before occupancy. The balance is to be paid directly to the rental owner or management company within a day or two of your arrival. Dollar travelers cheques are usually accepted, but credit cards seldom are. Cash is readily available throughout Germany by means of ATMs or cash advances on credit cards at banks.

This comfortable vacation home, just northeast of Frankfurt, features several multi-bedroom apartments that each house as many as six people. (Courtesy Interhome Vacation Rental Network)

Wire transfers are simply a matter of going to your bank and asking to have funds in marks wired to the payee's bank (to the account number shown on the bank form sent by ADZ). There is usually a fee of about $25 for the transaction. Keep the receipt and take it with you along with the receipt sent by ADZ.

If working with a travel agency, take the ADZ catalog with you to show them your chosen properties. They will be receiving a commission (actually a discount off the catalog price), so don't pay more than the catalog price (perhaps an additional 5 percent is reasonable if the service is good). They will issue a voucher to hand the German property owner or management on your arrival.

A refundable damage deposit is rarely required, but if it is it will be modest, not more than 10 percent of the rent. It is paid on site as are any local taxes.

This may sound a bit complex, but remember that the tight control assures you of the best possible value as well as a guarantee that the rental will match its description in the catalog.

Interhome (USA), Inc.   Throughout Germany
124 Little Falls Road
Fairfield, NJ 07004
Tel: (201) 882–6864   Fax: (201) 808–1742

As the independent U.S. agent for Interhome of Switzerland, the largest rental company in Europe, this is a good source for moderately priced properties scattered throughout Germany, concentrated in the most popular areas of the south and in the Rhine and Mosel valleys. It is a very efficient operation: Interhome USA communicates with the mainframe computer in Zurich, which keeps track of over 20,000 properties throughout Europe, about 200 of which are in Germany. Although the descriptions in their catalog are not very complete, there are small photos of the exteriors of the rentals, and a more complete description is sent when a client selects two or three properties. What you give up in display and descriptive information is compensated for by the large choice and moderate prices.

There is a commission charged, but the service and ease of booking (compared to ADZ) may be worth it. Order a free copy of their catalog *Self-Catering in Germany* from one of the German Government Tourist Offices; this will enable you to make a general comparison of prices relative to Interhome's. Being a private company, there is often some flexibility in prices, especially in shoulder and off seasons. Be sure to ask about discounted prices.

Your first step is to phone or fax and request the Interhome catalog and price list (specify Germany because there are several catalogs). The cost is between $3.00 and $5.00 and is worth it. Select and rank three choices and call or fax again with the reference numbers. Once they have your selections, they will let you know within twenty-four hours (often sooner) about availability on your dates. Or you can call or fax with your requirements of size, type, location, budget, and dates. The company will then quickly propose a number of possibilities that meet your criteria.

Once your rental has been selected the deposit can be paid by credit card or, if you prefer, an invoice will be sent showing deposit due and amount of balance due. Payment can be made by personal check (US$) or credit card. Be prompt in paying because this busy company will not hold the property very long. After the final payment is received by Interhome all instructions and directions to the property will be sent. If not stipulated in the catalog, be sure to confirm before paying that linens and towels are provided. The damage deposit, electricity and other charges, such as tax, are usually paid on site. Cancellation insurance is automatic with this company at a cost of 3 percent of the total rent. This is a fair rate, but if you do not want this insurance, say so at the time of booking.

Chapter 8

REPUBLIC OF IRELAND

Giant's Causeway

Londonderry

**NORTHERN
IRELAND**

Donegal

Belfast

Rossas
Point

Enniskillen

Ballycastle

Sligo

Cavan

Castlebar

Carrick

Westport

Roscommon

Enniskillen

Dublin ✪

Lettermore

Galway Bay

Ballyvaughan

REPUBLIC OF IRELAND

Irish Sea

Corofin

Atlantic Ocean

Ennis

Kilkee

Thurles

Limerick

Kilkenny

Prumcollagher

Tipperary

Wexford

Tralee

Waterford

Rosslare Harbour

Dingle

Lismore

Dingle Bay

Killarney

Cork

Kenmare

Bantry

Kinsale

Skibbereen

Bantry Bay

Baltimore

Irish Tourist Board

757 Third Avenue	160 Bloor St. East
New York, NY 10017	Toronto, Ontario M4W 1B9
Tel: (212) 418–0800	Tel: (416) 929–2777

International Telephone Country Code: 353

City Codes: Dublin 1; Cork 21

Example: To contact the central reservations office for Dublin city and county, dial 011–353–1–284–1782 or fax 011–353–1–284–1751.

Passport: Yes, but no visa.

Language: English and Irish

Currency: Irish pound, often called "punt"; symbol IR£; IR£ 1 = US $1.50.

Value Added Tax (VAT): 12.5 percent

Electricity: 220v AC, 50 cycles.

Credit Cards: VISA, MasterCard widely accepted, AMEX, ACCESS, and oil company cards accepted only in some stations; otherwise use credit card or travelers cheques.

Main Destination Cities from North America: Shannon International Airport (most air carriers) and Dublin.

The Country

Principally a rural country, Ireland attracts visitors who are looking for tranquility, escape from the pressures of high population centers, and a step back in time. As though the planners knew the desires of foreign visitors, most of the clusters of rental cottages in developments lie in peaceful settings: on farmland, along remote coastlines, and near isolated lakes. Some are near small villages, others independent of other habitation. They seem to be especially situated to take advantage of the beauties of rural Ireland.

But more than just the physical beauty attracts people to Ireland. In fact, the term beauty itself sometimes seems strangely misapplied, as when the winter countryside of the west looks as sere and barren as the Arctic. The scenery is breathtaking as one looks across a sweep of stone wall-crossed fields toward a distant sea, stirred by a sense of isolation. It's almost as though much of the beauty is psychological. But of course the beauty is legendary: It can be seen in the lush green hills of Tipperary, the forests, meadows, and flowers; castles, quaint towns, and fishing villages; Dublin's old Customs House and the Four Courts along the River Liffey; and the spectacular National Gallery.

As for the Irish themselves, it has been said that they enhance the stranger's visit; we agree. Our experience, however, has been that their famed gregarious and helpful nature reveals itself best after the first overture by a stranger. A friendly greeting, a question, or a request for assistance or advice from a visitor usually elicits an impressive response.

This is not a large country, so it is possible to conveniently explore a large part of it from a single location. If you are planning to stay for only two weeks, however, we suggest one week in one of the south counties and the other in the northwest.

A word about language: Irish is the official national language of the country, although English is almost universally used. Irish is called *Ghaeilge,* which literally means Gaelic, but "Gaelic" actually refers to Scots' Gaelic, and the proper term for the language in Ireland is, indeed, Irish. Be careful in the hinterlands: the word MNA on some of the restroom doors is the Irish word for "Ladies," not a mispelling of "Men."

Best Times of Year to Visit

The southern counties of Clare, Cork, Kerry, and Limerick are roughly on the latitude of central Labrador, the southern end of Hudson's Bay, Edmonton, Alberta, and not too far south of Ketchikan, Alaska. However, unlike these North American equivalents, the Atlantic Gulf Stream keeps southwestern Ireland virtually free from frost, with mild temperatures year-round. It is the area of the richest vegetation in the country, and even subtropical plants grow and flower in the more sheltered spots. The sea temperature is certainly not tropical, but summer swimming is enjoyed by many.

The high season for tourists throughout Ireland is early July through late August. The shoulder seasons are June and September, and low season is the rest of the year. Rental prices follow this schedule, so the optimum times are from late April through June and from September to mid-October.

For the northwest counties (Donegal, Galway, Leitrim, Mayo, and Sligo), the winter weather of the North Atlantic normally begins to overwhelm the warm Gulf Stream currents by early October. July and August are the best months in terms of weather, but like elsewhere, the northwest is crowded with vacationers at that time and prices are high. Optimum times in this region are May to mid-June, and again in September. To some travelers, however, the winter windblown clouds and mists that come in from the North Atlantic and top the cliffs of counties Donegal, Sligo, and Mayo add to the dramatic beauty and sense of isolation they come to Ireland for.

General Information About Rentals

There is no better way of spending a week or more in Ireland than by renting a self-catering cottage, bungalow, house, or apartment. Recognizing the advantages of this approach, the Irish Tourist Board, the Regional Tourism organizations, and Shannon Development have worked together to make finding and booking a vacation rental very easy. It is a sophisticated system, perhaps the best in Europe. It is efficient despite the large number of properties available for short-term rent. Like the French Federation of Gîtes, Ireland has in place a rating system that appears to us to be accurate and fair.

Overall, we feel that vacation rentals in Ireland are among the best accommodations values in Europe; the prices are reasonable, the properties well equipped and maintained according to their "standard" (between one and four stars), and a lot of personal attention is in evidence. The names of the owners or managers are published along with the properties in the self-catering catalog, even for many of the cottage clusters.

One minor problem is terminology. In Ireland (and Great Britain) the term "cottage" might describe a small, separate house, or it might be one in a row of what we would consider townhouses. The four words most commonly used to describe a rental accommodation are: "cottage," "bungalow," "house," and "apartment." The latter is self-evident, but if you need an apartment on one floor, look for a flat. A bungalow seems always to be freestanding, while a cottage or house may or may not be. Houses, in general, seem to be larger than bungalows and usually have two stories, but bungalows are larger than cottages. The key, if you are wisely using the Tourist Board's catalog, is to examine the little photos and look for the terms "detached" and "semidetached." The word "detached" ensures that the rental is a freestanding, one-family unit. "Semidetached" means that it is part of some other structure but has a separate entry. A semidetached house is usually what we call a duplex. In our search for definitions, one person said that a cottage is a dwelling too small to have a back entry and stairway to the maid's quarters. Our advice: Don't worry about the terminology, just study the descriptions and photos, and if you are seeking anything other than an apartment or flat, check to see whether it's "detached" or "semidetached." Manor houses, however, are quite distinct, usually larger and elegant, standing on private grounds. For large families or companionable groups, they are the best bargains in Europe.

Tourism is a large enterprise in Ireland, and cottage rentals are a large part of it. The country lends itself to exploration from a home base, and its rural and small-town nature means that there are not many hotels. The rentals are scattered throughout the land, many of them in small clusters built to capitalize on some dramatic or otherwise appealing setting. A preponderance of the rental properties, especially those in small developments, or holiday clusters, are along the southwest coast in the counties of Cork and Kerry. There are also many properties along the west coast, especially in the area between Shannon Airport and Galway to its north.

For a day or two in Dublin, it is not necessary to find a vacation rental in the vicinity. Hotels and B&Bs are numerous, and the city can be visited on a one- or two-night trip from any cottage rental area in Ireland. The distance from the towns of western Ireland to Dublin are not great; for example, Limerick to Dublin is 125 miles, Donegal to Dublin is 140 miles, and Killarney to Dublin is 190 miles. They are all easy and pleasant drives or a few hours by train (there are many departures daily). For a longer stay, however, there are apartments both in the city and nearby, all available through the Regional Tourism Office or through direct booking (see The Rental Companies and Organizations of Ireland, this chapter).

As for the other eastern and southeastern cities—Wexford, Waterford, and Cork—industry and commerce are their focus. This does not mean that they are devoid of interest, only that they are not themselves destinations around which several days need to be planned. For visits to these cities, plan to stay in western Cork or county Killarney and commute.

In addition to the more prevalent cottage parks, there are numerous independent private cottages available, as well as apartments in castles and some of the most elegant country manors in Ireland. These luxurious accommodations are available through the Dublin-based company, Elegant Ireland.

The Irish Tourist Board (*Bord Fáilte*) publishes a comprehensive catalog called *Ireland—Self-Catering Guide,* which lists and concisely describes many hundreds of properties throughout the country. If you are planning a first trip to Ireland, however, and are not sure where you want to rent a home base, the Tourist Board catalog does little to describe the nature of the various locales of the properties. It is important, therefore, to study a general traveler's guidebook to Ireland and a good map.

Where to Stay: The Regions

This guide divides Ireland into thirds: the Southwest, the Northwest, and the East. There are relatively few rentals available in the eastern half (except for Dublin) because it is not especially popular with foreigners. In addition, most transatlantic flights from North America to Ireland terminate at Shannon. This automatically brings virtually everyone from our side of the ocean into western Ireland, and the region capitalizes on this. In fact, one of the most popular vacation rental plans, Rent-an-Irish-Cottage, focuses on arrivals into Shannon, offering rustic but modern cottages the length of western Ireland.

The western half of the country is also more popular with visitors because it is the most scenic and offers a greater sense of remoteness, living up to our idealized view of what Ireland should really be like. And who is to say that it isn't? The crowds of French, British, German, Dutch, and Americans wandering through the old streets of Killarney and Tralee during the high tourist season are now part of contemporary Ireland, and indeed, have helped shape the nature of the towns themselves during the past few decades.

If you are interested in either a hosted or independent stay in a castle or in one of the elegant manor houses that dot the country, you will have to consider the eastern side of the country. Their locations have been dictated by the events of history, not by Shannon Airport. The castles stand at what were once strategic points for defense, many in the eastern lands. The manor houses are, of course, where the large estates were carved out all over Ireland during the past few centuries. Don't worry about the location—it is the experience of staying in such an elegant and historic place that matters.

The Southwest Quarter:
Counties Cork, Kerry, Limerick, Clare, and North Tipperary
Environs and Accommodations

In the southwest, from Skibbereen northward into Counties Kerry and Clare, the coastal areas are striking, and inland the countryside is rolling and rocky, yet green. The main towns of Killarney and Tralee are lively and attractive, and many of the smaller villages are little changed from earlier times. Cork (pop. 160,000) is the main city in the southern part of this region. Although it is principally an industrial city, it certainly offers visitors much of interest. Easily accessible from anywhere in the southwest counties, Cork is only 55 miles from Killarney, 75 from Tralee, and 75 from Shannon Airport, northwest of Limerick. (If you are looking at a map of Ireland, remember that the country is not large, so the distances may appear much greater than they are.) A vacation rental in any of the southwest counties allows for easy exploration of the whole. The main northern city of this region is Limerick (pop. 70,000), usually the first large town seen by new arrivals at Shannon. Built mostly in the Georgian period, it is also an industrial town, interesting for a short visit.

The vacation rentals are in the countryside surrounding the smaller towns of the region, which are so delightful to visit. The largest town of County Kerry is Tralee (pop. 13,000), an enjoyable place to while away a day or two, as is nearby Killarney. The fame of these towns, like most villages of Ireland, certainly exceeds their size. Killarney's population is only 7,500, and Tipperary is a market town of 5,000 people. The many towns of this region are not tourist destinations; they are where you go to shop for groceries and experience the rural life of Ireland, even for a short time.

The area of southwest Ireland is relatively small, and it is all accessible by making day trips from any location. Where to stay is therefore a matter of personal choice. The Dingle Peninsula, west of Tralee, has a dramatic coastline and provides a good sense of rural Ireland; the Ring of Kerry, which is the next peninsula south from the Dingle, is also a desirable area, and includes the Killarney Lakes country. The best way to choose a location is to obtain the Tourist Board self-catering catalog and brochures.

Location and Transportation

Ireland is not a country one usually thinks of as a jumping-off place to other destinations, but it is not difficult to cross the Irish Sea to England on ferryliners from Rosslare Harbour (near Wexford) and from Dublin. There are also port-to-port and round-trip sailings (of about twenty-two hours' duration) out of Rosslare for the French port cities of Cherbourg and Le Havre, and out of Cork for Le Havre and Roscoff, in Brittany. The ships are big, the cabins, pleasant; the food, satisfactory; and the prices, very modest. In the United States call (800) 221–2474 for information on Irish ferries.

The mainline railroad runs the length of the island from Belfast, Northern Ireland, to Dublin, and finally, to Cork. There is good connecting service to Killarney and Tralee; Limerick and Shannon; and to Kilkenny, Wexford, and Rosslare. There is also a fairly good town-to-town bus system, but for the most part the rentals, whether independent cottages or in cottage parks, are generally not accessible by public transportation. Further, the nature of the rural land and the coasts are such that without a car one is very hampered. The cottage rental agencies can also arrange vehicle rentals, usually for less than can be done independently. If you are booking your cottage independently then you will of course do the same for a car, but in any case economics dictate that you should book the vehicle before leaving home; the price of waiting until you arrive at Shannon or Dublin is high. (See chapter 4, Ground Transportation in Europe)

Prices

Most of the cottages are designed for families or groups of four to six persons, or more; very few are for only one couple. If there are two in your party, there will be plenty of room. The prices, relative to hotel rooms of similar standards, are very modest.

The rentals are rated with a star system by the Irish Tourist Board, and are awarded between one and four stars. A typical two-star, two- or three-bedroom cottage on or near the sea costs about $200 per week in winter (November to April), $275 to $300 in spring (through mid-June) and in fall (September and October), and between $600 and $700 during July and August. These are also the approximate prices of cottages on a river or lake. Simpler, privately owned cottages that are not on the water, such as a farmhouse or one of the few apartments in a rural house, can be rented for between $150 and $300 a week in the peak season. A well-located, four-star, four-bedroom house rents for about $750 in the peak season, $650 in June and September, and $450 the rest of the year.

While most of the private rentals adhere to a standard three-season price range, many of the cottage parks are assigned a complex variety of seasonal and holiday prices. This not only makes it hard for foreigners to figure out precisely when to go, but also makes it appear that the owners want to wring every possible punt out of the client. The price list in the Irish Tourist Board catalog, is interesting because it reflects the holiday periods as seen by Irish landlords, individual or corporate.

The following prices for a three-star bedroom on the water illustrate how some of the rental prices are broken down. They are shown in Irish pounds (IR£) per week, so use the current exchange rate to convert them to U.S. or Canadian dollars. The U.S. $ figures give an approximation to illustrate seasonal variances. It also shows some of the extras to look out for, although more and more extras are being included in the rent.

Period	IR £ 1.5	$
January 4 to March 31 (except Easter Week)	145	217.
Easter Week	300	450.
May 1 to May 31	185	277.
June 1 to June 26	240	360.
June 26 to July 3	330	495.
July 3 to August 21	385	570.
August 21 to August 28	330	495.
August 28 to October 1	185	277.
October 1 to December 18	145	217.
Bank Holidays (3-day weekends)	175	262.
Halloween Week	220	330.
Christmas to New Year	220	330.
Off season weekends & midweek breaks	135	202.
St. Patrick's Weekend	175	262.
Electricity	50p coin slot meter	
Fireplace turf extra after first bundle		
Bed linens available to overseas visitors—£8/person/week.		

The "50p coin slot meter" means that you need to have a pocketful of 50 pence coins when you arrive in order to feed the timer on the electrical meter. Some prices include electricity, however. The turf is peat used in open-turf fireplaces; in the modern cottages there is almost always central heating, so the fireplaces are more for atmosphere than heat. In simpler cottages, the fireplace and cook stove (cooker) are the only sources of heat. Linens and towels are becoming more and more standard, but sometimes must be rented. The Irish Tourist Board catalog shows a symbol for this, so be careful to check it.

In the low season, and even in the early and late periods of the shoulder months, you will rarely encounter a problem if you decide to find your cottage after arrival. Rent a hotel room in the area you choose for a day or two, ask for a list and directions from the Tourist Information Office in Dublin or Limerick or at Shannon Airport. Then drive around. Cottages can be rented on site, usually by VISA, AMEX, MasterCard, or Access credit cards. You might not find the best choice after early June or in early September, but you should have no trouble finding a rental. Do not try this method between mid-June and September 1.

Advance Booking Time
For July and August: six months
For June and September: two weeks to two months
Rest of the Year: two weeks from overseas, zero locally

The Northwest Quarter:
Counties Galway, Mayo, Sligo, Lietrim, and Donegal
Environs and Accommodations

The farther one travels northward from County Clare into northern Galway and counties Mayo, Sligo, and beyond, the more barren and empty the country seems. The coast of Donegal, the northernmost county, is surely the most ruggedly scenic and primitively stunning part of Ireland. After Cromwell crushed the Irish revolt in 1641 and confiscated the estates of the Catholic gentry, the former landowners became the peasantry. They were saved from starvation by the fact that potatoes grew fairly well, especially in the area known as Connaught. To the north, in Donegal, the land was so poor and the farm production so meager that the owners were pretty much left alone.

The physical and psychological isolation of the remote parts of this region explain why even now in some parts of the northwest Irish is still the main language spoken. Despite the popularity of the region among tourists, they are somehow swallowed up in its vastness, leaving only a minimal effect.

There are fewer vacation rentals in the Northwest quarter than in the Southwest. Dividing two or three weeks between the northern and southern areas may be a good idea. It depends on how long you can enjoy the northwest, with its rugged treeless mountains, moors, cliffs rising sheer from the sea, isolated fishing villages, and often inclement weather, especially in winter and at the change of seasons. But the late summer winds that blow across the bogs and moors are scented with heather, adding to the mysterious beauty of it all.

The Northwest can easily be explored from any location in the region, so the choice has more to do with the desirability of the immediate locale than where in the region it is situated. As in the Southwest, many of the cottages offered by rental companies are in cottage parks, usually fewer than ten, situated to take advantage of the sea, or lakes, or another view. The best approach to finding one is to study the photos and descriptions in the catalog or the brochure you receive. As for choosing between a privately owned dwelling or one in a cottage park, the main criterion is location, followed by your personal preference to be alone in a private place or in the company of a few neighboring travelers. The cottages in the parks are usually newer and slicker than the private ones, and may cost a little more, standard for standard. Some are constructed in a traditional way, including thatched roofs and stone floors, but if you are looking for authenticity, look for an older, private place.

Location and Transportation

Despite the sense of relative emptiness and space, nothing is too far away. From the village of Donegal to the city of Dublin, it is an easy four-hour drive, and less to Galway. From the airport at Shannon, it is about 55 miles (north) to Galway, and another 75 miles to the peninsula that comprises most of county Mayo. Virtually all the roads in the region can be covered in a few days.

It is possible to leave the Republic of Ireland by crossing the border of Donegal or Leitrim into Northern Ireland, and despite local unrest, a visit to Londonderry will prove to be most worthwhile. An extension of a trip to Londonderry of about 50 miles eastward will bring you to the "Giant's Causeway," an interesting geological oddity of myriad polygonal basalt pillars rising vertically from the sea. It has been a destination of travelers for well over a century. An overnight stay in the Causeway Hotel at the top of this unusual expanse of coast is a memorable experience.

As for the railways, it is almost as though "you can't get there from here." One line runs from Dublin to Sligo, one between Dublin and Galway, and one between Dublin and Westport. There is no line north and south along the coast except between Sligo and Donegal. It is not impossible to get from Shannon to Sligo by rail, but it must be done by going across the country to Dublin. There is local bus service and a long-route bus line between Londonderry and Cork via Donegal, Sligo, Galway, Ennis, and Limerick. A car is very important to have in this region, however, unless your plan is to stay put and explore by foot as many visitors do.

Prices

See the prices ranges for accommodations in the Southwestern Quarter section, listed above. The prices in this region are comparable.

Advance Booking Time

For July and August: six months
For June and September: two weeks to two months
Rest of the Year: two weeks from overseas, zero locally

Northeastern and Eastern Ireland

There is a fair selection of private cottages and other rental dwellings in the central and east coast counties available through the Irish Tourist Board, but fewer cottage park clusters than in the southern and western counties. Any of the privately owned rentals can be booked directly with the owners (whose names and addresses are in the catalog supplied by the Tourist Board) or through the computerized system of the Tourist Board and the regional tourism offices.

As we noted earlier in the chapter, with the exception of Dublin proper, we feel the east can best be explored from a home base in the west or from the central counties of Tipperary and Cork. The distances are not that great, and the heart of Ireland is not in its industrial east coast.

If you want to spend a week in Dublin or its immediate vicinity, there is a good selection of apartments and townhouses available through the Tourist Board and several of the following companies, all considerably less expensive than hotels of comparable standards. They may not be as centrally located as major hotels, but for the space and price they are a good value.

The Rental Companies and Organizations of Ireland

Brookman Town Homes   Dublin
3 Fitzwilliam Square
Dublin 2
Tel: 1–766–784   Fax: 1–763–166
U.S. agent: Keith Prowse & Co. (USA) Ltd., listed in this section.

One group of 25 three- and four-star townhouses of two, three, and four bedrooms is located in Donnybrook, a Dublin section just northwest of Trinity College, not far from the city center. These are priced in the range of 450 Irish pounds (approximately U.S. $675) per week for two bedrooms, to IR£ 490 ($735) for 3 bedrooms, and £550 ($825) for four bedrooms, all about 10 percent less in low-season. Another group of townhouses, also attractive, modern, and spacious, are also rated superior quality and are located a little farther out, in Ballsbridge. They are not far by bus or DART (Dublin Area Rapid Transport) from the city. Referred to as Shrewsbury Park, these are part of a secure residential complex of brick townhouses and include modern amenities such as a dishwasher, microwave, and washer/dryer. These range from $870 to $1,200 per week and are certainly worth it. There is parking available, the service is excellent, and you can count on a true home away from home.

Although the Brookman properties are not in the city center, they have the advantage of being sizable and in quiet neighborhoods. Short-term rental apartments of this size are simply not available downtown. These are like comfortable, well-managed, suburban townhouses in the United States or Canada. Call or fax the Dublin office for brochures and current prices before deciding which location to choose; those in Shrewsbury Park are the more luxurious, but they cost more. The deposit and rental payment can be made by credit card or a bank draft in Irish pounds. Electricity and phone are extra, payable at the time of departure.

Diamond Rocks Holiday Homes

Kilkee, County Clare
Contact: Limerick Travel Ltd.
Bedford Row, Limerick
County Clare
Tel: 61–413–844   Fax: 61–416–336

These are eight modern, well-designed, four-star, three-bedroom townhouses, beautifully situated on a slope overlooking Kilkee Bay in southwestern County Clare. Twice daily the low tide reveals a vast basaltic reef just below the townhouses, acres of a half-submerged wonderland to wander through, with some tidal pools large enough to swim in. The small row of townhouses could not have been better placed for capturing the feeling of this area. All have views of the bay and the sea beyond, as well as the green coastline to the north. Nor could they have been better designed. Linens and towels are included; electricity is metered and the cost is payable on departure. They are well-furnished, comfortable, and properly managed by a delightful and welcoming couple. For example, rents range from £475 (about $710) in July and August, £340 ($510) from mid-May through June and again in September, £240 ($360) from mid-April to mid-May, and £170 ($255) the rest of the year.

Although the town of Kilkee is less than exciting, it provides everything necessary for a stay. Enis is the closest large town, 35 miles to the east. This is a beautifully isolated area, yet only 50 miles west of Shannon International Airport. Overall, these townhouses are a true value, especially given their size, comfort, amenities, and location. We thoroughly enjoyed our stay here and found day trips easy and delightful. A car is essential.

Limerick Travel is a good company with fair prices. (Car rentals are also available.) Payment can be made by credit card or personal check.

Donegal Thatched Cottages

Connor and Mary Ward
Rosses Point
County Sligo
Tel: 71–77197   Fax: 71–77500
U.S. agent: Lynott Tours, Inc., listed in this section.

Eight three-star and two four-star modern detached cottages with thatched roofs are clustered on the rocky shoreline of lonely Cruit (pronounced Critch)

Island in County Donegal. They are accessible from the mainland by a bridge not far from the pretty town of Dungloe, in County Donegal. Rental prices are in range of IR£ 150 (approximately $225) per week in midwinter to 450 ($675.00) in July and August, with a variety of seasonal prices in between. Bed linens must be rented at about $6.00 per bed per week. There is an extra charge for the four-star cottages, which have good views of the sea and dishwashers; all have fireplaces. We did not stay here, but heard from the competition that they are very comfortable and cozy. The location is ideal for exploring Donegal, Sligo, and Mayo counties, but this north country is quiet and remote, requiring a car for exploration. Angling, kayaking, and golf are all available.

Contact Connor and Mary Ward for a free brochure. Payment can be made by credit card or bank draft in Irish pounds; or book through Lynott Tours, Inc. in New York.

Elegant Ireland   Throughout Ireland
Ms. Geraldine Murtagh
15 Harcourt Street
Dublin 2
Tel: 1–475–1665   Fax: 1–475–1012

This company offers what its name implies: manor houses, castles, stately homes, and other elegant rentals throughout Ireland. It also has a carefully chosen selection of more modest, and more modestly priced, properties. The large distinguished houses are, however, what Elegant Ireland is known for; they are rentals for persons, families, or groups seeking the ultimate stay, and rank among the most beautiful in Europe. Most properties include grounds, many with tennis court, some with pools. For many of these large properties arrangements can be made for domestic staff, and many are so large that a staff is required. Rental prices range anywhere from IR£ 500 to about IR£ 36,000 ($750 to $54,000) per week. The latter is for a fourteen-bedroom castle with 3 reception rooms, a billiard room, game room and a ballroom, nestled in approximately five hundred acres of grounds with a swimming pool, tennis courts, and a trout fishing stream. More typical, however, are what we consider to be the best rental values in Western Europe. There is no other country where so much space and elegance can be rented at such reasonable prices. Although many are in the range of $2,000 to $3,000 per week, there are some very nice ones for under $1,000. The four-double-bedroom, four-bath, Georgian country house "Corofin," 20 miles from Shannon, costs about IR£ 550–770 ($825 to $1,155), depending on the season. Travelers on moderate budgets should not overlook this company just because *some* of their properties are expensive.

Call or fax for a catalog and price list (which costs about $3.00), or let the company know what you are seeking, where, and the dates you prefer. The com-

Built in the 1880s and completely renovated in 1992, the Oysterbed House, located in County Kerry on the shore of the Kenmare River estuary, is one of many reasonably priced elegant rental properties available throughout Ireland. (Courtesy Elegant Ireland)

pany will mail or fax a booking form in addition to rental descriptions. The 30 percent deposit can be made by credit card, with the balance paid by bank transfer, bank draft in Irish pounds, or within at least sixty-five days or more of occupancy, by personal check.

It is difficult to overstate the character and elegance of these stately houses and castles, but, again, don't overlook the modest ones. Inquire about activities, such as hunting, shooting, fishing, and riding. If you wish to speak with someone about a particular property, ask for the director, Geraldine Murtagh, a most capable director. For independent planned tours or itineraries through Ireland associated with stays in these estate and castle rentals, contact Abercrombie and Kent in the United States at 800–426–7794; they work closely with Elegant Ireland and will probably have a catalog to send.

Irish Tourist Board
757 Third Avenue
New York, NY 10017
Tel: (212) 418–0800

Irish Tourist Board
160 Bloor Street East
Toronto, Ontario M4W 1B9
Tel: (416) 929–2777

Throughout Ireland

The Tourist Board of Ireland (Bord Fáilte) is unusual in that in one way it competes with private rental companies but in so doing offers to the public hundreds of privately owned houses and apartments, a considerable service to property owners. It publishes a comprehensive catalog containing hundreds of short descriptions along with a colorful commercial section in which companies and owners of larger properties are, for a fee, advertised. Many of the larger properties are the popular cottage parks, both family owned and company owned. Travelers benefit from the Bord Fáilte effort as a vast number of rentals is consolidated in a single catalog, which can be obtained by contacting the office in New York or Toronto. If you prefer to work with one of the companies, the group we have selected for inclusion in the guide includes those we recommend but are by no means the only ones to consider. Others can be contacted as shown in the tourist board catalog.

Selections can be made and booked through the many regional Computer Booking Service offices. We recommend going through one of the offices if you select a privately owned individual rental. (Not all private owners are in the system, but they can be contacted directly.) If you use a company, we suggest that you contact them directly and ask for their brochure and price list. Bookings through the central or regional tourism offices can be paid for with credit cards, and they can be booked either directly, if you wish to talk to a manager, or through a proprietor. If you choose to book through the appropriate regional tourism office (see telephone and fax numbers), refer to the described property in the *Self-Catering* catalog and its reference number—you will be asked for it by the reservationist.

Dublin City and County: Tel: 1–284–1782 Fax: 1–284–1571

Counties Carlow, Kilkenny, SW Tipperary, Waterford, Wexford: Tel: 51–52–444 Fax: 51–77–388

Counties Cork and South Kerry: Tel: 21–273–251 Fax: 21–273–504

Counties Clare, North Kerry, Limerick, South Offaly, North Tipperary: Tel: 61–317–958 Fax: 61–361–903.

Counties Galway, Mayo, Roscommon: Tel: 91–63–081 Fax: 91–65–201

Counties Cavan, Donegal, Leitrim, Monaghan, Sligo: Tel: 71–61–201 Fax: 71–60–360

Counties Kildare, Laois, Longford, Louth, Meath, North Offaly, Westmeath, Wicklow: Tel: 44–48–761 Fax: 44–40–413

There is a IR£3 fee charged by the tourist offices for bookings made through them, and it is well worth it. Deposit is one third of the rent, payable at time of booking. If the owner requires a damage deposit, it is also paid at the time of booking and is refundable if no damage is incurred. Cancellation charge details and other terms and conditions are shown in the catalog and are provided with company booking forms. For direct bookings with owners, be sure to clarify the owner's terms.

Bookings **cannot** be made through the tourist board offices in the United States or Canada, only through their catalog.

Island Holiday Cottages   West Coastal Ireland
(Tithe Saoire na n-Oilean)
Mr. Padraic O'Conghaile
Annaghvaan, Lettermore
County Galway
Tel: 91–81163   Fax: 91–81146

This is a group of thirteen modest, three-star, freestanding, three-bedroom cottages 30 miles west of the town of Galway. The setting is a sere coastal landscape of inlets and islets, stone and peat, small but neat white houses scattered along rustic roads. The Irish language is spoken by the people there along with English.

The cottages are simply but comfortably furnished, with beamed ceilings over the main living areas; bedrooms are upstairs as well as down. As in many traditional cottages in this area, the unusual floors are of glossy, black-painted slab stone. Heat is electric (paid for by coin box, so be sure to have a supply of 50-pence pieces), supplemented with turf-burning fireplaces. The first bale of compressed turf is free, but there is a charge thereafter. The kitchens are adequately equipped, including microwave ovens. Bed linen is provided at no extra cost, but ask in advance for towels. The location is very isolated, but only 90 miles from Shannon Airport and central for exploring counties Galway, Clare, and northward into County Mayo and the vast stone wilderness of the Connemara. The goods you may need can be purchased at the store at nearby Leitir Mor, but trips into Galway are easy, and the town is busy and interesting, full of good restaurants, shops, and stores.

Rents average IR£ 440 (approximately $660) per week in high season; £340 ($510) in April, May, and June; and £240 ($360) the rest of the year. The attentive manager, Mr. O'Conghaile (pronounced O'ConEEly), lives across the road from the entrance to the cottages, so there is always assistance when needed. A car is essential. It is easy to book direct (which we recommend) or through the Regional Tourist Organization, listed in this section.

Keith Prowse & Co. (USA) Ltd.
234 West 44th Street
New York, NY 10036
Tel: (800) 669–8697   Fax: (212) 302–4251

Keith Prowse is an agent for Brookman Town Homes in Dublin, listed in this section, and for Stephen's Hall Hotel in Dublin. The latter are well-located apartments, consisting of studios and one and two bedrooms. Stephen's Hall is at 14–17 Lower Leeson Street and comprises thirty-seven apartments altogether. Prices are published in U.S. dollars, and no commission is added. A brochure is available.

Kenmare River Holiday Cottages Southwest Coast

Mike and Bridie O'Sullivan
(Booking office) 45 Ard-na-Lee
Tralee, County Kerry
Tel: 66–26323   Fax: 66–23422
(Cottages) Lehid Harbour, Tuosist
Tel: 64–84258

A scattering of thirteen three-star contemporary bungalows occupies the banks of a small peninsula into the Kenmare River, which at this point is actually the sea. Waves batter the seawall at the bottom of the hill upon which the main group of cottages sit, and the dramatic view is of a distant horizon penetrated by the mountains of the Ring of Kerry across the broad estuary. The shore of the estuary as well as most of the coastal fringe of this part of Ireland is thick with growth: deciduous trees, conifers, ferns, vines, succulents, and subtropical plants abound. The roads are bordered with hedges of fuchsia. In this paradise Mike O'Sullivan has planted even more, making the surroundings of the cottages an imaginative garden, enhanced by juxtaposition with the rugged and formidable coastline of the peninsulas of the Ring of Beara and the Ring of Kerry.

The three-star cottages are contemporary in style. There are three smaller (one- and two-bedroom) cottages and twelve larger (three- and four-bedroom) ones, all simply but comfortably furnished, complete with fireplaces and dishwashers. In addition, there is Olde World cottage, a well-restored semidetached part of an older building, with 2 bedrooms (one with bunk beds, the other with a double) and the Villa, a three-star cottage with one bedroom and an open plan. This area of Ireland is most rewarded by the warmth of the Gulf Stream; it is a good spot if you plan an off-season visit (October through April). It is also an area remote from pressures and activity other than swimming, fishing, golfing, and exploring the spectacular coasts of nearby Dingle Bay, Bantry Bay, and the calm but deceptively named Roaringwater Bay. This is also a good location for travel into counties Kerry, Limerick, and Cork. The cottages are near the pleasant town of Kenmare, 18 miles south of Killarney and about 110 miles from Shannon Airport. There are tennis courts on site as well as a children's play area, and a barbecue. The nearby waterfront is good for swimming, boating, and fishing. There is an 18-hole golf course at Kenmare and a nine-hole course across the peninsula at Glengariff. The entire peninsula is a delightful and interesting area, from wonderfully bleak forelands to castle ruins, archaeological sites, small towns, and even the highest waterfall in Ireland.

Rents run about IR£ 500 (approximately $750) in July and August, $600 in the shoulder months, and $300 in low season. Linens are included, but towels must be rented at IR£ 3 per pair. May, June, and September are good months to visit. A brochure will be sent upon request, and bookings are easily made and paid for by VISA or MasterCard. We liked this area, the countryside, the cottages, and Mike O'Sullivan—he can tell Kerry jokes like few others.

Killarney Lakeland Cottages   Southcentral Ireland
Mr. Brian O'Shea
Muckross, Killarney
County Kerry,
Tel: 64–31–538   Fax: 64–34–113

This is a widely spaced group of three-bedroom cottages, all rated with three stars, in a wooded area adjacent to the working farm of Brian O'Shea's family. There is a tennis court and game room, and lake fishing nearby. These are very attractive cottages, well equipped and maintained. Linens and towels are included. The setting, however, in a tree-dotted meadow, is not very special. When on the premises, it is somehow hard to relate to being in Ireland. The cottages are 90 miles southwest of Shannon Airport and are centrally located for easy exploration of Counties Kerry, Cork, Limerick, and into Clare. The bays of the warm southwest coast are within 25 miles. The railroad runs from Killarney town eastward to Mallow and Cork and westward to Tralee. Although a car is a great convenience, this is one of the few cottage groups that can be reached from a nearby railroad station. Transportation can be arranged for at the time of booking.

Rents range from about IR£ 135 (about U.S. $200) per week in winter to IR£ 375 ($560) in the shoulder seasons and IR£ 475 ($710) per week in July and August. Booking and payment are easy; a brochure is available for the asking.

Lismore Tours   Western Ireland
106 East 31st Street
New York, NY 10016
Tel: (800) 547–6673   Fax: (212) 685–0614

This travel agency represents several Irish rental companies and includes some rentals listed in the Tourist Board's self-catering guide. The rentals are located in most west and southwest counties. A brochure available. The company has a good reputation and does not add on commission. Prices are equal to or may be better than booking direct or through the Regional Tourism Offices, but call and ask for quotes or order their brochure and compare. Lismore also offers escorted and self-drive tours as well as car rentals. Like Lynott Travel (listed below), they are specialists on Ireland.

Lynott Tours, Inc. Western Ireland
Empire State Bldg.
350 Fifth Avenue, Suite 2619
New York, NY 101118
Tel: 1 (800) 221–2474   Fax: (212) 695–8347

This is a travel agency that represents several Irish rental companies (as well as some properties listed in the Tourist Board's self-catering guide). Cottages are located in counties Clare, Kerry, Limerick, and Tipperary. Brochures are available. The company has a good reputation and does not add on commission. Prices are equal to or may be better than booking direct or through the Regional Tourism Offices, but order their brochure or get quotes and compare. They offer escorted and self-drive tours as well as car rentals. Like Lismore Travel (listed above), they are Ireland specialists. AMEX credit cards or personal checks are accepted.

Marfield House Southeastern Ireland
Mrs. Rachel Harris
Clonmel
County Tipperary
Tel: 52–25–444   Fax: 51–77–388

Marfield House is a privately owned, stately period home, which has been attractively converted to contain one-, two-, and three-bedroom apartments, all four-star rated. Each apartment differs somewhat in its furnishings and style, but all are comfortable and, given the prices, of very good value. The surroundings are parklike; the River Suir runs along the property. (Fishing is available.) The location (5 miles from Clonmel, the second largest town of the county) is excellent for exploring southeastern Ireland, including a visit to the famed glass and crystal manufacturing city of Waterford. Tipperary is 30 miles away. This is a modestly priced opportunity to stay in an Irish country house. One-bedroom apartments range from IR£ 125 $187.00 per week in winter to $360 in July and August; two-bedroom apartments are £160 to £295, and three-bedroom apartments from $285 to $525.

The Oysterhaven Centre Southeastern Coast
Oliver and Kate Hart
Oysterhaven, Near Kinsale
County Cork
Tel: 21–770–738   Fax: 21–770–776

Oysterhaven is far enough from the city of Cork to provide a sense of isolation, yet near enough to make easy trips into the city. The nearby town of

Kinsale is delightful, one of the oldest in Ireland, chartered in 1333. There are good markets, ruins, and interesting shop streets; it is also a center for deep-sea fishing. In retrospect, after months traveling through Europe, one of the best meals we had in terms of quality, service, style, and atmosphere was at the tiny Seasons Restaurant in Kinsale, of all places.

Oysterhaven itself is on the water at the end of the road, a small cluster of eight three-star rated, three-bedroom, two-story cottages looking out across the bay. Started as a simple resort for the purpose of teaching windsurfing and sea kayaking, the modern cottages were added later, along with tennis courts and boat rentals. The focus remains teaching: There are programs for every age, and now include sailing and canoeing. Oysterhaven is run by a hard-working and personable couple, the Harts, plus staff hired to teach the water sports. It is not necessary to enroll in a water program in order to stay, but the opportunity is certainly there to learn or to simply rent a sailboat or kayak.

The cottages are relatively new and comfortably but sparely furnished in a rustic style with everything included. The units are attached and form an L with a large community room at the corner, where events from parties to barbecues are held for guests. Oysterhaven provides a good base from which this south-eastern coast can be explored northward to Waterford and Cork and southward to Skibbereen. Rates are remarkably low: $225 per week in the off-season, $410 in April, May, June, and September; and $675 in July and August. June and September are ideal months. This is a good spot for families.

Rent an Irish Cottage   Counties Clare, Limerick, Tipperary
85, O'Connell Street
Limerick
County Limerick
Tel: 61–411–109   Fax: 61–314–821

This is a relatively large rental company with properties in seven locations in western Ireland. One of the oldest companies operating cottage clusters in Ireland, it has embarked on an extensive renovation program for its cottages. (Some had seen better days when we visited.) Feel free to make sure that the cottage you book is either one of their newer ones or has been refurbished. The locations are ideal. The accommodations are modern in most ways except for their adherence to traditional architectural style and the peat-burning fireplaces in many for atmosphere and supplemental heat.

The cottage parks are located at Ballyvaughan, Carrigaholt, Corofin, and Whitegate in County Clare; Puckane and Terryglass in County Tipperary; and Kilfinane in County Limerick. At Corofin the choice is between a group in the town and a scattering on a high ridge above the lake. (We stayed at the former but prefer the latter.) Much of the west-central part of the country is accessible from any of these locations, and none is more than 100 miles from Shannon airport. If you are not sure which location is best for you, contact the U.S. agent, Lynott Tours (see listing, this section) for advice; they know the properties well and their prices are the same or better than those published.

In general prices are around IR£ 150 ($225) per week in winter, $420 in the shoulder months, and $600 in July and August. With so many cottage types and sizes available, there are many variations, however. Everything is provided. These are very good accommodations, strategically located.

Springfield Castle   Southcentral Ireland
Mrs. Betty Sykes
Springfield, Drumcollogher
County Limerick, Ireland
Tel: 63–83–162   Fax: 63–83–255

Because a castle is normally considered a fortified dwelling, this is more properly described as a very large residence that was built with walled protection but not with the battlements of a castle. It sleeps twelve in seven bedrooms, has three bathrooms, one shower, three reception rooms, plus a living room and formal dining room. The estate is in a rural, wooded setting in south Limerick county, 35 miles from the city of Limerick and an equal distance from Tipperary. It is a rare experience to stay here, ideal for a large family or group of traveling companions.

This is an historic family home of moderate rental standards with unusual furnishings collected subsequent to a fire in the late nineteenth century. There is a repeat clientele, many of whom are Americans who have discovered the beauty of the area and the rare pleasure of staying at Springfield Castle. A wedding party was in residence for a week when we visited (an ideal use for the place). A short brochure is available for the asking, but it can be rented sight unseen in confidence if you are willing to overlook the worn character of some of its furnishings. Feel free to phone and speak with Betty Sykes.

The rent is remarkably modest: about IR£ 950 (approximately $1,425) per week in July and August; $1,075 in May, June, and September; $770 the rest of the year. Add 12.5 percent VAT for this company. In fact, we can think of no property we have visited where such space, atmosphere, and character is available in this price range. Book well ahead, and be sure to insist on specific directions (a map would be useful). Payment is made by personal check in dollars at the rate of exchange on the day of booking. A car is essential.

Trident Holiday Homes
Unit 2, Sandymount Village Centre
Sandymount
Dublin 4
Tel: 1–668–3534   Fax: 1–660–6465
U.S. Agent: Keith Prowse & Co. (USA) Ltd., listed in this section.

Throughout Ireland

Trident is a very capable company with a good selection of rentals dotted about Ireland. Most are townhouses of superior standard, but a few are austere but comfortable, well-furnished cottages. We stayed in the Landsdowne townhouses (sixteen two and three bedrooms) near the Ballsbridge town center, and found them spacious and comfortable as well as convenient. They are just southeast of Trinity College in a pleasant neighborhood. A little farther out is Trident's Park Court in Sandymount, a residential area south of the Liffey River and Dublin's city center (ten minutes from downtown via rapid transit). Here Trident has fourteen 2-bedroom and two 3-bedroom, three-star, townhouse apartments, well furnished and equipped. Both Landsdowne Village and Park Court are modern townhouses, nicely furnished, with all amenities supplied, including a phone, linens, a TV, dishwasher, microwave, and washing machine. Both are good choices for a stay in Dublin. The price of a two bedroom is about IR£ 430 (approximately U.S. $640) per week in June, July, and August and IR£ 370 ($550) the remainder of the year; this is less than a single room in a small hotel of equal standard. Electricity and phone are extra, paid at the time of departure.

Telephone or fax for Trident's brochure, which shows their properties in counties Galway, Limerick, Mayo, Clare, Kerry, and Waterford as well as Dublin. We were especially taken with the Old Head Beach Villas at Westport, County Mayo, one of the best locations for exploring the west-central coast. Even at a peak-season rate of about $625, these three bedroom beach houses are a bargain. Book direct or through the Prowse agency—the price is the same. Payment is made by credit card. We recommend Trident properties highly; they maintain good standards and good values.

Ventry Holiday Cottages
Mr. John P. Moore
Green Street
Dingle
County Kerry
Tel: 66–51588   Fax: 66–51591

Situated in a rather austere setting looking across Ventry Harbor, these cottages have plain exteriors that belie their comfortable interiors. We include this small group partly because of their location on the Dingle Peninsula, which juts into the Atlantic—a wildly beautiful area typical of Ireland's southwest coast. The cottages all have three bedrooms, and the prices are very fair, ranging from off-season lows of IR£ 150 ($125) to about $590 from the last of June through August. The cottages have open fireplaces, carpeting, and central heat, all linens, towels, and electricity are provided. Even for two persons, the price (as for most cottage rentals in Ireland) is reasonable. The closest town is Dingle; a car is needed.

West Cork Holiday Homes
26/27 Rossa Street
Clonakilty
West Cork
Tel: 63–33220   Fax: 63–33131

This company has groups of rentals at Clonakilty (near the bay), Baltimore, and Kinsale, all at the southwestern end of Ireland, none far from Cork. They are included here partly to suggest three places from which to explore this part of the country, and partly because they are comfortable, adequately furnished, and reasonably priced. Everything is provided. Of the three, the Kinsale group is the least attractive, although the lovely old town itself is a delight to wander through for shopping and browsing. The townhouses at Clonakilty are attractive and unusual (some are four-star), a gaily painted row directly facing the sidewalk, with outside space for residents at the rear. The Baltimore rentals are modern but traditionally built cottages. All three of these locations are near the sea, but are good for land explorations as far north as Waterford, throughout Cork, and even into Kerry via easy day trips. Prices at all three locations run from IR£ 200 (about $300) per week in winter to a high of £395 ($590) in July and August. The nearest railroad station is Cork, so a car is needed. Book through the Regional Tourism Office or directly with the booking office in Clonakilty, which handles all three properties.

Chapter 9

ITALY

Italian Government Travel Offices:

630 Fifth Avenue
New York, NY 10111
Tel: (212) 245–4822
Fax: (212) 586–9249

12400 Wilshire Blvd., Suite 550
Los Angeles, CA 90025
Tel: (310) 820–0098
Fax: (310) 820–6357

1 Place Ville Marie - Suite 1914
Montreal, Quebec H3B 3M9
Tel: (514) 866–7667
Fax: (514) 820–6357

International Telephone Country Code: 39
City Codes: Milan 2; Naples 81; Rome 6; Venice 41; Siena 577; Florence 55
Example: To contact Buckland & Abeti in Florence, dial 011–39–55–284–828.
Passport: Yes, but no visa.
Language: Italian; English spoken in tourist areas.
Currency: Lira (plural, lire), abbreviated L or Lit.
Value Added Tax (VAT): 15%
Electricity: 220v AC, 50 cycles.
Credit Cards: AMEX, VISA, MasterCard widely accepted in main cities and towns, not in smaller villages; no oil company cards accepted.
Main Destination Cities from North America: Rome, Milan

The Country

Italy has long invited travelers to savor its riches. Artists, scholars, poets, and writers have made the journey for centuries, and in more recent decades, photographers and filmmakers have come as well. Guides and other books, materials from the Italian Government Travel Office (ENIT), and brochures from travel agents help one decide where to go, but with so much to choose from, decisions can be difficult.

We are often asked, "If you were to return to Europe to spend some time, a few weeks or so, in a vacation rental, in what country or area would it be?" Of course we have many favorite places and countries, but if hard pressed for a reply, Italy would be very near the top of the list, and the hilly region of Tuscany and Umbria would be our first choice within the country, followed by the lakes of Lombardy and western Veneto.

Twenty regions, or states, make up the country, each with its capital city, and each somehow different from the others in terms of topography, climate, history, architecture, flora, cities and towns, and atmosphere. For example, on one visit we came into Italy from the northeast, driving in from southcentral Austria to Cortina d'Ampezzo, then through the Dolomites westward to Trento. High in this seemingly empty land of craggy mountains and precariously placed villages, we were astonished to see at an intersection of narrow roads a sign that read VENEZIA—165 KM, indicating that we were only 100 miles from Venice, a world so different from where we were that it was hard to believe that we could be sipping aperitifs on the Piazza San Marco within a couple of hours. This is a good example of the contrasts that Italy presents, manifested in a countryside of hills, mountains, fields, lakes, desert, and seashore. There is also the distinctive world of pre-Roman and Roman ruins, ancient living cities, and stone farmhouses that were built before Columbus came to North America.

The configuration of Italy makes it difficult to see everything in a relatively short time. There is a place in the Tosco-Emiliano mountains northeast of Florence where, it is said, on a clear day you can see the breadth of the country, from the Adriatic Sea on the east to the Mediterranean on the west—a distance scarcely over 100 miles. But from Reggio di Calabria at the toe of the boot, it is 440 miles north to Rome and another 450 miles to Como, near the border with Switzerland. From Reggio to Venice it is 750 miles and another 100 miles to Cortina. With distances such as these, a fundamental question must be answered by anyone planning to visit: Is it better to see a little bit of many things or to select one or two locations from which to explore some, but not all, of this unique country?

Best Times of Year to Visit

When to visit largely depends upon what areas of Italy you plan to stay in, but as we continually suggest, try to avoid the peak months of July and August and the peak prices and crowds that accompany them. Accommodations, restaurants, trains, and highways are also crowded in the weeks immediately before and after Easter. Otherwise, Italy is a land of benign climate, moderated by the Mediterranean and the Adriatic seas, which almost surround it, and by the high Alps along the northern border, which shield it from the winter cold of the rest of Continental Europe. Traditional vacation and holiday seasons during which Europeans travel, rather than the climatic season, determine when Italy is likely to be very crowded.

Midwinter in Venice, Padua, Verona, Bolzano, Milan, Torino, and other northern cities (as well as the northern lakes) can be cold and gray, so if you plan to visit from November through February, stay south of Rome. The obvious exceptions are ski vacations in the Piemonte, Valle d'Aosta, or Trentino-Alto Adige regions, where the winter peak is December, the shoulder months are November and March, and low season is January and February. The summer season is like other parts of Italy, peaking in July and August.

Considering rental prices, availability, crowds, and climate, the optimum months (except for skiing) for visiting northern Italy (Piedmont, Lombardy, Trentino, Venetia, and Friuli-Venezia Giulia) are June, September, and early October. Central Italy (the hill country of the Tuscany, Umbria, Emilia-Romagna, Marche, Lazio, and Abruzzi regions) beckon most strongly in May, June, September, and October. The season of mild weather can be extended as early as the first of April in the coastal region of Liguria and along the Mediterranean coasts of Tuscany and Lazio. In the southern third (the Amalfi Coast, coastal towns from Naples to Reggio Calabria, Sicily, and Sardinia's west coast) December daytime temperatures are typically in the seventies and in the sixties in January. Late summer temperatures approaching one hundred degrees Fahrenheit are not uncommon, especially inland. In this area, the best times to visit are April through June and September through October. It is usually delightful as early as mid-March and well into November.

General Information About Rentals

As the long list of rental companies at the end of this chapter demonstrates, Italy is a very popular country to visit, especially by travelers who have discovered that the best way to stay is by renting a villa, farmhouse, or apartment, rather than taking a hotel room. With such variables as size, quality, amenities, season, and location affecting price, it is difficult to infer what the rental companies charge for their services. It is, however, a very competitive business, and prices are determined in the marketplace. Most companies included in this chapter are Italian brokerage companies that represent owners directly; they are recognizable by their Italian addresses. These companies publish catalogs, communicate with would-be renters (and foreign rental and travel agencies), make the booking arrangements, and collect client rent deposits and rents. Also included are selected North American agencies that represent an Italian company or apartment block (usually exclusively); these charge no additional commission, so the rent price is the same. They are often called on by travel agencies and other rental agencies to find accommodations for their clients (for which the agency usually adds a commission).

Although there are confusing aspects to the procedure of renting from Italian companies (such as typically paying large damage deposits in lire upon arrival) most of the Italian companies are fair in their pricing. Some are prestigious organizations associated with Italy's aristocracy. The owners of the Best in Italy, which offers precisely what its name says, are a count and countess.

Minimum rental periods are one week and sometimes two during July and August. Some city apartments will rent for a three-day minimum during low season. Rental periods are from Saturday to Saturday.

Information on how to get to the property, where to get the key, what deposit is needed, and other details are well laid out by the agent at the time of booking.

Basically, there are four types of vacation rental properties in Italy: rural farmhouses, villas, and apartments; deluxe villas or summer homes; villas or apartments in developments (mainly in beach resorts); and city apartments.

Fattorie: The first type, the farmhouses are the most popular with foreign visitors. They dot the countryside, especially the hill country of Tuscany and Umbria, and are often surrounded by vineyards—many are in the Chianti region, producing some of the best wines of Italy. Called *fattorie* in Italian, the farms of the past few centuries have generally been large, usually family-run enterprises, and the houses were built to accommodate many people and much activity—and they were built to last. The typical Tuscan, Umbrian, or Emilia-Romagnan farmhouse is a large, square, stone building between a hundred and four hundred years old. A small one might have eight rooms and an area of 3,000 square feet, and a large one, a dozen or more rooms and an area of 10,000 square feet. Then there are the main houses of the larger estates that assume palatial proportions and, of course, there are palaces and castles.

In order to stem the abandonment of these great rural buildings and help maintain the life and age-old culture of the hill country, the government has encouraged and often assisted financially in the restoration and renovation of scores of *fattorie.* Private owners, too, have expended large sums turning their great old properties into comfortable, often elegant, rental accommodations. Some are apartments in the main building, some are individual stone houses, and some are clusters of apartments in renovated outbuildings. We are always impressed with the style of the properties and the way they have been modernized without destroying their essential character. Some of the larger companies, such as Cuendet, have helped with renovations.

By far the greatest number of these properties are in rural Tuscany, followed by Umbria. They range from simple to elegant; many are apartments and many are independent villas set on estate grounds with a swimming pool, tennis courts, and other amenities. In other words, don't let the term "farm" deceive you.

One final point is that hotels in the hill towns, especially the smaller ones, are rare. If you want to spend a week or more in this unusual and tranquil part of the world and be within easy traveling distance of such cities as Florence, Siena, Lucca, Pisa, Perugia, and Arezzo, then renting on a *fattoria* is by far the best and most economical way of doing it.

Deluxe Villas or Summer Houses: *Villa* is the Italian word for "house," and it can be small or large. It is possible to rent an apartment in a villa as well as rent an entire villa. Make sure that you and the company with which you are working are talking about the same thing, especially when dealing directly with a company in Italy. If you are not working with a catalog, or if the description of a property being proposed is not clear, don't leave things to chance. If you want a private, individual house, make it clear.

Although many deluxe villas are the main buildings on farms (and would fall into the above-listed category), the majority are the vacation homes of well-to-do Italians or foreigners. They are usually located in desirable areas, such as along parts of the Ligurian Riviera, the Amalfi Coast, Capri, Sardinia's Costa Smeralda, the lakes of Lombardy, and Lake Trasimeno (in Umbria). They tend to be upscale in quality, location, and price. Some are richly elegant, set in beautiful grounds, complete with pool, tennis courts, and resident staff.

Purpose-Built Villas and Apartments in Developments: Along sections of both the Adriatic and Mediterranean coasts are beach resorts popular with Italians and foreigners alike. The rentals in these areas have been built for vacationers and in the off-seasons are usually closed. Some are depressing in their sameness—row after row of motel-like stuccoed apartments—and some are attractive clusters of small individual villas, often with terraces and lawns and gardens surrounding a pool. Another style is the modern low-rise, basically an apartment hotel that can be found along the Mediterranean coast from Naples to southern Spain. These developments tend to reflect "tourist" Italy rather than traditional Italy.

City Apartments: There are comparatively few city apartments available. For anyone who plans to stay for a week or more in Rome, Florence, Naples, Venice, Perugia, Siena, Milan, or other major city in Italy, however, an apartment is certainly worth seeking out. Some are apartment buildings that specialize in short-term rentals (such as those represented by Keith Prowse & Company, listed at the end of this chapter), but most are privately owned and are being rented and managed by one or another of the Italian rental companies.

Two advantages to a city apartment over a hotel are space and price. Except in the most deluxe hotels in Italy, the rooms are rarely very large, and the prices are high; even a simple pensione can cost $100 per night. In contrast, even a studio apartment has more room and a one bedroom seems spacious, indeed. Unlike some rural rentals, linens and towels are provided in city apartments, and electricity is usually included in the rent. As for location, apartments in the cities are very much like European hotels—scattered about rather than concentrated in the city's center—but certainly available in central areas, if this is your preference. The best sources for Florence are Buckland & Abeti and Cuendet. For Rome, try

International Services for upscale apartments and Interhome for more modest ones.

Many city apartments are in ancient buildings, so don't be alarmed at outside appearances. And before you book, study a map of the city you plan to visit to make sure you will be where you want to be. Also, if you plan to have a car, it is essential that you determine from the company or agent what the parking situation is for the apartment you are considering. The central cores of many cities are closed to traffic (except buses, taxis, and residents with permits), and in others the parking problem is monstrous.

Prices

Despite the number of agencies, there are far fewer rentals available in Italy than in France or the United Kingdom, two countries with populations of similar sizes. The majority of the privately owned rural properties in those two countries, as well as in Austria, Germany, and Ireland, are cottages, small homes, or bungalows. In Italy most rural houses built during the past few centuries are large. Fewer numbers and larger accommodations as well as a high inflation rate in Italy mean that rentals command relatively high prices. By adding desirability of location to the formula and the tendency of owners to commit considerable effort and funds to the restorations of their properties, it's easy to see why rental prices on the whole are higher in Italy than in other European countries. The trade-off is that the rentals, especially rural ones, are often more attractive than in other countries (except for the estates of Portugal and the manor houses of Britain and Ireland). This does not mean that there are no modest or modestly priced rentals in Italy, only that it is more difficult to find a simple cottage in the Tuscan or Umbrian hills, for example, than in rural France or Britain.

To help put prices in perspective: A double room in a four-star, small hotel on the River Arno in Florence runs about L 320,000 per night in shoulder seasons (higher in July and August), roughly the equivalent of $1,500 per week, Continental breakfast included. For about the same price as the four-star hotel room, one can rent a pleasant apartment for two to four persons with one bedroom, a living/dining room, and kitchenette in the splendid and centrally located Palazzo Ricasoli (available through Cuendet). A less elegant, but nonetheless comfortable and well-located one-bedroom apartment for four in central Florence costs about $1,000 per week from Interhome. A modest one-bedroom, fourth-floor walk up we liked, two blocks from the Porta della Romana in Florence, rents for about $900 a week. This and other good properties in Florence and environs are offered by an excellent small company, Buckland & Abeti, codirected by an Englishwoman, who has lived in Italy since the early 1970s, and her delightful Florentine partner.

A rural rental that we are pleased to recommend serves as a good illustration of how style, location, and extras affect price. The Fattoria degli Usignoli, high in the Tuscan hills and 33 km (20 miles) southwest of Florence, has long been a vineyard and winery. The central 4 acres of the 20-acre vineyard are the estate grounds, with lawns, paths, gardens and cypress trees, statuary, a large swimming pool, and a tennis court, all overlooking the hills and the valley below. It is a working winery as well as a small, informal resort. The main, two-story house is three centuries old. Built of stuccoed stone, it has been beautifully renovated and converted into a dozen apartments, from studios to two bedrooms. Much of a large adjacent building, part of the winery operation from years past, has been artfully restored and converted to modern apartments. All are nicely designed and adequately furnished, complete with small kitchens and modern bathrooms with showers. Prices in the shoulder months (June and September) run about $700 per week for a one-bedroom apartment for two to four persons and $850 for a two bedroom. In peak season (July and August), the rents for these run about $900 and $1,000 respectively; and in April and October, $510 and $600. Linens and towels are included, but there is a charge for heat, and a cleaning charge of about $35, payable on site. A $250 damage deposit is paid to the owner, refundable on departure. This illustration (a Cuendet property) happens to be in the top range for rural apartments; prices for more modest yet comfortable two-bedroom apartments run from $300 off-season to $500 during peak.

For large families or groups of traveling companions, an ideal approach is to rent a single-family house. A large, nicely restored and thoroughly desirable stone house of five or six bedrooms with living room, formal dining room, and access to a pool will cost, depending on its quality, between $2,000 and $2,800 per week in the shoulder months and between $2,500 and $3,500 in July and August. These will easily accommodate up to twelve persons. Typical was one we visited that, although it is a farmhouse, is more like a small feudal castle; there is a cavernous vaulted living room, a large formal dining room, a large, well-equipped kitchen, five bedrooms, a swimming pool, a tennis court that has seen better days, and a sweeping view across the Chianti Region toward Siena. It rents for about $2,000 per week in the peak months and $1,200 per week from October through May.

Other properties run the gamut of prices, from modest farmhouses in relatively untrammeled southern Tuscany and Umbria in the $400- to $600-per-week range to a luxury four-bedroom home on 22 acres overlooking Lake Garda at $25,000 per month. Estate villas on the Amalfi Coast south of Naples (an expensive area) cost around $6,000 per week.

Although there are rarely changes in published rental prices due to weekly or monthly fluctuations in the currency exchange rate, if there is a long period of change in one direction or another, a blanket adjustment may be made. For example, in early 1993 at least two major companies cut their prices across the board by 25 percent and 34 percent respectively, mirroring the weakening of the lira relative to U.S. and Canadian dollars.

The substantial damage deposits required must be paid on arrival, often in lire. Figure on roughly 20 percent of the weekly rent. Determine before arrival whether it can be paid for with a credit card. Otherwise, go to a bank and buy lire. Many Italian rentals are furnished with antiquities or at least handsome pieces. We understand that when renting began in earnest a few decades ago, many renters took liberties with the owners' property, either through theft or carelessness. Hence, the deposits. If they seem a bit daunting, remember that the British have been renting Italian villas for many years, and handle the deposits with equanimity. North Americans can do the same.

Making Choices

Too many Americans who visit Italy independently act as though they are on a tour, setting up an overly demanding itinerary that allows them only a few days in each of numerous cities and regions. Those who know something of Italy or are more travel wise move only once or twice, concentrating on either the northern or the southern half of the country, but seldom both if they have two weeks or less to stay in Italy. A satisfying visit to Italy requires some hard decisions about where to locate.

The optimum arrangement for a visit to Italy would be a trip planned for spring or fall with enough time to settle in both the north and south. If you had three weeks, you might spend two in Tuscany or Umbria and one on the Amalfi Coast or in Rome. Limited to one week, you might select a place in the hill country of central Tuscany in the region of Florence, Chianti, or Siena. On a two-week vacation, one week could be spent in Veneto and one in central Tuscany. For anyone who prefers to be a little farther off the beaten trails, choose southeastern Tuscany or eastern Umbria.

Once hard to find from this side of the Atlantic, Venetian apartments and villas and villa apartments in the surrounding countryside (and even a few near the beautiful Lago di Garda, Italy's largest lake) are available from a new association, Laverda and Cuendet (see Cuendet listing at the end of this chapter). The other northern area of choice is the lake country of northern Lombardy (*Lago di Como* and *Lago Maggiore*) and the mountains of Piemonte. Because the northern Lombardy lakes region is shared with Switzerland, it is worth looking at rentals on the Swiss side of the border. (Try Interhome and IMO.)

The islands of the Tyrrhenian Sea off the west coast of Italy, which include Sicily, Sardinia, and the Aeolian and Lipari Island groups, are another possibility. These are discussed below in the section on Southern Italy but it bears noting here that we view the islands as somewhat culturally apart from mainland Italy. Sardinians see themselves as Sardinians first, Italians second; the same goes for Sicilians, it seems. We have never asked Panareans, Ponzans, or Lampedusans how they feel. If you are interested in a true getaway, seeking privacy and more time spent in your immediate surroundings (the beach, the sea, grocery shopping at the local village) than in visits to cathedrals, galleries, Roman ruins, and museums, then a stay on one of the islands is fine. In that context, a villa stay in Capri, Stromboli, Ponza, Ischia, and the Costa Smeralda of Sardinia also require a generous budget. Try International Services for the upscale island properties and Cuendet & Cie and Interhome for more modest rentals in Sicily and Sardinia. For a first visit to Italy, we suggest picking a mainland location and making day trips to various islands. All are served by boat, ferry, or hydrofoil. If three weeks are available, however, one spent on one of the islands would likely prove very worthwhile. Before deciding, we recommend that you study the excellent and detailed descriptions in any of the regional Cadogan guides to Italy by Dana Facaros and Michael Pauls.

Transportation: To, From, and Around

Rome and Milan are the gateway cities for transatlantic flights, so if you are planning to stay in south or central Italy you can either book a flight to Naples from Rome, or to Florence from either Milan or Rome. If Venice is your destination, your connecting flight will probably leave from Milan. Other flights to Florence and Venice can be made via Frankfurt, Paris, or other international airports in Europe. An important consideration, however, is your chosen means of transportation once you arrive, especially if you want to settle in a rural area but also want to explore a major part of the surrounding country via day trips and a few overnighters.

Although it is very good, Italy's railroad system is susceptible to labor stoppages ranging from one-day demonstrations to weeks long strikes. The regional and local bus systems seem to be less prone to disruption, and one can usually get around well using a combination of bus and rail. Even the remote and tiny hill villages are served by bus, but you may spend much precious time gathering information on local schedules and fitting your time into those schedules.

Although a car is convenient when your rental home is in a small town or a rural area, it is useless in the cities. Driving in most of the main large cities of interest can be harrowing. The main problems, however, are access to the city centers and parking: The cores of many larger cities such as Florence, Rome, and Bologna are closed to all except taxis, buses, and commercial vehicles. It is simply a fact of life; these ancient cities were not made for cars. One learns to live with the frustrations of sealed-off city centers and traffic congestion. For the visitor, it means combining modes of transportation.

If you are staying in a rural place and have a car, try to locate the railroad station in a village within ten or twenty kilometers of the city you plan to visit, park the car, and buy round-trip tickets (usually for less than the price of city parking). Some stations on spur lines are not in villages; they're small stops in the countryside; follow the distinctive electric power lines and watch for signs that say FDS or FERROVIE DELLO STATO (state railroad).

As we have stressed before, it is wise to arrange for a car before departing the United States or Canada—it will be much more expensive to arrange for a rental in Italy. If your stay is going to be three weeks or longer, consider paying a surcharge for delivery to Italy of one of the French automakers' cars or a purchase/buyback plan (see chapter 4).

Where to Stay: The Regions

Northern Italy (Piemonte, Liguria, Valle d'Aosta, Lombardia, Trentine-Alto Adige, Veneto, Friuli-Venezia Giulia, and Emilia-Romagna)

Rather than looking at northern Italy in terms of its eight individual administrative regions, we have divided this northern third of the country into five areas, each of which shares general physical and climatic characteristics or encompass a single destination of interest that lies in several of these regions. An example is Lago di Garda, a large, spectacular lake with shores in three of the regions. Liguria and Veneto are administrative regions as well as being two selected areas, the former because it is the delightful northwest coast and the latter because it contains Venice and is an area containing many outstanding rentals.

Liguria

For proximity to the sea, consider the Riviera di Levante, the eastern stretch of the Ligurian coast from just east of Genoa to Portovenere, which includes the justifiably well-known peninsula of Portofino. To the west of Genoa, the stretch known as the Riviera di Ponente is more crowded than the Levante and has become a populous strip of crowded roads and streets connecting high-rises that battle for a view of the sea. The prices now compete with those of the French Côte d'Azur, connecting from the west. The eastern Riviera, however, is less crowded, and the towns are more distinctive, making it a delightful area in which to spend a week or so, especially in the shoulder and low seasons.

The best selection of rentals on the Ligurian coast are from International Services, which has a few upscale villas, and from Interhome, which has a collection of more modest apartments in towns of the coastal region.

Advance Booking Time
For July and August: six months
May, June and September: three–four months
Rest of the Year: zero–one month

Valley of the River Po

Although the cities of this central area—Turin, Alessandria, Milan, Piacenza, Cremona, Parma, and Bologna—are all worth a visit, they are within reach of more attractive regions either to the north or south of the hills and flatlands of this area. Combined with endless days of fog in winter and into early spring, this probably explains why there are relatively few rentals available in this area. Nevertheless, a home base in Milan in late spring or fall is worth consideration; not only is it a city full of ancient splendors, it is central for exploring the region. (See Keith Prowse & Company for the Contessa Iolanda and Quark Hotel apartments in Milan.)

North of the Po Valley

The regions of Valle d'Aosta, northern Piemonte, and Lombardia occupy the northwest of Italy, which is mountain country, with Valle d'Aosta encompassing the southern slopes of Mont Blanc and the northern Piemonte sharing the Lepotine Alps and the lake country with Switzerland. This is perhaps the most spectacularly beautiful part of Italy, a magnet for skiers in winter and for hikers, walkers, cyclists, and lake sailors in the summer. The lake country of Maggiore, Como, and Lugano is an idyllic area of water, mountains, and shorelines dotted with beautiful small villages and covered with almost subtropical vegetation: oleanders, magnolias, palm trees, citrus, tulip trees, cedars, and nuts. It is a tourist-oriented area, with restaurants, hotels, villas, and lake steamers. The nature of the region plus its accessibility to other nearby European countries make it a busy place to visit. Visits to the cities of Milan, Alessandra, and Turin to the south can easily be made from a home base in the area, and Interlaken and St. Moritz in Switzerland are also accessible. Mainline railroads run through Stresa and Arona on Lake Maggiore and connect Como and Lugano on the route between Milan and Zurich.

May, June, and September are the best months to visit, followed by October. For skiing in Valle d'Aosta, January to mid-February is the best period to go; December is the peak month for crowds and prices. Try International Services and Interhome for villas and apartments in the lake region and Interhome for ski chalets and apartments in Piemonte. Because Switzerland shares the shores of major lakes such as Maggiore and Lugano, for a stay in the lake country consider rental properties on the Swiss side in the Italian-speaking canton of Ticino (see Switzerland chapter).

Advance Booking Time:

For July and August: six months
May, June, and September: two–three months
Rest of the Year: one–two months
Ski Resorts
December, February, March: six months
November and January: two–three months

The Northeastern Area

This is a large and remarkably varied area, incorporating eastern Lombardy, Veneto, Trentino-Alto Adige, and Friuli-Venezia Giulia. The first three regions share Lago di Garda, the largest lake in Italy at 32 miles long and 11 miles wide. Mountains rise from the northwestern shore, and looking up the lake from the more densely populated south shore is almost like looking out to sea. Along the eastern shore are numerous villages and resorts, some very pleasant and some very touristy. The little town of Desenzano, one of the largest on the shoreline, is a treat to visit, and the food in some of its traditional restaurants is excellent. Our favorite part of this lovely lake area, however, is the less tourist impacted west coast, from the town of Salo through Gardone and on north to Riva, where cliffs rise sheer almost a thousand feet, topped by pasture land and small villages. The climate is mild, but in the midwinter months the fogs of the valley can affect the southern end (to the benefit of the famous vineyards of Bardolino). The main city in this region is Verona, and it is easy from anywhere in the area to visit Parma, Padua, Bologna, and Venice. The mainline railroad between Venice, Verona, and Milan runs through the lakeside towns of Pescheria and Desenzano, and there is town-to-town bus service. A car is useful but not essential.

Veneto

Environs and Accommodations

This is the dominant region of the northeast, distinctive in part because of its remarkable capital, the city of Venice (*Venezia*). The region is also noteworthy because of the unusual, large country estates in which apartments have recently become available to foreign visitors through the association of a rental group called Laverda with the large, Tuscany-based Cuendet & Cie. The most elegant and unusual properties in Veneto are available through The Best in Italy. A week would be ideal here, with most of that time concentrated on Venice. Excursions are possible along the north coast to Trieste or into the Dolomite Mountains if you have a car. In Venice proper, however, a car is of no use, and must be left in the parking garage on the Piazzale Roma.

As for the best time to visit Venice, romantics would say anytime. But to better enjoy the city itself, from mid-April through mid-June and then September and October are the best months to visit. From mid-June through August the weather is fine, but Venice is packed with tourists, and the midwinter months can be chilly, rainy, and foggy.

A drive from the Lago di Garda area northeast into the region of Trentino-Alto Adige is like going into another world, as the road that turns off the autostrada north of Trento to Cortina d'Ampezzo goes through the heart of the famous Dolomites, mountains of astonishing ruggedness and a mecca for skiers as well as anyone who likes to hike and climb (or take gondolas to the heights). Contact Interhome for information on rentals in the Alto Adige.

Prices

Although rental prices are high in much of Veneto, especially Venice and the area nearby, compared to Venice hotel rooms they are reasonable. There is little more exciting than a stay in the city, but day trips from the countryside offer a good compromise. Typically between $200 and $250 per night is not out of line for a room in a two- or three-star hotel, whereas a first-class one-bedroom apartment for four from Cuendet & Cie, for example, runs about $1,400 per week, and a two-star studio averages less than $1,000. An apartment in a villa outside the city proper will rent for the same or a little less, but generally will be larger and more elegant. For luxury in Venice, including the magnificent Palazzo Albrizzi, contact The Best in Italy. It is easy to get into the city by bus or train from the surrounding area. If you are on a limited budget, Interhome properties tend to be more modest in both style and price.

The best agencies for Venice and the Veneto region, including Lago di Garda, are Cuendet & Cie, followed by International Services and Interhome. Although they have fewer rentals, Cuendet has American agents who charge no added commission, and they are the only company listed here with an office in the region.

Rail service runs from Venice and Padua as far as Calalzo, 20 miles south of Cortina, and connects with a bus. But to get into the Dolomites, a car is essential.

Advance Time for Booking

For June, July, and August: six months
May and September: four months
Rest of the Year: zero–one month

Central Italy: Toscana, Umbria, Marche, Lazio, and Abruzzi

This is the area most popular with North Americans (and other foreigners) who want to experience what is correctly perceived to be the heart of Italy. It ranges from the tree- and vineyard-covered hills of *Toscana* (Tuscany) and Umbria to the cities of Rome, Florence, Siena, Perugia, and Pisa and the ancient and enchanting hill towns such as Arezzo, San Gimignano, Cortona, Todi, Orvieto, Spoleto, and Assisi. This is a land whose shores are washed by two seas, and whose climate is made mild and vegetation made rich by the Tyrrhenian Sea on the west and the Adriatic on the east. Many weeks can be profitably and happily spent here. One can vary one's time between the hills, the mountains, the cities, and the seas, yet depart with the feeling that there remains so much more to experience that a return is essential.

Tuscany and Umbria
Environs and Accommodations
The complexity and wealth of things to see and do suggest that central Italy is divisible into two areas: Rome and the neighboring region of Lazio and Abruzzi are one and Florence and Siena and the regions of Tuscany and Umbria are another. Fortunately, the distances within central Italy are not great—less than 180 miles between Florence and Rome, with Perugia about halfway, and Siena less than an hour south of Florence.

Although there are hundreds of rentals in central Italy, the preponderance are in Tuscany, mostly in the hill country but also in the cities. If you plan to stay in Florence, we again suggest that you not try to deal with a car in the city, but if you must have one, tell the vacation rental company and ask about parking, either near the apartment or in one of the city parking garages. An alternative is to locate in Fiesole, a pretty hilltop village on the outskirts of the city, which has bus service to Florence.

As can be seen from the list of companies, almost all have rentals in Tuscany (country and cities), and most have them in Umbria as well. They all offer a variety of locations, sizes, standards, and prices that reflect these criteria. Choosing is simply a matter of studying maps and guidebooks to decide on a general locale and then poring over catalogs and price lists. It is a treat to look at Tuscan architecture through photos of villas, castles, and *fattorie* (farm estates) from the comprehensive list of properties in the catalogs of Cuendet, Buckland & Abeti, and the remarkable estates offered by The Best in Italy. The competition among owners and companies in this region is tough, so you can expect to get good accommodations.

Rome and Latium
Fewer companies offer rentals in Rome and the surrounding region of Latium, but given hotel and restaurant prices there, it is difficult to rent an apartment that is not lower in price and larger in size than a hotel of comparable standards. Rome is a complex city, full of ancient artifacts as well as modern, elegant stores, parks and restaurants, shopping streets and grand boulevards, and cities within cities; many rich weeks can be spent there. If, however, your

planned stay in Italy is limited to two or three weeks, then a week in Rome and the remainder in another area should be considered.

As for a location within Rome, the changing availability of private rentals makes a recommendation of little use, but there are a few that seem constant, available through Keith Prowse and Barclay International Group. Another approach is to contact the director of Rome-based International Services. Be forewarned that the rents are quite high; the apartments are usually privately owned and upscale; advice given by the director, or someone on the English-speaking staff is usually reliable—they specialize in finding Italian rentals that meet North American standards. Because many of these properties are elaborately furnished and equipped, prepare for a damage deposit of up to several hundred dollars. The company also has a U.S. contact who knows many of the properties. Interhome also has a few more modestly priced apartments, and Keith Prowse & Company is the contact for the apartments Palazzo Al Velabro, which run from $900 per week for a studio to $1,100 for a one bedroom. Buckland & Abeti are also worth a try.

A practical approach to visiting Rome is to rent an apartment in the beautiful lake country of Lazio, just to the north of the city, and then commute. Contact one of the two Cuendet & Cie agents in the United States.

Location and Transportation

There is no part of the central region of Italy that cannot be visited easily from any other part. Two *autostrade* run north and south, one along the spine of the country and one along the Adriatic coast. A third runs between Florence and the Mediterranean coast north of Livorno. The tolls on these *autostrade* are high, cumulatively about $15 between Florence and Rome, for example. The primary highways (without tolls) are good and often divided, such as those between Florence and Siena and along much of the west and east coasts. Secondary roads can be slow, winding through the hill country (all the better to see it), usually becoming the main street of each town they pass through.

Mainline railroads run roughly parallel to the *autostrade,* along the east and west coasts and along the spine. The trains are good, the prices are reasonable, and the service is dependable, except for occasional work stoppages. There are twenty departures daily from Rome to Florence, and vice versa and nine daily between Florence and Siena (plus twelve by bus). A car is invaluable, however, for exploring the hills and hill towns, which are the essence of Italy.

Unless you have considerable time, you may want to spend it all in central Italy, but wanderers can find numerous sailings weekly between Livorno and ports on Sardinia and the French island of Corsica; out of Civitavecchia, the port for Rome, there are four sailings daily on the eight-hour voyage to Sardinia. Tickets and information on the Civitavecchia-Sardinia route are available at main railroad stations. The ships are run by the government railroad, FDS. For other sailings, see an Italian travel agency or contact Tirrenia Line. (Also, see Sardinia, below.)

Advance Time for Booking

For June, July and August: six months
May and September: four months
Rest of the Year: one month
Rest of the Year (Rome): two months

Southern Italy: Molise, Campania, Apulia, Basilicata, Calabria, the islands of Sicily and Sardinia, and the Aeolian Islands

The southern third of Italy has a different quality from the rest of the country. Perhaps it is the climate, the soil, the foods, and the evidences of ancient Greece and the Orient as well as of Rome; maybe it is the winds of Africa across the Ionian Sea, the weeks on end of sunshine, hot summers in the interior, balmy winters, or the sense that Sicilians and Sardinians are different from mainland Italians. Whatever it is, a stay in the south is wonderfully different.

The Regions: Environs and Accommodations

There are few rentals in the southern region relative to the central and northern regions, but enough to make a visit of a week or more possible. The locations seem to be selected to capitalize on the best that the south has to offer.

The region is best explored by car, and most of it but not all can be reached by taking day trips or an overnighter from a home base anywhere in the area. If, however, you want to get very far into Sicily, it is best to locate a rental there for a week rather than try to do it from the area of Naples. Although the *autostrada* runs south from Naples to Reggio di Calabria at the tip and along much of the north and east coasts of Sicily, it is 750 kilometers (460 mi.), including a ferry trip, between Naples and Palermo.

Bay of Naples and Amalfi Coast. Although scattered rentals are available throughout much of the region, one of the most popular areas to visit and stay in is the *Costa Amalfinata,* the Amalfi Coast, which comprises the southern shore of the peninsula between Sorrento and Salerno, south of Naples. Here the villas and apartments in villas tend toward the deluxe and are priced accordingly, but it is arguably the most ruggedly beautiful coast in Italy. Its location close to Naples, Pompeii, Herculaneum, and Vesuvius and its easy access to the nearby isles of Capri and Ischia add to its virtues, which include sunshine, hot summers moderated by the sea breezes, and warm winters. The vegetation is both piney and subtropical, and the main coastal towns of Amalfi and Positano are not only beautiful examples of white-washed, southern Mediterranean architecture, but are small, manageable, and charming. Most of the rentals in Amalfi town·are individual villas, and in Positano both villas and apartments in villas are available. The best times to spend a week or two on this delightful coast are from mid-March to mid-June and from mid-September into early November. For swimmers, the sea temperatures are warmer in the fall months. This is an area where a substantial budget is necessary.

As for Naples itself, it is a strangely dramatic city, and it is sometimes hard to distinguish the rubble of antiquity from yesterday's debris. The traffic is mad, and traffic lights are often ignored. No unsuspecting visitor should actually try to cross a street just because the light has turned green. Yet the tumult of the city, the intensity of its citizens, the fine restaurants, its treasures, the setting, and the climate conspire to draw outsiders to it. A week in Naples is plenty, or as an excellent alternative, find a rental in the vicinity and take a train or bus (not a car) into the city for daily visits.

The drawback to the Gulf of Naples area, from the city itself south to Salerno and the islands, is the tourist crowds from mid-June through August, when the Italians and northern Europeans join with North Americans and Asians in the streets of Pompei and on the boats to Capri. You can avoid the crowds by renting a deluxe villa with grounds, or by visiting in the low or shoulder seasons.

The companies with the best selection of properties in the Amalfi Coast–Naples area are Cuendet & Cie, Coltur Italia Welcome (Sorrento), International Services, and Interhome. The rentals on Capri fall into the general luxury category. Like the Amalfi Coast, the setting is idyllic, and the large properties assure privacy from the tourist crowds making day trips from the mainland. If you are especially interested in Capri, contact International Services in Rome or New York.

Transportation In The Naples Area

In addition to the mainline railroads that connect Naples with Rome to the north, Reggio di Calabria to the south, and Bari and the Adriatic coast to the east, a local train called the Circumvesuviana leaves Naples every thirty to forty minutes for Pompei and Sorrento and points between and returns from Sorrento with the same frequency. It does not cross over the peninsula to the Amalfi coast, but there are public buses and taxis available for the short trip. If you have a car, and having one is very convenient in this region, on trips into Naples from the Amalfi area we suggest that you drive to Sorrento or Vico Equense, leave the car, and take the train.

Apulia (*Puglia*) and Basilicata. Except in the cities and larger towns, this southern part of the region seems very far away from the rest. Much of it is rugged and wild, and much of it is a serene joining of pine- and chestnut-covered hills with olive trees and tended farms. As for the Adriatic coast, aside from fine beaches we do not find much to recommend it, especially between Bari and Brindisi. Neither of these cities is of particular interest for travelers, especially with so many splendid alternatives in Italy. They are principally ports, and Bari is especially crowded in summer with North American and European tourists boarding or disembarking from the many passenger ships that sail daily between Italy and Corfu and mainland Greece. Otranto, near the end of the "heel" of Italy's famed boot shape, makes a good central base for exploring the unusual hill villages of Apulia and enjoying the good beaches north toward Brindisi. For something entirely different, rent a *trullo,* a stone house with a cone-shaped roof, unique to Apulia. Cuendet and Interhome offer a few of these.

Calabria. Calabria is the toe of Italy, separating the Ionian Sea from the Tyrrhenian Sea, which connect where the mainland and Sicily almost meet, across the Straits of Messina. In this southern reach of Italy, and especially on Sicily across the straits, it is the influence of ancient Greece, *Magna Graecia,* whose importance is most strongly felt, especially in the ruins from Eraclea to Selinunte.

This is a region with a benign climate in which orange and lemon orchards compete with vineyards and olive groves, and flowers and citrus bergamot are grown for the perfumes of Italy and France. The main city of Calabria, Reggio, is a fairly modern town, commanding from its palm-lined promenade a vista across the straits to the city of Messina, on Sicily. A home base in the hills or in a villa along the Riviera Calabrese between Reggio and Gioia Tauro makes an excellent center from which to explore all of southern Italy and even Sicily. Two weeks can easily be devoted to the enterprise, especially if a journey to western Sicily is included. Rentals in Calabria are relatively scarce, but a few are offered by Cuendet & Cie, Interhome, and International Services.

Transportation in the Mainland South

The railroad and a primary highway circle the "toe" of Italy, connecting Reggio di Calabria and the Adriatic coast. To get into the hill country of Calabria and the unique villages of southern Apulia, a car is helpful but not essential. Travel westward from Reggio di Calabria to Sicily is across the straits by boat or ferry to the port of Messina, from which *autostradas* and railroads go in two directions to circle Sicily.

Sicily (*Sicilia*). To rent in Palermo, Catania, Messina, Marsala, or Trapani is not, in our view, the way to visit Sicily. The cities are crowded, easy to get lost in, and

little English is spoken outside of tourist areas. Although there are treasures to
see in them, they are best visited on day trips from a home base elsewhere on
the island. These are rental villas and apartments scattered near such places as
Cefalu, Ragusa, and Sambucca di Sicilia. The idea is not necessarily to find the
best place in Sicily to stay (because that is debatable), but to find a comfortable,
modestly priced villa from which to explore all of Sicily. Contact Cuendet & Cie,
followed by Interhome.

Transportation

The railroad follows the north coast between the port of Messina at the eastern tip to Trapani on the west coast and between Messina and Syracuse along
the east coast. It also cuts diagonally across the island between Catania and
Palermo, with a spur to Agrigento on the south coast. Bus service is fair between
Trapani and Syracuse, some 365 kilometers (225 mi.), but the length of the
southwest coast has no rail service. In the low season there is limited bus service
from Trapani to Erice, and none to the ruins at Selinunte on the extreme southwest coast.

Much of Sicily is off the main paths, and a car will enhance your visit.
Arrange for it before your departure, to be picked up in any of the Sicilian main
cities or in a mainland city. You can then transport it on the short-run ferry from
Reggio di Calabria. In the past we have brought ours to Sicily on a long-run
ferry, once from Genoa into Palermo (twenty-three hours) and once from
Cagliari, on the south end of Sardinia, to Trapani (ten hours). The sea travel is
pleasant, and an entire itinerary can be built around it. Ships also connect
Trapani and Palermo with Naples, and if you want a glimpse of yet another culture, book a cabin for the eight-hour voyage out of Trapani to Tunis (and return,
or sail on to Marseille if you have given up your villa or apartment). Contact any
Tirrenia Line office in the port cities or else a travel agency. (In the United
States, call 813–394–3384.)

Sardinia (Sardegna). This large island, almost the size of Sicily, differs greatly
from it as well as from the mainland. Its isolation, 250 kilometers (155 mi.) off
the coast at its closest point, has over the centuries created a society distinct
from the rest of Italy, based largely upon agriculture and sheep raising.
Politically it is an autonomous region, self-governing in matters of its own development, which has been stimulated by the rise of tourism.

It is a physically beautiful place, with a craggy eastern coast and a central valley of green, rolling fields and hills with mountain vistas. The main highway
between Porto Torres in the north and Cagliari runs for 330 kilometers (200
mi.). The cities are not of special interest. If you are looking for an out-of-the-
way, deluxe resort area blessed with sunshine, beaches, shops, and social life, it

can be found concentrated on the northeast coast, the famed Costa Smeralda. There is very little in the way of rentals outside of the Costa Smeralda, but the properties there tend to be luxury-class villas. Most visitors are content to spend their week or two in this splendid isolation, but we recommend at least a train trip to Cagliari just to see the countryside. If you have a car, a drive along the east coast is very dramatic, and on the west coast a visit to Neptune's Grotto, near Alghero, is very worthwhile. The best contacts for booking a villa on Sardinia are Interhome, and International Services. Cuendet has a few.

Getting to Sardinia is not difficult: There are flights from major mainland Italian cities and from Nice and Paris into Cagliari, and from the major Italian cities to Alghero, Sassari, and Olbia. By sea, there are large ferryliners from Genoa, Livorno, Civitavecchia (Rome), Naples, and the four Sardinian ports, and between Cagliari and Trapani, Sicily.

Other Islands. Off the northeastern tip of Sicily, west of the mainland, lie the six Aeolian Islands, among which Stromboli is the best known. They exist as a mix of past and present: Some islands are almost primitive, and some are dotted with luxury villas and the modest homes of permanent residents, many of whom are fishermen. One of the Aeolian Islands, Panarea, is rich with vegetation and has moved quietly into the world of tourism; but it is only for those who want to get away, who want tranquility and privacy, who can deal with the absence of restaurants and hotels, and who can afford rents in the $1,500-per-week range (and much higher). The off-season rents drop substantially.

Ponza, another island, is north of the Aeolian group, almost due west of Naples. Another getaway, it is a more populous and developed island than Panarea, but nevertheless a pleasant and unusual place to stay. Information on rentals on Ponza and in the Aeolians can be obtained from International Services.

Advance Booking Time

For all locations in the south of Italy, except for the Costa Smeralda of Sardinia and the Aeolean Islands, we recommend the following advance times to book:

For June, July, and August: 6 months
May and September: 4 months
Rest of the Year: 1 month

For Sardinia's Costa Smeralda, Stromboli and other islands of the Aeolian Archipelago, as well as the Egadi and Stagnone Islands and Capri, few rentals are available and are in high demand. It's best to make your inquiry a year in advance and take the rental company's advice on when to confirm the booking.

A Special Note on Prices in Southern Italy

There is a marked contrast between the fashionable international spots such as Sardinia's Costa Smeralda or the Amalfi Coast and the simple rural areas of much of Sicily, Italy's "toe," and the Adriatic coast towns. This contrast between luxury and relative simplicity of accommodations is reflected in rental prices. Although comfortable rentals can be found in the $500 to $700 per week range (principally from Cuendet and Interhome), rents of $4,000 to $15,000 per week are not uncommon, with not much in-between. Be prepared for this wide difference, especially on islands such as Panarea and Stromboli.

The Rental Companies of Italy

Of the many companies offering rentals in Italy, the following were selected because they represent a broad and varied spectrum of properties in terms of geography, style, price, and historical character. Together they offer well over 2,000 rentals, from some of the most elegant palaces and villas in Italy to ancient stone farmhouses and rare apartments in Venice, Florence, and Rome. Inflation in the 1980s and early 1990s has raised hotel room prices in Italy to astronomical heights and, along with them, prices of rentals. Beginning in 1992, however, rental costs began to moderate, partly because of the increased number of properties available and partly to beat the hotel competition as renting became more and more popular. They remain the best accommodation bargains in the country.

Barclay International Group   Rome and Few Other Areas
150 East 52nd Street
New York, NY 10022
Tel: (800) 845–6636 or (212) 832–3777   Fax: (212) 753–1139

This company is listed because it represents several apartments in Rome. Their properties are all carefully selected and periodically inspected by someone on the New York staff. The company has been in business for nearly thirty years and represents properties in most major European cities. A color booklet and price list are available (call for the latest prices before booking). Booking is easy and the terms are included in their booklets, one for the Continent and one for England. Barclay offers some very good values and is worth contacting.

The Best in Italy   Throughout Italy
Via Ugo Foscolo, 72
50124 Florence
Tel: 55–223–064   Fax: 55–229–8912

The name of this unusual and relatively small company emphasizes its specialty: *palazzi* (palaces) and elegant villas, among them the most beautiful and unusual in Europe. The eighty or so properties are scattered throughout various regions; many are in Tuscany, Venice, and Veneto and also on the Ligurian coast, the island of Capri, and Rome. The rentals are personally selected by the company, and virtually all the villas come with staff, lovely furnishings, and many with pools. A few rentals have tennis courts and stables. Many of the villas and apartments belong to friends of the company owners, the Count Girolamo Brandolini d'Adda and his American wife, the Countess Simonetta Brandolini d'Adda.

Managed by the Contessa, the company is expanding its interests to offer the finest properties in selected countries throughout the world. It is indeed unusual, and the properties The Best in Italy represents can be rented with absolute confidence.

If the price of these luxury and rather exclusive accommodations seems beyond your budget, they may be ideal for sharing with traveling friends and families (although there are some restrictions regarding small children). All guests are personally greeted, and company staff will assist in securing tickets to the theater, concerts, opera, and other events. We cannot overemphasize that this is a most unusual organization, offering a chance to stay at any of a number of exquisite estate homes.

A catalog in color is available from a family member in the United States. Mail $10 in cash or travelers cheques or send a personal check, payable to Simonetta Brandolini d'Adda, to The Best in Italy, 4409 Dexter Street N.W., Washington, DC 20007. No credit cards are accepted for rental payment. Use a personal check, a bank draft in dollars or traveler's checks for the deposit and full payment.

Best Realty / Best Umbria S.R.L.   Perugia
Via Manzoni, 354
06154 Ponte San Giovanni (Perugia)
Tel: 75–599–0952   Fax: 75–599–0740

Principally a real estate agency, this relatively small company also lists moderate to upscale rental properties, mostly in the Perugia area and other parts of Umbria. No catalog is published. The booking procedure is to contact the company with your requirements. They then find several choices and propose them via letter or fax. Make your selection and notify them; they will confirm, and upon payment, will send all directions. The process should begin six months in advance for summer, two months for off-seasons. Payment is by bank draft in lire. The best prices and value can be assured. This type of agency is best when planning stays of a month or more.

The Big   Milan
Via De Cristoforis 6/8
Milan
U.S. agent: Keith Prowse & Co. (USA), Ltd., listed in this section.

An unusual name, but this is one of the few short-term rental apartments in Milan. We did not stay there, but rely on the reputation of the U.S. agent.

Buckland & Abeti Associates   Florence, Tuscany hills and coast
Via della Stuffa, 3
50123 Florence
Tel: 55–284–828   Fax: 55–289–448

Formerly called Soggiorno Italia, this relatively small company is well deserving of its good reputation. Its villas, stone houses on working farms (*fattorie*), and apartments in rural and coastal Tuscany are carefully chosen in an area that can easily be reached and monitored by the central office staff in Florence. The selection of apartments in Florence city, although not large, is the best we know of and certainly the most fairly priced. They also work with a smaller company called Il Ghibellino (and the delightful Mrs. Caloni), which restores apartments for rental purposes. They have a few apartments in Rome and Venice.

We have known Leslie, the "Buckland" part of the partnership, for several years. We met Antonella Abeti recently for the first time and think they make a dynamic duo, promising a good future for their company. The staff, too, is helpful with anything from prebooking advice to the best places to eat. With offices in central Florence there is always someone about to help out if needed. English is spoken.

The company makes everything easy. A catalog is available for the asking (there may be a small fee to cover mailing); just make two or three choices and fax or phone the information. Alternatively, tell the reservations office of your requirements and they will propose some properties. Upon selecting, they will confirm availability for your dates. Deposit and full payment can be made by credit card or by mailing a bank draft in lire or a personal check in dollars at the exchange rate prevailing on the day of the booking. This is a popular company, especially well known in Britain, so be sure to book well ahead for summer. Buckland & Abeti has our unqualified recommendation.

Coltur Italia Welcome   Sorrento
Piazza St. Agnello 17
80065 St. Agnello di Sorrento
Naples
Tel: 81–87–82–966   Fax: 81–87–83–483

This is a very small company with a few rare properties in Sorrento—under ten at present. The Sorrentine peninsula combines nature's beauties as rugged coast meets the sea. There are colorful houses and exclusive, almost hidden villas. To avoid peak season prices and crowds, the best time to visit this small, distinctive area is October to mid-November and mid-March through April.

English is spoken at the company, and a brochure will be mailed upon request. It is not, however, an easy company to work with from overseas. The best approach is to send a letter requesting a brochure and price list; enclose $4.00 cash for postage. When you find what appeals to you, contact the company and ask about availability and, if all is well, tell them that you will be airmailing a bank draft. Purchase a draft from the bank in lire, fax a photocopy to the company (which will hold the property until the draft is received), and airmail the draft. Confirmation and instructions will be sent to you by fax or mail.

Contessa Iolanda Apartments   Milan
Via Murat, 21
Milan
U.S. agent: Keith Prowse & Co. (USA), Ltd., listed in this section.

This is another of the rare, short-term rental apartments in the city of Milan; we have not seen it, but again rely on the reputation and selections of the agency.

Cuendet & Cie.   Throughout Italy
53035 Monteriggioni / Siena
Tuscany
U.S. agents: Suzanne T. Pidduck-Rentals in Italy
Grand Luxe Cuendet USA, listed in this section

This is the largest and one of the most efficient rental companies in Italy, with approximately 1,500 rental properties in the central states of Tuscany and Umbria, in the south of Italy, in the lake country north of Rome, in Sicily and Sardinia, and in northeastern Italy (Veneto). Apartments are also available in the towns of Venice, Florence, Lucca, Pisa, Siena, Assisi, Orvieto, and Perugia as well as throughout the countryside. Modest houses and elegant country villas are carefully chosen by this outstanding company. Mr. Cuendet, who is Swiss, manages a remarkable operation and staff in a large, ancient stone house in the vineyard-covered hills near Siena. The contrast between the rural surroundings and the computer system, phone, and fax banks, and the international staff inside the big villa is striking.

Through a recent association with Laverda, a smaller company in Veneto, a new area of rentals is available through the Cuendet operation and its two U.S. agents. Until this association, rentals in Venice and in the towns and countryside of this rich and beautiful region of Italy were hard to find and were usually handled by rental companies based elsewhere in the country, as far away as Rome. Paola Laverda knows the Veneto area, the people, and the properties, speaks a lilting, accented English, and is delightful to work with. She has done a superb job of finding a variety of very good rentals, ranging from the simple to the elegant. We especially like the Lago di Garda area, not so much the overvisited south end, but the rugged west coast from Saló north to Riva, and the northeastern coast.

We stayed at the Residence Florida in the little town of Gardone, near Saló, on the southwest coast. Our small, plainly furnished apartment had a view of the lovely grounds, the pool, and the southern end of the 30-mile-long Lake Garda. The Cipani family, which owns the residence, are not only excellent hosts but a storehouse of information about the region. From there we visited four of Cuendet's Lago di Garda rentals, among them an elegant 1,900-square-foot apartment in the fabulous, restored estate building called Byron in the town of Riva, an eagle's nest villa high above Limone, an elegant villa with pool on the east coast (L'Erta in the catalog), and a modern, very pleasant apartment hotel on the water.

A stay in an apartment in Venice is wonderful. We rented a small but efficient, bright, architecturally designed and perfectly located studio (Columbina 2 in the Cuendet catalog). At about $850 per week, it is priced well below a hotel room of equal standards and half the size.

Cuendet prefers to work through its foreign agents and will not accept direct requests for information or bookings. The price of the rentals is the same, booked directly or through the U.S. agents. These agencies are the source for the large and attractive Cuendet catalogs, which are themselves a wonderful pictorial introduction to historic rural Italian architecture, as well as the details of renting. All the prices (in U.S. dollars), terms, and conditions are included. The procedure is to phone or fax Suzanne Pidduck or Grand Luxe and ask for a catalog; the price is $15 (payable by personal check) and well worth it. Choose three or four favorites, phone or fax again, and wait for a reply from the agent confirming which choice is available for the dates you want. There is a $50 booking fee, again worth it for the good service provided and the quality of virtually all the properties. The directions to the villas, farmhouses, and apartments are clear, but be sure to tell how you are arriving (car, train, or bus). Suzanne Pidduck also provides useful personal advice and suggestions about everything from local customs to buying groceries. Payment to both agencies is by personal check. Although we generally do not single out one particular property from a large number offered, we must note that a stay several years ago at the Fattoria degli Usignoli near Florence was excellent. We are confident that it remains one of the nicest small, moderately priced, farm resorts in Italy, especially convenient to Florence.

Grand Luxe Cuendet USA   Throughout Italy
165 Chestnut Street
Allendale, NJ 07401
Tel: (201) 327–2333   Fax: (201) 825–2664

This is one of the two principal U.S. agents of Cuendet & Cie. (see above listing). This agent serves the eastern United States, but can be contacted from anywhere. The catalogs and prices are the same as Cuendet's, the service is very good, and they know the territory intimately. Call or fax for a catalog, make choices, and contact again.

Interhome (USA), Inc.   Throughout Italy
124 Little Falls Road
Fairfield, NJ 07004
Tel: (201) 882–6864   Fax: (201) 808–1742

The independent U.S. agent for Interhome of Switzerland, the largest rental company in Europe, this is a good source for relatively modest to moderately priced properties in out-of-the-way as well as mainstream places in Italy. If you are interested in a getaway in, say, Schiavonea, Calabria, or on the beautiful Levantine coast, Interhome is where you'll be most apt to find it. The company also has apartments in Venice, Florence, and Rome as well as rural villas and farmhouses.

The catalog property descriptions are not very complete, but there are small photos of the exteriors, and a more complete description is sent when two or three possibilities are selected by a client. Interhome is a very efficient operation: Interhome USA communicates with the mainframe computer in Zurich, which keeps track of more than 20,000 properties. Once you have chosen two or three rentals, you will know within twenty-four hours about availability on your dates.

We are sometimes concerned about the long chain of command between an office in New Jersey and the rental owners in Sardinia or Calabria, but an Interhome operation in each country finds properties and looks after client interests. It's not very personalized, but it works, and the wide range of styles, locations, and prices offered is the trade-off. There is a commission charged. In shoulder and off-seasons, always ask about discounted prices.

The first step is to phone or fax for Interhome's catalog; specify the country because there are several catalogs. The cost is from $3.00 to $5.00. If using the catalog, select and rank three choices and call or fax again with the reference numbers. Instead of requesting a catalog, you can call or fax your requirements, and a number of possibilities that meet your criteria will be proposed. Once the choice is made and a deposit is paid, all directions and instructions will be sent.

Payment is by personal check or credit card. The damage deposit, electricity, and other charges, such as taxes, are paid on site. Cancellation insurance is automatic with this company at a cost of 3 percent of the total rent; this is a fair rate, but if you do not want this insurance, say so at the time of booking.

International Services   Throughout Italy
Via Babuino 79
00187 rome
Tel: 6–3–6000–0018   Fax: 6–3–6600–0037
U.S. (Chicago) Office Tel: (708) 549–9957   Fax: Same

Operated by an American living in Rome, this company offers a variety of services including arrangements for conferences, theater tickets, and tours in addition to its rental business. Their rentals are an eclectic assortment of apartments and villas in most price ranges, though prices lean toward the luxury end. They have no catalog but instead furnish property profile sheets that match the client's requirements. Some sheets do not have photographs, which makes it a little difficult to choose. The position of the company, however, is that their properties are so well chosen that clients need not be concerned. Our experience has been that generally this is correct, but we urge you to get all pertinent information before making a decision.

The best approach is to contact the Rome office by phone or fax with your requirements: location, size, style, amenities, budget, and dates. If you prefer, contact the U.S. office with this information, but be aware that they are not personally familiar with the properties. They will answer questions and otherwise assist in the booking process, but your request is forwarded to Rome and the Rome office will respond. After a selection is made and confirmed, a 20 percent deposit is required; the balance is payable six weeks before occupancy. Payment is best made by personal check to the U.S. office upon receipt of invoice. As with many Italian companies, the damage deposit and local taxes are paid to the owner or keyholder after arrival.

Invitation to Tuscany   Tuscany - Mostly Chianti Region
U.S. Agent: Suzanne B. Cohen Agency
94 Winthrop Street
Augusta, ME 04330
Tel: (207) 622–0743   Fax: (207) 622–1902
Contact in Italy (Monteguidi): Susan Wrightson; Tel: 0577–96–3078

The Suzanne B. Cohen Agency is a very small, efficient, and personal operation that represents this British company. The company has located a handful (about 50) rental properties in central Tuscany, most in the region southwest of Florence as far as Siena and the tower town of San Gimignano. There is a good variety, including complete villas and farmhouses as well as apartments in rural and village houses. Prices range from $320 per week for a small one-bedroom apartment in low season to $7,500 for an immense eighteenth-century estate. Most, however, are unpretentious, typically Tuscan rural properties rented at modest prices. The best approach is to peruse the catalog and make selections, but do so early as they are very popular and fill quickly for summer.

A principal agent of the company, Susan Wrightson, lives in Tuscany and is available for assistance if needed. The U.S. agent, Ms. Cohen, has visited many of the properties and believes them to be ideal for North Americans looking for a good Tuscany experience at a fair and reasonable price. We agree.

There is no commission added, the price list is up front in British sterling, and booking and paying are easy. Phone or fax for a catalog, specifying the country of choice (properties in Spain, Portugal, France, and Greece are also represented by Ms. Cohen). The catalogs cost $3.00 to $4.00, postpaid, but are worth it for the photos and descriptions. Booking is very easy and efficient: pay by VISA, MasterCard, or personal check.

Keith Prowse & Co. (USA) Ltd.   Rome, Milan
234 West 44th Street
New York, NY 10036
Tel: (800) 669–8697; (212) 398–1430   Fax: (212) 302–4251

This U.S. agency is included here for several reasons: its prices are very competitive, equal to those that can be obtained by direct contact, the New York staff knows their properties well and offer good advice, and no commission is added.

A color brochure with prices is available. Prowse also represents apartments in London, Dublin, Paris (and throughout France), Amsterdam, Barcelona, Madrid, Geneva, Brussels, Helsinki, and Stockholm. Payment by check or major credit card. Unless there is a reason you want to speak directly with the apartment management in Rome, contact Keith Prowse & Company. (Also see Keith Prowse in chapters France, Spain, and the United Kingdom.)

Mansley Travel Apartments   Rome
No. 1 The Mansions
219 Earls Court Road
London SW5 9BN
Tel: 44–71–373–4689   Fax: 44–71–373–2062
U.S. agent: Grant Reid Communications, Box 810216, Dallas, TX 75381. Tel: (800) 327–1849 or (214) 243–6748   Fax: (214) 484–5778

This competent British company represents a very nice selection of apartments in major cities of Europe as well as elsewhere in the world, including two apartments in Rome located on Via Sicilia and Via del Velabro. Although we have not seen them, we are assured by Mansley that they are inspected at least twice annually and meet high standards. Mansley is a fast-growing company that specializes in city apartments for short-term rent. We find the properties they represent, of which we have visited six and stayed in three, to be dependably good, mostly three-star and four-star properties at fair prices. Contact the U.S. agent for a brochure and prices. (See chapter 13, United Kingdom, for a profile of Mansley and their apartments in London.) Prices are the same whether booked through London or the U.S. agent. Payment may be made by check or credit card.

One Holidays   Tuscany
Piazza Arnolfo, 5
53034 Colle Val d'Elsa
Tel: 577–922–619   Fax: 577–92–1195

This is a small company, eager to rent to North Americans, just as they have to the British and other Europeans for ten years. The properties they represent are modest; look to them not for luxury but for relatively inexpensive getaways in typical, rural Tuscan accommodations. Most are in Chianti. Linens and towels are not always provided, but can always be hired at a small extra cost. Let them know in advance.

English is spoken, but ask for Sylvana if you have questions. Pay by major credit card or use a credit card for the deposit of one third of the rent, and pay the balance on arrival. A refundable damage deposit will also be required on arrival. Telephone or fax for their small brochure or let them know what you want. They will reply with proposals.

Palazzo al Velabro   Rome
Via del Velabro, 16
Rome
U.S. agent: Keith Prowse & Co. (USA), Ltd., listed in this section.

This is an apartment hotel in central Rome that we have not seen, but rely on the reputation of the U.S. company. They will provide information and details by fax or phone.

Suzanne T. Pidduck   Throughout Italy
1742 Calle Corva
Camarillo, CA 93010
Tel: (800) 726–6702   Fax: (805) 482–7976

Suzanne Pidduck is one of the two U.S. agents of Cuendet & Cie., a large and prestigious rental organization in Italy (see profile above). Our experience

The living and dining areas of an apartment in Le Case Gialli exemplify the typical architecture and furnishings of the Villa Saulina apartment cluster, located just west of Florence. (Courtesy Villa Saulina)

with Ms. Pidduck's agency has been excellent: She offers good service, represents a splendid collection of European properties, responds quickly, and gives good advice. Ms. Pidduck visits Europe annually to look at properties and knows the territory. No added commission is charged, just a flat booking fee. The Cuendet catalog, which now includes the excellent new selection of rentals in Venice, Veneto, and Lago di Garda area as well as Tuscany and the south, is worth the $15 price, if only for the glimpse it provides into Italy's culture and countryside.

Ms. Pidduck is also an agent for an Italian company with the "un-Italian" name Country Service. The office is based in Tuscany, and a local manager is available at all times to assist clients if necessary. The properties are quite selective; according to Ms. Pidduck they lean toward the upscale, but at moderate prices. Most accommodations are apartments in large country villas in Chianti (such as Villa Pitiana, where *Much Ado About Nothing* was filmed), on the south Tuscany coast, and in Florence. The properties add a variety and dimension that complement those available from Cuendet. Ms. Pidduck is also a representative of Riviera Retreats, an excellent company with luxury properties on France's Riviera, and for Cuendet France, with some 600 rentals in that country. (See the listings in chapter 6, France.)

Villa Saulina   Tuscany (near Florence)
Via Maremmana, 11
50521 Ginestra Fiorentina
Florence
Tel: 55–872–9511 Fax: 55–878–065

This is one of the working farms, *fattorie,* thoroughly renovated for the comfort of its guests. It is a very attractive complex, including the main villa plus apartments scattered about in restored farm buildings, surrounded by 170 acres of vineyards, olive groves, and fields. There are twenty-six one- to three-bedroom apartments in the outbuildings and eight double bedrooms in the villa itself. There are three swimming pools, a small but very good restaurant, and gardens at the disposal of the guests.

The apartments in these old stone buildings are all pleasant and comfortable, with red tile floors and country furnishings and decor. Although all are appealing, of the different buildings we favor *le Case Gialli,* the yellow houses. Not all the apartment kitchens have ovens, so if you plan to use one, ask specifically at the time of selecting. If you are seeking complete tranquility, book *Spicchiello,* a small building containing four pretty apartments next to a pool about a kilometer from the main villa and group. There are no telephones, no TV, no noise, just bucolic scenery combined with simple comfort and ease.

The farm, Fattoria Mori, produces red and white still wine, a bubbling dessert wine *(spumante),* olive oil, and honey, all available for purchase at the office. The location is ideal: 10 miles southwest of Florence and within an easy day trip to Pisa, Lucca, Siena, San Gimignano, and the coast. There are bicycles for rent, tennis, and a horse stable where lessons are available as well as horses for rent. Treks are arranged here. Groceries are available at Lastra a Signa, a village about 4 kilometers north.

The English-speaking staff are quick to respond and provide information; booking is easy. Phone or fax for an attractive color booklet and price list. Major credit cards are accepted; you can either pay in full before departing for Italy, or pay the one third deposit by credit card and the balance on arrival. Everything is included. There is a wide range of prices; the least expensive is a studio, at about $225 per week in winter and $410 in the peak season. One of our favorites, Il Forno is for two to four persons and runs about $345 in winter to $600 in peak; Il Portico, for up to six persons, is about $650 in winter and $870 in peak. Book early for July and August, or, better, try to go in May, June, September, or October.

Chapter 10

PORTUGAL

Lima River

Viana do Castelo • • Ponte de Lima

Porto •
Douro River

COSTA DA PRATO

•Coimbra

•Figueira da Foz

Atlantic Ocean

Spain

•Foz do Arelho
Obidos • •Caldas da Rainha
•Rio Maior

Sintra •
Estoril
Cascais • •✪ Lisbon

Évora •

Monsaraz •

Guadiana River

ALGARVE

Lagoa   Tavira
Carvoeiro •   • Loulé
Sagres   • Albufeira   Faro
Salema   Lagos   Portimao

Portuguese National Tourist Office

590 Fifth Avenue
New York, NY 10036
Tel: (212) 354–4403

Concourse Level
2180 Yonge Street
Toronto, Ont. M4S 2B9
Tel: (416) 487–3300

International Telephone Country Code: 351
City Codes: Lisbon, Cascais, Estoril 1; Lagoa, Carvoeiro 82
Example: To contact Carvoeiro Clube, dial 011–351–82–357–262
Passport: Yes but no visa.
Language: Portuguese; English is spoken in tourist areas and by people under thirty because it is a language requirement in the schools.
Currency: Escudo (pronounced esh-KOO-doe), abbreviated Esc or esc; 200$50 is 200 escudos and 50 centavos.
Value Added Tax (VAT): 16%
Electricity: 220v AC, 50 cycles.
Credit Cards: AMEX, VISA, MasterCard widely accepted; some accept Diners Club; No oil company cards.
Main Destination Cities From North America: Lisbon; airports are at Oporto and Faro.

The Country

Portugal, the westernmost country of Europe, is a little smaller than Ohio and slightly more populous (about 10 million people), but there the similarities end. The sea, the benign climate, and the relatively low prices join to make Portugal a magnet for tourists, mostly Europeans. The better the weather, the more tourists there are, and the more tourists there are, the more expensive the development, especially on the sun-drenched south coast, in the Province of Algarve. Much of the resort development is financed by northern European companies, the rest by Portuguese firms and some multinational companies.

In the interior, where Spain and Portugal have a common boundary, and along the south coast, similarities in climate and topography exist between them. Spain's Costa del Sol, however, faces the Mediterranean, while the Algarve coast is on the Atlantic. The countries are different in many other ways, from architecture to language, and in Portugal the pace is slower. Fewer visitors are seen off the main tourist trails of Portugal. Some observers say that Portugal today is like the Spain of twenty years ago. The differences go far deeper, however, into the Portuguese character itself. This is a rewarding country to visit, not just for the sunshine of the Algarve, but to see the treasures of its luminous past, to visit its castles and cities, and to feel the warmth of its people.

With its green northern region, the drier east-central section, and the sun-bathed beaches of the south, Portugal is a country of contrasts. Equally note-worthy is the contrast between life in the rural areas and life in the cities and resorts. In rural Portugal, little seems to have changed from the past century. The entire nation remains relatively poor but is dotted with industrial and commercial cities, resorts, and some of Europe's most captivating and undervisited ancient towns, alive with shops, markets, and bustling streets.

Along the route from Spain to the Algarve (crossing the border near Badajoz and traveling south), the olive and almond groves covering the rolling hills are impeccably tended. In the village of Entradas, south of Beja, we stopped for coffee and got the feeling that the people in town were not accustomed to foreigners. But their smiles were friendly and the cups of espresso were generous and inexpensive.

In the south, cultivated fields of olives and grapes, rolling hills, and forests of pine and cork oak provide many of the nation's principal commercial products. The north, except for the absence of high mountains, is similar in many ways to northern California, with rich vegetation and vineyards. Portugal is a physically beautiful and a peaceful country. There has been no political violence in Portugal in recent memory. The prices are among the lowest in western Europe, and as for language, there is rarely a problem. For years English has been a mandatory subject in schools, so it is hard to find a person under the age of thirty who doesn't speak some English. This has been for years one of the main playgrounds of the British, who come on inexpensive flights to break the monotony of the British winters.

It seems that Portugal has not kept pace with most other western European countries in developing and promoting its many virtues. There are comparatively few places to stay outside of the principal cities, the resorts of the Algarve province, and along the coast west of Lisbon. Although it is necessary to look a bit harder for the right rental in the hinterlands the situation has improved during the early 1990s. The opening to visitors of some of the estates and country houses (known as *quintas* and *casas*) has also opened up new areas of the northern province of Minhos and the Costa Verde and even the scarcely populated regions east of Lisbon. One thing is fair to say: Once a place is found, it will undoubtedly be rewarding.

It is approximately 730 kilometers (450 mi.) between Portemão in the south and Valença do Minho on the northern border with Spain. The distance from east to west is less than 323 kilometers (200 mi.) at the country's widest point.

To explore a large part of the country from a single location in the central west coast near Lisbon is possible, especially if you have three weeks or more. The most rewarding approach, however, is to divide your time, devoting a week to the north, including the Lisbon area, and a week or two in the Algarve, or vice versa.

A note on pronunciation: Since many towns and other proper names have an S in them, it is useful to know that with few exceptions an S after a vowel is pronounced as a very soft "sh." Cascais is pronounced "Cash-caeesh," Silves is pronounced "Sil-vesh." The often-seen cedilla, ç, is pronounced like a soft S, almost a Z. Açores is pronounced Azores. The tilde, ã is pronounced "ah" in Portuguese, as in Portemão, pronounced Port-eh-maho.

Best Times of Year to Visit

In the Algarve, the largest, most developed, and most popular destination area in Portugal, the average daytime temperature in January is 55 degrees Fahrenheit and there is an average of only five days of rain. In April the temperature rises to 70 degrees or more and rainy days drop to four. By midsummer clouds are rarely seen, and temperatures in the upper eighties are common; by September, the temperatures have moderated to the low eighties with an average of twenty-eight days without rain. The seasons, which affect prices considerably, are a little complex, but they follow a fairly standard pattern in the Algarve and throughout the country, taking into account holiday periods such as Christmas and Easter. The dates given in the table below are approximate.

Tourist Seasons

Low	Shoulder	High	Peak
Nov. 1–Dec. 23	Dec. 24–Jan. 6	June 1–June 20	June 20–Aug. 30
Jan. 6–Mar. 12	Mar. 12–May 30	Sept. 1–Sept. 30	Oct. 1–Nov. 1

To those who live in the Algarve, April, May, September, and October are the finest months. The weather is good, the sea is pleasant, and many of the tourists have gone home. Even November has a large share of sunny days, and the sea is almost warm enough to swim in.

As for the rest of Portugal, or more specifically, the resort towns just west of Lisbon, a few spots along the coast north of Lisbon, and the *quintas* and *casas* in the Oporto, Braga, and Ponte de Lima regions of the north, May and September are ideal. April and October are also excellent, and March and November are generally pleasant but do have a greater chance of rain and clouds.

General Information About Rentals

Villas are independent houses, and apartments and townhouses are much as they are everywhere. An aparthotel is the combination the name suggests: apartments (usually not large) in a building run like a hotel, with a reception desk, sometimes a restaurant, usually a pool, and hotel services. A scattering of the villas are homes, but many are individually owned houses in resort areas especially built for part-time occupancy. Some may be owned by the company responsible for developing the resort, but more often they are the holiday homes of well-to-do Europeans and are managed by the company. These villa clusters dot the Algarve, and many of the development companies have U.S. agents. The villas are predominantly upscale in their standards, amenities, and high-season rental prices, although true bargains can be had in the off-season. Most of them are built in the curvilinear, Moorish-influenced architecture for which much of southern Portugal is famous. A white building with a red tile roof is the nearly universal color combination, with other colors supplied by bougainvillea and other vines and garden flowers.

Apartments and townhouses in attractive, low-rise buildings are usually in resort settlements on the outskirts of coastal towns. As land becomes more precious, too many of these settlements are being built like cells in a beehive, but it is easy to find those that are tastefully designed, offer space both within and without, are arranged around a pool, and are near a restaurant and cluster of shops. These are included in this book. In the large coastal towns of the Algarve, both on and away from the beaches, the apartments are more conventional, often in modern buildings. Some of the buildings are pleasant and some are jammed together, as builders vie for space.

The villas in the resort area west of Lisbon and the developing Costa da Prato, north of Lisbon, are for the most part individual properties. More resorts and villas and apartment complexes in developments are surely not far off, however. In Lisbon proper and in the towns of Estoril and Cascais most of the rentals are apartments and aparthotels; the few villas available are elegant, fairly expensive, and, usually rent for one- or two-month minimums. There are several resort communities of bungalows in the outskirts of Cascais. The best bet for ferreting out rentals in the Estoril-Cascais area is Ferriasol (see listing later in this chapter).

Where to Stay: The Regions

Portugal is divisible into thirds: the resorts, the cities, and the countryside. The latter can again be divided between the rural poor and the historical holders of vast estates. To stay in a villa in an Algarve resort or in the resort towns near Lisbon puts one at risk of missing the real Portugal. As in any country whose general populace is poor, these resorts are set apart from the daily life of the country. Visitors have a tendency to remain in the beautiful isolation of the resort areas, buying groceries only at the resort stores, eating at the resort restaurants, drinking on the terraces of the resort bars, lying on the resort beaches, and hearing only English, German, or Scandinavian languages. Yet inland from the beaches you can see ancient churches, ruins from Roman times, and the influence of the Moors in old villages and fortresses. It is possible to eat in small cafes where good local food is served at lower prices. One approach, then, is to make excursions from that comfortable villa or apartment and take in all the rest that Portugal has to offer.

Another approach, which few tourists adopt, is to spend a week on one of the old estates, which are mainly in the north. They are often places from an elegant past, still rich in furnishings, gardens, history, and beauty. The owners, who are the hosts, open up their great houses after much time and effort (and money) have been invested in restorations and conversions. The rooms and apartments may be in the main *quinta,* or house, or one of the estate outbuildings. You may not only meet the owners but also learn much about contemporary and historic Portugal from them. The American company with the best access to *quintas* and *casas* is Pinto Basto USA; in Portugal it is Ferriasol (see company listings, this chapter).

Madeira and the Azores are not included here because until recently there have been too few apartment or villa rentals to warrant the journey there. Madeira is off the coast of Africa about 500 miles southwest of the southern tip of the mainland. The twelve islands of the Azores lie nearly 800 miles west of Lisbon. There are, however, many hotels, and we have heard good reports about studio apartments at the Hotel Apartamento Belo Sol, Caminho Velho da Ajuda, São Martinho, 9000 Funchal, Madeira; tel: 91–76–2322; fax: 91–76–2358. To book call Pinto Basto, listed at the end of this chapter.

The Algarve

Environs and Accommodations

Highway EN–125 runs east and west for 175 kilometers (108 mi.) along the southern coast of Portugal, from the Spanish frontier at the Guadiana River westward to Ponta de Sagres, the southwesternmost point of Europe. The northern border of the province roughly parallels the coast and the highway, some 64 kilometers (40 mi.) inland. This long narrow band is bisected by a new high-speed freeway. The Algarve is thus a narrow stretch of land running east to west, influenced by the Atlantic Ocean that forms its southern and western coasts. An even narrower band actually delineates what visitors and developers alike think of as the Algarve. It is a 5 to 10 mile wide strip that edges the coast, roughly back to where Highway EN–125 runs. Short side roads lead off the highway to dozens of beaches, fishing villages, and resort communities. North of the highway are the hills of the Algarve and a scattering of small villages, some of which retain evidence of the Moors, who built cities and fortifications there in the tenth and eleventh centuries. One of these cities, Silves, the Moorish capital of the Algarve, was a center of art, culture, and learning rivaling Lisbon and Granada, Spain. The remains of several crusaders are entombed in Silves's unusual thirteenth-century cathedral. Silves is worth a visit, and is most easily reached from a home base around Carvoeiro.

Much of the strip between the highway and the seas is slightly rolling land that slopes gently toward the coast, where cliffs rise from the sea. The bases of the cliffs are scalloped by beaches of clean white and yellow sand. All the beaches are named and ranked for beauty and degree of surf in English language tourist publications. During the past decade, most of the tourist development has taken place along this narrow strip, beginning around Porternão and slowly moving eastward and westward. Faro remains the transportation hub, with express train service and buses to and from Lisbon. It has the only international airport in the Algarve.

White villas dot the hillsides, but the field plowman and his family do not live in any of them. These villas are among the thousands in the Algarve owned by sun-starved northern Europeans who have found an almost year-round holiday paradise. There are even a few houses owned by well-to-do Americans, Spaniards, and Portuguese.

It helps to have a car in order to leave the beach and the pool for excursions to the hill country villages. Visits to the ancient walled town of Evora, to Santiago do Caçem near the west coast, or even to Lisbon and its environs are feasible. There is little that is exotic about the Algarve resorts themselves, where English is commonly heard, so venture out and enjoy older Portugal.

The Carvoeiro Clube near the highway town of Lagoa is illustrative of the better resort areas in this region. A typical villa is set on about a quarter of an acre of tended lawns and gardens, separated from other villas by a low white wall. There are about seventy individual luxury two- and three-bedroom villas in one group, separated by curving streets, lawns and low walls, very much like an elegant neighborhood. Like other better rental accommodations in the Algarve, the Carvoeiro Clube's villas have terraces, pools, garages, fireplaces, baths, televisions, telephones, and daily maid service. They are spacious, light, comfortable, and stylish.

The Carvoeiro Clube complex is one of the largest, but there are many resort developments along the coast of the Algarve. Some cost less, but very few are more expensive. Some resorts are associated with nearby golf courses and others have their own. There are also three- and four-star aparthotels. A few rentals are quite modest in style and amenities as well as price, but many are budget stretchers in the peak season. If you are not looking for a deluxe villa, be sure to make this clear to any company you are dealing with.

From November through March (except three weeks around Christmas) apartments can be rented on the spot. This can also be done in October and May, but it may take longer to find a suitable place. The best approach is to go to an office of the *Região de Turismo do Algarve* (regional tourist agency) in any of the larger towns and inquire. They invariably have lists of available rentals. From June 1 through September, Easter season, and Christmas week, the season peaks and you should book well ahead.

In addition to the resort areas, the larger towns of the Algarve have become centers in which young Europeans gather, especially Albufeira and, to a lesser extent, Portemão. It is not difficult to find simple places for less than $150 per week in these towns. Food and wine are inexpensive, the beaches are great, the sun shines, and the towns are lively at night. Remember that some of the young people come from other parts of Europe with very little money, planning to pay for their holidays from someone else's pockets.

A cautionary note: The rush to take advantage of the Algarve's relatively newfound popularity has resulted in some gross overbuilding, especially in the towns along the Highway EN–125. Competition among apartment house owners has meant reduced rates, but we seldom hear about them in North America, and, in any case, a large proportion of these apartments are not in desirable locations. One of the worst offenders is the town of Albufeira, followed by Portemão and Lagos. The saving features in these towns are the old parts. Once quaint fishing villages, they remain at least partly so despite the rampant construction going on in and around them. There are still a few small, isolated seaside villages at the extreme west and east with a few villas or apartments. One we found is Salema, about 10 miles (16 km) west of Lagos, which has several very attractive villas for rent. There is also a modest apartment building as well as camping facilities near the beach. Contact Quinta dos Carricos, Praia da Salema, 8650 Vila do Bispo, Algarve; tel: 011–082–65201. The proprietors speak English.

Location and Transportation

The Faro airport is usually the first (somewhat disheartening) glimpse visitors get of the Algarve. Rental cars are picked up there, and some of the resorts run shuttle service for their clients. Even if you plan to spend all of your time in the resort area, we recommend a rental car because of limited public transportation.

Along the Algarve coast, rail service runs from Vila Real de São Antonio at the Spanish border through Albufeira and Portemão to Lagos in the west, connecting at Tunes for the mainline run to Lisbon. For the smaller hill towns and west of the end of the line at Lagos there is adequate bus service. For example, to get from Lagos to Salema, it is easy to catch the bus, which stops at two points in the little town.

For a visit to Spain, it is only 260 kilometers (165 mi.) from Portemão to the city of Seville and under 325 kilometers (200 mi.) to Cádiz. The Portuguese rail line ends at Vila Real São António, across the Guadiana River from the Spanish rail terminal at Ayamonte, but a ticket includes ferry passage across the river. (The ferry also takes cars.)

Prices

Rents in the Algarve vary considerably and are affected by size, location, standard, season, services provided, and external amenities such as a resort shopping center, community pool, tennis courts, and a golf course. The following approximate rental prices give an idea of what to expect. Refer to the section Best Times of Year to Visit for information on low, shoulder, and peak seasons. The figures are in U.S. dollars per week at an exchange rate of 150 escudos per dollar.

	Low	Shoulder	Peak
Simple village studio	$200	$250	$300
Simple 1 bedroom (Salema)	225	350	400
Three-star city studio (Portemão)	225	320	475
Three-star city 1 bedroom (Portemão)	250	375	500
Four-star city 1 bedroom (Portemão)	450	550	700
Resort aparthotel studio	300	500	750
Resort luxury 1-bedroom townhouse, maid	495	600	1,050
Resort 3-bedroom villa, pool, maid	850	1,375	2,100

The marked difference in rates for each season is obvious from the table, especially for peak season. It is also obvious that low- and shoulder-season prices are true bargains. Where else in Western Europe, except possibly Greece, can an elegant three-bedroom three-bath private villa with pool and daily maid service be rented for as little as $850 per week? These are typical prices for November and April, both pleasant months in the Algarve. Meals away from the resort communities are very modestly priced; a good dinner and wine for two can be had for under $15. Groceries in the town markets are also inexpensive.

Advance Booking Time

July and August: six months
Mid-April to late June and September through October and Christmas Season: three months
Rest of the year: two weeks from overseas or rent on site

Lisbon Area
Environs and Accommodations

The resorts west of Lisbon are smaller, older, and more settled than the resorts in Algarve. They are centered in the towns of Estoril and Cascais, 10 and 18 miles, respectively, from Lisbon proper. Once the playground of the rich and titled, Estoril remains sedately attractive, but despite the few elegant hotels and the famous nineteenth-century casino, it has seen better days. If you want to rent in a town, we suggest Cascais, west of Estoril. It is a popular, bustling place filled with good restaurants and shops and easy to manage. This is a relatively small region, but because of its concentration of diversions, a week spent here will be full.

Lisbon itself is a busy city with a population exceeding one million, not hard to manage except in a car. With seven museums, three noteworthy ancient churches, galleries, excellent restaurants, the opera, and all the other offerings of a large city (at prices much lower than can be found in most other European cities) there is much to do here. Don't miss the Castelo de São Jorge, which has brooded over the city for fifteen centuries. Originally built by Visigoths and expanded and rebuilt by Moors in the ninth century, it also affords the best possible view of Lisbon.

First-time visitors will be amazed by the similarity between Lisbon's colossal suspension bridge, Ponte Salazar, and San Francisco's Golden Gate Bridge designed by the same architect. Built by U.S. Steel, the graceful span across the estuary of the Tagus River was completed in 1966.

Although apartments are available in the city, the Estoril coastal area is so close and the transportation so good that we see little reason for staying in Lisbon itself; stay in the vicinity and commute. In addition to Cascais or Estoril, there is the more distant (57 km/35 mi.) but beautiful Sintra. Sintra is a hill town of about 25,000 people. Its magnificent palace and elegant mansions were occupied for generations by royalty and European aristocrats. In a setting lush with vegetation and pine and eucalyptus forests, Sintra captures the imagination with its still-visible opulence. The ruins of a seventh-century Moorish wall and castle rise from a rocky promontory above the town. At even greater heights, the nineteenth-century Palacio da Pena commands a magnificent view of the entire area. Sintra is a romantic and beautiful place to stay; it is convenient to Lisbon, to the Estoril coast to the south, and to the fine beaches near Cape Roca, Europe's westernmost point. For rentals in the Lisbon-Cascais area and northern Portugal we recommend Pinto Basto and Ferriasol, listed later in this chapter.

Location and Transportation

It is possible to explore northward to Coimbra and Porto from the Lisbon-Cascais area. The outstanding Spanish cities of Santiago de Compostela and Salamanca are both a day's drive through interesting country. Trains run locally every fifteen minutes (every thirty minutes on Sunday and during off-hours) between Lisbon's Cais do Sodre station and Cascais, stopping at Estoril and several other points along the route; the travel time is thirty minutes. Suburban trains also run frequently between Lisbon's Rossio station and Sintra, a splendid, forty-five-minute trip.

Mainline rail service runs south to Algarve Province; north to Porto, Vigo, Spain, and beyond; and east to Salamanca and Madrid. Large ocean ferries travel between Lisbon and the island of Madeira.

Advance Booking Time

July and August: six months
Shoulder months: two–three months
November through April: three weeks for overseas, or on site

Just north of Lisbon, including Costa da Prata
Environs and Accommodations

This small area of Portugal is not really defined as a region, but it is included here because a few rentals have been found there and it is such a delight. The Costa da Prato offers a taste of Portugal usually limited to foreign visitors on day trips or overnighters from Lisbon and its vicinity. To urban Portuguese, however, the villages and beaches of the Costa da Prato have long been a destination for Sunday picnics or weekend excursions.

To stay in this area happily one must enjoy tranquility and simplicity; there are no resorts or championship golf courses, as in the Algarve. The beaches of the rugged coast are vast and empty, and big-wheeled carts pulled by donkeys, oxen, and even cows are a common sight along the roads and highways. Excellent regional foods, especially seafoods, are served in unpretentious restaurants and cafes, and the prices are still modest. Although not much English is spoken, we found people friendly and helpful, and language was not a problem.

Neat, clean villages dot the coastal countryside, some of them historically important and physically beautiful. Óbidos, for example, is a medieval walled town of cobbled streets, small restaurants and shops, and whitewashed buildings with gaily colored trim. If you decide on a villa or apartment in the area, arrive before your Saturday occupancy date and stay in the castle, now one of the most beautiful government inns, called *pousadas,* in Portugal.

Most of the few short-term rentals in the area are available through Pinto Basto, listed below. Although we have not visited the specific properties, we would also not hesitate to book into the Solar da Vicarica (Vivarica, 3050 Mealhada; tel: 31–93458) or Quinta do Carvalhinho (Ventosa do Bairro, 3030 Mealhada; tel: 31–29343). Both are near Coimbra and we have heard good reports. There is also a small enclave of villas in the tiny coastal village of Foz do Arelho, just west of the main town of Caldas da Rainha. Mostly British owned, the villas are not worth the effort of booking in advance, but stop by in the off-season to check on availability. Foz do Arelho has the advantage of being on the coast. Also in Foz do Arelho are two apartment buildings with full service, the Aparthotel Atlantico (a modern high-rise) across from the beach, and the Aparthotel Sottomayor, a short walk to the beach. (See the Pinto Basto listing.) Quinta do Corticada and Quinta da Ferrarya, owned by one family, are beautiful examples of rural *habitaçaos*—elegant, old but modern, stylish. The former (where we stayed) offers rooms and meals only; the latter has apartments.

(Contact Ferriasol or book direct; see listing.)

Nothing is very far away from anything else in this region. For example, it is a twenty-five-minute drive from Óbidos to the beach and lagoon at Foz do Arelho, and both Foz and Óbidos are within a half hour of Caldas da Rainha.

Best Times of Year to Visit

Midwinter temperatures in the sixties are not uncommon, indicating a mild year-round climate, but the shoulder seasons (late spring, early summer, and fall) are optimum for good rental prices, fine weather, lovely flowers, and reduced tourist traffic.

Location and Transportation

Two rail lines run from Lisbon into the regions north: One goes through Caldas da Rainha, the main southern town of this area (approximately 105 kilometers from Lisbon) and terminates at Figueira da Foz. The other runs to Porto, stopping at Coimbra and other towns en route. A car is very useful in this rather rural area, facilitating trips to remote beach and coastal areas and drives south to Sintra and Lisbon. There is intertown bus service throughout the area as well as long-distance rail service.

Prices

Prices in many private *casas, solars,* and *quintas* are established by the government. A studio apartment in a house like Quinta Carvalhinho, noted above, will cost about $400 per week in the low season, $500 in the shoulder seasons, and $650 in July and August. A one bedroom will cost from about $500 to $800. A two bedroom in Solar da Vicarica costs about $1,000 per week in high season, less in off-seasons. If booked through Pinto Basto, there is a modest booking fee. Nevertheless, we think booking with this company is worth the extra money.

Advance Booking Times

July and August: six months
Shoulder months: two months
Rest of the year: two–three weeks, or can be rented on site

Minhos Province and the Costa Verde
Environs and Accommodations

This is the land of the great *casas antigas* (historic estates), of pine-covered hills, vineyards in the valleys of the Douro and Lima rivers, and stretches of golden beach—and it is relatively undiscovered by North American tourists. Its main cities are Viana do Castelo, near the Spanish border on the coast, Porto on the coast to the south, and Braga, an eleventh-century city, in between. This is the cradle of Portugal, inhabited by Celts, Romans, Visigoths, and Moors in a succession of civilizations leading to modern Portugal. Many of the remains are in evidence, such as the twelfth-century cathedral at Braga, the medieval town of Guimarães, and the fortified town of Moncão.

Our advice for spending a week here is to rent an apartment in one of the estate homes. Not only will you find yourself in historic surroundings, immersed in Portuguese culture, but you will be able to explore the entire area on day trips. Although you will have a kitchen and dining area, enjoy the restaurants, which are relatively inexpensive and known for the abundance and quality of the foods they serve. Contact Pinto Basto listed at the end of this chapter, to discuss the right place for you.

Transportation

A car is vital. However, a mainline railroad runs between Lisbon and Porto, then on through Braga, Viana do Castelo, Valença do Minho on the border, to Vigo, Spain, and northward. The trip to Lisbon by rail takes about three and a half hours, making an overnight visit feasible (and fun). If you plan to do this, we suggest rail over driving—it's easier, and more relaxing.

The Rental Companies of Portugal

In the off-season from mid-September through April and even until mid-May (except for Christmas and Easter periods) it is not essential to book ahead. One may go to any of the local tourist offices for a list of available apartments or villas or, in the cities, call the aparthotels. This is particularly true for the Algarve and the Lisbon areas, both popular tourist destinations. In the Algarve, the best bet is to drive into any of the resort communities and inquire. It bears repeating, however, that this should not be attempted from late spring to midfall, nor should it be attempted for accommodations in any of the rural estates.

A stay in an apartment in one of these estates is an unusual experience, in part because they provide insight into the lives and histories of the landed families of Portugal. The government has poured great sums into loans and grants to promote tourism in the poor rural countryside, essentially funding the conversion of parts of these estates into vacation rentals. One problem we see is that these conversions seem to have been overdone. There are literally dozens of these old/new great rural houses vying for tourist income. Of the *quintas* and *casas* we stayed in and visited, all were comfortable and beautifully restored with their historical character intact. Many of the larger *quintas* are managed by extraordinary, multilingual young persons, who are graduates of government-approved tourist schools. Those whom we met were fluent in English, sophisticated, knowledgeable, and very hospitable.

Some of the estates are hard to book without the assistance of an agent, such as Pinto Basto and FeriaSol. We also learned firsthand that because they are in very rural locations, they can also be difficult to find (especially on a rainy night). Getting detailed directions and the manager's or owner's telephone number prior to departure is essential.

Aparthotel Village Cascais   Cascais (Lisbon Area)
Rua Frei Nicolau de Olivera
Parque do Gandarhina
2750 Cascais
Tel: 1–284–7044   Fax: 1–284–7319
U.S. agent: Pinto Basto USA, listed in this section

Cascais is our favorite town in the Lisbon area, a bustling but manageable community of shops and restaurants on the sea near the mouth of the great River Tagus (Rio Tejo).

The Village Cascais is an elegant, modern, resort apartment building offering hotel services and amenities. The studio apartments are fair sized, well designed and comfortable, air-conditioned and attractive, and the one- and two-bedroom apartments are quite spacious. The compact kitchens are well equipped, and balconies offer a broad view of the sea or the gardens. There is a restaurant, bar, pool, and sauna on the premises, and although it is not directly on the beach, it offers views of the broad Tagus estuary where it becomes the Atlantic Ocean. Mountain or sea-view apartments are available. The service is excellent, the staff speaks English, and secure parking is available. It has a government four-star rating, and can be booked directly and paid for by credit card. Or, contact Pinto Basto in New York.

Aparthotel Solferias   Central Algarve
Sitio do Mato Serrao
8400 Lagoa
Algarve, Portugal
Tel: 82–357–401   Fax: 82–357–157

This is an apartment building in a pleasant rural setting, well located 1½ miles south of Lagoa and ½ mile from the fishing village of Carvoeiro. The apartments are small but adequate. We cannot recommend these for a winter stay, when weather is unpredictable and much time may have to be spent inside. This is listed principally because of its good location near the center of the 100-mile-long Algarve coast, its proximity to Carvoeiro, and the modest rental prices, around $200 per week in off-season and $500 for a studio in high season. A restaurant and bar are on the premises. Maid service is provided daily. Aparthotel Solferias will send a brochure and a current price list. Book by fax or

The villas and townhouses of Algarve Atlantico, one of three resort communities of Carvoeiro Clube, lie low on the palisades above the clean beaches of Portugal's Algarve Province. (Photo by Michael and Laura Murphy)

phone, paying the deposit by credit card, and the balance on arrival.

AR/Proalgarve   Algarve
1a. Transversal a Rua Egas Moniz, no. 15
Apartado 123
8900 Vila Real de Santo Antonio
Algarve, Portugal
Tel: 81–43–839   Fax: 81–43–839

This is a small company that markets its properties principally in Europe. It is worth a stop if you're in the vicinity or if nothing satisfactory can be found from other sources. They will send a list of rentals on request. AMEX, VISA, MasterCard, and personal checks are accepted. A 35 percent deposit is required on booking, and the balance is due on arrival.

Carvoeiro Clube   Central Algarve
Actividades Turisticas, S.A.
Apartado 24
P8401 Lagoa Codex
Algarve, Portugal
Tel: 82–357–262   Fax: 82–357–726

The three resort complexes that comprise Carvoeiro (pronounced carv-WER-oh) under a single management are in themselves almost the complete answer to a wonderful stay in the Algarve. They are ideally situated along a 3-mile stretch of a sloped palisade above the sea. Dramatic sheer cliffs rise along this section of the coast, and the yellow sand beaches that lie at their base are reached by easy paths. The area is well located near the center of the Algarve, making for easy day-trip exploration in either direction. A road intersecting the main highway at Lagoa (not to be confused with Lagos) runs 3 miles south to the little fishing village of Praia do Carvoeiro.

One resort community, Carvoeiro Clube, has mostly standard to deluxe villas with swimming pools, plus a few townhouses. East of it lies Monte Carvoeiro, a cluster of apartments and townhouses around a central pool and a restaurant and bar. There are also scattered villas with private pools. A mile or so farther east is Clube Atlantico, which is also a mix of townhouses and villas.

This complex, although large, is so spread out that there is no sense of crowding. An array of choices are available, from one-bedroom apartments to 2- and 3-bedroom townhouses and three-, four-, and five-bedroom villas. There are levels of quality: standard, luxury, and super-luxe. Contrasted to rentals in other parts of Europe, even the standard grade properties are comfortable, spacious, and modern. Moorish-Mediterranean architecture prevails: white stuccoed walls, red tile roofs, open and dramatic designs. This is an ideal destination for couples, families, and traveling companions sharing accommodations.

The rentals are well furnished and well equipped, with everything provided. Daily maid service is included in all accommodations. Golf is available at nearby championship courses and tennis courts are on the premises. Riding, boating, and deep-sea fishing are easily arranged. There is even a kindergarten. Service is excellent, the beaches are splendid, and the sea is clear and clean.

Prices vary, depending on the season, accommodation size, and standard. The lowest price is for a luxury apartment for two, which costs $285 per week from November to early April (except during the three-week Christmas period). The same apartment costs about $560 from April to July, September to November, and Christmas. In July and August the same apartment rents for about $800 per week. The seasonal price changes are dramatic, especially in the large, super-luxe villas. A four-bedroom, four-bath, luxury villa for eight persons rents for a very modest $1,050 in low season, about $1,650 in the shoulder periods, and $2,600 in high season. A villa of this class near the sea on France's Riviera would cost at least double these prices at any season of the year.

There are English-speaking staff. Fax for Carvoeiro's attractive brochure and fax or phone for booking or to discuss details. Pay a deposit six weeks in advance and make the final payment four weeks in advance or upon receipt of an invoice; major credit cards are accepted.

Clube Praia da Oura   Central Algarve
Praia da Oura, Apartado 27
Albufuera
Algarve
Tel: 89–589–135   Fax: 89–589–157

Praia means beach in Portuguese and *oura* means gold. This is a large complex of midpriced apartments and townhouses owned largely by British people
who spend their winter breaks and other holidays here and turn their properties
over to the management for rental and maintenance. The accommodations are
not of luxury quality, but the prices are fair and the living style is relaxed and
comfortable. The complex is located along the sea near the town of Albufuera.
This area is not as built up as the region nearer to Portemao, 20 miles to the
west. Albufuera town itself is not especially attractive, but is busy with the bustle of foreign visitors (many of them young) who can find very inexpensive apartments and pensions there.

Amenities include two pools (one for children), Jacuzzis, a bowling green,
and, of course, the sea. Services are like those of a hotel; maid service is included. Booking is easy: Phone or fax for a brochure and price list, decide on size
and style, and contact Praia da Oura again with your dates. The deposit can be
paid by credit card; you can also pay in full by credit card before departure, or
pay the balance on arrival. English is spoken universally. This is a good spot for
moderately priced comfort, and prices are modest, indeed, in the off-season.

Suzanne B. Cohen, Agent
94 Winthrop Street
Augusta, ME 04330
Tel: (207) 622–0743   Fax: (207) 622–1902

Suzanne B. Cohen is a small agency representing a fairly large British company called CV Travel, which does an excellent job of locating, displaying, and
renting properties, mostly villas and other independent houses, in Spain,
Portugal, and the islands of Sardinia, Corsica, and Corfu. This company has a
good reputation, has marketed its rentals to British travelers for several years,
and has a very nice selection available. Ms. Cohen's agency adds no commission
and makes finding and booking easy. Ms. Cohen is herself careful about the
companies and properties she works with, and seems at all times to have her
client's best interests in mind. Her association with PLUM Courtesy (see listing,
below) in the Algarve adds to the range of choices and prices.

The Portugal properties are in the Algarve, located in prime spots along 80
miles of the coast. Some of the villas are within resort communities, but most
are more individual. All are of superior to luxury standard, most with pools, and

all desirable. Even the few townhouses offered are bright, airy, and spacious. A typical two-bedroom two-bath villa with a private pool costs about $600 per week in low season and $1,000 in high. A secluded five-bedroom, four-bath villa with a pool is about $2,300 in peak season and $800 in low season. These are good values.

All of the CV Travel properties throughout the Mediterranean countries and Portugal are in a single catalog available from the Suzanne Cohen agency; the cost is $3.00 postpaid, but well worth it. The catalog is colorful, descriptive, and accurate. Payment can be made by personal check or credit card at the prevailing exchange rate on the day of booking.

FeriaSol   Lisbon, Cascais, and the North
Ave. Gonçalo Velho Cabral, 194-7C
P.O. Box 117
P2750 Cascais
Tel: 1–486–8232   Fax: 1–486–0783

For rentals anywhere from the Lisbon area to the northern border with Spain, we found this vigorous and competent company to be the best single source in Portugal. It is a small operation, but the owner, Antonio Imhof de Morais, has accumulated an excellent selection of properties, ranging from a pair of modest studios in the delightful town of Cascais to apartments in Sintra and along the northern coasts. Also in Cascais, in the forest near to the sea, are the bungalows and townhouses of the large Quinta da Marynha resort as well as a selection of very good aparthotels in the towns of Cascais, Estoril, and Lisbon city.

FeriaSol is also an excellent source for many of the estates noted in this chapter, including *quintas, casas, solars,* and other interesting properties. For an introduction to one of the estates that has been totally converted to a rural resort, the Quinta do Ferrarya is a good example. Just an hour's drive north of Lisbon, in the "middle of nowhere" but not far from Rio Maior, this white cluster of ranch buildings offers comfortable rooms, apartments, a restaurant, pool, museum, stables, and even facilities for a conference. The owners also offer rooms in their Quinta de Cortiçada, an elegant house.

Both the FeriaSol owner/manager and the staff, especially the capable Fernanda Mateus, are fluent in English and knowledgeable about Portugal and the properties they represent. They were most helpful as we traveled and stayed in the tranquil and seldom visited north provinces. They have not extended their energies to the overrepresented Algarve, concentrating instead on the region from Lisbon northward and working closely with the capable tourist organization of the Cascais-Estoril coast.

There seems to be a complete understanding of what North Americans are looking for and the standards expected. The properties are properly, if briefly, described and pictured in FeriaSol's small catalog. The best approach to booking is to fax or phone a description of what you are looking for: size, style (for example, an apartment in a rural *quinta,* a private villa, a bungalow in town, a modest studio, a modern aparthotel), and price. They will respond by sending descriptions and photos of proposed properties from which to choose. Make your selection and contact them again. Once you have booked, all the information you need will be sent. They are eager to work directly with North American travelers and certainly exhibited their ability to do so. If you are in the area without a reservation, telephone FeriaSol. Prices are fair and controlled by the government, so expect good value. Booking and payment are made easy; credit cards, travelers cheques, or bank drafts in escudos are accepted.

Hotel Apartamento Impala   Lisbon City
Rua Felipe Folque, 49
1000 Lisbon
Tel: 1–528–914   Fax: 1–575–362

A typical city aparthotel, this one rates three stars and is less than two blocks from the Eduardo VII Park in central Lisbon. Rooms are small but provide much more space than a hotel room; kitchenettes are also small but adequate. These apartments are comfortable and clean, but are not intended for entertaining. They make a good home base for a week in Lisbon city, but unless you specifically want to be in the city center, consider the aparthotel Cascais Village in nearby Cascais (profiled above). The deposit and balance can be paid for with a major credit card. There is a three-night minimum stay.

The Owners' Syndicate   Algarve (Also Spain's Balearic Islands)
79 Balham Park Road
London SW12 8EB
England
Tel: 44–81–767–7926   Fax: 44–81–767–5328

This is an interesting company we came across in Britain. Rather than the conventional way of adding a commission to the owners' prices, owners and villa management companies pay the syndicate for the promotion and administration of their properties. The syndicate, in turn, offers the properties to the public at direct, on-site prices. The brochure indicates that the properties are mostly large and well above average in standards. To book a rental contact the company with your requirements; they will send a number of very descriptive pages along with prices. We spoke with the principals in London, and although we did not visit any of the villas, we are fully confident that they are as advertised. This is an especially good source for villas in out-of-the-way places.

Pinto Basto USA   Throughout Portugal
40 Prince St.
New York, NY 10012
Tel: (800) 526–8539 or (212) 226–9056   Fax: (212) 966–1697

This company represents the largest and most diversified collection of Portuguese properties available through a North American company. Formerly the U.S. branch of the Portuguese company of the same name, it now operates independently and has approximately 2,000 rentals throughout Portugal, maintains all its former ties, and offers services from tours to car rentals, air transportation, and hotel bookings. Pinto Basto USA is a source of hard-to-find rentals in the northern provinces and along the Costa Verde, including the elegant manor houses in the region north of Porto near Ponte de Lima, Braga, and Viana do Castelo. They also have a selection ranging from aparthotels to *quintas* in the central provinces of the Costa de Prata and apartments in the area of Lisbon, especially nearby Estoril, Cascais, and Sintra. There are also a good number of properties in the Algarve, where Pinto Basto represents individually owned villas away from the built-up resort areas as well as a few of the better resort complexes.

Specializing in Portugal, Pinto Basto knows the territory. A good example of one of their estate rentals is the Quinta do Baganheiro near the northern town of Ponte de Lima. Here we found a great house which was built by the Knights of Malta. The estate has passed through generations of the Norton de Mateos family. The family has completed a successful conversion and now offers a few apartments and rooms in a tranquil, wooded setting. Its staff and owners take pains to make any guest feel completely at home and seem to especially enjoy meeting and talking with foreign travelers.

Also tucked away near an ancient village is the estate Paço d'Anho, across the Rio Lima from the town of Viana do Castelo. There half a dozen comfortable one- and two-bedroom apartments have been built in three of the outbuildings of this working farm.

The prices are fair and no commission is added. A small surcharge is applied for manor house accommodations, because manor house owners generally provide no discount to agencies. A catalog is available, or simply phone or fax your requirements. Pinto Basto USA will quickly search for available properties and propose one or more for your consideration. Pay one third on booking, balance a week or so before departure. Pay by personal check or major credit card. Good service, good selection, fair prices.

PLUM Courtesy   Algarve
Apartado 43
Santa Barbara de Nexe
8000 Faro, Algarve
Tel: 89–90–359 or 898–399–011   Fax: 89–92–630
U.S. agent: Suzanne B. Cohen Agency (see listing)

Englishman Peter L. Marriott and his expatriate associates operate this rather unusual service: a combination of greeter, villa and apartment rental agency, car rental arranger, and all around helper to travelers arriving and staying in the Algarve. They are a group that knows the Algarve. From their desk at Faro International Airport they meet arriving clients; arrange transportation to hotels, rented villas, and *quintas;* recommend restaurants; and arrange ground tours—any and all for a very modest fee. In sum, they help arriving travelers become situated in the Algarve, and are available to see that all goes well during the stay.

PLUM Courtesy is the contact for the clients of the British rental company Something Special, but they also have their own inventory of rental apartments and villas. Their prices are among the lowest possible because Mr. Marriott and staff are on the scene and they are able to negotiate with prospective clients on behalf of the owners. This is especially important during low and shoulder seasons when, it seems, a low rent is preferable to an empty villa, *quinta,* or townhouse, or, for that matter, an idle rental car.

There is no catalog of properties. The best approach is to telephone or fax PLUM or Suzanne B. Cohen Agency with your requirements and let them respond with some ideas. If you know where you want to be, they will limit their proposals; if you are not sure, they will make some suggestions. Although they seem to have properties scattered along the entire Algarve, most are in the hills and along the coast from Albufuera in the center eastward to Faro. They are the only company we have dealt with that knows and can arrange rentals east of Faro to the Spanish border. They are familiar with the eastern coastal towns like Tavira, where not many North Americans go.

Whether or not you rent a car or villa or apartment through PLUM Courtesy, if you don't know the Algarve, they are a good contact, especially if you are arriving by air. By phone or fax you can arrange for any of their services. We came to know and like Mr. Marriott and his staff and feel that their services are excellent, their knowledge abundant, and their prices fair.

Prainha Club Hotel   Western Algarve
P-8500 Portemao
Tel: 89–45–8951   Fax: 89–45–8950
U.S. agent: Best Western International

A new, white, low-rise apartment building surrounding a large swimming pool, Prainha Club Hotel is a good choice for people who prefer a single apartment building over independent villas or townhouse clusters. It is fresh, well designed, and comfortable, offering studios and one- and two-bedroom apartments at modest to moderate prices. The winter (November 1 through April 1) rate for a studio is a very modest $30 per day or $210 per week; in June and September the same studio is $650 per week. A nice two-bedroom apartment in peak season (August) costs about $1,650 per week. On the premises are a restaurant, coffee shop, two bars (poolside and inside), tennis courts, a sauna, and other amenities.

Located near the sea close to the town of Portemão the aparthotel is well situated for exploring the Algarve coast, especially the very rural west, toward Sagres, where the beaches are often quiet except for the waves. The city of Portemão itself seems to have been developed chaotically with little apparent planning. There are big resort hotels and apartments, many in various stages of construction or work stoppage. However, the cliffs and beaches of the western outskirts of Portemão, in the Praia do Vau area, are among the most beautiful of the Algarve. Contact the Prainha Club for a brochure and their latest price list; then book direct or through Best Western, and pay upon arrival. Credit cards are accepted.

Promoçoes e Ideias Turisticas S.A.
Torre D2-8A, Alto da Pamphilheira
2750 Cascais
Tel: 1–486–7858   Fax: 1–284–2901

This is an organization for the promotion of tourism. Bookings can be made from overseas, but it is somewhat difficult to get the information needed to select a rental property. But if you are planning a visit from late fall through early spring and prefer not to book in advance, this is a good contact to arrange in Portugal for a stay in the Lisbon-Estoril-Cascais-Sintra area. The rental prices are very good. For the summer season in central Portugal, especially in and around Lisbon, it is essential to book well in advance, so we suggest using the services of Pinto Basto (see their listing above) rather than making the effort through this organization.

Something Special   Algarve
10 Bull Plain,
Hertfordshire, SG14 1DT
England
Tel: 992–55–2231   Fax: 992–58–7057
Portuguese contact: PLUM Courtesy, listed in this section.

A moderate-sized British company, Something Special is well named. They do a good job of locating, displaying, and renting properties, mostly villas and other independent houses, in Spain, France, Portugal, and the island of Corfu in Greece. This company has marketed its rentals to British travelers since 1980, and in our view it has one of the nicest selections available. Although it is a bit awkward booking rentals in these Continental countries (and Corfu) through an English company, the nature of the properties they represent makes it worth the effort. Make sure, however, that you are totally satisfied with directions and instructions.

Phone or fax for a catalog, specifying your interest in Portugal. The cost is $3.00 postpaid, but well worth it. The catalog is colorful, descriptive, and accurate. All of the information needed is in the catalog; the price list is in pounds sterling. Payment can be made by credit card or, a month or two in advance, by personal check at the exchange rate of pounds to dollars on the day of booking.

TURIHAB   Throughout Portugal
Association di Turismo de Habiticão
Praca da Republic
4990 Ponte de Lima
Portugal
Tel: 58–94–2729   Fax: 58–74–144

A quasi-governmental organization through which villas, apartments, and *pousadas* (large estates, castles, and historic buildings that offer rooms by the night) can be rented. This is not the easiest organization to deal with from overseas, but it is a contact if you are traveling in the north of Portugal in the off- or shoulder season without an advance reservation. TURIHAB can also be contacted from overseas for a listing of rentals. They cannot make recommendations of one property over another.

Quintas: The Manor Houses of Portugal
The following rental properties are privately owned and comprise separate houses and apartments in houses and estates. They are among dozens listed in the booklet "Manor Houses of Portugal" published by the Portuguese National Tourist Office (and available for the asking). Named "Casa," "Quinta," "Vila,"

and "Solar," the distinguishing characteristics are fuzzy. There are three government categories: "Turismo de Habitacão" (distinguished manor house), "Tourismo Rural" (more rustic, reflecting the rural environment), "Agroturismo" (part of a working farm, ranch, or vineyard). A casa (house) is usually the larger of the habitations, often more suburban in location; a quinta is usually a rural farmhouse, but may indeed be an elegant farm estate. "Vila" also means house, often in a rural setting but more a residence without farm grounds; a "solar" seems to be smaller, less commanding than a casa or quinta. That said, the best way to decide is to pay attention to the property description in descriptive materials, not the name of the type of building.

Although the government oversees rates of hotels and certain private accommodations for tourists, the prices shown in the tourist office publication are not always accurate. Both inflation and currency exchange rates bear on current prices, and although the escudo is fairly stable against the dollar, there is an effect. You can, however, count on prices being very fair and the accommodations among the best values in Europe.

These are a few properties that we especially like and for which gathering information on and booking is made easy by going through Pinto Basto in New York and FeriaSol in Cascais. Our advice is to contact them for their catalogs and make selections; ask their advice if you remain unsure. Some telephone contact numbers are provided in case you wish to call to compare direct vs. agent prices. We have found them to be quite close. Only a few of these estates are open year around.

Casa do Ameal
Rua do Ameal, 119
Meadela
4900 Viana do Castelo, Minho
Tel: 58–822–403

One of the rare historic estates on the coast just outside the city of Viana do Castelo. More simple than some of the larger estates but in an ideal location due to its proximity to Viana do Castelo. There are two one-bedroom and one two-bedroom apartments in the main building plus a three-bedroom apartment in a separate building.

Casa do Baganheiro
Queijada
4990 Ponte de Lima, Minho
Tel: 58–949–612

Near Ponte de Lima, Minho, northern Portugal. One one-bedroom and one two-bedroom apartment plus rooms in an elegant, beautifully furnished historic home. The original was built by the Knights of Malta; also a two-bedroom cottage on the estate grounds. The Norton de Mateos family are exceptional hosts. Arrange directly or through Pinto Basto or FeriaSol.

Quinta do Benatrite
P.O. Box 17
Santa Barbara de Nexe
8000 Faro, Algarve
Tel: 89–90450

This beautiful old house in a tranquil setting near the eastern Algarve town of Faro is owned by an Englishwoman who occupies her own quarters and rents rooms, all of which have complete access to the house (except for the kitchen), the pool, and the grounds. A full breakfast is brought to your room, and, if desired, lunch and dinner can be ordered on a daily basis with the manager, a British gourmet chef. The furnishings are an elegant mix of Portuguese and English furniture along with art and objects gathered from many parts of the world by the diplomat traveling family.

As there are no apartments here, we see this as a good place to spend a few days immediately after arriving in Portugal to get over jet-lag before going on to your rented apartment or villa. Book direct or through PLUM Courtesy (see profile in this section).

Quinta do Cortiçada and Quinta da Ferrarya
Rio Maior, Estremadura
Tel: 43–478–182

Just 60 miles north of Lisbon, this is a beautiful example of a "Turismo de Habitacão," worth the journey from Lisbon if only to stay for a night or two. There are large, beautiful rooms, a dining room, a pool, lovely grounds, and peace. Another example just a few miles away from Cortiçada, the Quinta da Ferrarya, is owned by the same family Nobra and offers several very attractive apartments as well as rooms, pool, restaurant, museum, and conference facilities. Arrange directly or contact FeriaSol.

Quinta Horta do Moura
Monsaraz,
Alentejo

This *quinta* is 35 miles in southeast of Evora, in southcentral Portugal near the border with Spain. An ancient walled city of especial archaeological interest for its Roman buildings, amphitheater, and artifacts. This is a new and unusual "resort." Built in architecturally old style, it is modern in every other respect: air-conditioned rooms with refrigerators, room service, and other grand hotel amenities including tennis courts and nearby golf. Magnificent horses are available (guided rides unless guests are very qualified). Apartments are two-bedroom and three-bedroom, two bath. The people of the walled town seem to be of another time. Government rating is four-star but is very conservative. Rates vary but are very modest for the quality of the place. This is a true retreat in a very out of the way area. Information and booking through Pinto Basto.

Quinta do Lomba
Gandomar, Douro
(Near Porto)

Here is a small two-bedroom private house with three rooms available in the main house. Although the town of Gandomar is not very appealing, this is a good base for anyone wanting to be in the Porto area and near the Douro River. Arrange through Pinto Basto or FeriaSol.

Casa das Requeijo
Requeijo
4970 Arcos de Valdevez, Minho
Tel: 58–65272   Fax: 58–63310

Apartments for two and four persons; an especially attractive ancient building in Arcos de Valdevez in the wooded hill country up the Rio Lima from Viana do Castelo. Arrange directly or through Pinto Basto or FeriaSol.

Quinta de Santo Antonio
Albergaria de Sa
4950 Monçao, Minho
Tel: 51–542–06 or 02–68–3228

This name was given to us by a Portuguese shop owner in Viana do Castelo, a woman who had lived in the U.S. and Canada for many years and who has returned home to Portugal. She thinks this is one of the best *quintas* of the north and is sure it would be a delight to North Americans. We did not visit it, but knowing the nature of most *quintas* and trusting our new Portuguese/American acquaintance, we would certainly give it a try. Contact direct for brochure and book direct; the owner/manager is Judite Ranhada Moreira.

Casa do Tamanquiero
Ponte de Lima, Minho

An ancient two-bedroom stone house on a farming estate near Ponte de Lima. A very private getaway but close to town where there are food stores and some good restaurants. Arrange through Pinto Basto or FeriaSol.

Casa das Torres
Arribao
4990 Ponte de Lima, Minho
Tel: 58–941–369

Apartments of four-star class in one of the most beautiful and much pho-
tographed ancient houses of Portugal. Splendid grounds. Near the little town of
Ponte de Lima, Minho Province, northern Portugal. Arrange directly or through
Pinto Basto or FeriaSol.

Chapter 11

SPAIN

Bay of Biscay

France

Santander   Biarritz

San Sebastián

Andorra

Roses

Estarif

San Feliu de Gixols   Palagrugeli

Lioret de Mar

Barcelona

Sitges

Tarragona

✸ Madrid

Toledo

BALEARIC ISLANDS

MENORCA

Palma

IBIZA   **MAJORCA**

Valencia

Ibiza

Benidorm   Moraira

Vila Joiosa

Alicante

Portugal

Córdoba

Ayamonte   Seville

Huelva

Mediterranean Sea

Málaga   Nerja   Almuñécar

Cadiz   Marbella   Almería

Estepona   Motril

Benalmádena

Algeciras   Sotogrande

Atlantic Ocean

Ceuta (Sp.)

Tangier

Morocco

National Tourist Offices of Spain:

665 Fifth Avenue
New York, NY 10022
Tel: (212) 759–8822

845 North Michigan Avenue
Chicago, IL 60611
Tel: (312) 642–1992

1221 Bricknell Avenue, Suite 1850
Miami, FL 33131
Tel: (305) 358–1992

8383 Wilshire Blvd., Suite 956
Beverly Hills, CA 90211
Tel: (213) 658–7188

60 Bloor St. West - 201
Toronto, Ontario M4W 3B8
Tel: (416) 961–3131

International Telephone Country Code: 34
City Codes: Madrid 1; Barcelona 3; Nerja 5
Example: To contact El Capistrano in Nerja, dial 011–34–5–252–2814.
Passport: Yes, but no Visa.
Language: Spanish; in addition, Catalan is spoken in the northeast, Buskadi in most of the Basque region bordering France, and Gallego in the state of Galicia. English is spoken in cities and areas frequented by tourists.
Currency: Peseta, abbreviated Pta., approximately 110 ptas. per U.S. dollars.
Value Added Tax (VAT): 15%
Electricity: 220v AC, 50 cycles.
Credit Cards: AMEX, VISA, MasterCard widely accepted; some Diners Club. Oil company cards not accepted for fuel; use cash or another credit card.
Main Destination Cities from North America: Madrid, Barcelona.

The Country

Spain has an area larger than California and almost double the population, which is heavily concentrated in the four largest cities: Madrid, Barcelona, Valencia, and Seville. The north-south and east-west highway distances, each almost 975 kilometers (600 mi.), makes it almost impossible to explore Spain from a single home-base location. This difficulty is further complicated by the fact that except for Madrid and Barcelona there are very few short-term rentals that are not on one of Spain's famous coasts.

Almost half of the country's 1,900-mile mainland coastline is washed by the Atlantic and the other half by the Mediterranean. Two thirds of the coastline is rugged, spectacularly beautiful, and beachless. The remaining 600 miles or so comprise some of the most desirable beaches in Europe. As for the seas, the Mediterranean is the warmest year-round, especially along the southern coast. In either ocean, swimming is possible from late April through most of October and is excellent between mid-May through September.

For foreigners, especially other Europeans, the popular destinations in Spain are the mainland south coastal areas and the Balearic and Canary islands. The south coast, being more easily accessible, is where the majority of vacation rentals are. Despite construction before the Olympic Games at Barcelona, there are relatively few short-term rental apartments available there. Nor is there a large selection in Madrid, Valencia, or other cities. This poses no great problem, however. A villa or apartment may be booked in an area close to a city or cities of special interest, enabling you to commute by train or rented car. In this way, the home base can be away from the crowded, more expensive city centers, while providing access to its resources. Each of the principal coastal areas has at least one city nearby. Clockwise around the peninsula from the north, Barcelona is on the Costa Brava, Tarragona is on the Costa Dorado, Valencia is a focus for the Costa del Alhazar, Alicante and Cartagena share the Costa Blanca, and the Costa del Sol runs from Almeria to Algeciras.

The two other coasts of mainland Spain, the Atlantic coast between the Strait of Gibralter and the border with Portugal (Costa de la Luz), and the north coast along the Cantabrian Sea are still not well developed for contemporary tourism. Perhaps it is a matter of time before they, too, become destinations dotted with resorts and villas. At present, however, except in urban areas, they are not heavily populated. Two of the cities in the north, San Sebastián and Santander, are old style resorts, developed in the last century and still enjoyed by travelers who prefer elegant nineteenth-century surroundings. We could find no company with rentals in or near these cities. Because the British, Scandinavians, and other Northern Europeans favor the break that the sunny south coast provides, the 30-mile-long Costa del Sol section is fairly congested. For many who drive south to the Costa del Sol or who fly into Málaga, it seems the only way to turn is westward to Torremolinos and Marbella and points in between. To North Americans who have never visited Spain, these towns on the Costa del Sol are the most recognizable. However, as the high-rises and villa clusters fill the space, developers are moving eastward. Despite the rampant development that has taken place along some of this beautiful coast, there remain many excellent places in which to spend several weeks. It just takes some effort to find them.

Best Times of Year to Visit

The coasts of Spain enjoy a relatively benign climate, but in the dead of winter there can be many uncomfortable days, even in the south. In fact, some of the apartment hotels and condominiums close during late November and December. Typically, however, March brings sunny, warm days to the south, and by April days on the northern Mediterranean coast and Balearic Islands are delightful and remain so into October. As elsewhere in Europe, it seems that the high season for prices has less to do with weather patterns than with the habits of European vacationers. Rental (and other) prices are therefore highest during the hot days of July and August, while in spring and fall they are either in the low or shoulder range.

Given the nature of the weather, the seasonal prices, and the patterns of European tourist travel, the best months for visiting the Costa del Sol are April, May, and early October. For visiting the Costa Blanca the best times are April, May, and September. For the northeast coasts (Costa Brava and Costa Dorada), May and September are optimum. The effect of the tourist seasons on rental prices can be seen in the table below.

As for Madrid and the interior, the winter months can be cold and unpleasant, and summer hot and dry. "Nine months of winter and three months of hell," is the saying for Spain's high, interior plateau. Apartment rates in the city seldom change with the seasons, so your decision on when to go can be determined by the weather and the tourist crowds. From mid-April to the end of May and again from late September to mid-October are the best months.

General Information About Rentals

Unlike the other large countries of Europe, the variety of vacation rentals in Spain is fairly limited in terms of type, style, and locations. For example, there are few rural farmhouses such as the *gîtes* of France or the big stone buildings that dot the countryside of Italy. There has been little done in the way of restoring and converting ancient buildings, either in the cities or rural areas. There are, however, many rentals to choose from, most of them newer apartments and villas, many built especially for purposes of renting. As described later in this chapter, they are located in the most popular areas along the seacoast and a small selection in the major cities.

Spain has long been aware of its attraction to visitors from around the world and has made an effort to make them comfortable. The apartments in the coastal resort towns are pleasant and adequately furnished and equipped. Villas in these areas are even more so, being spacious and usually well located. Unfortunately, many of the apartment buildings in the tourist population centers of the coast are overbuilt, crowded together in a way that detracts from the otherwise pleasant nature of the individual apartments. One solution is to carefully choose an individual villa. Another is to locate in one of the areas such as in Nerja and Sotogrande, where the rentals have been thoughtfully arranged to allow for plenty of air and green space. We have sought out such places and include them later in this chapter while avoiding inclusion of companies and apartments whose rentals are in locations of high population. It is always easy to find the excitement of crowds and bustle of markets and nightclubs, but it's nice to be able to leave them for some peace and privacy.

Rentals run the gamut in their standards from simple, inexpensive apartments and small houses to elaborate, elegant villas. Our impression from visits and having lived near Barcelona for half a year is that the best values are in the moderate to luxury range. That is, economy rentals, while neat and clean enough, may lack sufficient and suitable furnishings and kitchen and dinner supplies. Small beds create a problem for persons over six feet tall. Not many of these types of rentals are included in this book. Interhome is so large that there are economy rentals included, but they select well and provide adequate catalog descriptions. Companies like International Lodging Corp., established years ago in the U.S. by a Spanish family, help to make sure that apartments and individual villas of the south coast meet the requirements of discerning travelers.

Price Ranges

Although some price schedules show four or five seasonal prices, in general there are three, plus the Easter season. Called *Semana Santa,* Easter week begins to affect prices and availability two weeks before Easter Sunday, and takes a week to dwindle off. Much of Europe is on the move at this time, especially in predominantly Catholic countries such as Spain. On the one hand, the experience of spending the weeks around Easter in a Spanish city is profound, but crowded restaurants, hotels, and trains are to be expected. The Easter weeks are not included in the following seasonal price schedule, but prices at that time would be comparable to the high season and sometimes higher. These are *average* prices for a range of property types along the south coast. To these prices may be added local tax up to 6 percent and often a cleaning fee in the $30-per-week range. Some luxury villas can run up to $5,000 per week.

	Low Season Nov. 1–April 30	Shoulder Seasons May 1–June 15 Oct. 1–Oct. 30	High Season June 16–Sep. 30
Basic 1-bedroom apartment	$350	$450	$550
Deluxe 1-bedroom apartment	450	550	800
2-bedroom resort villa	650	800	1,050
2-bedroom private villa	900	1,000	1,700
Deluxe three-bdrm villa	1,500	1,650	2,000 +

All else being equal, the prices in the resort areas of the Costa del Sol and the Balearic Islands are somewhat higher than on the other coasts. Rents are lower if you are willing to take a place away from the sea in the hills above the Costa del Sol or a few kilometers back from the Costa Brava. If you want to spend less of your travel budget on your *finca* or apartment, tell the agency you are willing to be back from the coast. A *finca* is the Spanish word for a country house; it may be a farmhouse or a converted outbuilding of some sort. (It is always best to study the property description rather than be concerned with what it is called.)

If you are planning a week in Madrid and its vicinity, few apartments are available, but with the price of hotels there, renting for a week makes economic sense. A room in the five-star Ritz costs about $400 per night, and a small room in a modest hotel is about $85. By contrast, large, fully serviced, one-bedroom apartments in a good location can be found, such as the Apartamentos Plaza Basilica or Apartamentos Plaza de España which cost about $1,300 per week ($185 per night) for four persons in high season; a studio is about $1,000 per week.

Where to Stay: The Regions

The decision on where to locate your home base depends on whether the primary purpose of your visit is to explore as much of Spain as possible, or to remain within a single area and enjoy the beaches, sea, sunshine, and regional towns and cities. If you want to see such far-flung cities as Barcelona, Tarragona, Valencia, Granada, Córdoba, and Seville, for example, you will need two locations. Three weeks could reasonably be divided by spending one of them on the Costa Brava or Costa Dorada, with easy access to eastern Spain, and two weeks on the Costa del Sol or the less developed Costa Blanca. If Madrid fits into your plans, the best approach might be to take an apartment there for a few days. If so, visits to Toledo and Ávila should be included.

Personal inclinations are also important. If you prefer resort life, then the area between Málaga and Marbella, noted above, offers attractive choices, from condos to villas. A good apartment in this area is the Flathotel International in Benalmadena Costa between Málaga and Marbella. International Services also has a good selection there. (See the listings for both companies at the end of this chapter.)

For a less developed area, look into the resorts east of Málaga, in or near the villages of Torre del Mar, Nerja, Almuñécar and as far east as Almería. If more privacy is desired than a high-rise resort area affords, locate a villa (or an apartment in a villa) near a village. (See El Capistrano, in the rental companies section of this chapter.) Two other inviting destinations are the Balearic Islands, in the Mediterranean off the east coast, and the Canary Islands off the coast of Morocco, some 500 miles south of the Spanish mainland. More information on rentals on the islands is included in the regional sections below.

The competition among the companies with properties in resort developments is pretty fierce. At last count there were eighteen agencies in England alone representing properties on the Spanish coasts, mostly on the Costa del Sol.

For Europeans, who are accustomed to seeing great cathedrals, museums, and ancient buildings and monuments in their daily lives, but who have relatively little access to sun-warmed sandy beaches in the spring and autumn months, the resorts have a great appeal. Fortunately for North Americans, there are numerous cities and towns on the coast and nearby, behind the Sierra Nevada range, that are rich in the culture, history, and ambiance of Spain. A home base on the Costa del Sol or on the less tourist-impacted Costa Blanca, which stretches on to the northeast beyond Alicante, is ideal for exploring southern Spain as well as for basking in the sun.

The Regions

The forty-eight provinces in Spain are divided among ten formal regions, which include the Balearic Islands and the distant Canary Islands. As we have noted earlier, the vacation rental properties in Spain are concentrated in the coastal areas and the island groups. With the exception of Madrid and Barcelona, there are not many rentals available in the interior rural areas and cities. For the purpose of providing practical information or vacation rentals, we divided the country into four sections: the east and southern coasts on the mainland and the Balearic and Canary islands.

The Southern Coasts: Costa del Sol and Costa de la Luz
Environs and Accommodations

Andalucia, Spain's largest province, occupies the entire southern area of the Iberian Peninsula east of the Portuguese border. The coast east of the Strait of Gibralter along the Mediterranean is the very popular tourist area called the Costa del Sol. To the west of Gibralter, the Atlantic coast as far as the Portuguese border is the Costa de la Luz, far less populated and lacking the tourist magnetism of the Costa del Sol. Because of the differences in the development along the Costa del Sol, we have divided the long stretch in two for purposes of description.

Costa del Sol, West. Some of the communities of the western Costa del Sol are developments of villas clustered around swimming pools and resort shops. Some are arrangements of apartment buildings with access to pools and tennis courts, and some are combinations of both, replete with resortlike shopping centers to serve vacationers living in the high-rise condominiums and aparthotels. These resorts can be found scattered along most of the Costa del Sol, but are mainly concentrated along the 65 kilometers (40 mi.) between Málaga and Marbella. Beyond Marbella the resorts thin out a bit, but extend as far as Gibralter, across the small bay from Algeciras.

The most popular area in the western reaches of the Costa del Sol is in the vicinity of Sotogrande, where one of Europe's best golf courses shares the recreational space with tennis courts and riding paths. The resorts in this area are largely British and Northern European enclaves. (Inexpensive flights are available between Britain and British Gibralter, half an hour's drive away.)

Away from the coast lies what Andalusians regard to be the "true Spain." Here the ancient history of the country is still evident. It ranges from the Moorish influence seen in such marvels as the thirteenth-century Alhambra at Granada and the Mosque at Córdoba and also in the white villages that seem to spill from the hilltops. It is an area so rich with places to go and important things to see that a few weeks will seem like not nearly enough time.

The decision of where to stay along the 140 kilometers (85 mi.) west of Málaga is somewhat perplexing. An effective solution is to contact two or three companies or an apartment complex (like Flatotel International) listed at the end of this chapter and ask for brochures and prices. If you are looking for a resort in a less populated area, remember that the farther west from Málaga, the less is the concentration of resorts. (Or look east of Málaga.)

Costa del Sol, East. The coastal zone east from Málaga becomes less populated, punctuated by fewer towns and resorts than the western half, and toward its eastern extremities the landscape is drier and the summer days hotter. Development, of course, takes time, and it is under way in this region. Thirty miles east of Málaga, the town of Nerja, which we knew from an earlier visit as a quiet fishing village, has become the site for large-scale development, including villa "villages" and the Aparthotel Marinas, whose garish architecture vaguely resembles Caesar's Palace, or perhaps the Dunes, in Las Vegas. Although Nerja's city fathers placed a three-story limitation on buildings heights, the large proportions of many of these white resort buildings seem incongruous. Still, relative to the western part of the Costa del Sol, the area around Nerja and east to pretty Almuñecár is uncrowded and peaceful. Night life in the resorts and towns makes it interesting for those who like to play day and night.

If you are less inclined toward a resort atmosphere, then a villa or apartment along this eastern stretch is worth seeking out. A home base even as far east as Almería does not rule out visiting the region and cities of Cádiz, Seville, and Córdoba, although it adds a few hours to the journey. (It is approximately 230 kilometers between Almería and Málaga.) The stretch between Nerja and Almuñecár provides the best of both worlds, and both towns are good centers to be near.

An example of a restrained resort for this area is El Capistrano in Nerja, listed later in this chapter. With some 500 units in three "villages," it is nevertheless one of the most pleasing complexes in the area and offers separate villas, apartments, and what they call *pueblo villas*, villas with an upper and lower apartment in each one. The pueblo villas cascade down the hill, so there is a bit of walking involved. The lower units open onto small gardens, while most of the upper ones have views. The individual villas are arranged like a compact Mediterranean neighborhood and the apartments are in low-rise buildings. Most of the units are privately owned and are managed by the resort.

Costa de la Luz. The Atlantic coast from the Strait of Gibralter west to the town of Ayamonte on the border with Portugal is devoid of larger development for foreign tourists. Yet it is a beautiful coastline with long stretches of sandy beach, much of it bordered by pine-covered hills, and the climate is even better and the sea warmer than the popular Costa del Sol, to the east.

The beach resorts at Punta Umbria, Ayamonte, Sanlucar de Barrameda, and many others are good locations for enjoying the sea and for visiting the essential cities of Seville and Córdoba. We have found no agency that offers rental properties on the Costa de la Luz to overseas travelers. If you are interested in exploring the western provinces of Andalucia for a week, go in spring or early summer or fall. Take a hotel in Huelva, Sanlucar, or Cádiz and drive to the smaller coastal towns to look for apartments or villas to rent. Except in high season, you will see signs that read ALQUILER (to rent). The city of Cádiz is easy to manage, and the restaurants are very good. The countryside is strikingly beautiful, especially between Algeciras and Cádiz, with white villages spilling from the hilltops. A fruitful week can easily be spent in this area; before long it will surely be another sunshine mecca for northern Europeans, as is the Costa de Sol.

Location and Transportation

Andalucia is a region rich in resources, a place to get a good feeling for Spain. Except for Cádiz, the main cities of interest in the region are away from the coast, so although a home base on the Costa del Sol is great for sunshine, beaches, shops, and nightlife, it is not what can be experienced as the real Spain.

Flights from North America usually land in Madrid, with connections to Seville or Málaga. There is mainline rail service between Madrid and Cádiz via Linares, Córdoba, and Seville, and between Málaga and Madrid via Córdoba. There is also service to Algeciras, Granada, and Almería. Trains run every thirty minutes on the twenty-five-minute trip between Málaga and the resort towns just to the west, as far as Fuengirola via Torremolinos. There is no rail service along the Costa del Sol west of Fuengirola or east of Málaga; Marbella, Nerja, Almuñecár, Motril, and the stretch beyond Motril to Almería are not served by rail. The bus service is good, however, so much of Andalucia and all its principal cities can be seen by a combination of train and bus. For convenience and the freedom of getting into the smaller towns and exploring the stimulating scenery of the usually snow-clad Sierra Nevada, a car is very useful.

In addition to traveling within this region, consider getting a glimpse of North Africa. It is a simple matter to visit Tangier, Morocco, on a one-day trip.

Passenger ships leave several times daily from the commercial dock at Algeciras for the two and a half hour trip to Tangier. The easiest approach is simply to drive or take a taxi to the terminal of the ship line Trasmediterranea-Limadet, buy a round-trip ticket, and board. Before boarding, however, it is important to have your passport stamped for exit by the Spanish authorities. (See the sections on the Balearic Islands and the Canary Islands below for more information on travel to and from the mainland.)

Advance Booking Time

For July and August: 6 months.
For June and September: 4–5 months.
For the rest of the year: 3 weeks, or rent on arrival

The East Coast: Costa Blanca, Costa del Alhazar, Costa Dorada, and Costa Brava

Environs and Accommodations

The Costa Blanca is the southernmost section of the east coast, connecting to the Costa del Sol as the peninsula turns northward. It runs some 230 miles and includes the east coast of Andalucia, the region of Murcia, and the southern half of Valencia region. The "nose" of Cabo San Martin and Cabo San Antonio, northeast of the city of Alicante, delineates the line between the Costa Blanca and the Costa del Alhazar, which runs northward along the sweep of the Golfo de Valencia. The next coastal segment is the Costa Dorada, which begins south of Tarragona and runs past Barcelona, where it becomes the more rugged Costa Brava, running northward to the border with France. There are many miles of beaches, a half-dozen important cities, and dozens of resort towns along this sun-bathed Mediterranean coast. Development for foreign tourists has been selective and is concentrated in the most attractive areas.

The Costa Blanca and Costa del Alhazar have been declared by some meteorologists to have the best climate in the world. The Costa Blanca stretch of the Mediterranean coast is second only to the Costa del Sol in popularity among travelers and vacationers who come to Spain. Whether to stay in this area or on the Costa del Sol is a difficult decision, as both have similar resort styles and much to do to occupy one's time and interest. The sense of a less concentrated tourist population than in the Málaga-Marbella area is certainly a plus, and it is not hard to find isolation in the dry country south of Alicante.

To the north of the Costa Blanca, along the Gulf of Valencia, is the Costa del Alhazar. The northern half of this area is a mixture of ports, resorts, industrial towns, rice paddies, and the vast groves that produce 25 million tons of oranges and lemons for Europe's markets. The main city of the Costa del Alhazar (orange blossom coast) is Valencia, the colorful river city of oranges and flowers.

In the hinterlands, Albacete and Murcia can be visited on day trips.

The best of the independent villas are offered by the British company Something Special, listed at the end of this chapter. By far the greatest number and variety of properties have been amassed by the giant Swiss company, Interhome, also listed below. Some of the coastline is dominated by hotels and apartment complexes, but there are scattered, often privately owned, villas available in the hills overlooking the coast. Look especially at smaller towns like Altea, Javea, and Moraira. A good, typical, mid-rise resort apartment hotel is the Eurotennis at Vilajoyosa (see description below).

In May to mid-June and from mid-September on it is possible to find a rental in this region after your arrival. Check the local tourist office, real estate agents (*immobilieres*), or look for signs saying ALQUILER (to rent). Book a hotel in Alicante or Valencia for a day or two and look for a place that suits your tastes on the coast. English is widely spoken.

Location and Transportation

An international airport serves Valencia, but often the best arrangement for transatlantic flights is via Madrid. Mainline rail service runs between Valencia and Madrid, Alicante and Madrid, and along the coast between Valencia and Alicante (except for a section between Gandia and Denia). The only way of going by train between the resort towns of Denia and Javea, mentioned above, and Valencia, is to go through Alicante and change there to a local. Good bus service is available also.

Other than journeys to the inland cities and up and down the coast, a voyage to the Balearic Islands for two or three days is interesting and fun. Passenger ships depart six days a week from Valencia and Palma de Mallorca on the seven-hour voyage between them. There are sailings between Valencia and Ibiza four times a week (two in winter); plan carefully, as you will need to stay on Ibiza at least two days. The fares are modest, the ships are pleasant, and the food is good. Unless you want a cabin, just take a taxi (or your car) to the terminal at the dock, buy your ticket, and board. If the taxi driver doesn't speak English, say "Trasmediterranea, al Grao de Valencia." (It is pronounced TRAS-Mediterranea—without an N in the first syllable.) For an extended adventure, many travelers book a round-trip from Valencia to Ibiza, sail on to Mallorca, and then either return or continue to Barcelona, returning to Valencia by rail. If you want a cabin or would like to plan the longer itinerary, it is best to book in advance through a travel agency in Valencia, Alicante, or another major town, or from North America, telephone 011–44–71–491–4968 two months in advance.

Prices

Prices are a little less on the east coast than on the Costa del Sol. They vary widely, but typically a studio in a resort high-rise can be rented for under $300 per week in the shoulder months; a one-bedroom in the same type of building is under $400. A small, modest, but comfortable two-bedroom private house is in the $500-per-week range, jumping to $700 in the peak months of July and August. A good quality three-bedroom private house for seven persons with a pool, terrace, and sea view is properly priced at about $1,100 per week year-round except for the peak months when it costs $1,500. Linen may cost extra.

Advance Booking Time:

For July and August: 6 months.
For June and September: 2–3 months.
The rest of the year: 0–six weeks.

The Coasts of Cataluña

The region of Cataluña, comprising the provinces of Tarragona, Lérida, Gerona, and Barcelona, is a complex area of cosmopolitan cities and simple villages. The mix of languages (Spanish and Catalán), the seaside resorts and snow-capped Pyrenees, and the monasteries, cathedrals, and vineyards provide variety and interest for any visitor.

The rental properties in this region are mostly along the coasts, but even there they are not as concentrated as they are on the Costa del Sol. Nevertheless, summertime means crowded beaches and full accommodations, especially along the south end of the Costa Brava, which is popular with European tourists. Considering the crowds and the weather, by far the best times of year to visit Cataluña are from mid-April to mid-June and again in September (except for the two weeks around Easter).

The coast of Cataluña is about 250 miles long; the southern two-thirds is designated the Costa Dorada and the northern third the Costa Brava. In the center are many miles comprising the busy port of Barcelona.

Costa Dorada. Valencia's Costa del Alhazar becomes the Costa Dorada or coast of gold, just south of Tarragona. The resort towns along the southern two-thirds of this coast and the land that borders it are not impressive, which may explain why this is not an area particularly favored by British or American tourists (or rental agencies). Our view is that a wonderful week or more can be spent in Cataluña exploring, shopping, eating, and looking. Wander through the wine country of Penedes and make the compelling trip to Montserrat. For a beach-based vacation we would go to the south. In this region there is too much else to see and do, and the beach areas will likely be a disappointment. Although we lived for several months in the delightful small town of Sitges (pronounced SEE-jus), this is about as far south in this region as we would want to stay. From

Sitges, which is just 20 miles south of Barcelona, or from Barcelona itself, day trips are the way to visit Tarragona and the important monasteries of Santus Creus and Poblet.

North of Barcelona, the Costa Dorada extends another 40 miles or so, its southern reaches distinguished by the impact of Barcelona's population on formerly quiet fishing towns such as Premia de Mar, Mataró, Arynes de Mar and Canet de Mar. There is little point in trying to find a home base there when there are more favorable areas just up the coast.

As for Barcelona itself, like most large cities it is a mix of the good and the bad, and like cities everywhere, it is expensive. It is vital and busy, full of great restaurants, stores, museums, parks, theaters, and churches. A week or more spent there in an apartment would be stimulating and full. It is also a good home base from which to explore surrounding Cataluña. The railroad runs along the coast and into the interior, so it is easy to visit the main cities and towns of the region. If you have two weeks or more for this region, a week in the city and one somewhere on the Costa Brava would be an excellent combination. The bus and subway systems are very good, so a car is not necessary.

Costa Brava. Forty miles northeast of Barcelona, the main coast highway turns inland toward Girona, and a branch highway continues along the Costa Brava. It is an exciting coastline; craggy mountains lift from the sea and the road follows their contours, rising to the heights and then dropping back to sea where the towns settle along the coves and sandy beaches.

The largest of the resort towns of the Costa Brava is the southernmost, Blanes (pronounced BLAH-ness), with 3 miles of sandy beaches. Other popular towns strung along the coast are Lloret de Mar, Tossa de Mar, San Feliú de Guixols (pronounced gwee-SHOL), and Platja d'Aro (pronounced PLAT-ya), pleasant places that are crowded in summer. Northward other small towns dot the coast: Palamós (which is not enticing), Estartit, Playa de Pals, and around the Golfo de Rosas, the villages of La Escala, Roses, and Cadaques. These are less affected by tourist development than the resorts nearer to Barcelona. In general, the farther north of Barcelona, the less is the impact of other tourists. The dilemma is that the farther north one stays, the more time-consuming is the travel to the Barcelona area. The 75 miles between Figueras and Barcelona on the *autopista* (toll freeway) pass quickly, however.

Because the Catalan coast stretches out with one major city in the middle, where to stay is a hard decision. We suggest eliminating the southern half (south of Sitges) from consideration. The next decision depends on whether a city base or a village base has more appeal. The city, of course, means Barcelona. For a coastal town base not far from Barcelona and within reasonable striking distance of Montserrat and Tarragona, look to the southerly towns of the Costa Brava:

Blanes, the larger Lloret de Mar, and Tossa de Mar. If you don't mind being as far as 100 miles from Barcelona and might be interested in forays into France, the towns of Rosas and Santa Margarita would be good choices for smaller towns, while the larger Escala and Ampuriabrava have a greater selection of rentals.

In the off-season, especially from October through March, it is not difficult to find a rental by simply driving around looking for ALQUILER signs. This is a good way to find the best possible value: renting directly from the owners. Look especially along the Costa Brava highway north of Lloret del Mar and south of Palamós; attractive villas and small villa groups are tucked along this winding and dramatic road.

When describing to a rental company what you want, make sure you specify whether or not you are seeking an apartment in a high-rise or in a smaller building; it is often assumed that Americans like high-rise living.

Location and Transportation

It is hard but not impossible to explore Cataluña from one home base in the region. If you stay near Barcelona, for example, it is a four-hour drive up the Costa Brava to the French border (two hours by *autopista*), two hours south to Tarragona, and another two hours south to Valencia by car or train. Overnight visits to the French cities of Narbonne and Carcassone are possible, and four hours northwest from Barcelona will find you high in the Pyrenees, into the Principality of Andorra. The railroad follows the coast south of Barcelona all the way to Valencia. It travels northward only as far as Blanes, however. There is bus service between all the towns of the Costa Brava.

Port-to-port passenger ships sail daily between Barcelona and the Balearic Island ports of Palma de Mallorca, Ibiza, and Mahon. The voyage durations vary from eight to ten hours, and it is possible to take an itinerary through the Balearics, stopping for an hour or so at each port or staying over and catching a ship the next day. The ship line also offers relatively inexpensive weekend cruises called *cruceros-fin de semana* through the Balearics, returning to Barcelona. Contact any travel agent in Barcelona, or go to the Trasmediterranea terminal at the harbor in Ramblas. For high season, book two to three months in advance (phone 011–44–71–491–4968).

Prices

With the exception of apartments in Barcelona, rent prices along the coasts of Cataluña are much as they are along the entire east coast. In low and shoulder seasons a typical studio in an area on or near the sea will cost about $300 per week, jumping to $450 in July and August. A one-bedroom apartment will range from $400 to $600, while a luxury villa with a pool for six to eight persons will average $1,000 in the shoulder months and $1,500 to $2,000 in the peak months. Apartments in Barcelona can often be rented by the night or for a three-night minimum and cost from $100 per night for a studio to $150 for a one bedroom. We had a comfortable one-bedroom apartment at the four-star Victoria apartment hotel in a fashionable part of the city for $175; a block away a five-star hotel charged $325 for a standard room.

Advance Booking Time

July and August: 6 months.
June and September: 1–2 months.
Rest of the year: 0–3 weeks.

The Balearic Islands:
Mallorca, Menorca, Ibiza, and Formentera
Environs and Accommodations

Clustered between 70 and 210 miles off the east coast of the mainland (or peninsula, as it is often referred to) lie the *Islas Baleares*, the Balearic Islands. There are three major islands, one smaller one, and a scattering of islets. By highway across the largest island, Mallorca (pronounced May-OR-cah), it is roughly 100 kilometers (60 mi.), while Menorca is about 50 kilometers at its widest, and from Ibiza town to the north tip of the island it is under 35 kilometers. Much is packed into the relatively small area of these islands, from beautiful isolated beaches to the international sophistication of Palma de Mallorca, the largest city of the Balearics, with a population of over a quarter of a million people.

The islands had for years been a playground for Spanish and other European aristocracy before they became increasingly popular with vacationers, beginning in the 1920s. They are now the destination of hundreds of thousands of tourists each year; about half of them visit during July and August.

Mallorca is, on the whole, the most settled island and has the greatest permanent and summer tourist populations. Its capital, Palma is a settled resort city, the sweep of the Paseo Maritima along the harbor conveying a sense of permanence. Elsewhere on Mallorca, the small coastal towns have become resort towns developed around the older villages. Many are in beautiful settings with good beaches, restaurants, and shops. In addition to the apartments available in the vicinity of Palma, and in villages like Valldemosa and Soller, and in large new developments, there are numerous private villas and *fincas* available for rent. They are scattered throughout the island; some are fairly basic, but most are deluxe, and many have pools and gardens. The best place to stay for one or two weeks on Mallorca naturally depends to a large extent on your budget. The privacy of a *finca* will cost more than an apartment in a resort development or in Palma, and the island is small enough that all of it can be explored from any location. Mallorca is the only one of the islands with a small, low range of hills, which makes its northwest coast especially pleasant.

Ibiza is as popular as Mallorca, providing an unusual mixture of luxury *fincas* and private villas. Ibiza town surrounds a harbor on the southern coast of the island and is dominated by D'Alt Vila, the old city, built on a hill over the foundations of the Moorish settlement. Outside the walls of D'Alt Vila, the town can hardly be called modern, although many of the old buildings house a great variety of the most modern and trendy boutiques and shops in the Balearics. Three cultures exist on the island: the culture of the past, as manifested in the rural people and their ways and language; the neon culture of the young; and the culture of the mix, permanent residents and the tourists which flow through the resort enclaves.

Ibiza is different things to different people who go there. The nightlife of the town and its sidewalk cafes and discotheques draw some, while the tranquility afforded by an exclusive villa in an isolated part of the island appeals to others. Everyone's pleasure is heightened by the sea, the beaches, and the laid-back life. The entire permanent population of the island is only about 20,000.

Second largest of the Balearics, Menorca is the one off the beaten track, although that is a relative matter. There are indeed tourist developments, a golf club or two, delightful small towns and restaurants, but overall Menorca is less directed toward the tourist economy than the other two destination islands. The 125 miles of coastline is scalloped with coves and sandy beaches and is far less crowded than the more popular beaches of Mallorca and Ibiza. Life is slower paced here, and it is easier to get away from the developed areas and find isolation. Both the capital, Mahon (pop. 18,000), and Ciudadela across the island are very nice towns. The latter is one of the most attractive on the islands. As for deciding on which of the islands to stay, one solution is a week on each, or if your time is short, a week on each of two.

After the *Semana Santa* period, two weeks before Easter and the week after, there is a period until early June when the weather is generally excellent, the tourist crowds are thinner, and the prices are lower. Peak summer season is July, August, and most of September. Shoulder seasons are between the end of the Easter holidays and July 1 and again in October. April, except for Easter weeks, is sometimes a fourth season for prices, which are just a notch above the lowest. Low season is November through March, with a possible peak for the Christmas holidays. Winter is mild, but as Chopin discovered while staying in Valldemosa, Menorca in 1839, it can be depressingly gray and rainy. The sad music he wrote there must have reflected the weather.

A look at price lists indicates that rentals are perhaps a little less on Menorca than on the other islands, but this is bound to change. In addition, the properties tend to be in the upper middle to luxury categories, with only a scattering of the more modest. There are not the hundreds of rentals to choose from on Menorca as there are on the Costa del Sol and other mainland destinations, but there are certainly enough to offer a good choice.

Transportation

There are several flights daily between Barcelona, Valencia, Madrid, and other mainland cities and the Balearics as well as direct flights into Palma from other major cities of Europe. The bus system on all the islands is adequate, but there are no railroads. If you rent a place outside of the main towns or resort areas, a car is a must. If you have a car on the mainland, it can be ferried with you from Barcelona or Valencia and, once you are there, between the islands. Rental cars are available in Palma, Ibiza, and Mahon, however, and the cost of ferrying a car is fairly high.

One of the most pleasant, leisurely, and inexpensive ways to travel to and from the mainland and between the islands is on one of the ships of the government-owned Trasmediterranea line. (See Barcelona and Valencia, above.)

Prices

There is of course enormous variation in rental prices, depending on season, size, and standards, but the prices listed below will give you an idea of what you can expect. The high season is longer and later on the islands and can stretch from mid-July through September and often into October (check the price lists carefully). The shoulder and low seasons are not easily distinguishable here; sometimes there is a single, off-season rate or else very little difference between the prices of the two seasons.

	Low	Shoulder	Peak
Simple studio apartment (Menorca)	$350	$400	$700
Modest 2-bedroom apartment in villa (Menorca)	425	475	750
Seaside studio (Mallorca)	500	525	800
Two-star, 2-bedroom sea view (Mallorca)	700	750	1,150
Two-star, 3-bedroom seaview villa (Ibiza)	950	1,250	2,100
Luxury 3-bedroom seaside villa (Ibiza, Mallorca)	2,700	2,700	4000 +

Advance Booking Time

July, August, September: 6 months.
June and October: 2–3 months.
Rest of the year: 2 weeks from overseas or rent on site

The Rental Companies of Spain

The rental companies, resorts, and apartments profiled below represent a wide range of standards, styles, and prices in desirable areas to visit. There are others, but these are the easiest to work with, the most responsive to inquiries, and the fairest in pricing.

Along the popular coastal areas, especially the Costa del Sol, are literally hundreds of rentals; during the off-season it is not difficult to find a rental by inquiring at a local tourist office or stopping at any of the many resorts and apartment hotels. At other times and to find a choice villa, it is important to book ahead.

Albaida Club Menorca

Menorca, Balearic Islands

Urbanazacion Torre Soli Nou
E-07730 Alayor, Menorca
Tel: 71–37–2423   Fax: 71–37–2423

This is a four-star resort comprising twenty attractive looking villas in an ecologically protected area near Son Bou Beach on the south coast of Menorca.

Prices range from about $440 for two in off-season (May and October) to $1,225 for a villa for four in August. Given the beauty of the island, we would not hesitate to book a week here. Contact them for a brochure and weekly rates. Reserve by credit card; payment can be made after arrival.

Apartamentos Playa Club

Lanzarote, Canary Islands

Pedro Barba, 3
E-35572 Puerto del Carmen
Lanzarote,
Canary Islands
Tel: 28–82–619   Fax: 28–51–0906

Playa Club is a low-rise resort on the southeast coast of Lanzarote, not far from Arrecife, the capital city. The gardens are a beautiful surprise in the desert landscape, the resort overall we remember as being a gem. There is a restaurant, bar, and we assume that the apartments are as attractive as the rest of the surroundings. Prices for a studio for two or three persons costs about $450 per week in low season (May, June, and October to mid-December); at peak it is only 7 percent more. An apartment for four or five persons runs from $575 to $600. Payment is made by credit card. A rental can be booked for less than a week here. If we were planning a visit to Lanzarote we would be comfortable booking here.

Apartamentos Waldorf   Madrid city
Eustaquio Rodriguez, 8
28003 Madrid
Tel: 91–553–5201   Fax: 91–535–1622
U.S. agent: Barclay International Group, listed below.

This is a small building with sixteen apartments in a residential setting due north of the city center. Prices and standards are moderate, and the apartments are well kept and clean. This is not the most convenient location, but it's easy to get to the city center and the apartments are otherwise a very good value. Pay with a personal check in U.S. dollars or with a credit card.

Barcelona Las Ramblas   Barcelona city
122, Ramblas
08022 Barcelona
Tel: 1–47–25–5454   Fax: 1–47–25–4918
U.S. agents: Barclay International Group and Keith Prowse & Co., listed below.

Because it was under construction, we did not see this building of 131 studios and two-room apartments, but we have stayed in and enjoyed other apartments of the French Citadines chain, which owns this property. It is in an ideal location in the city center on the famous Ramblas, just off the Plaza Cataluña. From the literature, this looks like a very good bet for a stay in Barcelona. On the premises are a reception desk, lounge, bar, breakfast room, laundry, solarium, and car park. We would book this with confidence, knowing the location and the Citadines' reputation for comfortable and well-equipped formulaic apartments at moderate prices.

A brochure and price list are available. Book directly or try Barclay or Keith Prowse or contact Citadines (profiled in chapter 6). Deposit and payment are made by major credit card.

Barclay International Group   Barcelona and Madrid
150 East 52nd Street
New York, NY 10022
Tel: (800) 845–6636; or (212) 832–3777 Fax: (212) 753–1139

One of the principal U.S. agents for Citadines' Barcelona Las Ramblas (see listing above) and Waldorf apartments in Madrid.

Can Negret Apartamentos   Costa Dorada
Avenida Balmins, 1
08870 Sitges (Barcelona)
Tel: 3–894–5360

We lived here for several months in 1984 and still find the town of Sitges a delight. These two small apartment buildings are adjacent to a vine-covered parking area and garden. One building is immediately across a quiet street from the crescent-shaped beach, and one faces the garden. Both have wonderful views along the beach to a promontory on which a church and museum stand. Along the crescent is a row of shops, cafes, and a small hotel. It is an idyllic setting, the northern end of a small resort town just 20 miles south of Barcelona. The new highway is excellent and trains run often into the city as well as south to Tarragona and on to Valencia.

The eighteen apartments are simple, comfortable, and quiet. The town is well located for day trips to Barcelona, Montserrat, the outstanding Monastir de Santus Creus, the wine center of Penedes and the Rioja region, and Tarragona. Can Negret is a small family operation. It is not marketed in North America and the apartments are not easy to book. Some of the family members speak English, so unless you are fluent in Spanish, the best approach is to telephone, ask for a person who speaks English, and explain your requirements and the dates you need. We have no preference for one building over the other. The one facing the garden is quietest; the one on the avenue is across from the sea.

The prices are very modest, ranging from about $250 per week from April through October for the smallest studio to $350 for a one-bedroom in peak (July and August) and about $395 for their best and most spacious. Because of these modest prices, we suggest booking one of the larger apartments with the best view. Their best apartments cost $320 per week in April, May, June, and September, ideal times to be there. Lower prices can be negotiated from November through March. Once you confirm your dates, tell Can Negret that you will be sending a bank draft in pesetas, then airmail it to Apartado Correos 143, 08870 Sitges. There will be a 6 percent tax and a $35 final cleaning bill added, to be paid on arrival.

El Capistrano
Urbanazacion El Capistrano - Centro Commercial
Apartado 193
29780 Nerja
Tel: 5–252–2813   Fax: 5–252–2814

Earlier, we described the town and area of Nerja as among the most pleasant along the rapidly changing Costa del Sol, and this resort village of townhouses, low apartments, small villas, and bungalows is the nicest in the area. There is little or no sense of crowding. A variety of accommodation types and sizes is available, some privately owned and therefore reflective of their owners' taste and style. We stayed in a bungalow with a rooftop terrace and walled garden that was modestly furnished but comfortable and pleasant. The prices are relatively low, ranging from about $225 per week for a studio in low season to

$500 for the same studio in July and August. A one-bedroom townhouse runs from about $270 to $610; a two-bedroom villa from $400 in low season to $980 in high. With these prices, one might consider renting a larger place than is required. The villas and larger accommodations are better located than the studios. If you rent one of the latter, request one back from the main highway.

On the premises are a central reception, small grocery store, laundry facilities, and restaurant. General Manager Manuel Martinez observes that the community of El Capistrano is operated very much like a full-service hotel, except that there are villas and apartments instead of rooms.

There is no problem at all with language, and booking is made easy. Phone or fax for a brochure and tariffs. Once you have decided, contact again to confirm and set dates. El Capistrano does not require a deposit, but we suggest that you give your credit card number to confirm. Final payment can be made after arrival. This is a well-managed and sophisticated operation, a delight to be in.

Suzanne B. Cohen Agency   South Coast, Balearic Islands

94 Winthrop Street
Augusta, ME 04330
Tel: (207) 622–0743 Fax: (207) 622–1902

Suzanne B. Cohen is a small, personal agency representing, among a select few, a fairly large British company called CV Travel. It does an excellent job of locating, displaying, and renting properties, mostly villas and other independent houses, in Spain, Portugal, and the Islands of Sardinia (Italy), Corsica (France), and Corfu (Greece). Based in London, CV (which stands for Corfu Villas) represents a very nice selection of rentals. Most of the rentals are large and of superior standard, ideal for families or for traveling companions looking for privacy, space, and beautiful locations. This is an excellent source of better villas in the Balearic islands of Mallorca and Menorca. The prices are moderate and fair, in the $700 to $1,200 per-week range for villas for four to six persons. Their U.S. agent adds no commission and makes finding and booking easy. Ms. Cohen is selective about the companies and properties she works with and always has her clients' best interests in mind. She also represents a selection of more modestly priced rentals, so be sure to ask for advice if you find no CV property that suits you.

All of the CV Travel properties throughout the Mediterranean countries and Portugal are in a colorful and accurate catalog available from the Suzanne Cohen agency; the cost is $3.00, postpaid, and is well worth it. Classic hotels are also available through the company. Payment can be made by personal check or credit card at the prevailing exchange rate on the day of booking.

Eurotennis   Central Costa Blanca
Paraje Montiboli, s/n
E-03570 Villajoyosa (Alicante)
Tel: 65–89–1250   Fax: 65–89–1194

This large combined hotel and apartment building is a three-star resort on
the beach, 2 miles from the small town of Villajoyosa (Vila Joiosa in Catalan), on
the sun-bathed southeast Costa Blanca. It is very much a tennis resort, with
twenty courts and a pro running the academy. Also offered are a well-equipped
workout room, mountain bike rentals, saunas, fitness programs, and a splendid
pool. The garden area is beautifully subtropical and the cove is small but pretty.
The nearest long sand beach, however, is at Paradiso, about ½ mile away.

Eurotennis is quite apart from the many high-rise hotels and apartments
that stand virtually next to each other in many of the resort towns such as
Benidorm and Villajoyosa along this coast. It stands alone at the end of a narrow
road that leads to a cove between two rocky hills. A full-service hotel is associated with the apartments, and its services can supplement the basic apartment
amenities. The restaurant, bar, and cafe/lounge are comfortable and appealing.
There is a small grocery store on the premises.

A brochure and price list will be sent for the asking; the rates are per night
(there is no minimum stay), with a 10 percent discount for rentals by the month.
Rates are reasonable, typically Pts 8,000 (about $70) per night for a sea-view stu-
dio in off-season and $120 in August. Go any month other than August if possi-
ble. The reservation can be held by credit card and the balance paid after
arrival.

Flatotel International   Central Costa del Sol
Puerto Marina
Darsena de Pontiente
Benalmádena Costa
29630 Málaga
Tel: 52–44–00–33   Fax: 52–44–04–67

On an isthmus between the marina and the sea, literally in the harbor of
Puerto Marina, this large "3 key" low-rise apartment building is in one of the
most pleasant locations of this populated area of the coast. It offers excellent services: twenty-four hour reception, maid service three times a week, linen change
weekly, towel change daily, and in season a rooftop pool, bar, and solarium. The
air-conditioned apartments are especially spacious, light, nicely designed, and
livable. There are one-, two-, and three-bedroom apartments available, all with
balconies and one bathroom for each bedroom. The kitchens are large, modern,
and equipped with dishwashers and microwaves; off each kitchen is a pantry

housing a washer-dryer. We found the staff delightful, helpful, and full of ideas on where to go and what to see.

Flatotel is a small chain of seven apartment hotels: the other six are located in Paris, Brussels, the French Riviera, and New York City. Its name derives from joining the words flat (for apartment) and hotel, signifying that they are serviced apartments with 24 hour reception and maid service. They are known for their good value. A large one-bedroom in Puerto Marina, for example, rents for about $375 per week in low season (January through March), about $550 in high season (last 2 weeks of July, September, and Easter weeks), and $700 in August (peak). A two-bedroom ranges from around $465 to $835, and a three-bedroom from $600 to $1,050. Given the size, high standards, and good location of the apartments, these are excellent values. Nightly rates are available.

Benalmádena Costa is principally a resort town, small but busy, less congested than Marbella or Torremolinos, and ideally located in central Costa del Sol. Its proximity to Marbella and its shops, restaurants, and nightlife is an asset, but Benalmádena is nice to come "home" to. A drive inland over the high coastal range to the old walled city of Ronda is very worthwhile.

Phone or fax for a brochure and price list, if you wish. Book as you would a hotel, confirming by credit card; the final payment by credit card (or cash or traveler's checks) can be made upon arrival.

Hotel Apartamentos El Rocio   Costa de la Luz
Sector - L Parcelas 68-69
E-21760 Matalascañas-Huelva
Tel: 55–44–0350 Fax: 55–44–0164

A rather boxy low-rise apartment near the beach, this is one of the few apartments that can be easily booked in this extreme southwestern coast, the Costa de la Luz, bordering Portugal's Algarve. One advantage of the location is that it is near one of Europe's main wildlife sanctuaries, the Doñana Natural Park; another is that the area is less developed than the Costa del Sol. It is also within easy visiting distance of Seville (60 mi.) as well as the interesting old city of Huelva. Unfortunately, this is a summer operation and is closed from October 31 to May 15. This says something about the state of development in the area. Although we could not visit the apartments, they are considered three-star by the government, so we are confident that they are quite acceptable. Telephone or fax for a brochure and price list. Payment can be made by credit card.

Hotel Apartamentos Victoria   Barcelona city
Avenida Pederalbes, 16 bis
08034 Barcelona
Tel: 93–280–1515   Fax: 93–280–5267
U.S. agent: International Lodging Corp., listed below.

We were initially concerned that the Victoria's location in a semiresidential area was too far from the city center, but we found that it is in a center of its own, close to the new U.S. Consulate, an immense new El Corte Inglés department store, shops, restaurants, and other major hotels. Although the immediate neighborhood is quiet, the aparthotel is just one long block off the great boulevard Diagonal, which provides direct access to the city center.

This is a four-star aparthotel with twenty-four-hour reception, an attractive lobby, a restaurant, pool, garage, and maid service. It is the only one of the respected HUSA chain's hotels that offers apartments, which must be requested specifically, or you may find that the kitchen and dining area are not equipped. A spacious one bedroom (there are no studios) rents for about 25,000 pesetas about $175 per night in high season. A two bedroom for four persons is about $235 per night. Ask the agent for the lowest price possible, and always request a weekly rate if you plan on staying more than a few nights. Bear in mind that this is a four-star city hotel in a desirable area. There is a parking garage beneath the building and a metro stop nearby, as well as buses. We recommend that you avoid driving to the city center. Payment is made by personal check in U.S. dollars or credit card.

Interhome   Throughout Spain including Balearics and Canaries
124 Little Falls Road
Fairfield, NJ 07004
Tel: (201) 882–6864   Fax: (201) 808–1742

With its home office in Zurich, Interhome is Europe's largest rental company. The prices will be higher than by booking directly with Spanish rental companies, but the trade-offs are the vast selection that Interhome offers and the color catalogs that not only describe properties and locations but also give a pictorial overview of the regional architecture. Note that not many Interhome rentals in Spain include towels and bed linens; they are customarily rented locally, so advise Interhome that you want them. Payment of the linen rent, local taxes, and any other extras (some charge for utilities) is made to the owner or keyholder upon arrival.

Contact the company for their catalog for Spain; the price is under $5.00 postpaid. Make your choices (at least three), contact Interhome again and give your dates and the property reference numbers. Discounts are often offered,

Located in Elviria, the La Mairena townhouse is situated high atop a hill overlooking the coastline. (Courtesy International Lodging Corporation)

especially in the off-season, so be sure to ask about them. Thanks to their hookup with a main computer in Zurich, they will notify you about availability either the same day or the next. They will inform you about payment—personal check is preferred—and procedures. Upon final payment, full directions and instructions will be sent. Note that with this company cancellation insurance is automatically provided unless you specifically say that you do not want it; at a fee of 3 percent of the total rent it is worth considering. (See the Interhome profile in chapter 12, Switzerland.)

International Lodging Corp.   Throughout Spain, including the Balearic
300 First Avenue, Suite 7C   Islands
New York, NY 10069
Tel: (212) 228–5900   Fax: (212) 677–1815

Perhaps the best North American source for apartments and villas in Spain, this company was founded over a decade ago by a Spanish couple. They have since retired, having turned over the operation to their daughter Josephine Santos. The company remains very specialized, focusing on Spain exclusively. International Lodging represents a number of hotels as well as apartments, aparthotels, and individual villas, and they know the territory very well. Ms. Santos and her staff select the properties carefully, inspect them regularly, never charge more than the published rates, and sometimes charge less.

Their Costa del Sol properties range from apartments on the sea to villas in the hills, mostly in the area between Marbella and Estepona, with a few more in the Mijas-Benalmádena area. In the Balearic Islands there are villas and apartments on Mallorca, Menorca, and Ibiza, all as carefully selected as on the mainland. Just ask for property descriptions.

In addition to Hotel Apartamentos Victoria in Barcelona, listed above, International Lodging represents two other aparthotels, the San Gill, in a restored historic building in Seville, and Los Jerónimos, a block from the Prado Museum in Madrid. Both are excellent choices.

There is a general brochure available for the asking, but the best approach is to let them know what you are looking for. They will respond with several detailed, illustrated description sheets for properties that meet your criteria. If you are not sure where you want to be, call them for ideas. Some of the larger villas include staff, or in most cases staff can be arranged for. Booking is easy: Just confirm the choice by fax or phone. Payment is by personal check or traveler's check. For hotels and aparthotels, you can secure your reservation with a credit card and pay on arrival (or upon checking out). Confirmation, directions, and any instructions will be mailed immediately. This is a well-managed company that knows its specialty: Spain.

Keith Prowse & Co. (USA) Ltd.   Barcelona and Madrid
234 West 44th Street
New York, NY 10036
Tel: (800) 669–8687 or (212) 398–1430   Fax: (212) 302–4251

Keith Prowse represents two apartment buildings in Barcelona and three in Madrid. This is the independent U.S. office of a large old English company with a good selection of apartments in Europe. The company is included here because it is a good resource, and no commission is added. Unless you want to discuss anything with the Spanish reservations offices, phone Prowse to book a rental in one of the apartment buildings. Ask for their brochure and price list, make your selection, and book. Prowse will stand behind the properties they rent.

In Barcelona both the Citadines Barcelona Ramblas and the Hotel Apartments Victoria, listed above, can be booked through Prowse. In Madrid, the three apartment buildings Los Jeronimos, Plaza de España, and Plaza Basilica are centrally located. The Los Jeronimos, at 9 Calle de Moreto, is an easy walk to the Prado Museum and the vast Parque del Retiro. The Plaza de España is located in the northeast corner of the central core, two blocks north of the Royal Palace. These two are best for vacationers, while the Plaza Basilica on Calle Commandante Zorita is closer to the financial district. The off-season (August) rent is approximately $700 for a studio in the Plaza de España and Plaza Basilica (no studios in Los Jeronimos), $1,000 for a one bedroom, and

$1,100 for a 2 bedroom. For high season in this city (April through July and September through November) the price increases by 25 percent. Payment can be made by credit card or check.

Mansley Travel Apartments   Madrid, Barcelona, Costa del Sol
No. 1 The Mansions
219 Earls Court Road
London SW5 9BN
Tel: 44–71–373–4689   Fax: 44–71–373–2062

U.S. agent: Grant Reid Communications
Box 810216, Dallas, TX 75381
Tel: (800) 327–1849 or (214) 243–6748   Fax: (214) 484–5778

This competent British company represents hard-to-find apartments in major cities of Europe as well as elsewhere in the world. Mansley is a fast-growing company that specializes in city apartments for short-term rent; we find the properties they represent to be dependably good, mostly three- and four-star properties at fair prices. Contact the U.S. agent for a brochure and prices; payment is by check or credit card. (See chapter 13, United Kingdom, for a profile on Mansley.)

The Owners' Syndicate   Balearic Islands
79 Balham Park Road
London SW12 8EB
England
Tel: 81–767–7926   Fax: 81–767–5328

This is an interesting company we came across in Britain, an organization that offers rental services to owners and villa management companies. Rather than the usual procedure of adding a commission to the owners' price, the owners pay the syndicate for promotion and administration. In turn, the syndicate offers the properties to the public at direct owner prices. A review of the brochure comprising color photographs shows that the properties are mostly large and certainly well above average in standards.

The best approach is to decide on one or several properties you are interested in, then contact the company with your requirements. They will send a number of description pages along with prices. Select what appeals to you and contact them again. We spoke with the principals, and although we did not visit any of the villas, we are fully confident that their properties are as advertised. Their villas are in the Balearic Islands, Portugal's Algarve, and elsewhere in Europe. This is an especially good source for villas in out-of-the-way places.

Playa Famara Bungalows   Canary Islands
La Calet
Lanzarote, Canary Islands
Tel: 28–845–132   Fax: 28–845–134

Perhaps the most exotic location in which rentals are listed in this guide, the island of Lanzarote is closer to Africa than to Spain.

The Playa Famara Bungalows comprise a large resort of 146 bungalows away from the main tourist areas, right on the beach. Although we haven't visited these bungalows, the literature indicates that their services and amenities are quite complete and include a small market, restaurant, tennis, swimming pool, car rental, library, money exchange, reception area, and maid service. The accommodations themselves appear to be upscale. The setting is much like the American southwest; place an Arizona resort next to the sea and it would be much like Playa Famara.

Phone or fax for their brochure and prices; English is spoken. The deposit can be paid with VISA or personal check, final payment is made before or upon arrival. Prices run from Pts 4,750 (about $35) per day for a bungalow for two in low season (May and June) to $40 in the shoulder season (July through October), and $44 per day in the high-season winter months. For a bungalow for up to six persons the rates are also very modest: approximately $65 to $80 per day. There is an airport at the capital city, Arrecife, or for an adventure, take the Trasmediterranea ocean ferry from Las Palmas (Gran Canaria).

Something Special
10 Bull Plain,
Hertfordshire, SG14 1DT
England
Tel: 992–55–2231   Fax: 992–58–7057
Agent: Suzanne Cohen
Tel: (207) 622–0743   Fax: (207) 622–1902

A moderate sized British company, Something Special is aptly named. It has done a good job of locating, displaying, and renting properties—mostly villas and other independent houses—in Spain, France, Portugal, and the island of Corfu, Greece. This company has marketed its rentals to British travelers since 1980, and in our view offers very attractive rentals. The small selection of villas in Spain are located on the Costa Blanca, the southeast coast, in the little towns of Javea and Moraira, both delightful. A beautiful two-bedroom, two-bath villa with pool runs about Pts 66,600 (roughly $490) per week in low season and $850 in peak (August). These are good values.

Phone or fax for a catalog, specifying your interest in Spain. The cost is $3.00

postpaid, but well worth it: The catalogue is colorful, descriptive, and accurate. All of the information needed is in the catalog, and the price list is in sterling. Payment can be made by credit card or a month or two in advance, by personal check at the exchange rate on the day of booking.

Sotoestates   Western Costa del Sol
Puerto Sotogrande
11310 Sotogrande, Cádiz
Tel: 956–61–5351 Fax: 956–61–5721

This is the largest and one of the nicest resort complexes of the western Costa del Sol. Less built up than the better known Marbella-Torremolinos area 50 miles to the east, it is within day-trip distance of the Atlantic coast west to Cádiz and Jerez, the British enclave of Gibraltar, plus the tip of North Africa (Tangier and Spanish Ceuta). In addition, Sotoestates provides a nice setting, good beaches, apartments, villas, and a nearby golf course. The highway between nearby Tarifa and the city of Cádiz is the route of white villages and a dramatic coast. The big ferries of the Trasmediterranea/Limadet line depart four times daily on the one-and-a-half-hour trip across the Strait of Gibraltar between Algeciras and Tangier, Morocco, an interesting journey.

Apartments range from moderate to very high standards and are completely furnished and equipped. Many are privately owned, so they reflect the taste and style of the owners. There are three groups of apartment buildings about half a mile from one another. In one area, one- to four-bedroom apartments are available in low-rise buildings set back but looking across the harbor. These would be our choice for off-season, when the marina area is busy but not crowded with tourists. In summer the central group of apartments is quieter and more private, yet still a short distance to the marina area and its shops and cafes. We suggest that at the time of booking the reservationist be told that you are coming a long way and expect the most desirable accommodation.

The third cluster is the most exclusive, comprising luxury villas and townhouses along the banks where river meets sea. They are isolated, which is great in July and August when the rest of the area is crowded with vacationers, but rather lonely in winter. Luxury villas for rent are also scattered about the hundreds of acres of woods and palms. The entire area is much like a large, well-planned resort community in southern California or the Carolinas coast except that the Rock of Gibraltar looms in the near distance.

Call, write, or fax for a free brochure. Rents range widely, depending on size and season. A one-bedroom apartment in the low season (October through May) runs 48,000 pesetas (about $350) per week; in August it is about $600. An apartment for four is about $450 in the low months and $1,250 in August. The prices in June, July, and September are in between. Unfortunately, credit cards from overseas are not accepted. Upon booking, ask them to fax or mail you a bill for the 50 percent deposit. Send traveler's checks (or a personal check) payable to Sotoestates, S.A. Fax a photocopy in case of a mail delay. Or, make a bank transfer in pesetas to: Banco Atlantico de Sotogrande, account 11 019526 00 35.

Chapter 12

SWITZERLAND

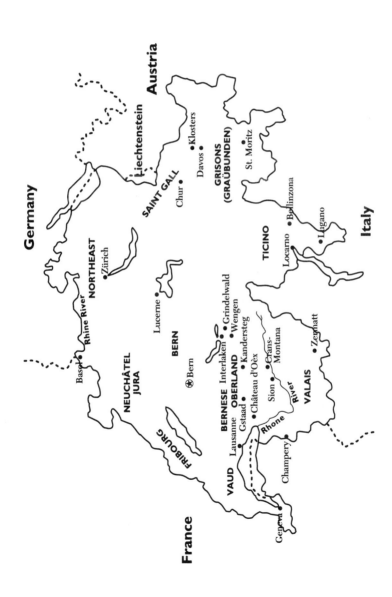

Switzerland National Tourist Offices:

Swiss Center
608 Fifth Ave.
New York, NY 10020
Tel: (212) 757–3737
Fax: 262–6116

250 Stockton Street
San Francisco, CA 94108
Tel: (415) 362–2260
Fax: (415) 391–1508

Commerce court
Ark Mori Building
Toronto, ONT M5L 1E8
Tel: (416) 868–0584
Fax: (416) 868–6702

International Telephone Country Code: 41
City Codes: Zurich 1; Geneva 22; Bern 31
Example: To contact IMO Tours in Bern, dial 011–31–260–101
Passport: Yes, but no visa.
Language: German, French, Italian, and Romansh. English is widely spoken.
Currency: Swiss Franc, abbreviated S.F.
Value Added Tax (VAT): None
Electricity: 220v AC, 50 cycles
Credit Cards: AMEX, VISA, MasterCard widely accepted, some Diners Club; no oil company credit cards accepted.
Main Destination Cities From North America: Geneva and Zurich

The Country

From Geneva at its western border with France across the country to Austria near Bregenz is a five-hour trip by car or train. But despite its small size, Switzerland's diversity, beauty, and facilities for travelers are legendary and chalet rentals are extremely popular. The character of the villages, the location of so many on alpine slopes, and the diminutive nature of much of the architecture make chalets the accommodation of choice. The Zurich-based company Interhome has over 3,000 rentals listed in this tiny country alone.

Best Times of Year to Visit

Most of the winter resort towns of Switzerland are reborn each year with the coming of summer. It is not just that the snow disappears but as the nature of the visitors changes, the character of the towns change also. The decks and terraces of restaurants are filled with a clientele that is generally older than the winter skiers, although many return in summer to hike or walk through the alpine meadows, wander around the narrow, sunny streets of alpine villages, ride horseback, play tennis, sail, or take one of the steamer cruises that stop at the villages dotting the shores of Switzerland's large lakes.

From late October until the beginning of ski season and again from the end of the ski season until the beginning of the late spring tourist season, many of the alpine resort towns and nearby valley cities such as Interlaken are quiet. Some of the hotels, rental properties, and tourist activities are closed, which means you might have to look a bit harder to find one, but there are still many to choose from in these off-seasons.

Although the crowds from mid-June through August can be frustrating, summer can be delightful if you are willing to get off the beaten track into the high country, especially by setting up a home base in one of the smaller communities. Taking into account, however, seasonal prices, weather, crowds, and the availability of tourist activities, the optimum nonski periods to visit are from mid-April to June and again from mid-September through October. In early spring there may still be some snow around the higher towns, and in late fall the fog often lies in the valleys, but the towns at higher elevations remain in sunshine.

In winter only Austria, the Trentino Alto Adige and Valle d'Aosta of Italy, and the Savoie region of France rival Switzerland for the number and variety of ski resorts. The names Gstaad, St. Moritz, Davos, Wengen, and Zermatt conjure accurate images of the young, the rich, and the stylish. You'll find them on the slopes, on the decks of fashionable alpine hotels, and in the restaurants and nightclubs of towns nearly buried in snow. In fact, many visitors, dressed in the most fashionable togs, come only to watch and to shop.

As for the best skiing, it depends on the altitude of the resort area and the height of the mountains. Gstaad, for example, is a popular and glamorous ski resort, but is among the lowest in altitude, so good snow conditions early (December) and later (Easter) cannot be counted upon. On the other hand, Zermatt, which has the highest runs in the country, and the less glitzy Wengen, whose runs are in the shadow of the Eiger, tend to have better snow conditions both early and late in the season. One factor, however, is constant: In the ski resorts, December is the peak season for prices and crowds. It's followed by a relatively low period in January, and then picks up in February and March. If snow conditions are more important to you than nightlife and being seen or watching the rich and famous, go early or late in the season to one of the higher altitude resorts.

The exception to the general rules of seasons and best times to visit is Ticino, Switzerland's southernmost canton, which enjoys a mild Mediterranean climate. See the overview on Ticino later in this chapter.

General Information About Rentals

The term "chalet" is the one most commonly used for rental properties in the villages and smaller towns of Switzerland. It can mean either a separate, individual house (sometimes referred to as a bungalow), or a larger building built in the chalet style but containing two or more apartments. Larger buildings may simply be called apartments or aparthotels, even if they are constructed in chalet style. Chalet style generally means a cube-shaped building with a peaked, gently sloping roof, balconies, and real or decorative window shutters. They are made of wood or are wood trimmed and often are gaily decorated.

In the southeast, especially in the Italian-speaking region of Ticino, a Mediterranean influence is manifested not only in the mild climate, vegetation, and lifestyle but in the architecture. Here rental properties are often in villas or in apartment buildings of modern design.

In the larger cities throughout the country, the rentals are in apartment buildings as varied in type and style as they are in North America. Large, modern apartment complexes have been built in some of the valley towns, so do not assume that anything you rent will be in a quaint chalet.

Swiss rentals are invariably immaculate, even the more simple country houses and alpine chalets. There is a certain Swiss reputation to live up to, and most owners do so, maintaining comfortable and attractive properties. They are cozy in winter and light and airy in summer and are usually situated to take advantage of their surroundings. Utilities are sometimes not included in the rent, and although linens and towels are usually supplied, check the catalog carefully or verify this with the rental company. They are for hire if not supplied.

The good quality of most of the rentals, combined with the mountains, lakes, the scenery, and the orderly towns and villages makes the majority of Swiss rentals both desirable and costly. The extensive use of wood as the construction material of choice gives even the largest and most expensive rentals a rustic charm. Perhaps luxury/rustic is the most apt term, because they offer every comfort and modern convenience.

Prices

Prices vary immensely, influenced not only by the size and standards of the rental but by its location. For example, you may pay extra to be close to the ski lifts, adjacent to a lake, or within view of the Matterhorn. Season also affects price. Zermatt, for example, is principally a winter resort, so seasonal prices are lower in summer than in winter. The following schedule shows the varying prices for a standard studio apartment in a well-located, large, chalet styled building in Zermatt. It is also a good example of the complexity of the seasonal changes. The dates and prices are approximate, and are per week, per apartment.

Dec. 15 to Jan. 7 and Feb. 1 to Mar. 15 $725
Jan. 8 to Feb. 1   600

Mar. 15 to April 15	700
April 16 to July 1 and Aug. 26 to Dec. 15	450
July 1 to August 26	600

In Lucerne, Interlaken, and other lower altitude cities and in the villages along the large lakes, the reverse dates apply: July and August are the costly months. The shoulder periods are the same. For example, a studio in a chalet-style private home in Interlaken costs about $400 per week November through April, $510 May through June and in October, and $620 July through September and the ten days or so around Christmas.

For more spacious four- and five-star private chalets and apartments in the most popular resorts, rents of $2,000 to $4,500 per week and more can be expected during peak seasons, dropping by about one third in the off-seasons. These rentals, however, are not only of exceptional standards but are usually large enough to accommodate four or more persons.

A double room in a modest, three-star hotel in Interlaken, including Continental breakfast, runs about $100 per night ($700/week) in winter, $110 per night ($770/week) in the shoulder months, and $125 per night ($875/week) in June, July, August, and September. A room in the top hotels in the ski resorts can run about $300 per night.

Overall, Switzerland is among the more expensive countries in Europe. Comparable accommodations in alpine towns and smaller cities in Austria, for example, cost less. But rental prices can be quite reasonable in the off-seasons, and standard for standard they are always cheaper than hotels.

Transportation

It is only 275 kilometers (170 miles) between Geneva and Zurich; and Bregenz, Austria, is only 75 miles east of Zurich. From Zurich in the north to Lugano in the south is only about 160 miles. The point is that Switzerland is very small, easy to drive across in either direction in a matter of a few hours. The highway system is outstanding, and the highways themselves are excellent. There are no tolls, just a single autobahn permit good for a year; it costs about U.S. $11 and is paid upon entry into the country or upon renting a car.

Interesting cities in adjacent countries can readily be explored from locations within Switzerland. For instance, it is a short journey from Geneva westward into France (95 miles to Lyon) and southeastward into Italy (about three hours by rail or car to Turin). From the southernmost canton of Ticino it is only 45 miles to Milan; an overnight visit to Venice is even possible. In the east, day-long drives or rail journeys into Austria as far as Tirol can be taken, and tiny Liechtenstein can be explored along the way.

There are more than three thousand miles of railways in Switzerland.

Mainline railroads border Lake Geneva and Lake Neufchâtel and connect all the major cities of the country as well linking those beyond. Secondary lines serve a large number of smaller towns despite the rugged terrain of the east-west spine of the Alps. Where regular trains cannot run, cog railways take over, taking passengers to amazing heights.

If you are planning to spend the greater part of your visit in an alpine village, be sure to determine from the rental company if vehicles are allowed. Although driving is an excellent way to travel and explore Switzerland, you might want to consider travel by rail and cog alone if the village you plan to stay in does not allow cars. You can, however, leave your car parked at the facility, which is always associated with the base terminal of the cog railway.

Where to Stay: The Regions

Switzerland's small size means the entire country can be explored from any location within it, given a week or more. The country has a large number of vacation rentals available, primarily in the most popular alpine resorts but with a good selection scattered elsewhere.

Among the major winter resorts, Gstaad and St. Moritz are generally rated the glamour resorts, and are fun if your budget is unlimited; the rentals available there are generally in the deluxe category. Zermatt has great scenery, character, the steepest ski runs, varied slopes, and good restaurants. St. Moritz is a winter playground with something for everyone: great downhill skiing, miles of Nordic trails, bobsledding, skating, polo on the frozen lake, and even curling. Davos and Klosters in the eastern canton of Grisons, north of St. Moritz, provide excellent skiing and a good selection of rentals.

The character of Switzerland is as variable and complex as its topography. Three basic regional cultures exist, each manifested in different language, architecture, food, style, and atmosphere. In general, 75 percent of the population is German speaking, 20 percent is French speaking, 4 percent Italian, and 1 percent speak the ancient language, Romansh. There is no Swiss language.

Along with other considerations such as mountains, lakes, ski resorts, and cities, these cultural characteristics may tell something about where you might want to stay. The western area and cities such as Geneva, Basel, Lausanne, and the resorts in the mountains of the canton of Valais, have a decidedly French atmosphere. In northern and central Switzerland, from Zurich south into Lucerne and the popular Bernese Oberland and eastward into the canton of Graübunden (Grisons), the language spoken is Swiss-German (Schweizerdeutsch). It is in Grisons (Graübunden in German) where there remain a few speakers of Romansh. The lake country of the canton of Ticino and the towns of Lugano, Locarno, and Bellinzona are definitely Italian in their language and flavor. Don't be concerned if

English is your only language—it is widely used. For a concise overview of the country, request the publication *Switzerland* from the Swiss Tourist Office.

The following regional profiles are generally divided according to language and culture. They turn out to be geographic as well because adjacent nations have, for centuries, influenced the character of neighboring lands: France in the west, Germany in the north, and Italy in the south. Beyond this, each region is briefly described in terms of its physical nature and the rentals available there.

The West—French Speaking
The Cantons of Jura, Neuchâtel, Vaud, Western Fribourg, Western Valais
Environs and Accommodations

This region encompasses the low hills and pasturelands of the sparsely settled north and borders the rugged Alps of the south. Lake Neuchâtel, the largest lake totally within the borders of Switzerland, lies in generally flat land ringed by towns and resort villages, some of them among the most picturesque in the country. To the south lies Lake Geneva (*Lac Leman*), its south shore in France and its north shore in Switzerland. At the lake's western tip is the city of Geneva, and near the center of the north shore is Lausanne; both are high on the list of cities to visit. Steamer voyages on these two great lakes make for delightful days.

The Rhone flows from east to west through Valais, bordered by high mountains, before it empties into the eastern end of Lake Geneva. In these mountains are some of Switzerland's major ski resorts, as well as towns and villages that, during summer, become ideal for short stays for alpine hikers. Among them is Montana, better known as Crans/Montana, an area where five towns support the largest ski and winter sports complex in Switzerland. There are literally hundreds of vacation rentals in this area. Another ski resort is Verbier, a spot especially popular with the European youth, while Chateau d'Oex (pronounced day), Villars, and Campery are more family oriented and are excellent summer alpine getaways.

Two weeks in spring, summer, or fall could be spent in this region alone, perhaps one in Geneva or the more manageable and less expensive cities of Fribourg or Lausanne and one week in one of the alpine villages or on Lake Geneva. A winter visit could be divided between two resorts: one in Valais or Vaud and one in the east such as Davos, Klosters, or St. Moritz.

Central Switzerland—North to South; German Speaking
The Cantons of Basel, Bern, Eastern Wallis (Valais), Luzern (Lucerne) Eastern Fribourg, and Zurich
Environs and Accommodations

These six cantons (or parts of cantons) are a few of the nineteen in which

German is the predominant language spoken. They are the principal ones in which rentals are available and represent the areas of greatest interest to foreign visitors. The region is bordered by Germany on the north, Austria on the east, and Italy on the south. To the west lie the French-speaking regions of Switzerland. Topographically this is a varied area, comprising the rolling hills and broad valleys of the Plateau in the north, range after range of midheight mountains toward its center, and the high Alps in the south. Lake Zürich (*Zürichsee*), Lake Constance (*Bodensee*), and Lake Lucerne (*Vierwaldätter See*) are in this area, along with the lesser-known and smaller Lake Thun (*Thunersee*) and Lake Brienz (*Brienzersee*). These two lie along the northern base of the Jungfrau/Eiger massif.

Zürich is the principal city of the area and is the largest in Switzerland (pop. about one million). It has its own attractions for tourists, and there are apartments available. If you are inclined toward a city stay, Zürich or Lucerne are good choices.

In an area as scenically beautiful as this, it is difficult to recommend one region over another for a home base. Despite the lure of the big lakes of the north, it is the Alps and lakes of central Switzerland (Lucerne canton), the Bernese Oberland (southern Bern canton) and the canton of Wallis that draw travelers from all over the world. In fact, because so many come in the summer, we again urge you to try to visit in April, May, September, or even early October, when your stay will be much more rewarding and less expensive.

Canton of Lucerne. The area of Lucerne (*Luzern* in German) is a special delight for people who love mountains but are not climbers or hikers. The Alps are amazingly accessible—with no more effort than it takes to walk a city block or two you can take a cable car to the top of Mount Pilatus. Or you can take an elevator to the Bürgenstock, or the cog railway to 6,000-foot Rigi for a view hard to rival. Lake Lucerne itself, like most of the Swiss lakes, is also easily accessible, affording great views of the mountain country from the decks or dining rooms of the lake steamers that call on the villages along its shores. For winter visitors, Lucerne canton does not offer the number or quality of ski runs offered by the canton of Wallis (*Valais* in French) or the Bernese Oberland, but cross-country skiing is very popular.

Bernese (Berner) Oberland. Surrounding Lucerne to the west and south is the canton of Bern, divided into the Bernese Mittelland and the Bernese Oberland. It is the Oberland and the canton of Wallis to the south to which the majority of visitors come. There are many alpine villages and resorts, and in them are most of the vacation rentals available in Switzerland.

Lakes Thun and Brienz, long and slender, lie end to end, with the town of

Interlaken between them. The lakes are bracketed by the city of Thun to the west and the pretty village of Brienz to the east. From much of Interlaken there are unobstructed views south to the peaks of the Jungfrau, Monch, and Eiger. Interlaken itself is an old-fashioned resort town that serves as a popular base for everything from boating or taking a steamship cruise on one of the lakes to exploring the Bernese Alps. Its population of 14,000 almost doubles in the summer months and increases again during ski season. It is possible to commute daily from Interlaken to any of several resorts in the vicinity.

From late spring to late fall these mountain villages are themselves perfect centers in which to stay and hike, take a cog railway or gondola to the heights, or descend to the large lakes below. Deciding which village to settle in for one or two weeks may be difficult, but it is also hard to go wrong.

Wengen: There are no cars in this mountain village. It is busy but not glitzy in winter and a peaceful base for summer hiking. There are great views, excellent ski runs, and good restaurants, grocery stores, and shops. The town is accessible by train from Interlaken or by cog railway from the car park at Lauterbrunnen.

Grindelwald: This mountain village is accessible by car or train, 20 kilometers (12 mi.) from Interlaken. Access is also possible by cog railway from Lauterbrunnen. Great views of the high valley at the base of the Eiger and Schreckhorn, a popular ski and hiking area. Many restaurants, grocery stores, shops are accessed via the Jungfraujoch railway, which runs almost to the mountain top.

Brienze: This small town on the shores of Lake Brienz 20 kilometers east of Interlaken is a center for woodcarving. Restaurants, shops, and boating serve the many tourists in summer, but the town is pretty and peaceful at other times.

Mürren and Gimmelwald: There are no cars in these relatively high altitude villages of 1,645 m/5,345 ft. They are principally ski areas, but are good bases for hiking as well. Just 15 kilometers (9 mi.) south of Interlaken, both are accessible by cog railway from Lauterbrunen.

Gstaad: This major international summer and winter resort in an area of many smaller resort villages boasts swimming, tennis, horseback riding, good skiing in winter, and an elevated social life. Fine restaurants cater to an international clientele. It is 75 kilometers (47 mi.) southwest of Interlaken by highway or rail. Prices here are high.

Kandersteg: A pretty, traditional summer and winter resort village at the foot of Blümlisalphorn. Hiking, swimming, tennis, riding are offered in an unaffected atmosphere. There are restaurants, grocery stores, and shops 60 kilometers (37 mi.) southwest of Interlaken via Spiez by highway or rail.

Beatenburg: This small village is a ten-minute funicular ride above the north shore of Lake Thun. It is convenient to Interlaken and the lakes without having to stay in the larger, busier towns.

Oberhofen and Merlingen: Two very pretty lakeside villages on the north shore (south slope) of Lake Thun, and just a few minutes drive to Interlaken and the town of Thun. Or you may take the boat which runs between Interlaken and Thun on a regular schedule, calling at both Oberhofen and Merlingen.

Darlingen is a small lakeside village on the south shore of Lake Thun, 6 kilometers (3½ mi.) from Interlaken.

Canton of Wallis (Valais). In the preceding section on the French-speaking region of western Switzerland, we described the western half of the canton of Valais. The eastern half of this canton is called Wallis by its German-speaking populace. As in the west, the eastern half is dominated by the valley of the Rhône River (*Rotten*) from which the Alps rise on either side. Over fifty peaks are above 4,000 meters (13,000 ft.), and in the valley fertile farms grow strawberries, tomatoes, and apricots. There are many alpine resorts here. One of the most charming and internationally popular ski resorts is Saas-Fee. This village, surrounded by high Alps, is also for summer visitors who want a sense of isolation. It is located 26 kilometers (16 mi.) south of Visp, on the Rhône. Thirty-six kilometers (22 mi.) southwest of Visp is Zermatt, the most famous ski and summer resort of the region, known not only for skiing but for good restaurants, hiking, sunny terraces, and as the base for assaults on the nearby Matterhorn. Cars are not allowed in either Saas-Fee or Zermatt and are parked at the railroad station where service by rail or minibus is available. It is 110 miles from Zermatt to Lausanne, and another 55 miles on to Geneva.

The Southcentral Region: Canton of Ticino
Environs and Accommodations

Entering Ticino is like crossing an international boundary into Italy rather than a provincial one in Switzerland. There is a marked change in language, food, architecture, music, and dress. Yet Ticino has been Swiss since the sixteenth century. The unusual atmosphere is a mix of the Italian good life and the order and efficiency of the Swiss.

On the sunny south side of the Alps the mountains are high enough for plenty of snow, but this region is equally appealing in spring and summer when you can enjoy the magnolias, mimosa, palm trees, flowers, and the mild weather. The predominant language of Ticino is Italian, but about 10 percent of the population speaks Swiss-German and 30 percent are foreign residents who may speak anything from Danish to Portuguese. The common language is English.

Lakes Maggiore and Lugano, both shared with Italy, are the main attractions for visitors to the region. They add to the complex juxtaposition of the Mediterranean influences and alpine grandeur, making the area a very attractive one in which to spend a good part of one's visit.

Many of the rentals available are in or near the towns of Locarno and Lugano. Locarno is the smaller of the two, a charming but busy place on the shore of Lake Maggiore. Lugano, on the shore of the lake by the same name, is the grande dame of resort towns in the lake country. Like Locarno, it would be a good base in which to stay except in July and August, when it is jammed with tourists. It is of manageable size, with a population of 30,000. It has smart shops, good restaurants, and an atmosphere of elegance. If you prefer not to stay in town, there are rentals available in many of the smaller villages.

Unlike most of the other small towns and rural areas of Switzerland, there are few chalet-style buildings in Ticino. Single-family rentals and smaller rural apartment buildings are often built of stone; many are old with tile roofs. They are mountain places perched in the lower reaches of the Alps that surround the lakes and are generally well kept and clean. Most rental accommodations, however, are in the towns and cities around the lakeshore, typically modern apartments such as found in the U.S. One of the most pleasant, high above the lake, is the Parco Paradiso Lugano, as comfortable as one could desire. Its description later in this chapter characterizes the better apartments in this region.

Bellinzona, the capital of Ticino, is a midsize town north of the lakes. It makes a good base for anyone wanting to avoid the press of summer tourists in the better-known Lugano and Locarno and have easy access to the eastern cantons. The autumn harvest festival in Lugano in October involves the entire village in a celebration of wine, food, and traditional music and dance. The central piazza is decorated to resemble a vineyard, and wine flows freely from open kegs to everyone there. Lake steamer excursions are a must, and drives through the mountain valleys are a delightful mix of splendid scenery and charming small villages where one may stop for excellent coffee and pastries or glasses of local wine or beer.

Best Times to Visit Ticino

A drawback to this area is one that afflicts the most attractive places in Europe: summer crowds. Because of the mild climate, however, the region is pleasant long before summer. Flowers begin their displays in February, and by April the wisteria, azalea, and cherry trees are in bloom. If possible, go in March, April, May, September, or October, and avoid the months of June, July, and August.

Advance Booking Times

June, July and August: six months
February through May: two months

September and October: two months
November through January: two weeks, or rent after arrival

The Southeast—German, Italian, Romansh Canton of Grisons

Environs and Accommodations

This is where the Swiss go to get away from it all. Grisons (*Graübunden* in German) is the largest and least populated canton in Switzerland. Three languages are spoken: ancient Romansh along the central east-west axis, German to the north and south, and Italian in the south.

It is a few hours drive from Interlaken to Chur (pronounced Koor), the principal city of the Grisons. Because the highway is not an *autobahn* and climbs through passes over 7,000 feet high, this approach to Chur makes the area feel somewhat isolated from the rest of the country. This feeling is compounded by the town names and signs in the unfamiliar Romansh language. Lakes are now called *lei* instead of the Italian *lago,* French *lac* and German *see;* no more German *"horn"* names, or Italian *"monte,"* but *"piz,"* meaning "peak."

Engadine Valley

For mountain lovers who must visit Switzerland during the summer tourist months but want to avoid the crowds, a week in the Engadine Valley southeast of Chur is ideal. The villages of the Lower Engadine uniquely retain their character from other days, and most of the valley remains unspoiled. St. Moritz, on the other hand, is the principal community of the Upper Engadine. It is one of the world's best known resorts: a fashionable, dynamic, and expensive international play spot. In winter St. Moritz hits its stride, but in the other months it is also a place to go for hiking, swimming, tennis, riding, and shopping in exclusive and expensive stores. Here is where most of the rentals in the Engadine are. The majority are deluxe in standards and high in price—and some are moderate in standards and high in price. Nevertheless, with midstandard hotel rooms about $220 per night or more, a studio apartment at $1,000 per week seems reasonable, as does a one-bedroom apartment at $1,500. Less expensive and more in character with the Romansh culture are the towns of Zuoz, Pontresina, and the main town of the Upper Engadine, Samedan. Most of the rentals in these Engadine Valley towns are recently built, modern-day versions of the old balconied chalets. The apartment buildings are small, typically two to four apartments in each, a few larger. Count on them being neat, clean, and cozy.

East of Chur

Elsewhere in the Grisons, the two most popular village resorts are Davos and Klosters, both in the alpine country less than 70 kilometers (43 mi.) east of

Chur. Davos is a large and busy ski and summer resort where almost everything costs slightly less than at St. Moritz and the more fashionable Klosters, a few miles north. Charles, Prince of Wales, has often come to Klosters for the skiing and the relatively restrained and elegant atmosphere.

West of Chur
Off the highway leading to the St. Gotthard tunnel and Interlaken are the smaller, quieter villages of Laax and Flims. It is an area of wooded hills and small lakes that lends itself to a relaxed stay. There is easy access to Chur, and to the west, the Bernese Oberland is within easy striking distance.

The Rental Companies of Switzerland

IMO Tours   Throughout Switzerland
Belpstrasse 11
CH-3001 Bern
Tel: 31–260–101 Fax: 31–262–645

U.S. agent: Europa-Let, Inc.
92 North Main St.
Ashland, OR 97520
Tel: (800) 462–4486   Fax: (503) 482–0660

This midsize company markets very little in North America but is a good source of rentals at low prices. Its concentration of properties in the desirable, Italian-speaking canton of Ticino are of special interest. There are helpful English speakers on the staff, but the catalog, although illustrated, is in German. The prices and selection are worth the effort of booking, however. Request a catalog and recontact the company with several property reference numbers or fax a description of your needs and the dates and then follow up with a phone call. There is always an English speaker to help, and he or she will make suggestions. Alternatively, contact the agent in Oregon; there will be a commission, but IMO prices are low and the end result is fair.

We have been acquainted with IMO for several years and have heard of no one with a complaint. Be sure to mention your need for linens and towels. Rents of between $250 and $350 per week for a one-bedroom chalet or apartment in the shoulder seasons is not uncommon. Reasonable prices explain why IMO is very popular with Europeans, so book early. Payment must be made in the form of a bank draft in Swiss francs, or you can book through the U.S. agent.

This six-room chalet, located in the popular mountain resort of Verbier, can accommodate up to eight people. (Courtesy Interhome Vacation Rental Network)

INTERHOME, INC.   Throughout Switzerland
Backhauserstrasse 26
8000 Zurich
Tel: 1–497–2777   Fax: 1–497–2760

U.S. office:
Interhome Inc. USA
124 Little Falls Rd.
Fairfield, NJ 07004
Tel: (201) 882–6864   Fax: (201) 808–1742

With nearly 4,000 rentals in Switzerland and 22,000 throughout Europe, this Swiss company is the largest vacation rental company in Europe. Readers will see it referenced in most of the country chapters of this book.

With this many rentals it is clear that they run the gamut of type, style, standards, and price. Whether large or small, those that are not are in the larger cities or in the flatlands of the valleys are predominantly chalet style: pitched roofs, shutters, and balconies. In the busy resort centers like Zermatt, Crans Montana, and Davos, many of the "chalets" contain dozens of apartments. Single family chalets are hard, but not impossible, to find. Interhome sets specific standards for owners to meet and monitors the properties. Value in general is good. A scan of the long price list shows a four-star nine-room house in

Chateau d'Oex for about $5,200 per week during peak ski months (drops to $2,600 in spring and fall); a simple but adequate studio can be rented for as little as $250 per week.

Complete information on its thousands of rental properties is stored and constantly updated in a mainframe computer at the Zurich headquarters, accessible to many country agencies, such as Interhome Inc. USA in New Jersey. These Interhome offices can make immediate contact with the Zurich computer, offering clients a choice of properties available at the dates specified. It can cross-reference client requirements and perform a computer search of many parameters.

Because the independently owned U.S. Interhome company is only one step away from the European company, there is only one commission involved. Rent will be higher than booking direct, but inquiries made to the Zurich office will be referred back to New Jersey. Fortunately, this arrangement is offset by the fact that the service of the New Jersey firm is personal and overall worth the commission. Ask about discounts early in your communication; there may be a number of properties discounted to clients who make direct contact, especially in low and shoulder seasons.

There are two approaches to finding and booking: Call or fax the agency and request a catalog and price list; there is a small charge, from $3.00 to $5.00, depending on the country catalog requested. (The Europe-wide catalog is only pictorial, not descriptive.) The Switzerland catalog is almost 150 pages and offers a provocative selection to choose from. This is a distinct advantage, and makes the catalog worth the price.

The other approach is to phone or fax with your choice of dates and list of requirements (locations, size, number of bedrooms, baths, amenities, special needs, such as proximity to railway station, and budgetary limits). If these are laid out clearly, the computer will find all such properties available during the period you specify, and you will be notified of the choices almost immediately.

If using the catalog, select and rank at least three rentals of interest and phone or fax again with the reference numbers from the catalog. You will be notified of availability, usually within twenty-four hours.

If all is satisfactory, Interhome will ask for a deposit check for 30% of the rent (or full rent if within less than four weeks of arrival date). Upon final payment, all instructions and directions will be sent by mail or fax. A damage deposit is paid to the keyholder or owner on arrival. Not all the properties are supplied with towels and linens; read the catalog carefully, or specify that you need them. If they are not supplied, they can be rented.

The U.S. office prefers personal checks in U.S. dollars; VISA and MasterCard are also acceptable. Rates are guaranteed in U.S. dollars at the time of booking.

If you do not want cancellation insurance, say so or it will be automatically included. The fee is 3 percent of the rent, a very good rate.

Mansley Travel Apartments   Geneva, Zurich, Basel, Lugano
No. 1 The Mansions
219 Earls Court Road
London SW5 9BN
Tel: 44–71–373–4689 Fax: 44–71–373–2062

U.S. agent: Grant Reid Communications
Box 810216
Dallas, TX 75381
Tel: (800) 327–1849 or (214) 243–6748   Fax: (214) 484–5778

This competent British company represents a nice selection of otherwise hard-to-find apartments in Geneva on rue de Lausanne, rue Richemont, rue de la Navigation, and an especially attractive group, ideal for a longer stay, on rue Thalberg. In Zurich they have apartments on Bienenstrasse, and in Lugano they represent the marvelous Parco Paradiso, listed below. Mansley is a company that specializes in city apartments for short-term rent; we find the apartments they represent, of which we have visited nine, to be dependably good, mostly in the upper-middle and luxury categories, three-star and four-star. Because of high standards and city locations, prices are also high but are good value. (See chapter thirteen, United Kingdom, for a profile on Mansley and its excellent apartments in London.) Prices for booking through the U.S. agent are the same; payment is made by personal check or credit card. (We recommend the latter to assure exchange rate of the day.) Contact the U.S. agent for a brochure and prices.

PARA Apartments AG   Zurich
Baselstrasse 107
8048 Zurich
Tel: 1–491–4116   Fax: 1–401–1068

This is a good source for apartments for business and leisure travelers in and around Zurich. There are apartments in three locations, all desirable: Baselstrasse 107, Leutholdstrasse 19, and Morgartenstrasse 15. Weekly rates run from about 630 Swiss francs (about U.S. $450) for a small studio to about $1,200 for a two-bedroom, 950-square-foot apartment, with many prices in between. A brochure is available on request. This company does not market in the United States or Canada, but English and French are spoken. Payment must be made by a mailed bank draft in Swiss francs.

Parco Paradiso Lugano   Lugano
Via Carona 27
CH-6902 Lugano
Tel: 91–55–1111   Fax: 91–55–1011

U.S. agent: Grant Reid Communications
Box 810216
Dallas, TX 75381
Tel: (800) 327–1849, (214) 243–6748   Fax: (214) 484–5778

The name may sound a bit overdone, but this beautiful combined hotel and apartments takes its name from the Paradiso section of Lugano where it is located. Given its perch high above the lake and the city, the grounds that surround it, and the quality of the apartments and hotel rooms, it is aptly named. Were we to pick a place in Europe in which to spend a week or more, Lugano and the Parco Paradiso would be top contenders.

The small city itself curves around the shoreline of Lake Lugano, a great, clear jewel filling the broad valleys of the southern Alps. Steamships of other times sail often from the Lugano quays, taking passengers to picturesque villages that dot the shore. The town of Lugano is an old style resort, filled with restaurants, museums, monuments, parks, and a multitude of shops, among which are the most elegant in Europe.

The Parco Paradiso is in a quiet neighborhood, beautifully situated on a sloping hill with outstanding views of the lake and the city below. It is five minutes by car or bus to the town center. The building is fairly new and is designed and decorated in a contemporary, upbeat style. It is not a cozy sort of place—it is light, angular, and classy. The apartments are spacious, well designed, and stylishly furnished and decorated. There are balconies and modern, well-equipped kitchens. Overall, we think the apartments rate four stars. Because the views vary, ask for the best available location, the higher up the better. The premium apartments are in the main hotel section; they can be rented as full-service hotel suites in which the kitchens remain unused, or as self-catering apartments at a lower price. All services are available à la carte, from room service to a very nice restaurant, a bar, lounge, pool, and in summer a terrace dining room. The Parco Paradiso is well managed, offers twenty-four-hour reception, porterage, and parking. We found the on-site management to be especially hospitable and helpful and concerned with the comfort of their guests.

Call or fax for a brochure and current price list, or book with confidence. Booking is easy, just like a hotel. A deposit payment can be made by credit card or personal check. The balance can be paid by any method of your choice either upon arrival or departure. Feel free to work with the U.S. agent; we have been assured that the price is the same. There is never a problem, however, in calling or sending a fax directly to Parco Paradiso. The apartments are not inexpensive, in the U.S. $1,500 per-week range for a spacious one bedroom, but it is a good value and a place sure to please.

Travel Together   Zurich
Lagerstrasse 95
8004 Zurich
Tel: 1–242–0012   Fax: 1–242–8200

This is a small company we know little of, but the staff are courteous and helpful on the telephone. The company has not marketed in North America— it emphasizes apartments for business travelers who like to bring their families along, thus the name. If a few days in Zurich are planned, call or fax for details and prices.

Citadines   Geneva (Gaillard)
163–167 avenue Georges Clemenceau
Batiment E
Parc des Fontaines
92022 Nanterre Cedex, France
Central Reservations, Paris Tel: 1–47–25–5454   Fax: 1–47–25–4918

The Citadines apartments in Gaillard, a suburb of Geneva, are actually in France, not Switzerland, so are appended here as a convenience inasmuch as there is no reason to stay in Gaillard other than for access to central Geneva, and the fact that prices are less. Citadines is a large chain of apartments best characterized as upper moderate in their standard and prices. They are generally attractive, comfortable, and well maintained, and are very well priced. It's easy to get to central Geneva from Gaillard, just a few blocks to the border, then ten minutes by car or bus. The apartments are somewhat formula in their nature, but are neat, spotless, comfortable for a few days stay and much more spacious than a hotel room of equal standard and higher cost. The neighborhood is busy semi-commercial, but the apartments on the back and sides are quiet. There is reception, a pleasant lobby and breakfast room if you don't want to prepare your own. Contact direct (credit cards accepted, booking just like a hotel) or in the U.S. contact Keith Prowse & Co. (USA), Ltd., (800) 669–8687 Fax: (212) 302–4251 or The Barclay International Group, (800) 845–6636 Fax: (212) 753–1139.

Chapter 13

UNITED KINGDOM

John O'Groats

Inverness

Aberdeen

Pitlochry

Dundee

Perth

Scotland

North Sea

Edinburgh

Glasgow

Melrose
Jedburgh

Newcastle-upon-Tyne

Carlisle

Ambleside
Windermere
Kendall

Isle
of Man

Irish Sea

York

Leeds

Liverpool

Lincoln

Holyhead
Chester
Caernavon
Llanberis
Porthmadog

Birmingham

Warwick

Norwich

Stratford-upon-
Avon

Cambridge

Aberporth

Wales

Tewkesbury
Cheltenham

Colchester

Harwich

Fishguard

Cirencester

Oxford

Swansea

Cardiff
Bristol
Bath

London

Tunbridge Wells

Atlantic Ocean

Salisbury
Southampton

Portsmouth

Rye

Brighton

Exeter
Bournemouth

Plymouth
Torbay

Isle of
Wight

Land's
End

English Channel

British Tourist Authority (BTA) Offices:

40 West 57th Street
New York, NY 10019
Tel: (212) 581–4700
Fax: (212) 265–0649

350 So. Figueroa St., Suite 450
Los Angeles, CA 90071
Tel: (213) 628–3525
Fax: (213) 687–6621

625 No. Michigan Ave., Suite 450
Chicago, IL 6611
Tel: (312) 787–0490
Fax: (312) 787–7746

2580 Cumberland Pkwy., Suite 470
Atlanta, GA 30339
Tel: (404) 432–9641
Fax: (404) 432–9641

94 Cumberland St., Suite 600
Toronto, Ontario M5R 3N3
Tel: (416) 925–6326
Fax: (416) 961–2175

Northern Ireland Tourist Board Offices:

551 Fifth Avenue, Suite 701
New York, NY 10176
Tel: (212) 922–0101
Fax: (212) 922–0099

111 Avenue Rd, Suite 450
Toronto, Ontario M5R 3JS
Tel: (416) 925–6368

International Telephone Country Code: 44

City Codes: London central 71; London outskirts 81; Exeter 392; Edinburgh, Scotland 31; Bath 225; Belfast, No. Ireland 232

Example: To contact The Independent Traveller, dial 011–44–392–860–807

Passport: Yes, but no visa.

Currency: Pound sterling. Symbol: £; divides into 100 pence.

Value Added Tax (VAT): 17.5%

Electricity: 220v AC, 50 cycles.

Credit Cards: AMEX, VISA, MasterCard, Barclay Card, ACCESS, and Diners Club.

Main Destination Cities from North America: London (Heathrow and Gatwick airports); Manchester

The Country

The United Kingdom comprises England, Scotland, Wales, and Northern Ireland. As for size, it is claimed that there is no point in Britain more than 80 miles from the sea, which makes the country seem rather small. Its configuration nevertheless makes distances between its extremes too long for day trips or short excursions. London is about 735 highway miles from John O'Groats, at the northern tip of Scotland. (Miles, not kilometers, are used in Britain.) Even east to west is deceivingly distant: Norwich, near the east coast, is over 400 miles from Penzance, on the tip of Cornwall. If you want to see a lot of Britain in a limited time, two home bases need to be selected. Because of the large number of rentals throughout Britain, no lack of accommodations will limit your choice.

No other country in Europe, or perhaps the world, has been written about as extensively as Great Britain. The British document themselves and their country prodigiously in everything from guides to their stately homes and detailed histories of the royal families to ordinance survey maps, which show every bend in the road and everything there is to see along the way. Guidebooks to Britain covering every imaginable topic occupy several feet of shelf space in any bookstore of even modest size. This chapter does not, therefore, concern itself so much with Great Britain as with an overview of how to spend a few rewarding weeks there in a self-catering home base.

Best Times of Year to Visit

Spring comes early in the south country, normally by mid-March. By early April the weather is usually very pleasant in the southern two-thirds of the country. In Scotland, spring comes later, especially in the Highlands. So if consistently good weather is important, wait until May.

The warmest and sunniest months are June, July, August, and September, which are the months most tourists flock to Great Britain. School lets out late, however, often mid-June or later, and until exams are over, most Britons with children stay home. Thus, May and early June are the best times to go of the warmer months.

General Information About Rentals

It would be confusing and of little purpose to attempt to profile all of the rental organizations in Great Britain. Approximately 280 companies and apartment managements offer an estimated 60,000 to 65,000 rentals in Great Britain. A relatively small proportion of these companies are profiled, but they are sufficient to offer a vast number of choices in style, type, size, price, and location. They were selected because of their good reputation, fair prices, availability of catalogs and other information, ease of booking, speed of response, the variety of their properties and interest in the North American market. We have known many of the companies for a number of years.

Most Americans who have never been to Britain before are surprised to discover how different, how foreign, it is. The differences are most evident in the small towns and rural areas where central marketplaces have not yet given over to malls, where small shopkeepers have kept their individuality and seven-day-a-week, around-the-clock hours for stores, restaurants, bars, and other commercial enterprises has yet to be accepted. These differences are what we travel to foreign places to experience. Because of a common national language and historical ties to Great Britain, however, Americans seem to expect it to be more like the U.S. than it is.

In terms of rentals, unexpected differences can be disconcerting, but if you are forewarned they can easily be dealt with. The American expectation of a "cottage" is, for example, usually quite different from how one is thought of in Britain. It's good to know that in some properties the electricity is turned on and metered by means of putting 50 pence pieces into a coin box, which is often concealed in a cupboard. The solution of course is to always carry a few coins and to always look for the coin box if the lights don't come on when switched.

To make matters easier and to help avoid misunderstandings that could lead to undesirable ends, a few definitions and explanations are in order.

Definitions, Terminology, and Details

"Self-catering" is the term used in the United Kingdom for vacation rentals; "holiday" is the word for vacation. "Cottage" can be used to describe what *we* think of as a cottage—a small, single-family dwelling—in which case it is referred to in Britain as a "detached" cottage. Or a cottage can be one unit or apartment among several in a larger house (usually rural or in a village) or a unit in an attached row, which we would call a townhouse. A cottage can also mean half of a duplex, which the British would describe as "semidetached." When communicating with a rental company, it is essential that you clarify what you want. If it is a cottage as we think of the term, make sure to specify that you want a single-occupancy, detached cottage.

A "unit" generally means an accommodation that shares the laundry room, terrace, and perhaps garden and hallways with others in similar units. The first floor in Britain (and all of Europe) is what we call the second floor. The floor or street level is called the "ground floor," and a "lower ground floor" or "garden level" means the floor halfway below the street level.

A bathroom must contain a bathtub or shower in addition to the other facilities. What Americans call a half bath is described as having a hand basin and WC (water closet, or toilet).

"Apartment" usually means the same as in American and Canadian English. The term "maisonette" refers to one side of a duplex, often on more than one floor. A "flat" is an apartment occupying a single, and usually an entire, floor.

Rental Periods. Except in London and other major cities, Saturday to Saturday is the normal rental period. In the low season (roughly late September to early June in most areas) midweek bookings can often be made of three or four days duration. In the cities, three- or four-day minimums are usually available, except in the peak summer months, and changeover days are far more flexible than in rural cottages. In the low and shoulder seasons, many rural rentals can be taken for a weekend or a "midweek break" of three days. For rural rentals during high season, consider arriving in Britain a day or two early and taking a hotel or B&B in the vicinity of your rental before the occupancy date, especially if you want to take advantage of lower midweek air fares.

Electricity. The cost of electricity is sometimes not included in the rent. As mentioned, many rural and village properties are set up with a coin-operated meter. In some properties, the renter is asked to read the meter upon arrival and departure and then settle with the owner on the spot. British electrical plugs are immense, and a plug converter should be taken with you for any personal appliances.

Electrical Switches. The British seem to be mad about electrical switches (or perhaps it is a safety precaution). There are almost always switches on the wall or baseboard sockets, so if a lamp or appliance does not operate by its own switch, look to the socket it is plugged into. This includes the TV, the range (called a "cooker"), the cooking surface (called a "hob"), and even the oven, refrigerator, and electric hot-water heater. If nothing electrical works, make sure your metered time has not run out before calling the owner or agent.

Towels & Linens. In rural and village properties towels and linens are often not provided for British renters, but they are available to renters from overseas. There may be a small extra charge.

Welcome & Information. If you are not met on arrival by the owner or an agent, look inside the rental for a folder or booklet containing information about how to operate things, the location of the laundry, grocers, and other services, and telephone numbers in case you need assistance.

Appliances and utensils differ from what Americans may consider standard equipment. Long-standing tea drinkers, the British use instant over brewed coffee. In some rural and village rentals you will not be supplied with a coffeemaker of any kind, but an electric kettle. Dishwashers are also uncommon in most rentals, so if this is important, it needs to be made clear to the rental agent; you will, however, be limiting your choice of properties.

Prices and Seasons

Prices for rural cottages and village apartments are lower than comparable properties in many parts of France, Italy, Germany, and even Spain. Many of the rental companies' price schedules are, however, exceedingly complex, with as many as ten seasonal or periodic changes throughout the year. In addition to the standard tourist seasons, there are domestic holidays such as bank holidays, celebratory national holidays, and school-break holidays when the domestic demand for cottages increases and so do the prices, often by just a few pounds. Competition among the rental companies is very keen, keeping prices fair.

Prices for apartments in London are expensive, but they are 30 to 40 percent less than hotel rooms of equal standards. There are also bargains and good values available. More information follows in the section on London. Most catalogs are quite well done; they are accurate and descriptive. Price schedules will be in pounds sterling and will show the various rate periods.

Where to Stay: The Regions

Putting ourselves in the place of North Americans planning to visit Britain for the first time, we developed an itinerary to take us to where we had been in the past and particularly enjoyed, and where we had not been but had wanted to visit. The process took us to properties from the tip of Cornwall to the north of Scotland, from the waterlands of East Anglia to the coast of Wales and, of course, London.

We chose to focus on twenty areas and cities because of their variety, their proven interest to American visitors, and their interest to us. We visited them with an eye toward rentals available and their suitability as a home base from which to explore and enjoy the surroundings. These areas are covered in geographical order. The counties or areas of our concentration are:

In England: Kent, Norfolk, Lincolnshire, North Yorkshire, The Lake District, The Cotswolds, The Chilterns and the Thames Valley (west of London), Gloucestershire, Dorset, Devon, Cornwall, Hampshire, West Sussex, and the cities of London and Bath.

In Scotland: Borders Region (Roxburghshire), Grampian Highlands, Dumfries and Galloway, Edinburgh and Aberdeen.

In Wales: Gwynedd (northern Wales) and Dyfed (southern Wales).

Although they do not exhaust the interesting places in which to stay in Britain, these regions encompass the large majority of where the rentals are available and provide many good starting points, especially for people planning a first visit.

If you want to stay in an unusual rental—such as a manor house, castle, gatehouse, or converted fort—a study of the companies section at the end of this chapter will lead you to the appropriate organizations, such as Sudeley Castle, the Landmark Trust and National Trust. If you are an avid walker seeking seclusion, let the rental agent know. There are rentals scattered across the remotest areas of the Scottish coast and the hinterlands of the Northwest Highlands, for example. For island lovers, rentals are available on the Scottish islands, the Isle of Man, the Isle of Anglesey in Wales, the Scilly Isles off Cornwall, and the Channel Islands off the coast of France.

A good first planning step is to contact the nearest office of the British Tourist Authority or Northern Ireland Tourist Board. They are very busy offices, especially from January to June, so try to be specific about the information you are seeking. British Airways is also a good resource, as is the Keith Prowse Agency, listed below.

A note on Northern Ireland: It offers a beautiful, sometimes rich, sometimes austere countryside. We suggest spending little time in Belfast and, rather, following the breathtaking north coast of counties Antrim and Londonderry, visiting the towns of Bushmills, Portrush, and Portstewart, and the interesting cities of Londonderry and Armagh. Because of the continuing political unrest, we neither recommend nor discourage a visit there, but we found our visit memorable and would feel quite comfortable going again. There are rental accommodations for Northern Ireland listed at the end of this chapter.

This section of the chapter is divided into three sections: England, Scotland, and Wales, followed by a section on the city of London. England, in turn, is divided into three tiers or divisions, South, Central, and North. Each tier has been divided lengthwise into eastern and western, resulting in six geographic regions.

The first step in planning your trip is to get a good general guide and a map of the whole country. If you are considering a stay in London, as all visitors should, also purchase a London map that shows the districts by name—for example, Chelsea, Bloomsbury, and Mayfair—so that you can see where these are in relationship to the things you especially want to see and do. Once you have narrowed down the areas of interest find and contact the companies or apartment managements in this chapter that offer properties in these areas.

England

Prices

Cottages throughout England range from small and simple to large and elegant, and can be rented for anything between £100 (about $155) and £800 (about $1,280) per week. For the higher figure you can expect a fairly large country home replete with gardens, grounds, and, rarely, a pool. For half of that amount you will find very comfortable, nicely furnished, one- and two-bedroom detached houses in choice locations. This is about the cost of a room in a three-star hotel in one of the larger towns. At the lower end, for about $240 per week, the cottages are typically studio or one-bedroom apartments in small buildings with three to six units, often converted outbuildings of a former farm.

There are also a scattering of manor houses for rent throughout England, usually large and beautifully furnished. Staff are often available, and gardening and maintenance are of course included in the rent, which typically runs from about $2,700 to $3,600 per week. For example, among the 140 or so unusual rentals of the Landmark Trust, the most expensive is Wortham Manor, a beautifully restored eight-bedroom, five-bath, medieval country home that rents for about $1,600 per week in low season and $2,700 in July and August. Twelve persons can be comfortable there and fifteen is possible.

Environs and Accommodations
Southern Tier

The Southeast. This compact area includes the rolling hills, woods and farmlands of the county of Kent in the east to the county of Hampshire in the west, and the Channel coast from the estuary of the Thames westward to Portsmouth and the Isle of Wight. The northern part of the area is surrounded and impacted by the city of London. The main advantages of locating in this area are the tranquil but not remote beauty of the countryside, the number of attractive and historically interesting towns, its castles and stately homes, and its proximity to both the sea and to London. The eastern towns of this region—Canterbury, Rye, Lewes, Rochester, Tunbridge Wells, and Maidstone—are particularly worth locating near and visiting. In the western half of this region, the Hampshire towns of Winchester and Lymington are of special interest and beauty. The prettiest countryside is in the Kent Downs, the High Weald, Sussex Downs, New Forest or, closer to London, the Surrey Hills. We once settled in Tunbridge Wells, Kent, because we especially liked the wooded, uncultivated countryside of the High Weald, an area of several hundred square miles that stretches from the coast near Hastings westward into West Sussex.

If day trips into London from a rural setting are your preference, avoid the suburbs by staying well outside the M25 motorway that rings the city. Rail service is very good, so visits to the city from anywhere in the region can easily be accomplished. (See Location and Transportation, below.)

Few North Americans will likely find the larger resort towns of Brighton, Hastings, and Eastbourne and the cities of Portsmouth and Southampton very appealing, but the smaller coastal towns, such as Bognor Regis, and the towns set back from the coast, such as Chichester and Arundel, have something to offer.

Numerous companies offer rentals in this area, so contact any with properties in the counties of Kent, Surrey, East and West Sussex, Hampshire, and Berkshire, listed in the companies section of this chapter. Rentals in the more desirable areas are booked well in advance for the summer season, mid-June to mid-September. Among the regionally based companies is Freedom Holiday Homes in Kent, a small, personalized company with a good selection in Kent and East Sussex.

A drive along the coastal area from Dover at one end to Southampton at the other can be done in half a day or less, but two weeks can be spent exploring the region and taking day trips to London (by rail, preferably), still leaving much to see and do.

Location and Transportation

Highways and railroads serve this area well, partly because much of it is within commuting distance of London, and partly because the ferry ports at Dover, Sheerness, Folkestone, and Portsmouth are the conduits for traffic between Britain and the Continent. Crossings to the Channel Islands or short trips to Belgium or the coastal cities of France are not difficult, so it is easy to spend a weekend in Bruges, Belgium, or in Boulogne, Calais, Cherbourg, Le Havre, or Roscoff, France. Large ocean ferryliners sail between Portsmouth and Bilbao, Spain (201–768–3852 in the U.S.) and between Plymouth and Santander, Spain (011–44–752–221321 in the U.K.) Contact any travel agency in the region for information and ticketing.

No place in the region is more than two hours apart by car or train. A car enables you to get off the main thoroughfares into smaller communities, castles, stately homes, and other sites. This can, however, also be accomplished by public transportation.

Advance Booking Times (Dates are approximate)

Peak - June 25 to Sept. 10: six months
High - mid-May to June 25 and Sept. 10–Oct. 1: three–six months
Mid - April 1 to mid-May and October: one–two months
Low - November, December, January, most of March.: none

Odd periods about which most foreigners know nothing, such as school term endings, and bank holiday weekends, affect both prices and advance booking times. These often vary from year to year but are always shown in rental price lists.

The Southwest. Except for Wiltshire, all the counties of this region are coastal. Dorset is on the English Channel. To its north, Somerset and Avon lie along the coast of the Bristol Channel and the banks of the industrialized Severn River estuary. Devon and Cornwall share the southwest peninsula and are washed by the Channel at the south and the Atlantic at the north. The Southwest comprises four somewhat distinct areas: the English Channel coast; the rolling hill country of Wiltshire and Dorset; the forests, moors, and orchard land of Somerset and Devon; and the rugged Atlantic coast of Devon and Cornwall.

The English Channel coast from Southampton west to Penzance and Land's End (at the tip of Cornwall) is dotted with resort towns, and punctuated by the larger industrial port cities of Bournemouth, Weymouth, and Plymouth. These larger cities are rich with the evidence of maritime British history. They are certainly worth a visit, but there is no need to rent in or near any of them. Many of the smaller coastal towns are attractive and pleasant, especially when the sun shines, but are not especially noteworthy. Several are worth visiting, however, such as Fowey and Falmouth in Cornwall and Lyme Regis in Somerset. If you must rent a place on the coast, advise the agent that you want to avoid the larger resort towns.

Back from the coastal zone, along the east-west axis from London to Land's End, is an orderly rural land dotted with beautiful small towns, any of which would be an ideal setting in which to stay for a week or two. Some of the most interesting and historic towns of England are in this region. Visiting Bath, Exeter, Wells, Taunton, Glastonbury, and Salisbury alone will occupy many days.

Perhaps because Cornwall and Devon occupy the western reaches of the southwest peninsula, or perhaps because they are the land of Camelot, they seem somehow remote from the rest of England. The farther west, the more tranquil and remote it seems, but it is still only four hours by motorway or rail between Plymouth and London. Cornwall is an area for those seeking quiet pursuits, who enjoy poking around small towns, walking across the moors, and exploring rugged coasts. Devon is much the same but slightly more populated, especially on the Channel coast and around the city of Exeter. From a cottage in Devon, day trips to Cornwall are an easy matter. Perhaps the deciding factor between staying in Cornwall or Devon is that Cornwall seems more rural and distant. The eastern reaches of the estuary of the Severn River toward Bristol are more industrialized and less attractive, although Weston Super-Mare, near Bristol, is a popular resort with the British.

Several years ago we spent time in Devon around the tiny village of Thorverton, just north of Exeter, where we learned a great deal about the rental business in Britain from Mary Spivey, the very knowledgeable proprietor of the Independent Traveler. Although it has no slick catalog, this small company is one of the best for working personally with clients and ferreting out good rentals not only in Devon but elsewhere in the south, the Thames Valley, the Cotswolds, and in London. Another company with rentals in this area is Haywood Amaro.

The headquarters of Cornish Traditional Cottages are near the small village of Lostwitheil in a wing of a large, beautifully restored old stone house. In addition to a few apartments in the building, there are about 300 well chosen properties in Cornwall handled by this company. From any Cornish rental all of Cornwall is easy to explore. Warmed by the Gulf Stream, the area is particularly popular with vacationers from the eastern parts of England. There are between 500 and 600 vacation rental cottages available in Cornwall.

The counties of Wiltshire and Avon seem less rural and more orderly than the western counties. The beautiful valley of the Avon River (not the Avon River upon which Stratford lies) flows through both counties and through the cities of Bristol (on the north coast), Bath, Warminster, Salisbury (inland), and Bournemouth (on the Channel). A cottage in the valley in the vicinity of any of the three inland towns would be ideal for anyone wanting to be closer to London and willing to forego the more isolated beauty of Cornwall and Devon.

For those preferring an urban location, the small city of Bath is an excellent choice. Numerous apartments are available. For elegant, centrally located apartments, contact Fountain House. For more modest apartments, contact Bath Holiday Homes, which has a good selection. Bath is a very popular city, rich with the history of Britain's Roman occupation, so book well in advance: six to nine months for summer and two to three months in advance for the periods from mid-March to mid-June and September through October. These spring and autumn months are ideal.

A sampling of the cottages in this region suggests that the owners and the companies that represent them are very serious about the rental business, maintaining high standards of neatness and cleanliness. Few of the rural properties, however, could be called elegant. They tend to be simple, comfortable, English cottages, rather than manor houses or large homes that have been converted.

Transportation

There is rail service between London and the tip of Cornwall and along most of the Channel coast, with spurs to the Atlantic coastal towns of Barnstaple, Newquay, and St. Ives. The area is, nevertheless, best explored by car, especially Devon and Cornwall, where many of the interesting smaller communities are not served by rail. An alternative is the public bus system.

For a visit to France, large ferries sail between Plymouth and Roscoff and between Weymouth and Cherbourg. There are also sailings out of Weymouth to the Channel Islands (Jersey and Guernsey). For something entirely different, a long route port-to-port ship runs on a regular schedule between Plymouth and Santander, Spain. (Contact Brittany Ferries at the Plymouth harbor.)

Advance Booking Time (Dates are approximate)

Peak - June 25 to September 10: six months
High - mid-May to June 25 and September 10–Oct. 1: three–six months
Mid - April 1 to mid-May and October: one–two months
Low - November, December, January, most of March: rent on arrival.

The Central Band

East Central England. East Anglia is the low country of England, the waterland, and the area least touched by industrial change. It comprises the counties of Cambridgeshire, Essex, Norfolk, and Suffolk, and is noted for the remarkable changelessness of the cities, towns, and villages, rather than for dramatic scenery. The past seems to be the present and is evident in Norman castles, churches, and other buildings of medieval times, and in thatched cottages, timbered Tudor houses, and eighteenth-century manor houses. Much of the prosperity and cultural development of the period from the fourteenth through sixteenth centuries is manifested in the great university town of Cambridge as well as in the area's principal cities—Norwich, Ipswich, and ancient Colchester. For those who enjoy beautiful examples of England's past, this area abounds in cathedrals, abbeys, castles, and museums. Each little market town has its own character and unusual melding of ancient and new.

Blakes Holidays was established in 1909 as a rental company for boats, skiffs, and flat-bottom sailing vessels called wherries on the vast inland waterways known as the Norfolk Broads. It has continued in this popular business and now rents every kind of pleasure boat and yacht from sailboats and houseboats to big motor cruisers and canal boats. In addition to renting vessels on the Broads, Blakes now operates on the Thames, Avon, and other rivers and on the long chain of highland lakes in Scotland. From this interesting beginning they have expanded into one of the largest cottage rental companies in Britain and even have rentals in Continental Europe. Many of their rentals in this area are near the lakes and waterways, such as the attractive townhouse complex in Wroxham, 10 miles north of Norwich by highway, or 50 meandering miles by water. A nice approach to staying there is to arrive a day or two before the Saturday changeover and stay in the nearby Norfolk Mead Hotel, a handsome Georgian country house. (The Mead also has a few apartments and can be booked through Blake's Holidays.)

Also located in East Anglia, in Fakenham, Norfolk, is the headquarters of English Country Cottages, one of the largest and most respected rental companies in Britain. Many of their rentals are in East Anglia, but they also handle hundreds more throughout Britain. Another large rental company is Hoeseasons, which, like Blakes, rents boats as well as cottages. Many of the latter are "holiday parks"—functional, modern, resort developments that, to Americans, may seem strangely out of place. All of Britain, however, is not made up of narrow lanes and quaint houses, and these holiday park rentals are good for young children and inexpensive, in the range of $150 to $200 per week, and adequate for those who plan to spend most of their time exploring the countryside.

Adjoining East Anglia to the northwest are the counties known as the "Shires." In a continuation of the coast of East Anglia, miles of beaches are dotted with towns where many Britons go for their holidays. The main interest in this area is the juxtaposition of quaint market towns and historic cities and the green countryside. Less flat than East Anglia, the Shires is scenically more interesting, ranging from the undulating Lincolnshire Wolds to the Peak District National Park in the northwest county of Derbyshire. The highland moors rise to 2,000 feet at the northern end of the park. Between the park and the wolds lies Nottinghamshire and Sherwood Forest, smaller but still much the way it must have been in the days of Robin Hood.

More populous than East Anglia, the Shires are rich with towns and cities of historic interest, among them Nottingham, Chesterfield, Lincoln, Louth, and Stamford. It is also an area popular with walkers and bikers, who enjoy the wolds and the Peak District. An apartment or cottage in one of the smaller towns or a cottage in the countryside makes an ideal base for exploring all of central England as well as the area of the Shires.

There are surprisingly few rental properties in the Shires, but they can be found through Blakes and English Country Cottages.

West Central England. Located between East Anglia and the Shires on the east and Wales on the west, this region has perhaps the most orderly scenery in England, where even the meadows appear to be well tended and each turn in the road opens a new picture-book scene. The Thames and Chilterns are to the northwest of greater London, and the Heart of England is farther west.

Rolling hills rise into the Peak District National Park to the north and also along the border with Wales. The low hills of the Cotswolds and the Chilterns form the watersheds for the beautiful rivers of the area: Avon, Severn, Wye, and Windrush; and Evenlode, Cherwell, and Thame, which join and feed the Thames. Farther north is the Trent River. The hills are gentle and shelter dozens of villages, some with just a few houses, while in the broad river valleys the yellow limestone of the region brings a warmth to the buildings of the cities and the castles, abbeys, and country homes.

The tranquil Thames that runs through Wiltshire, Oxfordshire, and most of Buckinghamshire appears quite different from the tide-influenced Thames that flows through London. North of the Thames Valley, the Avon flows through Warwickshire and, of course, through Stratford-upon-Avon, Shakespeare's country.

Day trips from any point in this region can be made to some of the best known and most interesting towns and cities of England: Cheltenham, Cirencester, Broadway, Gloucester, Stratford, Shrewsbury, Warwick, and Worcester in the Heart of England, and High Wycombe, Marlow, Newbury, Oxford, St. Albans, Windsor, and Woodstock in Thames and Chilterns. For castle and palace lovers there is Warwick Castle, Berkeley Castle, and Windsor, and at Woodstock, Blenheim Palace. For a stay at a castle estate, the cottages at Sudley Castle are excellent. A number of the outbuildings have been converted for rental use and any would make a well located and delightful home base.

Toward the west is Birmingham, Britain's second largest city. Despite being an industrial center, it has excellent shopping and numerous museums and historical sites. It is easily accessible from anywhere in the area.

Several regional companies have rentals in this area; many are in the Cotswolds and in Shakespeare country. Most rentals are modestly priced and can usually be counted on to be attractive and well maintained. Try The

Independent Traveller, Rural Retreats, Tony & Diana Soutar: The Moretons, and Sudeley Castle; if no success, try one of the larger rental companies.

Closer to London, the Thames and Chilterns area is not unlike the adjacent Heart of England. At least to the foreigner, the gentle hills of the Oxfordshire Cotswolds are hard to distinguish from those of Gloucestershire, and the towns of the wooded Chiltern Hills are as appealing as those farther to the west. Of course the closer to London, the more the impact of the city can be felt, and there is no reason to stay too close. A cottage in the countryside around Oxford, if you like proximity to a city, is a good choice, but anywhere in the area will make an ideal home base.

For persons seeking larger, distinctive, and elegant homes, this area has a good selection of manor houses and country homes with grounds in private settings. Some of these more distinctive properties can be rented with or without staff, others offer rooms for a few guests. Contact Castles and Country Estates in London or The Landmark Trust.

The fact that virtually all the large British companies offer self-catering properties throughout this region attests to its desirability. If there is any place in England that fits our idealized images of the country, this is it. There are many tourists here from mid-June to mid-September.

Transportation

A good network of railroads in the central tier of England radiates from London. Many of the smaller towns, however, are not on a line. This is especially true of East Anglia but also of the Cotswolds and Chiltern Hills. If you plan to depend on rail, advise the rental company or study *Cook's European Timetable* (see chapter 4, Transportation).

If you rent a car in London and are headed for East Anglia, in peak traffic times try to avoid the Dartford Tunnel, where the M25 ring motorway goes under the Thames east of the city.

From East Anglia and the Shires, day trips can be made into Kent and its special places, such as Canterbury and Rye. Harwich, on the coast of East Anglia, is the most active port in England for long-run ocean ferryliners, so if an ocean adventure is of interest, take one of the almost daily sailings to Hamburg (Germany), Esbjerg (Denmark), Göteborg (Sweden), Hoek van Holland (Holland), and in summer, Kristiansand (Norway). Voyage durations are from nineteen to twenty-four hours, so a cabin is recommended. The price is modest and the food on board is good. One-way or round-trip tickets can be purchased. Contact any tourist office or travel agency in Britain for information.

From the west central area trips into the southern counties of Dorset, Somerset, Devon, and even Cornwall and west into Wales can be easily undertaken.

Advance Booking Times (Dates are Approximate)
Peak - Mid-June to mid-September: 6 months
High - mid-May to mid-June and mid-Sept. to Oct. 1: 3–6 months
Mid - April 1 to mid-May and month of October: 1–2 months
Low - Nov., Dec., Jan., Feb., March: rent after arrival

The North

The Rose Counties. The Rose counties are the southernmost of this region, north of and bordering the Shires, the Heart of England, and, on the west, Wales. They extend from coast to coast, about 135 miles at the widest point. The principal features of the countryside are the reknowned Yorkshire Moors and the Yorkshire Dales, large areas that are now national parks. The Moors suggest ominous and brooding scenes from Emily Bronte's *Wuthering Heights* and Sherlock Holmes's *Hound of the Baskervilles,* but their wildness can be tamed by exploring them from a cottage base in the vicinity of Helmsley, Thirsk, Pickering, or any other of the stone villages in the area, or, for that matter, from an apartment in the city of York.

The Yorkshire Dales occupy much of the northwest of the region; it is a countryside easily identified by anyone who has seen the television series "All Creatures Great and Small." Southwest of the Dales the pretty area of Lancashire's Forest of Bowland borders the more industrial zone of the county of Cheshire and the cities of Liverpool and Manchester. In the region's southern reaches, the Peak District National Park is shared with the central counties.

Towns of considerable historical interest are encompassed by the region, from the walled city of Chester in the extreme southwest to Ripon in North Yorkshire and the old seaside town of Scarborough.

The architecture changes here from the daub and wattle, timbered buildings or thatched-roof houses of many of the counties of the south to gray stone. Virtually every rental property in the region is a cottage of stone. The severity of the architecture is softened by the countryside, and the rentals seem to be almost universally neat and plain but comfortable, perhaps projecting the nature of the independent people of the region.

One way to select a specific locale in which to spend a week or more is to decide whether you prefer moors or dales. The former tend to be more wild and isolated and the latter more tame. From any spot in the region all others can easily be visited. If you are inclined to stay near a city, an area called the Vale of York is especially appealing.

The companies offering the widest selection of rentals in the area of the Moors, Dales, Yorkshire coast, and Vale of York are Harrowgate Holiday Cottages and Blakes Holidays, listed below. You can also try Holiday Cottages Yorkshire Limited (Water Street, Skipton, North Yorkshire BD23 1PB; Tel:

756–700–510). It is a local company with about 150 rentals in the area.

Toward the west, in Lancashire, Red Rose Cottages has a small but good selection of modestly priced rentals with easy access to the Lake District as well as the Dales. Given the often crowded conditions in the Lake District, this is a good alternative during summer high season.

Location and Transportation

Travel throughout the area is best done by car, but there is intercity bus service and mainline rail service connecting York with London to the south and Newcastle and Edinburgh to the north. There is also rail service into Leeds and across the country to Carlisle, with a somewhat roundabout connection into the Lake District at Windermere. Southeast of York is the port city of Hull, the largest city of the area.

For a complete change of scene, there are daily sailings between Hull and Zeebrugge (Belgium) and Europort (Rotterdam/Netherlands). The voyages take about fifteen hours, so a cabin is a good idea for an overnight trip. The ships are large, new, and attractive, the food is fair, and the prices are modest.

Advance Booking Time (Dates are approximate)

Peak - mid-June to early-Sept.: 6 months
High - May 15 to June 15 and Sept. 10 to Oct. 1: 4–6 months
Mid - April 1 to May 15 and October: 1–2 months
Rest of the year: 2 weeks or rent after arrival

The Lake District. Occupying the northwest corner of England, the Lake District, in the county of Cumbria, is one of the most popular areas of the country, especially for British vacationers and weekenders, but also for foreign visitors. The countryside is a beautiful blending of hills, mountains, and lakes, including Windermere, the largest lake in England. During the summer months and on long weekends in the spring and fall, many of the narrow roads that wind through the hills are lined with the cars of picnickers, walkers, and climbers. At times it may seem as if there are as many people on the hillsides as there are sheep, and that's saying a lot. Those who are not climbing hills or hiking the lakeshore paths are in the shops, restaurants, and on the sidewalks of the pretty towns of Ambleside, Grasmere, Bowness, Keswick, and Windermere. Then there are those who come to sail on Lakes Windermere or Ullswater or travel on the lake steamers or on the steam train.

Except in July and August, most of the nonresidents are British, not foreign tourists. In those two high-season months, when Continental Europeans and Americans join the British, crowded conditions prevail. The lesson is obvious: To enjoy this beautiful area and its charming towns, go in the late spring (May to mid-June) or early fall (September). Much earlier or later than these times increases the chance of inclement weather—it rains considerably here.

Not all of Cumbria is occupied by the Lake District. The area surrounding the district is rich with important places to visit, including castles, stately homes, and to the north, the ancient gray-stone city of Carlisle. The distances in this narrow section of Britain are not great, and day trips to York, for example, or the Yorkshire Moors or Dales can easily be taken. Any of the large companies offering properties throughout England can arrange bookings in this popular area. Two small regional specialists we like are Lakelovers and Lakeland Cottage Holidays, both with a good selection of cottages in the area.

Transportation

The nature of Lakeland is such that a car is very useful, although there is bus service between the lake towns. Windermere is served by a spur rail line off the mainline, which runs between London, Lancaster, Carlisle, and Glasgow. East-west rail routes connect Carlisle and Lancaster with Newcastle-upon-Tyne and York.

Advance Booking Time (Dates are approximate)

Peak - mid-June to early-Sept.: 6 months
High - May 15 to June 15 and Sept. 10 to Oct. 1: 4–6 months
Mid - April 1 to May 15 and October: 1–2 months
Rest of the year: 2 weeks, or rent after arrival except on weekends, national and bank holidays.

Borderlands. This region, comprising the counties of Cleveland, Durham, Northumberland, and Tyne and Wear, is among the least visited by North Americans. Many travelers, however, do go specifically to visit this area of ancient battlegrounds and the castle fortresses built to defend the almost indefensible no-man's land. They are always rewarded by the visit. The castles of Bamburgh, Alnwick, and Dunstanburgh are especially impressive, and Barnard Castle is softened somewhat by the attractive town that surrounds it. This is also a country of old abbeys, priories, pele towers (fortified houses), and a scattering of stately homes.

There are relatively few vacation rentals in this area. Northumberland National Park and vicinity is the most attractive countryside, and the town of Durham is the most interesting. For rentals in this region, contact Blakes Holidays and English Country Cottages.

Transportation

The only north-south rail service is by the mainline between London and

Edinburgh, serving Newcastle and another through Berwick-upon-Tweed, England's most northern town. The single east-west line runs between Newcastle and Carlisle, just north of the Lake District. From this region, day trips into Scotland as far as Edinburgh, Glasgow, and Pitlochry are possible.

In the summer months, port-to-port ships sail between Newcastle and Bergen (Norway), Esbjerg (Denmark), and Göteborg (Sweden), all fairly long voyages. Contact any British travel agency for details.

Advance Booking Time

For July and August: 3–4 months
May, June and September, October: 1–2 months
Rest of the year: 2 weeks; book in advance because it is hard to find rentals by driving around.

The City of London

To go to Great Britain, especially for the first visit, and not spend some time in London would be a sad omission. How long you choose to stay will depend on your personal interests and budget. There are so many things to enjoy in this great city that choosing how best to spend a limited time can be frustrating.

Planning Your Visit

It is useful in dealing with a city of this size and complexity to have a basic plan of how to best utilize your time. For example, the prospect of buying tickets to London theaters, the National Opera, Covent Garden, the Promenade Concerts, Shakespeare at Stratford, and other events can be daunting, and the mechanics time consuming. One solution is to let someone who knows London help out, either with advice or direct assistance. We have found the British Travel Authority very good on the first count, and British Airways excellent on the second. In addition to helping out with tickets for everything from theater to dinner cruises on the Thames, British Airways has a selection of London apartments and townhouse hotels at discounted prices. Unlike staying in a country cottage, the complexity of London makes everything time consuming, so the more that is worked out in advance, the easier it is when you arrive.

Best Times to Visit

The lower winter rates in most London apartments are in effect from around November 1 through March 31; in a few places there is an increase for a short period before Christmas. Although the price differences between the seasons are not as great as in rural rentals, they can often be in the range of 25 percent, which means that an apartment that rents for £600 (about $950) per week in high season will rent for $700 in the winter months. Unfortunately, the winter season as interpreted by London apartment owners and rental companies is relatively short, and those five months are indeed wintry: The days are short and chilly at this latitude, and rainy days punctuated by a rare sunny one are the norm. The tourist population, however, is small. The crowds peak in July and August but are large from early June through September. They begin to grow again in mid-April. April, May, and late September through October combine the virtues of thinner crowds and usually good weather.

Where to Stay

Assuming that you have found good reason to stay for a week or even three or four days, the next steps are to find the right location and the right price. According to the British Travel Authority, short-term rental apartments in London earn nearly four times the rate of complaints from North American visitors than any other vacation rental properties in Britain. The reasons are complex. Mainly it is a matter of expectation versus reality. North Americans who live in large homes or in spacious city apartments are often disappointed in the relative small size of London rental accommodations. A small hotel room may be expected, but we usually imagine something larger than the average London flat or apartment turns out to be. Spaciousness, especially in London, comes at a premium but is available.

Another factor is the age and often, therefore, oddity of the buildings. Many were built well before modern plumbing, for example, so pipes are on the outside and in strange places. Many bathrooms are without a shower of any kind; some have hand-held showers to connect to the bath spigot. Elevators, "lifts" as they are called, may not exist or may have been installed later in the building's life, necessitating small size and unusual location. The key is to look carefully at the descriptions of any apartments under consideration.

Central London is a large, complex, and varied area that deserves study of a good map and guide before deciding where to locate. Without advice or some good research, first-time visitors often don't know where to settle. Fashionable neighborhood names are most recognizable, but apartments in them may be expensive or, if modestly priced, quite small. But if affordable, such prime areas as Knightsbridge, Sloane Square, and Mayfair are convenient and pleasant. Areas less visited by tourists or thought of as less fashionable, such as Bloomsbury and Kensington, provide, in general, the most space for the pound. Remember that the transportation system is excellent if, as with any great city, you avoid rush hours. There are also a few rentals in the suburbs available from such out-of-London companies as The Independent Traveller. They require a commute, but they are the best values in the London area in terms of price and space.

These brief profiles of the areas where the majority of rentals are located will help you decide where to look.

Bloomsbury

Rental prices are relatively modest in this quiet area of residential streets, small shops, restaurants, pubs, and cafes. This is the academic and museum district, which includes the British Museum and the University of London. There is good transportation via railroad, underground, and bus. Most apartments are within walking distance of Russell Square and the British Museum. Apartment Services, Ltd. is a principal supplier of Bloomsbury apartments.

Mayfair

Rental prices are high in this area. Surrounded by Oxford Street on the north, Bond Street on the east, Green Park on the south, and Hyde Park on the west, this is a desirable area. Many of the larger and better hotels, and the U.S. Embassy are here. Shopping is on Oxford Street, Old Bond Street, and Shepherd's Market. There is good intracity transportation but no railroad station.

Bayswater

Rental prices are moderate here. Located along the northern edges of Hyde Park and Kensington Gardens, this is a quiet area of apartments and large old residences, many of which have been converted to apartments. There are offices, smaller hotels, and a few restaurants. Although not one of the more exciting areas of London, it is convenient to Oxford Street shopping. There is good underground and bus service, and Paddington Station makes out-of-city day trips by rail convenient.

Kensington and Earl's Court

Rental prices are moderate here. Areas to the west and southwest of Kensington Gardens are a little distant from the core of the city, so the rental prices there are lower. The location of 51 Kensington Court Apartments is excellent, and the apartments themselves are comfortable and fairly priced. During our stay there, we found the court itself is quiet, while nearby Kensington High Street was bustling with many shops and an assortment of restaurants. Kensington High is a good transportation artery. In addition, Kensington Gardens, Albert Hall, the Victoria and Albert Museum, Science Museum, and Natural History Museum, and a Safeway are all within easy walking distance. Book 51 Kensington Court through London Apartments Ltd.

South Kensington and Knightsbridge

Rental prices are relatively high in this area south of Kensington Gardens and Hyde Park. Toward the west is the Victoria and Albert Museum. Knightsbridge, in the east, is close to Harrods and the stores of Brompton Road. There are many good restaurants in the area. Kensington Road, Brompton Road, and Sloane Street are all good transportation arteries, and underground stations are convenient.

Chelsea

Rental prices are high in this area, especially toward Belgravia to the east, and they are lower toward the southwest. This is considered a fashionable area of residences, better apartments, elegant boutiques, good small restaurants, and antique stores. If you find a modestly priced apartment with a Chelsea address, it is probably either quite small for the price or fairly distant from the city center. Good transportation runs along the Chelsea Embankment, King's Road, and Fulham Road, but there are only two underground stations.

Belgravia

Rents are high in this fashionable area. Between Sloane Square and Hyde Park to the north at least a dozen countries have their embassies. There are good restaurants, shops, pleasant residential streets, and easy access to popular spots like Harrods, Buckingham Palace, and Victoria Station. Sloane Square is an interesting example of the paradox of London. Addresses on Sloane Street, Sloane Gardens, Holbein Place, and others in the vicinity of the square are quite in vogue, and indeed most of the residences and apartments are elegant, but they are best viewed from the inside. Like many of the fashionable areas of inner London, the external neighborhoods disguise the elegance of the residences and apartments in them. This is, nonetheless, a desirable location.

Pimlico

Rents here are moderate. The location is excellent for persons preferring to be near the Tate Gallery, Westminster Abbey, and Houses of Parliament, rather than to the shopping streets of Mayfair and Knightsbridge. Victoria Station and the British Airways terminal are in this area. References in guides or rental company material to the Victoria area mean Pimlico near Victoria Station. One of the largest apartment complexes in London, Dolphin Square, is in Pimlico. Neither quaint nor elegant, it is secure, comfortable, and self-contained, with a swimming pool, shops, and a small grocery within the building complex. It can easily be booked (tel: 71–834–3800; fax: 71–798–8735).

Westminster

Rents are moderate here. The Thames-side area of Westminster is the most recognizable to foreigners, comprising the Victoria Embankment, Parliament, Big Ben, Westminster Abbey, the Tate, and No. 10 Downing St. This east area is not residential, but to the west it joins Pimlico and Belgravia. It is a good area for access to museums, the National Theaters across the river, and other city sights.

The City and Barbican

Rents are relatively modest. The central financial core of London, called "The

City," is here, with few residences and apartments except near the Barbican Center. The area merges with Holborn and Bloomsbury to the north and is convenient to Covent Garden, the theater district, and St. Paul's. Transportation throughout London radiates from here.

Across the River

Not the most popular of London areas to visitors, there are a few rentals in Lambeth and Vauxhall, modestly priced because they are across the river. Mostly residential, many Londoners who live here find it an easy walk across the bridges to the area surrounding Westminster Hall and the Houses of Parliament. There are good apartment values here, and the river is far more a psychological boundary than a real one.

Prices

London is an expensive city but not outrageous, as cities go. To visitors from New York, Chicago, or San Francisco, it does not seem unreasonable.

A rating system is being introduced for short-term rental apartments and cottages that is similar to the star system used for hotels. For the time being, many owners and rental companies tend to classify apartments according to an "A, B, C" ranking or the terms "Luxury, Superior," "Comfortable," and "Economy." Comparisons indicate that the prices of central area London apartments run from about 70 to 80 percent of hotels of equivalent standards.

Unlike country cottages, London serviced apartment prices include all utilities (except telephone charges), a change of linens once or twice per week, and a change of towels from daily to once a week. Better apartments generally provide maid service daily, mid-category apartments usually three to five times per week, and those in the economy class, once or twice per week. The approximate prices in the table below are average for each category, and are per apartment per week, including the VAT. On the average, deduct 15 percent from these rates for winter occupancy.

Category	Studio	1 Bedroom
Luxury	$1,500	$2,240
Superior	1,000	1,360
Comfortable	700	880
Economy	575	700

In the economy category the furniture will be simple and the rooms not much larger than hotel rooms. There is weekly maid service and change of linens. Many of these apartments are occupied year-round and are being rented while the owners are temporarily away; so until the time of booking, there is no way of knowing exactly where the property is located. It will, however, be in the area you specify. The saving over a hotel room of equal standard may not be great, but you will have more space, and a kitchen.

A typical one-bedroom flat in the moderate price range will also usually have a sitting/dining room with sofabed, a bathroom with a bath, WC and basin, and a well-equipped kitchen. Services: weekly cleaning, telephone, washer, entry-phone. Electricity, heat, and linens and towels would be included in the price.

A typical one-bedroom apartment in the superior category should be fairly centrally located, perhaps in the residential areas of Mayfair, Kensington, Chelsea, or Knightsbridge, convenient to shopping and entertainment. Expect 600 square feet of space, period furnishings, six or seven days maid service, porterage, all utilities, security entry system, telephone, towels changed daily, linens every second day.

In the luxury category, expect elegant furnishings and perhaps antiques and art. There may be welcome provisions awaiting you in a modern kitchen and the space would be much larger than a suite in a five-star hotel.

People on limited budgets who want the best value should be willing to locate in outlying areas. In this category are addresses in Maida Vale and St. John's Wood. The rents drop considerably the farther the property is from central London. For example, within a forty-five-minute commute, a comfortable two-bedroom house in the Thames Valley west of London will rent in the range of about $400 per week in winter to about $560 in summer. For information on outlying properties, contact The Independent Traveller. Barclay International Group has apartments in East Croyden, about fifteen minutes from central London by train.

In summary, it takes some care to assure that you are getting fair value. Economically priced apartments can be very poor indeed and, unfortunately, so can moderately priced ones if you are not careful. This is especially disturbing when "moderate" prices are actually quite high in North American terms. With the basic information provided about the areas of London, the difference in rental prices among them, and an idea of what to expect in apartments and rents, you should be able to find the right apartment. The next step is to consult the rental company listings at the end of this chapter.

Transportation

We can see no particular reason to have a rental vehicle in London. A London newspaper article pointed out that the average speed of traffic in central London during the peak hours is much slower than the rate of carriages in Victorian times. Taxis are plentiful and cost relatively little; the underground is the fastest and most efficient; and the double-decker buses are the most fun.

Advance Booking Time (Dates are approximate)

May 1 to September 31: 4 months

April and October: 2–4 months
November 1 to April 1: 0–1 month

Scotland

We have divided Scotland into two areas, the Lowlands and the Highlands and Islands. The former is roughly the southern half of the country, and the Highlands rise north of the axis between the Firth of Forth on the east and the Firth of Clyde on the west. The Islands are offshore from the Northwest Highlands and include the Inner Hebrides, comprised of Skye, Mull, Jura, Islay, and smaller islands; and the Outer Hebrides, consisting mainly of North and South Uist, Lewis, Harris, and Barra. Rentals are available on some of them.

Traveling north from England, once the Scottish border is crossed, a sense of isolation sets in and prevails. This happens twice, actually; once, upon crossing the Cheviot Hills and dropping into the Lowlands of the counties of Borders and Dumfries and Galloway, and again, more profoundly, upon leaving the narrow, populated zone anchored by Edinburgh and Glasgow and moving northward into the Grampian Highlands. In this northern region, occupying nearly a quarter of the area of Britain, fewer than 2 percent of the population lives. This statistic conveys the nature of the Highlands and suggests that it is an area where visitors go for peace, solitude, hiking and walking, fishing, and enjoying the beautiful and rugged countryside, free from the pressures of cities and tourist throngs.

A problem for travelers from overseas is that Scottish rentals are very popular with Britons and Continental travelers, so they are booked early, especially for the summer months. For any stay in Scotland, either avoid a stay in July and August or book well in advance.

The Lowlands

Short-term rentals are available throughout Scotland, including apartments in Edinburgh, Glasgow, Aberdeen, and other cities and towns. Where to stay is a matter of individual choice. Although the name "Lowlands" suggests flat, low countryside, in actuality it is higher and more rugged than much of England; it is low only in contrast to the more mountainous region to the north. The South Uplands occupies most of the Lowlands, odd as that may sound. Except for journeys to the Inner and Outer Hebrides, the area can be explored by day trips from any home location.

Rolling farmland, soft mountainous areas, ancient and interesting towns, castles, and the cities of Glasgow and Edinburgh are in this region. Its variety makes it an excellent region to settle in for a week or more, perhaps divided between a cottage in a village and an apartment in Edinburgh. It is only 45 miles between Edinburgh and Glasgow. Even from the southern reaches of Borders, it is not a difficult journey into the northern region to visit towns like Perth and Pitlochry.

We once stayed in a delightful little apartment in the center of Borders (Roxburghshire), in the little one pub village of Lilliesleaf, and found the area rich in atmosphere and historical places. Nearby Melrose, Jedburgh, and Kelso are all interesting towns, whether for marketing, dining, or visiting the ruins of twelfth- and thirteenth-century abbeys and castles. Abbotsford House, in Melrose, home of Sir Walter Scott, is worth a visit. Edinburgh is less than a two-hour drive. Lilliesleaf, incidentally, is the improbable location for one of the best rental companies in Scotland, Holiday Cottages (Scotland) Ltd., listed later in this chapter.

In Edinburgh, a small gem of an apartment at the improbable-sounding address of Lady Stairs' Close on the Royal Mile provided us with an ideal home base from which to explore this great but manageable capital of about half a million people. The apartment, across the close from Lady Stair's House, is one of two in a delightfully strange old building. It can be booked by contacting owner Jill Bristow (tel: 835–870–417; fax: 835–870–417) or through Holiday Cottages (Scotland). Another rental company for this region is Royal Mile Enterprises. Seasonal flats are also offered by the University of Edinburgh through the Campus Educational Exchange Foundation. Both are listed at the back of this chapter.

Glasgow, with a population of nearly a million, is a bit more complicated than Edinburgh. Despite its rather industrial appearance from the motorways, it's worth visiting. Days can be spent seeing historic buildings, including Glasgow Cathedral, the only standing example of pre-Reformation Gothic architecture in Scotland, and one of Britain's finest art collections at Kelvingrove Park. Unless you specifically want a city stay, Glasgow can be visited by day trips from a rural rental in the vicinity.

To the north of Glasgow, Loch Lomond lifts the spirits, and introduces visitors to the beauties of Scotland's spectacularly large lakes. In the county of Fife, directly across the country from Loch Lomond and an easy trip from Edinburgh, is the town of St. Andrews: It is to golf what Wimbledon is to tennis.

The Highlands and Islands. The Grampian and North West Highlands can best be described as extensive and open. Except in the cities—Aberdeen, Perth, Dundee, and Inverness—little evidence of the pressures of the twentieth century intrudes. In winter, the Cairngorm Mountains rising from the Spey Valley are the skiing and winter sports centers of Britain, with peaks rising well above 4,000 feet. In summer, they are an area for walks and hikes, especially into the Cairngorm Nature Reserve.

Northward beyond Inverness and westward beyond the long valleys of Loch Linnhe, Loch Lochy, and Loch Ness, the countryside becomes even more grudging of modern incursions. Although there are rental cottages available on the mainland and on the islands of Skye, Mull, Colonsay, Tiree, and a few others of the Inner and Outer Hebrides, they are widely scattered. Anyone who wants privacy and peace can be guaranteed it here, but one can also find delightful fishing villages and summer resorts to break the isolation. If planning a summer visit, it is best to wait until at least mid-May to improve the chances of good weather.

Closer to the population centers but still quite isolated and peaceful, the main highway between Edinburgh and Inverness runs through the valley of the River Spey, with an occasional spur leading to the west coast. We found this area appealing because of its physical beauty and its central location in the Highlands region. Day trips or easy overnighters can be made to the western coast, the western offshore islands, east to the city of Aberdeen, or back south to Perth and Edinburgh.

Many estate houses of the area have become available for short-term renting. Some of the larger estates, comprising thousands of acres, raise produce, cattle, timber, and even husband herds of deer. Thanks to modern machinery, greater efficiency, and changing business focus, these estates no longer need large staffs of workers for the lands. Many of the estate homes where workers and their families formerly lived have been renovated and modernized as rental properties. Such is the case with the Ardverike Estate on Loch Laggan, about 50 miles south of Inverness. The stream, meadows, hills, long slender lake, old stone houses, castle-like estate mansion, and the hospitality of the property manager (known as a "factor") typify all that is good about a stay in this part of Scotland. Ardverike Estate rentals are offered by Holiday Cottages (Scotland) Ltd., listed below.

Prices

Prices run the gamut in Scotland as do the types of rentals available—from simple, isolated cottages to apartments in larger estate homes and large, detached houses. There is a considerable difference between low and high season prices. Typically, the simplest one-bedroom cottage will cost about $160 per week in low season, about $210 in midseason, and about $240 in high. Most rural or village rentals in the middle to upper price ranges are usually very comfortable and fairly large, with between two and four bedrooms. A typical rent is roughly $265 per week in low season, $305 in mid, and between $400 to $560 in high season. Apartments in Edinburgh and Glasgow cost more, although not nearly as high as in London. The one-bedroom apartment we stayed in, nicely located on Edinburgh's Royal Mile, is typical of the prevailing prices at about $500 per week in low season and $650 in high.

The Landmark Trust has a select few properties in Scotland of distinctive character, as does the National Trust for Scotland, both nonprofit organizations. There are so few, however, that they are usually booked many months in advance for the period from mid-April through October. But don't let this discourage you—plan well ahead or rent off-season.

If you want to rent an Edinburgh apartment directly from an owner or manager and do not mind booking without the benefit of a description and illustration, write the City of Edinburgh Advance Reservations Department, Waverley Market, 3 Princess Street, Edinburgh, EH 2 2QP, Scotland, and ask for their list of self-catering accommodations and an order form. There is more effort and risk involved than if you were to work with a rental company, but there will be no commissions involved. When dealing directly with an individual, you will probably be required to pay with a sterling bank draft purchased at a U.S. or Canadian bank. If you are in Edinburgh during the off-season it is not difficult to go into the Princess Street office and find a rental on the list. The same holds true for the rest of Scotland. If your visit is planned for any time between mid-October and mid-May (except Christmas week, bank holidays, and school midterm breaks), you can always count on finding something on the spot without reservations. Just telephone or go to the offices of the Scotland-based companies profiled in the listings at the back of this chapter. For the summer months, however, almost every good property is rented by February, so book well ahead.

Transportation

Mainline railroads connect all the major cities of Scotland, and they connect Scotland with the cities of England. Less frequent service is available all the way north to Scrabster and west to Mallaig, Oban and to Kyle of Lochalsh where there is a ferry to the Isle of Skye. There is also ferry service between Oban and the Isle of Mull and the Hebrides. The isolated Orkney Islands off the north coast are served by ferry from Scrabster. Although we are aware of no rental companies with cottages there, a visit of a few days is worth looking into. Another interesting journey is by a P&O ocean ferry from Aberdeen to the Shetland Islands well north of Scotland's north tip. Ships sail three times per week on the fourteen-hour voyage to Lerwick, Shetland (with connections in summer to Bergen, Norway, the Faroe Islands, and Iceland). Although we know of no rentals there, contact the British Tourist Authority or any travel agent in Britain for information.

Despite good rail and bus systems, most of the rural rental properties are off the main lines and tourist trails, and a car is essential.

Advance Booking Time (Dates are approximate)
Late-June to Sept. 1: 6 months

Late-May through June and Sept.: 2–3 months
Oct. to late-May (except holidays): 2 weeks or rent after arrival.

Wales

Geographically, Wales is the western end of the central tier of Britain. Its western border is the Irish Sea and its eastern border, the counties of the Heart of England. To cross the border from England, however, is to enter a different country, which it once was. In terms of history, culture, and language, these distinctions live side by side with the country's English identity. Although the country's Welsh history is reflected in signs that read CROESO I GYMRU (Welcome to Wales) and in the names of the counties—Clwyd, Dyfed, Glamorgan, Gwent, Gwynedd, and Powys—English is spoken universally.

Wales is not large: from a cottage rented anywhere within its borders the whole of it can be explored by day trips. The only two cities of any size, Cardiff and Swansea (pop. 280,000 and 180,000 respectively), are on the south coast, and from there northward the populace is thinly spread throughout farms, villages, and towns of fewer than 20,000 people.

There is much to enjoy in Wales: Inland are national parks of Snowdonia in the north and Brecon Beacons toward the south. Both are noted for the scenic beauty of their woods, mountains, and streams. The coast extends from Cardiff all the way to Prestatyn and includes the long, thin Pembrokeshire National Park along the southwest coast. The coast is lined with many villages, which lie on the promontories and along the estuaries and, in the north, around the Isle of Anglesey. In addition to the beautiful scenery, Wales has many sites of historical and architectural interest: cathedrals and abbeys, and, more impressive, castles—from the forbidding walls and mass of the ruined Caerphilly to the classic grace of Caernarvon. Finally, throughout Wales in the towns and villages there are hospitable people, good food, old and wonderful pubs, and an unhurried lifestyle.

The north of Wales, including Anglesey, seems especially remote from London and the Heart of England, even though it is less than four hours by train from London's Euston Station to Bangor. Welsh people we talked with seemed to feel that the needs of Northern Wales were not of high priority with the British government, and it is true that there is little sense of development and incursion of late twentieth-century British progress. To the outsider, of course, therein lies its charm and beauty. However, the replacement of a torturous north coastal highway of Clwyd by a four-lane freeway surely pleased weekenders from Liverpool and Manchester, who used to line the highway for miles trying to get home. Such is progress.

Prices

The owner of one Welsh rental company expressed concerns about whether some of the simpler cottages would meet American standards, but this should not deter anyone from staying in Wales. If this is a worry, the answer is to book a cottage of average standards or above, not the simplest. There is a wide variety of rentals available, from cozy cottages to beautiful larger homes and apartments in village buildings and even in castles. The main concentrations of rentals (as well as of castles and towns) are in the northwest and the southwest. Both are good locations for a home base. There is also a scattering of rentals in central Wales and the very pretty Brecon Beacons area.

For a stay in a castle consider Bryn Bras Castle, 6 miles east of Caernarvon, in northwest Wales. We took an apartment here to see what castle living was like. The fairly comfortable apartments are of average standard and can accommodate from two to six persons. Rates are reasonable, in the range of $160 to $290 per week in low season and double that in July and August. In castles it is usually best to book one of the better rooms, rather than the former staff quarters, in order to enjoy the surroundings. Write or telephone Bryn Bras Castle, Llanrug, Gwynedd LL55 4RE, Wales; tel: 011–44–286–870–210. Two castles with well above average apartments are in the southwest—St. Bride's Castle in Havorfordwest, Dyfed, and the elegant Roch Castle in Pembrokeshire National Park near St. David's, at the tip of the peninsula. (Both are available through Blakes Holidays.)

Another small and very nice group of cottages is on the Isle of Anglesey at Beaumaris. Called Henllys Farm House Apartments, they are on the grounds of Henllys Hall, now a hotel. The address is Beaumaris, Anglesey LL58 8HU; tel: 011–44–248–811–303. In southwest Wales, the apartments of the Hotel Penralt, listed below, are a good choice. Stays of only three or four days can almost always be arranged in the low-season months.

Wales is not a very popular place to visit in the low-season months from mid-October to April (except at Christmas, national holidays, and school midterm breaks), so rental prices drop dramatically. But even during the summer months, it is not difficult to find a comfortable, modernized cottage in the range of $240 to $320 per week. At the other end of the spectrum, the main part of Roch Castle, mentioned above, can be rented for about $1,280 per week from late fall through early spring and $1,920 per week in the peak months of July and August. These prices are for five bedrooms, two baths (with showers), four toilets, and 6 acres of grounds, which are shared with the renters of the slightly smaller, three-bedroom, west wing (which rents from $560 to $990). There are rental properties in every price between the two extremes, and the values are very good.

Transportation

From the south of Wales, day trips to London are possible; the travel time by motorway or train is a matter of two to three hours. There is a highway along the coast and several crisscross Wales, but there is no rail line along the southern part of the west coast. The north-south rail line runs between Swansea and into England, with connections at Shrewsbury west to the coast at Tywyn. The northern part of the west coast railway runs from Aberystwyth through Porthmadog and connects with the mainline running from London to Crewe to Holyhead. It is possible to get around the country fairly well by train, except for the southwestern coast and, of course, through much of the Snowdonia and Brecon Beacons national parks. These require a car and so do most of the rental properties. Wales is very rural, and even though there is fair bus service, without a car you will need to be prepared for long walks.

For an interesting change of scenery, there are daily sailings of large car/passenger ferryliners between Fishguard and Rosslare, Ireland, and between Holyhead and Dun Laoghaire (just south of Dublin). The former crossing takes about four hours, the latter less than two on an immense catamaran. If not traveling by car, rail passage can be booked from any station in Britain across to Ireland, the ferry voyage included. Of the choices, the trip to Dublin is the most rewarding, although Rosslare is the gateway to Cork and the south counties of Ireland.

The ferryport of Holyhead is on the tip of Holy Island, across a narrow channel from the west end of the large island of Anglesey, which in turn is across a narrow channel from the North Wales town of Bangor. Anglesey itself is an important area to visit, rich with ancient ruins and castles. Beaumaris Castle, one of Britain's most beautiful, is just a short trip by bus or car from Bangor.

From a cottage or apartment in North Wales, it is an easy and worthwhile trip by car or train to the city of Chester, just across the border in the English county of Cheshire. Liverpool is just to the north.

Advance Booking Time (Dates are approximate)
Mid-June to September: 3–4 months
Mid-May to Mid-June and Sept. and Oct.: 2–3 months
Rest of the year: 2 weeks or rent on arrival.

The Rental Companies and Organizations of the United Kingdom

Approximately 280 companies, consortia, trusts, and individual apartment managements represent well over 30,000 vacation rentals in Great Britain. The task of selecting the right place for a stay of a week or more is difficult indeed. This is especially true for foreigners who do not know the country well, much less the rental companies. We have tried to make some helpful suggestions about where to locate. As for finding the right company, we have done much of the sorting for you.

The companies selected for inclusion are a relatively small proportion of the total number. They were chosen for a number of reasons. First, viability: We favored companies that have been around, surviving in this competitive business because of client satisfaction and repeat business. Some companies are included because we have come to know them over the years and can personally recommend them. Others responded quickly and openly to our inquiries and welcomed our attention. We also made a point of including companies that make contact and booking easy from overseas. Finally, we included companies with a regional specialty as well as the large organizations that offer many hundreds of rentals throughout Britain. Together these organizations cover all of the United Kingdom. The full spectrum of available standards is represented, from modest apartments to manor houses.

A few U.S. companies are included, especially those representing London apartments. Unless otherwise noted, they charge no additional commission.

London companies are separate and follow those elsewhere in Britain. Northern Ireland follows London.

A & D Soutar: THE MORETONS
Central England (Gloucestershire)
Bredon, Tewkesbury
Gloucestershire GL20 7EN
Tel: 684–72294   Fax: 684–72262

The Moretons is a collection of nine houses and cottages on a centuries-old working farm estate. Seven of the houses were built around 1820 of Cotswold stone, as was the six-bedroom, four-bath main house, which can accommodate ten. The smallest cottage accommodates two.

The conversions have been beautifully accomplished, retaining the character of the Cotswolds while being otherwise thoroughly modernized and comfortable. All the accommodations are completely equipped and furnished with amenities such as central heating, dishwashers, microwave ovens, color TV, coffee maker, direct telephones, and hair dryer. The furnishings are tasteful, enhanced by personal objects collected from many parts of the world. The result is a level of comfort rarely found in rental accommodations. Anthony and Diane Soutar, the owner/managers, have done everything possible to provide for their clients, with an eye toward overseas visitors. The efforts have been rewarded by having created one of the most pleasant small rural complexes in England.

This is an excellent location from which to explore the Heart of England—it is 25 miles to Stratford-upon-Avon and 50 miles to Oxford. There are 5 acres of lovely gardens and trees, surrounded by farmland and orchards.

Contact the Soutars for a free brochure and price list. Booking is easy: a 20 percent deposit is required, with the balance payable after arrival and inspection of the premises, an unusual and generous offering. Details in brochure. Prices are surprisingly modest, ranging from about U.S. $225 per week in low season to $275 in July and August for the smallest cottage. Four cottages that accommodate four persons cost from about $280 in low season to $530 in high. Second and third weeks are at reduced rates. Add 17.5 percent VAT. No credit cards are accepted, but payment can be made with traveler's check or a personal check in U.S. or Canadian dollars at the rate of exchange on the day of booking. (Add the equivalent of £8.00 to cover the bank exchange fee on their end.) Or pay by sterling bank draft or wire transfer. (Instructions are given at time of booking.) The Moretons will make for a delightful stay—guaranteed.

Bath Holiday Homes   Bath and Environs
3 Franklcy Buildings
Bath, Avon BA1 6EG
Tel: 225–332–221   Fax: 225–442–388

A virtual must on a visit to England is this beautiful, busy, and intriguing city southwest of London. This small company specializes in apartments and maisonettes in and around Bath city and has done an excellent job of selecting and presenting them in a colorful and informative catalog. Many are in attractive Georgian buildings of the kind that makes Bath so distinctive in appearance. They are well furnished, traditional in style, well equipped, and generally spacious. Locations are excellent, including several in the heart of the city.

Prices vary considerably, but we are impressed with the overall value of these properties, especially compared to London apartments. For example, a beautifully appointed three-bedroom Georgian maisonette (two floors) in the city center runs £350 (about U.S. $575) in low season to £430 (about $700) in high. A cottage converted from an eighteenth-century shop reputed to have inspired Dickens's *Old Curiosity Shop* accommodates two in one bedroom for about $380 per week year-round.

Phone or fax for a brochure, select three, and recontact about availability. This is a popular city so book well ahead. Watch the catalog for booking periods—some are Friday to Friday. Payment is in the form of a bank draft in pounds sterling. Since you will have to mail it, fax a copy of the draft to assure that the booking will be held. Credit cards may be accepted in the future, so ask before booking.

Blakes Holidays Ltd.   Throughout Great Britain
Wroxham, Norfolk
Norwich NR12 8DH
Tel: 603–782–141   Fax: 603–782–871

One of the largest and oldest rental companies in Britain, Blakes has a large selection of properties in most price categories throughout England, Scotland,

The Norfolk Mead Hotel and Cottages, which are available through Blakes Holidays, Ltd., are situated on a beautiful estate near the town of Wroxham, Norfolk. (Photo by Michael and Laura Murphy)

and Wales, and some on the island of Guernsey as well as in the Republic of Ireland and many parts of France. Blakes began as a company renting boats on the vast waterways of East Anglia, the Norfolk Broads. It still does, and you might consider spending a week on a self-catering motor cruiser or sailing yacht on the Broads, a cruiser on the upper Thames, or in Scotland's Highland Lakes—an outstanding way to explore Britain. The prices are surprisingly modest, about the same as a London apartment.

The selection of rental properties is so large and the locations so varied and diverse that there seems to be a place to fit any requirement. You can either advise the company of exactly what you are looking for, with dates, or call or write for their catalog. If you want the catalog, add two weeks to your advance planning time. Booking is easy and payment can be made by major credit card. A company this large can be somewhat impersonal, but we find it competent and helpful. The properties are well maintained and fairly priced.

The U.S. agent, Blakes Vacations (tel: 800–628–8118), charges a fairly high commission but offers personalized service. The advantage of working with the U.S. agent is quick availability of the catalog and ease of payment.

Campus Educational Exchange Foundation   Edinburgh, Scotland
U.S. Agent: British Travel Network Ltd.
The Mews, 594 Valley Road, Upper Montclair, NJ 07043
Tel: (800) 274–8583 or (201) 744–5215   Fax: (201) 744–0531

Operated by the University of Edinburgh's Operations Department, these modest, inexpensive apartments are in University Flats, Mylne's Court, and Pollock Halls of the University of Edinburgh. They are available only in summer and fall. Mylne's Court is near the old town center, while the others are located on campus. The campus accommodations and atmosphere are somewhat institutional in nature, but they are all very good values. The company also handles Royal Court Apartments in London, listed below. For both Edinburgh and London the prices are the same booked through the New Jersey company as they are when booking directly. A brochure is available, and payment is made by check or credit card. The contact in Scotland is University of Edinburgh— Edinburgh Scotland, Commercial Operations, Dept. LB1, Pollock Halls of Residence, 18 Holyrood Park Road, Edinburgh EH 16 5AY, Tel: 31–667–1971, Fax: 31–668–3217

Castles and Country Estates   Throughout England (Including London)
55 Earls Court Square
London SW5 9DG
Tel: 71–373–0451   Fax: 71–370–0838

This small company specializes in well chosen, mid- to luxury-standard country and village houses in southern England and also has a number of very nice apartments in London. The company owner operates on a personal basis, seeking to match clients with exactly what they are seeking. The best approach is to phone or fax with information about what you are looking for, the general location, and dates. You will be contacted with one or more proposed property descriptions. We feel the prices are fair and that the service and attention are excellent. Discuss payment details at the time of booking.

Cornish Traditional Cottages   Cornwall
Peregrine Hall
Lostwithiel
Cornwall PL22 0HT
Tel: 208–872–559   Fax: 208–873–548

This is one of our favorite rental companies, offering a well chosen selection of cottages throughout Cornwall. They set high standards, even for the most modest properties. Interestingly, many clients are from the east of Britain, coming to Cornwall to enjoy the warmer climate. The company offices occupy part of Peregrine Hall, a large and stately building on grounds near the little village of Lostwithiel. The house contains several apartments in what we understand was once a chapel.

A well-illustrated catalog will be mailed for the asking; the descriptions and illustrations are accurate and informative. After making choices, phone or fax about availability. Alternatively, if you know where you want to be, provide your complete requirements and they will fax a choice. If you use the catalog, note the properties that provide linens and towels; if the one you want does not, be sure to request them at the time of booking. Prices are remarkably modest. Payment can be made by VISA and MasterCard, or by bank transfer. (The company will provide instructions.)

Edinburgh Royal Mile Apartments   Scotland (Edinburgh)
Lilliesleaf, Melrose
Roxburghshire TD6 9JD
Scotland
Tel: 835–870–417 or 835–870–481   Fax: 835–870–471

This is the name of the two delightful apartments noted earlier in this chapter in the section on Scotland. Located on the Royal Mile in Lady Stair's Close, they are owned by delightful and helpful, Jill Bristow. Although she is a director of Holiday Cottages (Scotland), and the apartments can be booked through that company, it's nice to talk with the owner. There is a one-bedroom apartment at £415 (about U.S. $665) per week and a studio at about $500, both with all amenities furnished. The kitchens, while not large, have everything you would expect of a modern kitchen. Call or fax for the little brochure, or book with confidence. Pay by VISA or bank draft in pounds sterling. A stay here will add to the experience of a visit to Edinburgh. And for something entirely different, try a few days or a week in Lilliesleaf, a "one-pub" village south of Edinburgh where Ms. Bristow has a gem of a studio apartment.

Fountain House England (Bath City)
9/11 Fountain Buildings
Lansdown Road
Bath BA1 5DV
Tel: 225–338–662   Fax: 225–445–855
U.S. agent: Utell International
Tel: (800) 448–8355

This is an elegant, small apartment building, actually a five-star, all-suite hotel, housed in a lovely Palladian mansion on a quiet street in central Bath. Everything from studios to three-bedroom apartments are available, all luxuriously furnished, spacious, and thoroughly desirable. There is a reception area, porterage, and daily maid service. Continental breakfast is delivered to the apartments. We recommend Fountain House highly; the prices are in keeping with other luxury accommodations. Studios cost about $225 per night and less by the week. A brochure will be sent on request.

The U.S. agency charges the published rate; feel free to phone or fax Fountain House to compare prices. Payment can be made to either Utell or Fountain House by major credit card.

Freedom Holiday Homes   Southeast England (Kent, Sussex)
Weaversden Cottage, Frittenden
Cranbrook, Kent TN17 2EP
Tel: 58–080–251   Fax: 58–080–455

Specializing in rentals in delightful Kent and Sussex, this small company offers personal attention as well as a good selection of rentals. There is much to say for regional organizations such as this: They know the territory intimately and offer good counsel. Another plus is that there is always someone with the company close by in case any problem should arise. Having lived in Tunbridge Wells (Kent) for six months, we can attest to the tranquil beauty of this part of England, plus easy access to London and to outstanding towns and sites such as Rye, Canterbury, Hastings, Bodiam Castle, and Leeds Castle. From this region it is easy to take the ferry, hovercraft, or the tunnel for a day or two visit to France.

The rentals tend toward the modest and traditional, including converted oast houses (pointed-roof-buildings used for drying hops). As for a specific area in which to stay, if you don't know Kent or Sussex trust company owner/manager Maggie Hoyt to find the right one. Phone her to discuss possibilities. Prices are very fair and the rentals are good value. Detached cottages sleeping four to six persons typically rent in July and August for around £275 (about $440), which drops to the £175–200 ($280–$300) range in winter, early spring, and fall.

Call or fax for a catalog, mailed at no cost. The company is busy and bookings need to be made early. At time of this writing the rent payment is made by bank draft in pounds sterling or through bank transfer, but Ms. Hoyt advises that they will likely accept VISA and MasterCard. We recommend this company, especially for people wanting pleasant accommodations at a modest price in a quintessentially English location.

G.M. Thompson & Co.   Throughout Scotland
27 King Street
Castle Douglas,
Dumfries and Galloway DG7 1AB
Scotland
Tel: 556–2973   Fax: 556–3277

Not a large company, G.M. Thompson has been in business for more than twenty-five years, specializing in southwest Scotland, with a few properties in Argyll and near the golfing mecca of St. Andrews, far to the northeast. It represents about 200 modest to moderately priced cottages.

The company is quick to respond and sends a catalog at no cost upon request. Unfortunately, it does not yet accept credit cards, so purchase a draft in pounds sterling at your bank, fax a copy of the draft to hold the property, and then airmail it. Confirmation and directions will be sent by return airmail or fax.

Grant Reid Communications   Throughout England and London
Box 810216
Dallas, TX 75381
Tel: (800) 327–1849 or (214) 243–6748   Fax: (214) 484–5778

This is a good source for travelers interested in staying for a few days or a week in London as well as in a rural or village cottage. They have a small but nice selection of cottages, and a large selection of apartments in London. (See profile under London, following this section.)

Harrowgate Holiday Cottages   Northeast England
127 Cold Bath Road
Harrowgate, North Yorkshire HG2 0NU
Tel: 423–520–476   Fax: 423–526–057162

Harrowgate specializes in rentals in North Yorkshire. This small company is included here because it is prompt to reply to inquiries and booking is made easy, but our main reason for including it is that it specializes in properties in this pleasant and relatively undervisited area of England. Almost all of the company's sixty-five or so rentals are within a 25-mile-radius of Harrowgate, itself an interesting and busy nineteenth-century town characterized by stately Victorian architecture. From a cottage anywhere in the region day trips can easily be made to the wonderful cathedral and market city of York, to the North Yorkshire Moors, and into the Yorkshire Dales National Park.

Rentals are in the modest to moderate price range. A catalog will be sent free upon request, or explain what you are seeking and they will suggest a few properties that will suite your needs. The deposit and final rent may be made by credit card. Confirmation and instructions will be sent upon final payment.

Haywood Amaro Cottage Holidays   Throughout Britain
Lansdowne Place
17 Holdenhurst Rd.
Bournemouth, Dorset BH8 8EH
Tel: 202–555–545   Fax: 202–558–144
U.S. agent: Heart of England Cottages
Eufala, Alabama
Tel: (205) 687–9800   Fax: (205) 687–5324

By British standards this is not a very large company, offering some 350 properties, most in the south counties of England but with a good representation in Wales and a few in Scotland. Its size makes it easy to work with, and the catalog is colorful, descriptive, and well laid out, including good locator maps. If you are not sure where in Britain you want to locate, a perusal of the catalog will help, especially if you are interested in unfamiliar places. (How about Curry Mallet in Somerset or Burton Bradstock in Dorset?) Prices range widely, as does the variety of properties. A stone cottage for two in Wales, for example, runs from $250 per week in low season to $450 in high. A very comfortable four-bedroom wing of an eighteenth-century country house with all modern amenities in Dorset rents for a low of $850 per week from November through March (except for Christmas) to $2,100 from mid-July through August. The properties are properly priced.

A catalog is available for the asking. The deposit and final payment are payable with VISA and MasterCard or a bank draft in pounds sterling. There is, however, an administrative charge of £15 for overseas bookings.

An alternative to booking directly with Haywood Amaro is to contact their main agent in the United States, Heart of England Cottages. Although a very helpful company, they add a commission. Compare prices.

Hoeseasons Holidays Ltd.   Throughout Britain
Sunway House
Lowestoft, Suffolk NR32 3LT
Tel: 502–500–500   Fax: 502–584–962
Boat rentals: Tel: 502–501–010   Fax: 502–586–781
For brochure only: Tel: 502–501–501

This is a large company with rentals throughout the United Kingdom plus France, Belgium, Holland, and Germany. Although in Britain they have a few independent cottages, they specialize in rentals in purpose-built resorts, clusters of cottages usually centered around common communal buildings with a pool, games, picnic facilities, and the like. Their properties will appeal more to families with young or adolescent children. They are also for travelers on a modest budget; it is rare to find a rental over £250 (about U.S. $400) per week for four persons, even in high season, and many off-season cottages for two or three are in the $160 range. There are even caravan (mobile home) parks, where six can stay for $200 or so per week, including the caravan.

The company's substantial catalog will be mailed upon request; payment can be made by VISA or MasterCard. A deposit of 50 percent is payable at the time of booking and the balance four weeks before occupancy.

Hoeseasons is one of the two large companies that rent boats by the week, especially for cruising the Norfolk and Suffolk Broads. Motor cruisers, houseboats, and sailboats can be rented as you would a cottage or apartment. Prices run about the same as for a London apartment of the same standards and guest capacity.

Holiday Cottages in Scotland   Throughout Scotland
Hillcrest, Lilliesleaf, Melrose
Roxburghshire TD6 9HX
Scotland
Tel: 835–870–7481   Fax: 835–870–471

This relatively small company has an excellent selection of rentals throughout Scotland, including a rare few in the sparsely populated far north and the islands of Seil, Colonsay, Tiree, and Argyll. In addition to independent, privately owned cottages there is a good selection of rentals on the properties of some of the great estates. Many of the houses formerly lived in by estate employees and their families have now been converted for short-term rental use. Typical is the Ardverike Estate on the shores of Loch Laggan, about 60 miles south of Inverness. We stayed there several years ago in a five-bedroom stone house overlooking the woods, river, and lake. We found it to be a new and wonderful experience. The setting is beautiful, the house not grand but certainly comfortable and central for travels into central and northern Scotland.

We know this company well and like its operations; it is large enough to offer a good choice and small enough to provide personal service.

A small but well-illustrated catalog is available. It is a little awkward to obtain because of a $2.50 charge for postage, but write for it enclosing currency or a VISA or MasterCard number and expiration date. Unless you already know exactly where you want to be, the catalog is a great asset in deciding. Booking can be made by phone or fax and payment made by major credit card. Once done, complete instructions and directions will be sent immediately.

The Independent Traveller   Mostly Southwest England, London Environs
Dinneford Springs, Thorverton
Exeter, Devon EX5 5NT
Tel: 392–860–807   Fax: 392–860–552

Mary Spivey, owner of this small company, is exceptionally resourceful at finding rentals, and is among the fairest in pricing. Although most of the properties are concentrated in the southwest counties (Devon, Somerset, Dorset, Wiltshire), they are also offered elsewhere, including in the Cotswolds, Thames Valley, and rural environs within commuting distance of London.

The catalog, available for the asking, is an informal assemblage property description sheets, which are kept current. Or you can phone or fax your requirements to the company. The prices are closely pegged to the overall quality of the property, so if you book at an economy price you will be booking an economy cottage; if you pay a considerable amount, the quality of the rental will reflect this. The company is also a good resource for late bookings. Phone or fax with your needs and the Independent Traveller will start a rush property search, often working cooperatively with other rental companies.

In our experience, although dealings with Ms. Spivey and the company are rather informal, the end result is that client and property are well matched. If you need advice, they are experts in helping. Payment is made by major credit card or bank draft in pounds sterling.

Lakelovers   Northwest England (Cumbria / Lake District)
The Toffee Loft, Ash Street
Bowness-on-Windermere
Cumbria LA23 3RA
Tel: 53–94–88–855   Fax: 53–94–88–857

Lakelovers is a small and very good company specializing in the Lake Country with a fine and fairly priced selection of properties, nicely presented in their catalog. The rentals are scattered about the area from Grasmere in the north to Stavely-on-Cartmel in the south. You will need to decide whether you want to be in one of the villages or in a more isolated area, and whether a lakeside location is essential.

Rental prices run a bit more in this area, but are relatively modest. A nicely furnished two-bedroom, "3-key" independent cottage, for example, will run about £250 ($400) per week from November through March and about $750 in August.

A catalog is available at no cost, or you can phone or fax with an idea of what you are looking for, and when. They will send descriptions of a variety that meet your needs. The deposit and final payment can be made by major credit card or bank draft in pounds sterling.

Lakeland Cottage Holidays   England (Cumbria / Lake District)
3 the Heads
Keswick, Cumbria CA12 5ES
Tel: 76–87–71–071 Fax: 76–87–75–036

The rentals of this very small company are all within a 10-mile-radius of Keswick, a busy small town in the northern section of the Lake District. Prices are quite modest and properties well looked after. Contact them for their brochure and pay by credit card. (Be sure to request towels.)

The Landmark Trust   Throughout Great Britain
Schottesbrooke
Maidenhead, Berkshire SL6 3SW
Tel: 628–825–925   Fax: 628–825–417
To request a catalogue in the U.S. and Canada: Tel: (800) 848–3747 or (802) 328–1353 Brattleboro, Vermont.

This is one of the most unusual rental organizations in Britain, a major non-profit foundation founded to save, preserve, and restore historical buildings of Britain. A noble enterprise, but what does a foundation do with ancient castles, old forts, an unusual farmhouse, an unused railway station, or a once-elegant manor house that has seen better times? It restores them, maintains them, and offers them for rent.

The properties are scattered throughout England, Wales, Scotland, and the Channel Islands. There are even two in Italy and one in the United States (the former Vermont home of Englishman Rudyard Kipling). They are varied in their nature. Some are odd, some quaint, and some elegant. All are old and, in one way or another, special. For example, with the approval of the Queen, two apartments in famed Hampton Court are on the rentals list (book a year in advance). So is the summer house in Scotland built by the Earl of Dunsmore in 1761 as a gift for his wife. (Dunsmore later became governor of New York and Virginia.) There is, it seems, an abode for every possible taste and whim. The range of prices is as great as the range of sizes, types, and styles.

With considerable wisdom the Trust has overcome the problem (and cost to the client) of mailing individual copies of their large and beautiful catalog overseas. They are shipped in bulk to a contractor in Vermont (The Landmark Trust, 28 Birge Street, Brattleboro, VT 05301).

To locate and book a property, call the U.S. office for the Landmark Trust and order its large catalog. It is less than $20 and well worth it for its photographs, drawings, and descriptions. Pick two or three of your dream or fantasy places and call or fax the offices in England with dates; they will advise you concerning availability. Payment can be made by MasterCard or VISA, or mail a personal check at the rate of exchange upon booking to the Landmark's U.S. mailing address.

Prices are surprisingly low, principally because the Landmark Trust is a non-profit foundation. The range is as great as the range of sizes, types, ages, and styles of the properties. Apartments for two or three cost as little as £200 (about $320) in winter up to $560 in July and August. Prices in the $400 to $700 range for four persons are typical. The most expensive are Wortham Manor (accommodates 15) at about $2,720 and Saddell Castle for eight at $2,250 in high season. Staying in one of these rentals is an outstanding way to visit Britain, but don't complain if the floors creak, the four-poster bed squeaks, the room arrangement is odd, or the walls are made of stone; they may all be centuries old.

MacKay's Agency   Throughout Scotland and in Northern England
30 Frederick Street
Edinburgh EH2 2JR
Scotland
Tel: 31–225–3539   Fax: 31–226–5284

McKay's offers a selection of some 3,000 rentals, making it the largest rental company in Scotland. Among these are everything from simple croft cottages to mansions, pictured and described in their catalog. The catalog, including a good locator map, is free for the asking and is itself a geography lesson, since it is divided into shires (counties).

This is a good source for travelers who want to get well away, out to the islands of Lewis, Scalpay, Harris, Uist, Jura, Islay, Arran, and others of the Inner and Outer Hebrides. There is also a fair selection of apartments in Edinburgh.

It's best to make your selection from the catalog and phone or fax with at least four possibilities. You will be told immediately of availability. The deposit is £80, which can be paid, along with the final payment, by major credit card or a bank draft in pounds sterling. Check the description for extras to be paid to the owner or keyholder, such as utilities, linens, and towels. The prices make for very good value; a comfortable freestanding house for four to six persons can easily be found for about $560 per week in peak season and $400 in off-season. For a family reunion or company holiday, try the elegantly furnished Mansion House on Eilean Aigas, a private, 60-acre island in Inverness-shire. It has eleven bedrooms and accommodates nineteen. The price is about $4,250 per week.

Mann's Holidays   Northwest Wales
Gaol Street
Pwllheli, Gwynedd LL53 5DB
Wales
Tel: 758–613–666   Fax: 758–612–485

Mann's is one of the very few regional companies specializing in the area of northwest Wales. It is not large, and the catalog is an assemblage of sheets with written property descriptions. Our suggestion is to send for the catalog (no cost) and work with a good map, deciding where you want to be and choosing several possibilities. Gwynedd is rich in rewarding diversions, from visiting great castles and pleasant towns to a lovely coast and Snowdonia National Park. The rentals are very modestly priced and can be booked by credit card.

The National Trust   Throughout Great Britain
Holiday Booking Office
P.O. Box. 536
Melksham, Wiltshire SN12 8SX
Tel: 225–79–2299   Fax: 225–70–6209
Brochures only: Tel: 225–79–1133

Founded in the late nineteenth century, The National Trust is Britain's major acquirer and keeper of great historical edifices, monuments, stately homes, gardens and ancient sites and, more recently, protector of many natural areas. Many of its trust holdings are the most well known in Britain, such as St. Michael's Mount, Chirk Castle, Bodiam Castle, the Stonehenge Downs, and Lindisfarne Castle. These properties are open to the public, and those who visit each year are counted in the millions. More recently, the Trust formed a division that deals with short-term rentals.

Like the Landmark Trust and the National Trust for Scotland, the rental operation is nonprofit and commits the proceeds from its operation to the acquisition and restoration of historical properties.

The National Trust offers about 200 rental properties throughout England, Wales, and Northern Ireland, ranging in price from £125 (about $200) to about $1,750, with standards and sizes to match (modest to elegant for two to ten persons). However, given the reputation of this venerable organization, even the most modest accommodations have been wisely selected. A look at the catalog will make clear that location has been an important consideration in the Trust's selection of "cottages" for rent.

The booking procedure is easy and direct: Phone or fax for a brochure, choose at least three properties of interest, then contact them again with your choices and dates. They will let you know immediately about availability. A deposit is required, with final payment within four weeks of occupancy, all payable by major credit card or bank draft in pounds sterling. Like the Landmark Trust and the National Trust for Scotland, this is an outstanding organization that also does a good job with its rental properties. It is very popular, so book early!

National Trust for Scotland   Throughout Scotland
Holiday Cottages
Dept. BTA
5 Charlotte Square
Edinburgh EH2 4DU
Tel: 31–226–5922   Fax: 31–243–9302

This nonprofit trust was established in 1931 to protect and maintain the fine buildings and gardens of Scotland's past. It has since added the protection of endangered lands to its duties and more recently began renting carefully selected apartments and cottages. Fewer than forty in number, they are scattered about, from Arran Island to Aberdeen. Many of the rentals are historical properties or apartments in castles and the like. Their scarcity, combined with their quality and fair prices, makes them very popular, so it is important to work three months ahead for winter and six to eight months ahead for the high season, mid-June through early September.

A catalog is available, but obtaining it is made awkward by the price of 50 pence. They will accept payment by personal check, postal money order, and credit card, but the processing cost exceeds the 50p price. Our suggestion is to either buy and mail an international postage coupon (available at the post office) or send $3.00 in cash and ask them to mail the catalog. Then call or fax with your choice of three or four properties and the dates needed. Booking is easy: Included with the catalog is a chart of all the properties, indicating which are available at the time the catalog is mailed. They will accept major credit cards or bank drafts in pounds sterling. If you are mailing the latter, they will hold your booking until the check arrives. Prices run the gamut, but a scan of the price list reveals that no rental costs more than about $785 per week, even in peak season (this, for a house on the northwest island of Canna that sleeps ten), and most are under $450 per week.

Hotel Penrallt–Holiday Homes   West Coast of Wales
Aberporth, Dyfed SA43 2BS
Wales
Tel: 239–810–227   Fax: 239–811–375

Or book through Hoeseasons Holidays at the same prices (see profile above).

The Hotel Penrallt is just outside the coastal town of Aberporth, near Cardigan. It sits on 32 wooded acres of grounds along with a number of cottages, villas, and apartments. The cottages are arranged in several rows, and are comfortably though modestly furnished. Some are around a swimming pool. The location is ideal for exploring everything from Snowdonia National Park to the Pembrokeshire coast. The hotel is full service, including a restaurant, swimming pool, sauna, solarium, and putting course. (Renters pay a small charge for some of these amenities.) Bed linens are provided, but towels must be requested and paid for at $4.50 per person per week. Be prepared to feed the electric meters with 50-pence pieces.

Prices range from about $115 for an apartment for two in low season and $410 for the same apartment in August, to $185 and $595 for a two-bedroom cottages for four in low and high seasons. We think these are good values, especially in the spring and fall shoulder seasons. The town of Aberporth has little to recommend it except that the beach is a nice one, and swimming is fine into autumn. Thirty miles down the coast is the more interesting town of Fishguard, busy and full of shops and restaurants. If you are not interested in more than a few days in this area, try the hotel. The rooms are spacious and pleasant, and the stay will provide insights into resort life in Wales. We sometimes felt that we had gone back to another era; after dinner we danced, along with fellow guests, to music of the 1940s.

Red Rose Cottages   Northwest England
16 Shawbridge Street
Clitheroe, Lancashire BB7 1LY
Tel: 200–27–310   Fax: 200–28–929

This small company specializes in rentals in the rather rural, forested, north central county of Lancashire, just south of the Lake District, which is near enough for day trips. The catalog is actually a pocket folio of individual, descriptive sheets, and a good map is needed to pinpoint the property locations. Most, however, are within 30 miles of the town of Clitheroe. Rather than request all the descriptive pages, phone or fax information about your requirements and dates. A packet of possibilities will be sent. Payment is made by bank draft in pounds sterling or a wire transfer.

Royal Mile Enterprises Ltd.   Edinburgh
3 Doune Terrace
Edinburgh EH3 6DY
Scotland
Tel: 31–225–7189   Fax: 31–220–6162

These are small one-bedroom apartments wonderfully located on what is

known as the Royal Mile, a street where the titled and the wealthy have for centuries had their homes and apartments. It is an easy walk to Edinburgh castle,
but a bit farther down the palisade and across the river for groceries at Marks
Spencer. For a sense of old Edinburgh, this is the area in which to stay. We have
not seen these apartments, but given the location and the company's informative brochure, we would book a week's stay with confidence. Weekly rates run
from about $480 in winter to $625 in July and August. The apartments can usually be rented per night at $95 in low season and $120 in high. These properties
are rated with three crowns by the Scottish Tourist Board.

Rural Retreats   Throughout Great Britain
Blockley
Moreton-in-Marsh
Gloucestershire GL56 9DZ
Tel: 386–70–1177   Fax: 386–70–1178
U.S. agent: Suzanne B. Cohen, Agent
Tel: (207) 622–0743   Fax: (207) 622–1902

Rural Retreats has a selection of some of the nicest rental properties in
Britain—not manor houses, but distinctive cottages obviously chosen because of
their character. They are what foreigners imagine an English cottage will look
like: well aged, built of stone, some with thatched roofs, nicely situated among
gardens and grounds. The properties are concentrated around the Cotswolds
northwest of London and Oxford, and are scattered through Yorkshire, the
Welsh borders, Wiltshire, Derbyshire, and north Wales, with one lodge in the
Scottish Highlands.

Accommodations include a welcome basket of groceries and wine, and in
Cotswolds rentals a complimentary membership in the elegant Walton Hall
Country Club and trout fishing privileges. Prices cover a wide spectrum but are
eminently fair. A pretty, one-bedroom cottage in Blockley for example, costs
about $500 in winter and $720 during peak season. A splendid old stone four-
bedroom, three-bath house is the most expensive at about $1,150 in winter and
$1,600 in mid-summer.

The brochure is free and a colorful, descriptive, and well-designed catalog
will be sent on request from agent Suzanne Cohen for $3.00 (worth it), or phone
or fax the agency your requirements. It adds no commission, provides very good
service, is familiar with the properties, and easy to work with. Make a selection
and pay by personal check in dollars or by credit card. We recommend Rural
Retreats, their rental properties, and their U.S. agent.

Shaw's Holidays Wales   Northern Wales
Celtic House, Maes Square
Pwllheli, Gwynedd LL53 5HA
Tel: 758–612854   Fax: 758–613–835

A midsize rental company, family owned and operated, Shaw's Holidays offers some 300 properties in the north of Wales. Their catalog, which will be mailed on request, is sparsely illustrated. (This seems to be the case with Welsh regional companies.) Read carefully, especially for location, and ask that this be pinpointed if it is not clear. The majority of the properties are owner-occupied for most of the year and rented only during the summer season, which means they are well maintained as regular dwellings.

There are a number of terms and conditions in the catalog, but nothing to make booking difficult. The best approach is to phone or fax for a catalog, make a selection of three or more properties and then contact them again. Payment may be made by credit card—a deposit, with the balance on arrival, or in full. Linens and towels are rarely provided but can be rented. Be sure to advise the company of your need at the time of booking.

Skene House   Aberdeen, Scotland
96 Rosemont Viaduct
Aberdeen AB1 1NX
Scotland
Tel: 224–645–971   Fax: 224–626–866

The gray stone buildings of downtown Aberdeen cannot help but remind one a little of Disney's Fantasy Land, and the rest of the city and surrounding countryside make this a delightful destination. The Skene House offers studios and one- and two-bedroom apartments, well located near the city center. Rates are quoted by the night, from about $105 to $135. Our suggestion is to try just a few nights. It is a nice city, but there are other good spots to visit in Scotland. The deposit can be paid by credit card, with the balance due on arrival. Consider a daylong (or nightlong) ocean ferry trip to the Shetland Islands and at least an overnight stay in the capital town of Lerwick. There is usually a sailing on alternate days; ask any travel agent there.

Sudeley Castle Cottages   West-Central England
Winchcombe
Gloucestershire GL54 5JD
Tel: 242–602–308   Fax: 242–602–959

Formerly the palace of Queen Katherine Parr and now the home of Lord and Lady Ashcombe, the gardens of Sudeley (pronounced SOO-dley) Castle and the castle in part are open to the public from April through October. Thousands visit annually to wander through the great halls, view the paintings by Rubens, Turner, and Van Dyck, and stroll around the magnificent English gardens.

A few buildings of the estate, others in what was once a paper mill, and several along a short street leading to the castle have been artfully converted for use as vacation cottages. Whether freestanding or within one of the Cotswolds stone buildings, the accommodations are delightful. The cluster of cottages around the cobbled square create the impression of a tiny English village from another century. There are seventeen independent cottages and apartments under the Sudley Castle management, ranging from one to three bedrooms, all well furnished and fully equipped.

In addition to its excellent location for exploring the Heart of England, the activities surrounding the castle itself add to the enjoyment of being there. There is a very good playground, a restaurant, shop, and in summer a group of working crafters. Just outside the town of Cheltenham, Sudeley Castle is less than a two-hour drive from London, half an hour from Birmingham and Oxford, and a little less from Stratford-upon-Avon and Broadway. By rail London is about 90 minutes from the station at Cheltenham, seven miles from the castle. The town of Winchcombe, in which the castle is situated, is itself busy and pleasant, with good pubs, restaurants, shops, and grocers. There are surprisingly few tourists, except in July and August.

Prices vary. They are, however, very fair, and all are a good value. The high season is from late May to early September, during which time the smallest flat costs about £400 (U.S. $640) per week and the largest cottages are about $865. All rents run some 40 percent less in winter (mid-November to early March), and 30 percent less in spring and fall. Vineyard and Duck cottages are away from the main group on a small street off the Winchcombe High Street, a good location for more privacy than on the small cluster.

Contact Sudeley for a brochure and current prices, or book sight unseen with confidence. Payment can be made by bank draft in pounds sterling, but ask about using credit cards, which may soon be accepted. This is a very popular place, so be sure to book early if planning a visit during their high season.

Americans will be interested in knowing that Lady Ashcombe of Sudeley Castle was Miss Elizabeth Chipps of Lexington, Kentucky. According to Ann Berry, the capable manager, Lady Ashcombe has had a prominent hand in setting the style of the cottage furnishings and decor.

Suzanne B. Cohen, Agent   Throughout Britain
94 Winthrop Street
Augusta, ME 04330
Tel: (207) 622–0743   Fax: (207) 622–1902

This small agency represents Rural Retreats of Gloucestershire, which has a selection of some of the nicest rental properties in Britain, mostly in the north Cotswolds. They are chosen because of their character: much stone, well-aged, some with thatched roofs, nicely situated with gardens and grounds. Request a catalog ($3.00), or phone or fax your requirements. This small agency adds no commission, provides very good service, is familiar with the properties, and is easy to work with. Booking is simple: make a selection and pay by personal dollar check or by credit card. Also see Rural Retreats, listed on page 298.

London

The listings below represent apartments over a range of standards (economy to luxury), prices, and locations, including all of the popular areas of central London. In addition to listing the more conventional rental companies we have included apartment house manager/owners and agents (brokers) who handle rentals in a number of apartment buildings. Many more listings appear in the booklet *City Apartments,* available from British Tourist Authority offices in the United States and Canada.

In London a deposit is usually required at the time of booking, most often as a charge against your credit card. If the company or management accepts credit cards for full payment, the deposit will be credited toward the full rent. If credit cards are not accepted for full payment, the deposit amount will be credited to your card account (the charge reversed) upon your arrival, and payment in full must be made in pounds sterling or traveler's check. You may also be required to pay a telephone and/or damage deposit, often up to £200 each, which will be refunded, less charges, upon checkout. All the U.S. agencies listed accept payment in full by major credit cards, however.

The terminology and customs involved in renting an apartment in London require explanation. "Serviced apartments" or "serviced blocks" have maid service and sometimes porterage or an in-house manager. The term "broker" indicates a company that has assembled a group of serviced blocks and offers apartments for rent in all of them. They may also represent a number of privately owned apartments. The broker may or may not be the exclusive representative, so don't be surprised to see the same apartment blocks in several brochures you may receive. In such cases, compare prices.

In general, the price for any particular apartment is the same, whether rented directly from the serviced block management or through a broker in London. The advantage of booking with a specific apartment house management or owner is that you know more precisely where the apartment is and what the accommodations are like. The advantage of booking through a London broker is the variety of locations and standards to select from. Also included in the listings below are a selected few U.S. representatives or agents who charge no additional commission. Some represent one serviced block exclusively and others are large enough to negotiate even better prices from the apartment managements. The anomaly is British Airways, neither an apartment owner nor rental agency, but a source of dependable apartments at fair prices for travelers on British Airways flights.

Apartment Services
2 Sandwich Street
London WC1H 9PL
Tel: 71–388–3558   Fax: 71–383–7255

A small personalized operation, this is among the best sources for modestly priced, individually owned apartments in the Bloomsbury, Regent's Park, and Holborn areas, with a scattering of apartments elsewhere. Owner Christine Ayling is careful about selecting properties, and the company enjoys much repeat business. Although a few luxury apartments are represented, most are of moderate and upper middle standards, good values in part because they are not in the high-rent districts, such as Mayfair and Chelsea. As for location, we like Bloomsbury. Transportation to and from other parts of the city is fast and convenient, via bus or by tube, with many tube stations.

There is no slick catalog, but property description sheets are accurate and include a sketch and layout of the premises. The best approach to booking is to phone or fax with your requirements. A selection of apartments meeting those criteria will be sent. Talk with Ms. Ayling or staff if you are unsure or want advice or more information. Count on good value and personal attention. Payment is by major credit card or bank draft in pounds sterling.

Ashton's Designer Studios and
Ashton's Budget Studios
39 Rosary Garden
London SW7 4NQ
Tel: 71–370–0737   Fax: 71–835–1419
Toll-free direct to London: 800–525–2810

U.S. agent: Keith Prowse & Co., listed in this section.

The tiny designer studios are a marvel of arrangement; everything needed has been tucked into a small space. The compact kitchens are well equipped for two persons, the furnishings are attractive, and the colors and decor are stylish. The bed is actually a sofa bed, but we find it comfortable. Bathrooms are in marble, with fittings in gold. Nice touches include air-conditioning, robes, and hair dryers. These little gems rent for about $640 plus the VAT—a London bargain. A very few one-bedroom apartments are also available for about double the price of a studio. Maid service is daily.

The budget studios are just that: simply furnished and outfitted, but neat and clean. At about $400, however, they are also a good value. Larger budget studios for up to four persons are also available.

Rosary Garden is a short residential street in South Kensington of mostly Victorian houses. It is within easy walking distance of the Victoria and Albert Museum and Exhibition Road. Phone or fax for a brochure; reservation is confirmed by credit card, but payment must be made by a bank draft in pounds sterling or travelers cheques a month in advance of occupancy.

Barclay International Group
150 East 52nd Street
New York, NY 10022
Tel: (800) 845–6636 or (212) 832–3777   Fax: (212) 753–1139

Barclay represents a number of the best-serviced blocks in London, all carefully selected and periodically inspected by someone on the New York staff. The company has been in business for nearly thirty years and negotiates prices with apartment block managements, often resulting in prices below those available through direct booking. They also may lease apartments for the long term and then rent short term to U.S. and Canadian clients at competitive prices. Among these is 64 Buckingham Gate, a superior grade serviced block in which Barclay has apartments on the ninth, twelfth, and fourteenth floors. It is in a short street that ends at Buckingham Palace on one end and Victoria Street at the other, not far from St. James's Park. These are well-furnished, well-maintained, and of excellent value. They look out either on the palace or across Westminster to the towers of Parliament. Studios run between $800 and $900 depending on the season, one-bedroom in the $1,150 range and $1,550 for two-bedroom.

Of approximately twenty-five apartment blocks in the Barclay group, we especially like Grosvenor House and 47 Park in the Deluxe grade. In the Superior, in addition to 64 Buckingham Gate, are 130 London (at 130 Queensgate, actually) and the Berkeley/Curzon Plaza. In the Standard, try Roland House and Nell Gwynn House. Lawrence Wharf is a good value if you don't mind being out of the city center by ten minutes or so by tube; they are modern in style and sit on the bank of the Thames. Also available are suburban apartments in East Croyden, with easy access to the countryside as well as the city.

A color booklet and price list are available (for the latest prices before booking, telephone). Some of the apartments are also represented by other U.S. agents and are advertised in the British Travel Authority booklet, so compare at least two prices. These prices, however, are hard to beat. Theater tickets and sightseeing tours can be arranged.

Barclay also represents apartments in Paris, Brussels, Rome, Amsterdam, and Madrid, and, most recently, many good villas and apartments in Italy. They also have an excellent selection of modest to moderate rentals in some of the most attractive destinations of France, from the Riviera to the Alps and in Brittany, Normandy, and the Atlantic coast (see chapter 6). Booking terms are included in their booklets, one for England and one for the Continent. Barclay offers some very good values and is well worth contacting.

B & V Associates
140 East 56th Street - Suite 4C
New York, NY 10022
Tel: (800) 755–8266 or (212) 688–9464   Fax: (212) 688–9567

B & V Associates is the capable U.S. representative of the large French chain of modestly priced apartments called Orion (see Residences Orion in chapter 6, France). In its first venture into Britain it has recently opened an apartment complex near the Barbican Center in central London. (See Orion–London, listed below.) Any Orion property in Europe can be booked through this agency. Payment by credit card or personal check. No commission is added.

Beaufort House
45 Beaufort Gardens, London SW3
Tel: 71–584–2600   Fax: 71–584–6532

U.S. agents: Barclay International and Keith Prowse & Co. USA, listed in this chapter.

This is a superior apartment block in Knightsbridge, well located and featuring an "old London" style and atmosphere. The apartments are relatively large and the surroundings very pleasant. The prices reflect location as well as comfort, ranging from around $1,000 per week for a one bedroom to $3,000 for a four bedroom. There is a concierge, washers/dryers, dishwashers, and microwave ovens in most apartments. They are good values for the area. Contact Beaufort House for a brochure and price list, but check with the U.S. agents as well.

Belgrave House
92-94 Belgrave Road
London W2 1QE
Tel: 71–834–3866   Fax: 71–834–3866

Belgrave House is in Pimlico, the area squeezed between Chelsea and Westminster, south of Victoria Station. It is principally residential with few boutiques and tourist shops and accommodations are good values. Such is the case here, where a studio costs about $550 per week and a one bedroom about $700. The apartments are not large but are certainly adequate, furnished rather simply.

British Airways

U.S. offices: Jackson Heights, NY
Tel: (800) 247–4000; (800) 247–9297 (Main air reservations numbers)
Tel: (800) 876–2200 (Holiday desk: apartments, hotels, car rentals, theater tickets, tour programs.)

This airline company offers passengers easy access to apartments in London and Paris (see chapter 6). Unlike other companies in this guide, British Airways is of course not a rental company or broker; it offers a group of apartments and townhouse hotels that can be booked through its Holiday Desk or central reservations number. The convenience is obvious if you are planning your flight on British Airways. The prices are very competitive.

In the British Airways publication *London Plus* (available by telephoning) the Apartments are listed as "Hyde Park, Mayfair, Kensington, Chelsea, and Brompton apartments." The ones in Hyde Park include several superior grade apartment buildings in and around the Hyde Park and Kensington areas. The Brompton Apartments is a single, standard plus building on Old Brompton Road which, despite being a little distance from Harrods, is a good value—especially if booked through British Airways. Both the Hyde Park group and Brompton Apartments have a minimum stay requirement of three nights. Additional nights can be added at a reduced rate.

All apartments come with fully equipped kitchens, tableware, and linens and towels (changed regularly). Because prices change with the fluctuating currency rates, it is best to get a current price from the company. Payment by credit card or personal check. Prices for all include VAT; as is typical of most London rentals. A £100 deposit for security and another for telephone usage is required on arrival, refundable less the charges incurred.

Brookman-Knightsbridge

20 Ovington Square
London SW3 1LR
Tel: 71–823–7159   Fax: 71–584–3615

These Knightsbridge apartments are of a high standard. Light and airy, they are sizable, well furnished, and gaily decorated. Equally desirable is the location, three short blocks down Brompton Road from Harrods. The neighborhood ranges from residential Ovington Gardens to busy Brompton Road. Bus transportation along Brompton Road (or a short walk) provides easy access to the Victoria and Albert Museum and Exhibition Road, while Picadilly can be reached directly in the opposite direction. It is hard to find a more convenient all-around location.

The prices are surprisingly reasonable for apartments of this quality and location, from about £650 for a one bedroom to £1,250 for a lovely three-bedroom apartment with a balcony overlooking the gardens. These are short of being luxury, but will nonetheless make for a very comfortable stay. Maid service is three times weekly; business devices are included (fax, copier, answering machine). Contact Brookman-Knightsbridge for free brochure and price list. Payment is made by bank draft in pounds sterling or by credit card.

Castles and Country Estates
55 Earls Court Square
London SW5 9DG
Tel: 71–373–0451   Fax: 71–370–0838

This small company specializes in superior to luxury-class apartments in London and moderate to luxury-standard country and village houses in southern England. The company owner, Melody MacDonald, seeks to match clients with exactly what they are looking for. The London apartments are carefully chosen, mostly in Kensington, South Kensington, Chelsea, and Belgravia.

The best approach is to phone or fax with information about what you are looking for, the general location, and dates. You will be contacted with one or more proposed property descriptions. We feel the prices are fair and the service and attention are excellent. This is a good company to contact if you are planning a stay both in London and the countryside. Discuss payment details at the time of booking.

Draycott House
10 Draycott Avenue
London SW3 3AA
Tel: 71–584–4659   Fax: 71–225–3694

On a quiet street a short walk from Sloane Square in Chelsea, the staid but unprepossessing Draycott House offers guests a nice flavor of London. The tree-lined streets here are quietly residential, yet close to many shops, pubs, and good restaurants. Straight up Sloane Street is Knightsbridge, Brompton Road, and Harrods.

This is a relatively small house of thirteen deluxe apartments with period furnishings, beautifully appointed. Many have balconies looking into a garden in the rear, and although they are not immense, all the apartments are certainly adequate in size. As should be expected of apartments of this class and style, almost anything can be arranged, from limousine pickup at the airport to theater tickets, interpreters, and couriers. There is an office on the premises, and the staff, headed by Linda Coulthard, assure personal attention. There is a resident housekeeper.

We found the apartments to be not only elegant but comfortable, and bright. The kitchens are well equipped and supplied. Prices range from £725 (about U.S. $1,150) plus VAT per week for the smallest one bedroom to about $3,000 for a large, luxurious, two-bedroom, two-bath apartment. This was about the price of a good double room at the Hilton. Five-day minimum stays are accepted. Overall, Draycott House is inviting and delightful. Contact them for a brochure and current prices if you wish, or book direct in confidence. Payment is by bank draft in pounds sterling or traveler's checks.

Euracom
76 New Cavendish Street
London W1M 7LB
Tel: 71–436–3201   Fax: 71–436–3203

This company offers a wide range of apartments in specific serviced blocks in Bloomsbury, just west of Bloomsbury, Earl's Court, Hyde Park, Kensington, Knightsbridge, and Mayfair. They range from simple and inexpensive to luxury (in Mayfair). For the most part they are in the £400 (about $640) range for studios, $830 for one bedroom, between $960 and $1,120 range for two bedrooms and around $1,600 for three bedrooms.

This is a reputable company with a good selection of fairly priced apartments, all in good locations. Those a bit farther away from central London, such as Earl's Court, cost less than those in premium neighborhoods. For the best values, we favor the modestly priced Bloomsbury block, not far from the British Museum. The apartments are neat and comfortable, at a good price.

Call or fax for a brochure and price list. A deposit of £100 (about $160) is required, payable by credit card or sterling bank draft. There is no commission, but there is a £25 booking fee for making the arrangements.

Five Emperor's Gate
8 Knaresborough Pl.
London SW5 0TG
Tel: 71–244–8409   Fax: 71–373–6455

U.S. agent: Keith Prowse & Co., listed in this section.

Modestly priced, standard apartments in South Kensington, these are good values, especially in the off-season, when special prices are usually announced. The apartments are a good choice for two people who want neat, clean accommodations at an economy rate. Contact them for a brochure and the latest prices, then book direct or through the U.S. agent.

Grant Reid Communications

Box 810216
Dallas, TX 75381
Tel: (800) 327–1849, (214) 243–6748   Fax: (214) 484–5778

Grant Reid is the U.S. agent for London Apartments Ltd. (and for Mansley Travel Apartments, except in England) listed in this section. They have a large selection of apartments in Mayfair, the Marble Arch area, Chelsea, Kensington, and South Kensington. The staff in Dallas knows London well and works closely with London Apartments Ltd. to assure the best accommodation for their North American clients.

Brochures and prices are available, but since the company represents approximately 700 apartments, the best approach is to phone or fax your requirements and price range and let them propose a few options. The service is good and you can rely on a fast response.

If you want to rent a cottage or a castle in rural England as well as an apartment in London, this is a good company to contact. Prices are the same as when you book direct. Payment can be made by personal check or, better, credit card to lock in the exchange rate on the day of booking.

Huntingdon House

200-220 Cromwell Rd., London SW5
Tel: 71–373–4525   Fax: 71–373–6676
U.S. agent: Barclay International, listed in this section.

On the busy corner of Cromwell Road and Earl's Court, this long, low red stone apartment building has an Old World appeal and is indeed international in its character and its clientele. It is convenient to bus and underground transportation to the city center. Earl's Court is a robust street busy with shops, restaurants, grocers, news agents, and pubs.

Huntingdon House is rather ordinary, a little worn in places, with wide halls, especially spacious apartments (from studios to four bedrooms), twenty-four-hour reception, and good furnishings and appointments. Overall, it is a comfortable place to stay and a fair value at prices ranging from £500 (about $800) per week for one bedroom to $1,500 for three bedrooms and $2,200 for four bedrooms. Request a garden-facing apartment rather than one on noisy Cromwell Road.

London Apartments Ltd.

11/12 Tottenham Mews
London W1
Tel: 71–436–4453   Fax: 71–436–4453

U.S. agent: Grant Reid Communications, listed in this section.

This excellent company, under the capable direction of Laurence Stockman (whom we have known for several years), represents a large number of moderate to luxury apartments around London, especially in and around Mayfair, Marble Arch, Kensington, and South Kensington. They have long served American and Canadian visitors and are very helpful and easy to work with. Formerly located at 51 Kensington Court (see profile), they managed this pleasant apartment house near Kensington Gardens for a number of years, and still represent it, among others. We find the prices very fair and trust the company to match their clients' requirements with a suitable place. The staff knows London and the rental business intimately and works closely with its U.S. agent in Dallas. The best approach is to contact Grant Reid in Dallas, the prices are the same, and the service is good. Pay by check or credit card.

Keith Prowse & Co. (USA) Ltd.

234 West 44th Street
New York, NY 10036
Tel: (800) 669–8697 or (212) 398–1430   Fax: (212) 302–4251

This is an independently owned company associated with Keith Prowse Ltd., a company founded in London some 200 years ago. It provides good service and a carefully chosen assortment of rental apartments, well located in and about central London, from South Kensington eastward to St. James's Park, into Mayfair, and north of Hyde Park in Bayswater.

The agency is included here for several reasons: Its prices are very competitive, equal to or less than can be obtained by direct contact, with no commission added, and the New York staff knows the London properties well and offers good advice. Were we to choose three in each of three categories from the thirty or so serviced apartment blocks handled by the company, we would lean toward: Roland House, Five Emperor's Gate, and Westminster Suites in the standard class; and Cheval Apartments, Beaufort House, One Thirty (130 Queensgate), and Twelve A Apartments (12A Charles St.) in the superior class. Of the luxury apartments, all are excellent, with Hyde Park Residence at the lower range end, the much smaller Carlos Place in the midrange and Grosvenor House the most costly.

A color brochure with prices is available. Prowse also represents apartments in other major cities in Western Europe. Payment is made by check or major credit card. Since the currency exchange rates vary, be sure to confirm prices. (See also Keith Prowse listings in the chapters on France, Italy, and Spain.)

51 Kensington Court
London W8 5DB
Tel: 71–937–4248   Fax: 71–937–4240
U.S. agent: Grant Reid Communications, listed on page 308.

We especially like the location of the 51 Kensington Court apartments. It is one block from Kensington Gardens and off busy Kensington Road and its many shops, restaurants, and pubs, yet it faces a quiet, residential court. It is a short walk east to Albert Hall and Exhibition Road and in the other direction to a Safeway and other shopping. Kensington Road is also a main conduit for buses, so access to Knightsbridge, Mayfair, Piccadilly, and the City is easy and fast.

Formerly the London residence of the Aga Khan, this red brick Edwardian building has been converted to a number of comfortable, unpretentious, one-, two-, and three-bedroom apartments of various styles. The kitchens are adequately equipped; there is maid service daily, a porter, and laundry facilities. Good service, fair prices, and pleasant apartments make for an enjoyable London stay.

Contact the management or the agent for a brochure and current prices; in off-seasons do not hesitate to ask about special rates. Although the management changed in early 1994, we believe that the apartments and service will remain as they have been. The U.S. agent knows the premises well, however, and will be candid about any changes. Payment is by major credit card, sterling bank draft or, to the agent, personal check.

Mansley Travel Apartments International
No. 1 The Mansions
219 Earls Court Road
London SW5 9BN
Tel: 44–71–373–4689   Fax: 44–71–373–2062

This capable company represents a very nice selection of apartments in London's Mayfair, and otherwise hard-to-find apartments in major cities of Europe and elsewhere in the world. Mansley is a fast-growing company that specializes in city apartments for short-term rent; we find that the European properties they represent are dependably good, mostly superior and luxury properties at fair prices. We assume that their other properties worldwide are of similar standards and adhere to fair prices.

Of special interest to visitors to London are Mansley's apartments at 44 Curzon Street and in nearby Charles Street, both in the heart of Mayfair near Shepherds Market, a five-minute walk off Park Lane. These are small, historic apartment houses with character. The period furnishings enhance the architecture and finish of the apartments, which, while not spacious, are very adequate in size and well designed. The compact kitchenettes are unobtrusive, yet equipped with everything needed. Dinnerware is in keeping with the high standard of the apartments overall.

Although Mansley price lists are printed in the client's home currency, they are available in pounds sterling as well. You can pay in either. Prices are shown by the day as well as the week. A Curzon Street studio costs about U.S. $900 per week, a one bedroom is $1,300, and a four bedroom is in the $3,000 range. For luxury apartments in London these prices are fair, especially for this location. Even the two-bedroom apartment is about the price of one twin room at the nearby Sheraton Park Tower or the Connaught.

The company also brokers other apartments around London, such as Beaufort Gardens, profiled in this section, and Roland House on Brompton Road, also profiled. Contact Mansley directly for their brochure and for the excellent Curzon and Charles Street apartments. For the other apartments in London, compare prices. Many of the apartments represented overlap with those of the U.S. agents Barclay International and Keith Prowse in New York. If the prices are close, it is always preferable to use a toll-free telephone line.

Orion - London

7–12 Goswell Road
London EC1
U.S. agent: B & V Associates, 140 East 56th Street - Suite 4C
New York, NY 10022
Tel: (800) 755–8266 or (212) 688–9464   Fax: (212) 688–9467

Residences Orion is a French company operating a large chain of modestly priced, short-term rental apartments throughout France. Their first venture into England is a new serviced apartment complex comprising 120 studios and nine one-bedroom apartments on Goswell Road near the famed Barbican Center in the area just east of Bloomsbury. This is not a traditional area of shops, but the location is within an easy walk of St. Paul's Cathedral and the London Museum. Although the London apartments opened subsequent to our stay there, we are very familiar with the French properties and have been advised that these follow a similar formula: a dependable consistency in the style, furnishings, decoration, equipment, and even dinnerware, all satisfactory.

The apartments are not large or luxurious but are very well-priced, comfortable enough, compact but adequate in size. The design makes the best use of space, a good formula. Orion's properties are good values, and we recommended them for travelers more interested in being out and about than in staying at the home base. They are especially good for families wanting reasonable prices and accommodations a cut above economy level.

U.S. agent B & V Associates will send brochure and prices; booking is easy and no commission is charged. Payment can be made by credit card or personal check.

Park Lane Estates
48 Curzon Street
London W1Y 7RE
Tel: 1–800–284–7385 (Toll-free to London) or 071–629–0763   Fax: 71–493–1308

This company manages six apartment houses; three are modest to moderate in price and standard and three are superior. All their apartments are very well located in Mayfair.

Among the superior apartments, 34/36 Clarges Street and 61 George Street are the most comfortable and have the best location. Forty-six Mount Street and 12 Hertford Street are the best bets among the moderately priced apartments. (For Hertford, which has the best location, ask if the renovations are complete before you decide to book.) There are house managers at the buildings on Hertford, Mount, and George streets.

Prices range from a winter low of about £550 (U.S. $880) sterling per week for a one-bedroom apartment on Mount Street or Hertford Street to $1,200 at 61 George Street. In summer, the prices are about 15 percent higher. A two-bedroom apartment costs from about $1,450 on Hertford in summer to $2,500 on George Street. For a 3 bedroom with two or three baths, the best bet is the Mount Street address at $1,900 in winter and $2,550 in summer, a bargain for a family or group of traveling companions.

For Park Lane's brochure and current price list, call the toll-free number. When your selection is made, telephone again and confirm. Payment is made by major credit card, against which there will be a £200 charge as a deposit. Upon your arrival, the charge will be held as a telephone deposit, and you will be expected to pay for the booking in pounds sterling cash or in traveler's checks at the prevailing exchange rate. All instructions and directions will be given at the time of booking. This is a well managed company offering a good selection. They are quick to respond to inquiries, and their prices are fair.

Roland House
121 Old Brompton Road
London SW7 3RX
Tel: 71–370–6221   Fax: 71–370–4293
U.S. agents: Barclay International and Keith Prowse & Co., listed in this section.

It seems that there are numerous agents for this large, rather ordinary but popular apartment block in South Kensington, suggesting that it is a solid value. The location is good—just a short walk from busy Earl's Court Road in one direction and the Victoria and Albert Museum in another, and within easy access of Knightsbridge. The apartments are spacious but simply furnished, some with well-designed kitchens. (Other kitchens are not so well designed.) Prices, in the $800-per-week range for a one bedroom, coupled with the location and the international character of the clientele make Roland House a good value.

The better choices are apartments on the upper floors, and the best approach to securing the right apartment is to contact one of the U.S. agents, rather than booking direct. The prices will be close, if not equal or lower, and the agents know the property well enough to request the best situation. For a brochure and price list, contact Roland House directly or either agency.

Royal Court Apartments

51 Gloucester Terrace
London W2 3DH
Tel: 71–402–5077   Fax: 71–724–0286
U.S. agent: British Travel Network Ltd.
The Mews, 594 Valley Road, Upper Montclair, NJ 07043
Tel: (800) 274–8583 or (201) 744–5215;   Fax: (201) 744–0531

Royal Court is a long and architecturally attractive row of Victorian townhouses that have been totally renovated and modernized. The ninety studios and apartments are comfortable but not luxurious, and except for the studios they are certainly of ample size. Amenities such as a conference room, exercise facilities, sauna, daily maid service, and twenty-four-hour reception raise the standard. The location is very good, on a residential street just one block off Bayswater Road, with its small hotels, scattered restaurants, and the walk bordering the park.

The prices range from a modest $650 per week for a studio to about $1,000 for a one bedroom and $1,800 for a three bedroom for seven persons. These prices are not especially low, but are in keeping with the standard, amenities, and location. Daily rates are available. Contact the agent, which charges no additional commission, for a brochure and current prices. They will likely be lower between Nov. 1 and April 1. Payment is by personal check or credit card.

Northern Ireland
(Dial the same as the rest of the U.K. 011–44–)

We did not visit Northern Ireland this trip and cannot offer personal observations on the rental properties. The best approach is to contact the Northern Ireland Tourist Board in New York for their brochures (tel: (212) 922–0101; Fax: (212) 922–0099), including the information bulletin on self-catering accommodation. This lists more than one hundred vacation rental properties, almost all privately owned. They range from single farmhouses to resort clusters of cottages and a few apartment buildings.

We think that the coast of County Antrim is spectacular, the area in which to begin a visit to Northern Ireland. If you arrive in Belfast or in the town of Larne (the ferryport just north of Belfast), drive north on the A-2. The first apartment rental of any significance is in Cushendall, 45 miles from Belfast. The second is at Portrush, 35 miles farther on. Because one should visit the Giant's Causeway, a remarkable internationally known geological oddity, we suggest staying at Portrush. This is also closer to the interesting and important city of Londonderry than Cushendall. When there a few years ago we had no sense of danger and thoroughly enjoyed the countryside and smaller towns. Belfast we see as a great but sad city with not many reasons to stay long on a leisure trip.

Following, then, are a few rentals that we have selected partly because of their location and partly because they appear from the materials we received to be comfortable enough.

Atlantic House Flats

Portballintrae, County Antrim
Northern Ireland
Tel: 265–823–226

Six flats in this interesting but quiet small town on the beautiful north coast. Sleep from four to six persons; rent under U.S. $400 per week.

161 Thronlea Hotel (Apartments)

6 Coast Road
Cushendall, Co. Antrim BT44 0RU
Northern Ireland
Tel: 26–67–71–223   Fax: 26–67–71–362

Several apartments sleeping up to four persons; hotel services. Rates from U.S. $250 to $450 per week, depending on standard and season.

O'Neill's Causeway Coast Apartments

36 Ballyreagh Rd.
Portrush, Co. Antrim BT56 8LR
Northern Ireland
Tel: 265–822–435   Fax: 265–824–495

Twenty three-bedroom apartments at a modest price ranging from $250 per week in winter season to $580 June through August. Open all year. Accepts credit cards.

York Apartments
Portstewart, County Londonderry
Northern Ireland
Tel: 26–583–833–594

This is the largest town on the north "Causeway" coast and the most interesting. The apartment building is typically small, eight apartments sleeping
three in each. Having not visited these particular apartments, we can only
observe that from past experience accommodations in Northern Ireland tend to
be plain, neat, and clean. The apartment building looks across the golf course
and the sea. There is a bar on the ground floor of this small building that, we are
told, features nationally renowned food. This location, as well as any of the
above, is ideal for exploring this beautiful north coast.

Index

INTERNATIONAL TRAVEL

Here are some other guides on various international destinations. All Globe Pequot travel titles are published with the highest standards of accuracy and timeliness. Please check your local bookstore for other fine Globe Pequot Press titles, which include:

Exploring Europe by Car, $12.95

Exploring Europe by Boat, $12.95

Exploring Europe by RV, $14.95

Guide to Eastern Canada, $15.95

Guide to Western Canada, $16.95

Britain by Britrail, $13.95

Europe by Eurail, $14.95

The Best Bed & Breakfast in England, Scotland, and Wales, $18.95

The Best Hotels of Great Britain, $21.95

The Best Restaurants of Great Britain, $21.95

Hotels and Restaurants of Britain, $18.95

Ireland: The Complete Guide and Road Atlas, $19.95

The Vineyards of France, $14.95

The Traveler's Handbook, $19.95

Berlitz Travel Guides

Bradt Travel Guides

Cadogan Travel Guides

Karen Brown's Travel Guides

Off the Beaten Track Travel Guides

To order any of these titles with MASTERCARD or VISA call toll-free, 24 hours a day, (800) 243–0495; in Connecticut call (800) 962–0973. Free shipping for orders of three or more books. Shipping charge of $3.00 per book for one or two books ordered. Connecticut residents add sales tax. Ask for your free catalogue of Globe Pequot's quality books on recreation, travel, nature, personal finance, gardening, cooking, crafts, and more. Prices and availability subject to change.